Crosscurrents in African American History
Graham Russell Hodges and Margaret Washington
Series Editors

Hitler's Black Victims

*The Historical Experiences
of Afro-Germans,
European Blacks, Africans,
and African Americans
in the Nazi Era*

Clarence Lusane

Routledge
New York   London

Published in 2003 by
Routledge
29 West 35th Street
New York, NY 10001

Published in Great Britain by
Routledge
11 New Fetter Lane
London EC4P 4EE

Routledge is an imprint of the Taylor & Francis Group.

10 9 8 7 6 5 4 3 2 1

Library of Congress Cataloging-in-Publication Data

Lusane, Clarence, 1953–
    Hitler's black victims : the historical experiences of Afro-Germans, European Blacks,
Africans, and African Americans in the Nazi era / Clarence Lusane.
        p.   cm. — (Crosscurrents in African American history)
    Includes bibliographical references and index.
    ISBN 0-415-93121-5   ISBN 0-415-93295-5 (pbk.)
    1. World War, 1939–1945—Blacks—Germany. 2. World War, 1939–1945—Blacks.
    3. World War, 1939–1945—African Americans. 4. Germany—Ethnic relations. 5. Race
    discrimination—Germany. I. Title. II. Series.

D810.N4 L87 2002
940.53'18'08996—dc21

                                                                                      2001041860

Contents

Acknowledgments

It is three months since turning in the manuscript and I am trying to remember everyone over the last five years or so who has had his or her fingerprints on this project. I am checking e-mails, scraps of paper (lots of scraps of paper), phone records, letters, the wall next to my computer, behind the trash can that I never empty, all the while recalling how boldly I thought "I will remember X gave me this absolutely essential information." Another self-delusion exposed. OK, here is my best shot and apologies way in advance to anyone I forgot.

I received critical support and comments from faculty colleagues, staffers, and students at American University, especially in the School of International Service, where I gave presentations on the research over the past few years. This includes Professors Mohammad Abu-Nimer, Phillip Brenner, Betty Dickerson, Carol Gallagher, Lou Goodman, Nanette Levinson, Linda Lubrano, Cathy Schneider, Stephen Silva, Gary Weaver, and Quansheng "John" Zhao. I was also fortunate to have some very talented and resourceful students work with me doing research and readings, including Helen McClure, Chris Campos, Titus Chin, and Marilyn Coucou.

Research institutions that provided not only invaluable data but friendly faces include National Archives, Moreland-Spingarn Research Center, Schomburg Center, U.S. Holocaust Memorial Museum, Museum of Tolerance, Black Wax Museum, Library of Congress, Berlin Central Library, British Museum, School of African and Oriental Studies, and other research institutions in many other places.

As usual, there was the endless array of friends and associates who diverted me when necessary, gave criticism when needed, and did everything they could to make me and this book better. Hey to Shirikiana Aina, Jewel Andrews, Karen Bass, Jelani Cobb, Derrick Cogburn, Cecelie Counts, James Early, Anita English, Haili Gerima, Charles Green, Cheryl Hanna, Mark Harrison, Sylvia Hill, Karen Jefferson, Keith Jennings, Mae King, Melvin Lewis, Carolyn Mathews, Joseph McCormick, Ife

Modupe, Lorenzo Morris, Julie Mostov (and her students at Drexel), Brother Mutota, Alain Patrice Nganang, Deborah Robinson, Jocelyn Sargent, Mike Simmons, James Steele, Lisa Sullivan, Nkechi Taifa, Nathalie Thandiwe, Makani Themba, Veena Vasista, Carline Watson, Walter Watson, and Joy Zarembka. A special appreciation to Hugh McCann for delivering to a stranger a most valuable asset.

Thanks also to American Friends Service Committee, Black Professionals in International Affairs International Possibilities Unlimited, Institute for Policy Studies, and the National Conference of Black Political Scientists.

The "G8" always had my back as well as insightful perspectives. Deep love and friendship to Robin T., Robin L., Tara, Kim, Chris, and, of course, Camille.

In Europe, an endless array of friends and scholars gave and gave and gave. This includes Brima Conteh, Donna St. Hill, Makeda Coaston, Etienne Bryan (and the whole crew), Josephine Ocloo, Kwame Dixon, Lou Kushnick, and Sameera Anwar. Thanks for the bagels, beer, and brains.

There have been so many Afro-Germans, both inside and outside Germany, who gave me answers to questions and queries that it is impossible to mention everyone. Some of the key folks that I must acknowledge and to whom I will always be grateful include Theodor Michael, Hans Massaquoi, Eke, Judy, ADEFRA, ISD, Eleanore, Dimitria, Nancy Scott, Paulette Reed Anderson, John Kantara, and Katherina Oguntoye.

I also want to express my gratitude to Harry Belafonte, one of the world's most valuable treasures. Our discussions about the book and the historic and contemporary situation of black folks were fresh and discerning. I felt honored and blessed to have his worldly perspective at my disposal on more occasions than I could have imagined.

I want to also thank the editors and staffers at Routledge. I feel a great deal of pride in having a book published by one of the most respected scholarly presses publishing today. To Karen Wolny, Vikram Mukhija, Farideh Kamali, series editor Graham Hodges, and the rest, thanks.

A very special thanks to Dr. Randolph Persaud. Though he may not know it, Randy continues to be as much a mentor as a dear friend. I am the better for each discussion and encounter that we share. I look forward to many years of shared discoveries, brilliant insights, profound understandings, and chilling time.

Finally, my very first exposure to the story and ideas that formed this book happened more than a dozen years ago when I first met some black Germans at a conference in London. One of those individuals was Nicola Laure al Samari. Originally from the former East Germany, she has become one of the people in my life whose presence is indispensable. She is a thinker of the first order and an unyielding advocate for human rights, women's rights, and cultural rights, and it is safe to say that without Nicola there would have been no book. More important, much more important, she plays a strong and determined role in the forging of the black German community.

Part 1

Beyond a
White German Past

Introduction

Black in Germany during the Nazi Era

The Undiscovered Country

In general terms, who constructs collective identity, and for what, largely determines the symbolic content of this identity, and its meaning for those identifying with it or placing themselves outside of it.

—*Manuel Castells*[1]

The date: 21 June 1933. The place: Düsseldorf, Germany. The time: five months after Adolf Hitler has become chancellor of Germany's Third Reich. An incipient resistance movement has emerged, but it is already coming to know the murderous ferocity of the Nazi state. That June day, in the luminous and buoyant blue waters of the Rhine, a brutalized and battered body is discovered under the Rhinebridge. It is the remains of another casualty of the expanding Nazi crusade that had only a short time ago come to power and would soon give the world a bone-chilling meaning to the phrase "racial purity." The victim, Hilarius "Lari" Gilges, was an anti-Nazi labor organizer, performing artist, and communist who chose to defy the state authority of Hitler and his followers. While millions of Germans saw in Hitler a national redemption and reassertion of Aryan might—a manifest destiny of the worst kind—aimed at Germany's internal and European enemies, Gilges was one who was willing to fight the onslaught of National Socialism and to make the ultimate sacrifice in the name of justice, democracy, and freedom. To many of those familiar with the history and politics of Nazi Germany, perhaps the most unusual fact in this saga was that he was also black.

The existence of blackness under Hitler raises not only the issue of identity and resistance but also the issue of an identity of resistance. The construction (in many ways imposition) of blackness from above struggled with the reality of an unformed blackness from below. This combination created a complex and unstable racial landscape for

3

people of African descent as they, with little choice, practiced what James Scott termed the "arts of resistance." Gilges's murder begs the questions "How did people of African descent fare under Nazism?" "Was there an indigenous 'black' community, and, if so, where did it exist?" "Were Blacks targeted and singled out for specific forms of repression?" "Where do their experiences fit within the Holocaust paradigm—or do they?" The answers to these questions, to the degree they have been asked at all, remain vague even for those scholars and researchers familiar with the Nazi era and the Holocaust in particular. In part, the vagueness is informed by a lack of historical rendering of the experiences of Afro-Germans and other Blacks during the period. Indeed, it is not unusual, when the question is raised, for the response to be one of surprise that there were any Blacks present in Nazi Germany at all. The Black presence is mystified, shrouded in whispers and innuendoes, dismissed as inconsequential, and lost in the popular and scholarly notions of an all-white Europe and in a reading of Nazi Germany and the Holocaust in which blackness is excluded.

Of those who are aware that Blacks did live in Germany during the period, some argue that the black presence in Nazi Germany was too small and too insignificant to warrant the kind of detailed and extensive research that has been afforded other groups targeted for Nazi oppression and extinction. A further implication of this notion is that Afro-Germans and other Blacks had no agency of their own: they were simply acted upon. This denies the fact that Afro-Germans and other Blacks were more than just the "other," but were subjects of their own history, subjects that engaged in "infrapolitics," anti-Nazi resistance, and a perpetual redefinition of Germany's cultural and social life.

To dismiss the antiblackness character of Nazism and the subjugation of its black victims is a historical whitewashing. This erasure abandons the important insights regarding the nature of racism and fascism offered by a more inclusive and rigorous investigation of the substantive level of oppression faced by Blacks under Nazism and their resistance. The reinsertion of Blacks into the historical process that gave rise to and drove perhaps the most decisive social and moral moments of the 20th century is a necessary corrective.

The relentless goal of Hitler's National Socialist Workers Party, as Michael Bureleigh and Wolfgang Wippermann point out, was to create a racial state that was built on the fantasy of breeding "pure" Aryans while eliminating all "others" including even some who would otherwise be considered white.[2] At the core of this framework was a pervasive anti-Semitism that consolidated state power with popular appeal resulting in Hitler's "final solution" that called for and attempted the murder of Europe's Jews. Other groups of people were also targeted for extermination, mostly notably the different Gypsy ethnic groups, as well as communists, homosexuals, Slavic peoples, and Jehovah's Witnesses.[3] Politically, Germany's response to the global crisis of capitalism was a racialized fascist state, supported by the German bourgeoisie and lingering nobility, that attempted successfully to consolidate its legitimacy among the middle and working classes upon the bedrock of anti-Semitism, the myth of Aryan superiority, and domination of the European landscape.

While this analysis is essentially sound and constitutes the consensus discourse on the racial politics of Nazism, it fails to demarcate the dynamics of the specific racisms that emerged under National Socialism. Multiracial societies in which racism is a major factor generate multiple racisms, that is, each identifiable and subordinated racialized group experiences a distinct relationship to the dominant racial class and to the state that has its own dynamics, history, logic, and path of development. These societies also ignite multidimensional forms of counterhegemonic, antiracist resistance. Though hardly alone, South Africa, especially during the apartheid era (and since), is perhaps the best example of this process given the rigid racial classifications that shape and drive that nation. Racism against Blacks, Indians, and the so-called Coloured took different forms as applied by the state and lived in practice.[4] In the discourse produced by Hitler and the Nazi leadership and its theoreticians, it is clear that a particular type of antiblackness gaze and praxis evolved that overlapped with anti-Semitism but had its own character, argument, and sociohistoric significance. Nazism's racial policies were also about politics, and a number of self-interest factors determined when and to what degree each particular racism was implemented despite what might have been the desires of Hitler and others. Local prerogatives were also a variable in the way in which racism was exercised. Additionally, while the Nazis could tap into an anti-Semitic predisposition on the part of the German masses, rooted in a long history of European antagonism toward Jews, it is not clear that a similar attitude existed regarding people of African descent although negative media images of Blacks were pervasive.[5] More important, the documented (and undocumented) lived experiences of Afro-Germans inform our understanding of the differentiated expressions of racism carried out by the Nazis and the German people. This study is an effort to excavate the nature and significance of "blackness" and "antiblackness" in Germany and the occupied lands in the periods preceding and constituting the Nazi era. This also includes identifying the oppositional praxis and resistance on the part of black Germans and other people of African descent trapped under Nazism, as well as the discourse and engagement regarding these issues from other parts of the black diaspora, including African Americans.

The dialectic between fascism and blackness is also an unexplored dimension of the period. In Paul Gilroy's *Against Race,* he contends that elements of fascism, in the form of ultranationalisms among contemporary black diasporic peoples, have appeared despite the apparent and real racist nature of fascistic ideologies. This provocation will also be explored in relation to the Nazi era itself and, in particular, the small but notable debate among African Americans whether they should oppose the war, support Hitler or National Socialism, or even embrace anti-Semitic thinking. This discussion was informed by some African Americans' limited knowledge of the desperate situation of Blacks in Germany.

Objectives of the Study

The purpose of this study is multifold. First, it is to expand our understanding of the Nazi Holocaust and all the peoples that were its victims. Necessarily, this project challenges and deconstructs the hegemonic discourse on the Nazi era that, for the most part, has written out or downplayed the presence of antiblackness and Negrophobia. In the thousands of books on the period, Afro-Germans and other Blacks, and their experiences are notable only for their absence. Classic works such as William L. Shirer's *The Rise and Fall of the Third Reich*[6] or more recent works such as Daniel Jonah Goldhagen's *Hitler's Willing Executioners*[7] are groundbreaking studies on the Nazi era and the politics of the time, yet offer no insight whatsoever into this particular slice of the pie.

In a similar vein, the large number of museums dedicated to remembering the Holocaust and the horrors of Nazism, including the U.S. Holocaust Memorial Museum in Washington, D.C., also give little, if any, exposure to the black experience.[8] At the USHMM, an important, unique, and indispensable archive of files on Blacks during the Hitler era is available to researchers, files that were critical to this present work. The museum, which opened in April 1993, has also held a number of special exhibits over time highlighting various aspects of the black experience. In 1997, for instance, it displayed the internment camp paintings and drawings of an Afro-Belgian artist (who was also Jewish by religion), Joseph Nassey. (See chapter 6) Despite these important efforts, in the permanent exhibits of the museum, which are the only exhibits seen by perhaps 90 percent or more of the two million visitors each year, there is virtually no black presence.[9] Located among the numerous museums on Washington's Mall, the Holocaust Museum receives the second-highest numer of visitors to the area, exceeded only by the U.S. Air and Space Museum, the largest museum in the world.[10] There are more than 100 Holocaust museums and research centers in the United States.[11] In a number of instances at the USHMM, displays note other victims of the Holocaust besides Jews, including homosexuals, Gypsies, and the handicapped, but consistently fail to include Blacks. Apart from a few photos of Blacks in an exhibit displaying identification cards of those who were sent to the camps, one could visit the museums' permanent exhibits and leave with no appreciation of this perhaps relatively small, but nonetheless important, aspect of the Nazi era.

Second, I argue that Nazism's racial agenda was complex, fluid, and contradictory as opposed to simple, straightforward, and unproblematic. A consensus reading of Nazism's racial agenda reduces it to its most vulgar expression: the implementation of the "final solution" of mass extermination. In fact, the Nazi racial agenda, rhetoric, and practice changed over time, was unevenly applied and carried out, and was often contradictory, especially in the case of Afro-Germans and the experiences of other people of African descent. In *Mein Kampf* and other works, Hitler and prominent Nazi leaders gave considerable and specific, though often incoherent, attention to antiblackness themes. However, despite a vicious and unyielding determination to create an Aryan-only society, and an ongoing rhetoric of Negrophobia and antiblack racism, the Nazis did not deport or (initially) exterminate Afro-Germans and Africans, or remove them completely from German social life. In fact, in many cases, they were allowed to attend schools and work while Jews and Gypsies were not. More important, a perpetual debate in Nazi ruling circles on the black question extended through the entire dozen years of

Nazi rule. These circumstances and occurrences demand a more complex reading of the will, capacity, and limits of the Nazis' racial agenda.

My third purpose is to deepen our knowledge of the experiences of the African diaspora. The European experiences of people of African descent are often forgotten when the diaspora is discussed, especially from an African American and, perhaps more broadly, American perspective. For example, in a number of comparative works on antiblack racism, the focus is invariably on the United States, South Africa, and Brazil, as a Ford Foundation–sponsored June 2000 conference, "Beyond Racism," held in South Africa, exemplified.[12] The tendency to privilege for research the large number of Blacks who reside in these nations and their overt and formal histories of legalized segregation misses the quality of the racial experiences of the much smaller numbers of Blacks in European societies: it also ignores the fact that the level of development of the United States and Europe, and how those states address issues of race and racism, are closer in nature than comparisons with vastly disparate societies.[13] There are, of course, some African American scholars who have given theoretical, historical, and contemporary attention to the European branches of the diaspora tree, including the sociologists Tina Campt and Charles Green, the political scientists Terri Sewell, Lorenzo Morris, and Ronald Walters, and the historian Allison Blakely, among others.[14] They are a welcome exception in terms of African American scholars. European race scholars, such as Stuart Hall, Paul Gilroy, and others, naturally are more cozignant of the need to connect and not just compare, this dynamic relationship.[15] *Diaspora* itself remains a contested term, one of social construction and fluid definitional character.

Fourth, I argue the need to reconceptualize our framework on racism and see racism as multidimensional, contingent, and intersecting. One of the lessons that we can glean from the Nazi experience is to view racism as differentially applied, contingent, and intersecting. The case has been made that in a given society multiple racisms may be in practice, that is, differentially constructed oppressed racial groups will face dissimilar experiences in terms of racism. This will include everything from portrayals in the media, the application of state authority, treatment in the criminal justice system, and opportunities related to education, health care, and housing. Relative to the Nazi period, the various racialized oppressed groups—Jews, Gypsies, Slavs, and people of African descent, among others—suffered distinct though overlapping racist encounters. The contingent nature of racism tells us that local prerogatives, in many cases, overrode national and general racial orders. This can be viewed in the experiences of Afro-Germans, who often lived isolated, where their individualized status—an "It's only one, so don't bother" attitude—allowed some of them a degree of protection that, in many instances, was enough for their survival. The contingent nature of racism also intersected with other exigencies such as the sexist-informed need to preserve a romanticized German womanhood even if it meant allowing a mixed-raced child to be spared the worst of Nazism's racial onslaught. More generally, the intersecting nature of gender, class, nationality, and race is inseparable in grasping the lived reality of Afro-Germans and other Blacks during the period, and in the present.

Finally, I examine the roots of contemporary European racism through the prism of the black experience under Nazism. The post–Cold War rise in incidents of racism and racist rhetoric in Europe on the part of both conservative and even mainstream political parties has among its features a distinguished Negrophobia. Manifest in the violent physical attacks on African workers and students, the criminalization of people of color, the slinging of the term "nigger," and the racialized discourse on immigration, antiblackness is not simply the contemporary expression of the so-called new racism, but is also derived from unresolved contradictions regarding antiblack racism from the Nazi era including the erasure of the black experience.[16]

Research on the experiences of Afro-Germans has a contemporary resonance. Since the end of World War II, there have been successful campaigns to seek compensation and reparations, estimated to be as high as $100 billion, for the victims of Nazism—those who were in the concentration and death camps as well as those who were forced into slave labor. It has been a struggle, mostly unsuccessful, on the part of older Afro-Germans to benefit from these victories because of the difficulty in proving their repression and specific targeting by the Nazis. The denial of compensation to Afro-Germans is due in part to the lack of a popular moral outrage over their experiences at the hands of the Nazis. Winning compensation is contingent not only on the justice that should be given but on the mobilizing of political and moral power that eases the process and embarrasses the German government and German corporations who still hold responsibility for the events of more than half a century ago. The postwar movement against racism that was a catalyst for the United Nations, the purging of notions of biological races, and the founding of the state of Israel, which played a key role in winning compensation agreements for Jewish victims of Nazism, virtually ignored the needs of surviving yet victimized Afro-Germans. It is time for a correction of the historical record.

A second compensation battle revolves around the descendants of the Herero peoples of Namibia. The 1904–1907 state-sanctioned German slaughter and near genocide of more than 80 percent of the Hereros ranks as one of the greatest atrocities of the twentieth century. A campaign in Namibia has been initiated to win reparations for a people who have never recovered economically from the theft and homicide inflicted upon them by German colonialism.

This inquiry also requires an interrogation of the German discourse and legal parameters regarding citizenship. Perhaps more than any other modern industrialized nation, Germany has fixated on blood linkages as the condition and determinant for full citizenship rights. Under German law, preceding, during, and even after Hitler, to become a citizen required that one be descendant from Nordic bloodlines, that is, the state sought to create, consolidate, and defend what Uli Linke terms a "community of blood."[17] In contemporary Germany, the issue of citizenship for a wide range of non-Germanic peoples who reside there remains a foundation on which everyone from neo-Nazis to politicians to the corporate and noncorporate media to "ordinary" German citizens can elaborate a xenophobic rationale masking a racism that has generally had state support, if not encouragement. Moderately successful efforts in 1999 and 2000 at changing the German citizenship laws operated within a context of new forms of German nationalism that seek again to close borders and shut doors. Within this discourse, Afro-Germans find themselves in a liminal position where their objective and legal citizenship is constantly questioned, while other people of African descent must fight alongside the Turkish, Roma, Sinti, and Arab communities against a rising anti-immigrant sentiment. Though not acknowledged as such—in fact, vehemently denied—the current anti-immigrant rhetoric echoes that of the Nazi era in significant ways.

This work is not about war heroes, war villains, or even the war itself. A large number of books regarding the black presence in the war are available, although it should be noted that again none mention the role of Afro-Germans or Africans in German society, or Blacks as prisoners of war captured by either the Allies or the Russians. Nor do those works document the experiences of African Americans or Afro-Europeans who were caught and imprisoned by the Nazis in the final years or months of the war. This is also not a study of fascism, which has been aptly done elsewhere. The story here is about completing the racial landscape upon which the Nazi era existed and unerasing the role that antiblackness played and the struggle for survival and perseverance waged by Afro-Germans and other Blacks who found themselves in a world where their very lives were at stake daily. It is about the intersecting dynamics of nationalist politics and the black diaspora at a time of great global military, economic, and political change, a time that was the last gasp of a period when racism was a central, overt, and acceptable dynamic in international relations.

Methodological Issues

One central question in a study of this sort is how to problematize our concern. It is not enough simply to identify a phenomenon—the repression and status of Afro-Germans and other people of African descent during the Nazi era and the contradictory nature of Nazism's antiblackness—one must decide how to approach the topic conceptually and theoretically. Critical concepts—race, racism, Nazism, fascism, the Holocaust, and diaspora—are highly contested and are not defined easily or compatibly. These concepts are examined more fully and critically in chapter 1. It is important to resist the temptation to generalize the application of these terms, though theorizing is necessary. It is most crucial to ground the experiences in a materialist reading of multiple causes and explanations within a general theory—employing Charles Mills's "racial contract" framework and Omi and Winant's "racialization thesis"—of racialized fascism.

Scholarly literature on Blacks in Germany during the Nazi era and the years preceding it remains thin. In German, Rainer Pommerin's seminal study—*Sterilisierung der Rheinlandbastrade* (*Sterilization of the Rhineland Bastards*)—of the so-called Rhineland Bastards, the mixed-race children born out of the post–World War I occupation, is one of a kind.[18] Although some other documents have been discovered in recent years, no other substantial work exists from that time that attempted to document the experiences of Blacks, German and non-German, from the end of World War I through the Nazi time. Even less exists in English.

Since the late 1980s, a notable and welcome upsurge took place in the research and publication of material about the Nazi era specifically focused on the experiences of

Blacks. These works, some in both English and German, run the gamut from the scholarly (*Showing Our Colors: Afro-German Women Speak Out* and *African-Germans: Critical Essays*) to the autobiographical (*Destined to Witness: Growing Up Black in Nazi Germany* and *Eine Afro-Deutsche Geschichte* [*An Afro-German History*]) to the research manuscript (Paulette Anderson), to the fictional (*Clifford's Blues*), and even a film (*Black Survivors of the Holocaust*).[19] These works are discussed in detail in chapter 1 and throughout and are part of a concerted effort to raise the profile of black history in relation to Germany's past and present. In addition, a number of dissertations, specifically by Tina Maria Campt, Fatimah El-Tayeb, and Nicola Laure al Samari, have been or are being done. Campt's dissertation, "'Afro-German': The Convergence of Race, Sexuality, and Gender in the Formation of a German Ethnic Identity, 1919–1960," focuses on the construction of blackness in Germany and the challenge to the dominant notion of Germanness as "white."[20] El-Tayeb's dissertation specifically focuses on Blacks during the Nazi era. Meanwhile, al Samari examines the distinct history of people of color on the East side of the Berlin Wall during the cold war era, an area of research that has been completely neglected by scholars. While not focused totally on the topic at hand, Paul Gilroy's *Against Race: Imaging Political Culture beyond the Color Line* also speaks to many of the subjects under consideration here and pushes the discourse to debate the penetration of fascist notions in contemporary black politics.[21] There is also a film production on the Rhineland children in the works by the journalist William Pleasant.[22] Collectively, these works reflect recognition of the need to correct the record and fill an important historical and intellectual void regarding the racial politics of the Nazi period and developments since then. This material does not argue that the Holocaust should be recast away from the Jewish experience, but rather that an expanded appraisal of the intentions, behavior, and perspectives of the Nazis toward Blacks should be included if a holistic view is to be obtained.

In addition to these works, this present study has benefited from several years of research using the many archives and depositories that perhaps themselves were unaware of the rich pool of history they held. Museums and special libraries in the United States and Europe have provided critical and indispensable information that simply was not available elsewhere. Buried in these articles and documents are gold mines of resources on the topic at hand. Among these materials are photos, cartoons, editorials, film and television scripts, diaries, interviews, declassified intelligence documents, and letters from a wide variety of sources.

An equally important and interdependent development has been the contemporary social and cultural evolution of an Afro-German identity manifest in the creation of a number of organizational and political activities. In 1986, the Black German Initiative (ISD) was created to unite Blacks across West and then later East Germany. This movement seeks to assert a positive identity for those of African descent. ISD sponsors an annual gathering for all Blacks that is mostly social but includes workshops, informal discussions, cultural presentations, and networking. While the ISD for the most part eschews political activism around issues such as immigration rights and compensation for discrimination, its very existence recognizes the difficult situation in which black

Germans find themselves and their determination to resist marginalization and erasure. Another very important group, whose members overlap to some degree with ISD, is ADEFRA, an organization comprising black German women. They initially came together around their common experience of being both women and mixed-raced, and the particular issues they faced at the nexus of gender and race. ADEFRA has also developed strong ties with black women from other parts of Europe, North America, and Africa. There has also been an explosion of publications, businesses, and nonprofit organizations aimed at people of African descent.[23] The contemporary face and fact of blackness are discussed in chapter 12.

Finally, I will note the crucial and determinant role of personal interviews, formal and informal, that were conducted in the research for this study or journey of racial discovery. My first encounter with Afro-Germans is linked to the collapse of Eastern European socialism. The fall of the Wall opened the door for diasporian contacts between people of African descent from the East and those in West Germany and in Western Europe in general. These encounters brought forth not only critical facts and thought-provoking insights but a surfeit of perspectives and viewpoints that matured this work over a number of years of research. From surviving and thriving Afro-Germans, to younger black Germans from throughout the diaspora embarked on their own paths of historical discoveries, to ex-patriot African Americans, who bring another kind of insight into blackness in Germany, and countless others, this work is a best effort at consolidation and synthesis of a wealth of input, a concert of many voices, instruments, tones, melodies, and rhythms.

"Afro-German" and the Nomenclature Problem

Throughout this work a number of terms are used to describe and categorize the different groups of people of African descent under discussion. I recognize from the outset that these terms are problematic at both the general level and at the level of specific use. Race (as described in chapter 1) is amorphous, fluid, socially constructed, and political, and any attempt to come up with precise descriptive terms must fail. Thus, the terms I use are compromises that serve my ability to discuss and perhaps better understand the reality of racial practices and racism.

Naming difference has historically been a site of vigorous contestation. In the United States, Brazil, South Africa, Australia, and other significantly racially stratified societies, how people of color have labeled themselves or been labeled by official bodies has never been settled for long because the racialization process continues.[24] This nomenclature problem affects all groups in society. In the United States, for the social group now generally referred to as African Americans, a number of labels have been used from the early seventeenth century when they first began to arrive in significant numbers up to the present. This includes "African," "Colored," "Negro," "Afro-American," "Black," and "African American." Complicating this process more have been terms to describe those of "mixed-raced" heritage such as "mulatto," "octoroon," and "quadroon," all terms that have been used on the U.S. and state censuses. Many of these individuals, faced with the unyielding racial structure in the United States, have embraced two or more of these racial identities, confounding a uniracial protocol. Neither African Americans nor the broader society ever completely or permanently adopted these appellations for reasons that span personal, group, state, and political decisions.

Again, to use the United States as an example, in a similar vein, "Hispanic," "Latino," and "Chicano," among others, have been used to conflate a wide group of nationalities whose primary basis of unity is the Spanish language and, in some instances, a common history of Spanish colonialism.[25] Even more troubling, the terms "Indian" and "Asian-American" seek to bring together widely different communities of people whose unity, to the degree it exists at all, is tentative and conditional, and in some ways externally generated by the dominant culture.

At the same time, Pan-African, Pan-Asian, Pan-Arab, Pan-Hispanic, and panindigenous movements have also been proactive and used these terms as a progressive assertion in the face of racist oppression and ideological assaults. The coming together of seemingly disparate groups under one banner is, in fact, a logical and even self-preservative motion driven by the nature and state of oppression that is indeed common across a number of boundaries. Forging an identity of resistance, even if on relatively fluid foundations, is a necessary stage in developing a counterhegemonic voice and sociopolitical movement. This development is a form of cultural struggle that embodies what the late African revolutionary leader Amilcar Cabral called "necessarily a proof not only of identity but also of dignity."[26]

In the quest for a cultural and political counter to a long history of erasure, "Afro-German," or *Schwartz Deutsch,* presents a number of answers, provocations, and challenges. First, it is a relatively new term. According to the authors of *Showing Our Colors,* the late Afro-Caribbean poet Audre Lorde made the first meaningful introduction of the term into the German racial discourse while teaching, a graphic demonstration itself of the intersecting diasporic nature of racial conditions.[27] The generally smooth acceptance of the term by some of the emerging Afro-German activists was conditioned less on its poetics or sound than on its naming an experience that could easily be identified with by many. However, as with the longer history of struggling over names that African Americans have gone through, "Afro-German" has not been embraced by all of those who would seem to fit under the label, that is, particularly many of the Africans who have immigrated or reside in Germany today. In fact, the term may be a transitional one that will reflect both the degree to which German society addresses the issue of racial difference and the political maturation of black people who may or may not make the issue of (anti)blackness a core concern in their movement for democratic inclusion. It is not a given that challenging antiblackness racism in Germany will need, in the long term, the particular Afro-German label, although the need for acknowledging black identity will remain. The struggle over Germanness will be just as important for many as the struggle over blackness.

A second challenge in using the term while describing the history of people of African descent in Germany is that it should no way be seen as reflecting a self-conscious racial awareness or group identity. In fact, there is plenty of historical evidence that while a black race consciousness existed among people of African descent in

Germany at the individual level, given the individual racial experiences that occurred, at the group level a collective race consciousness was minimal or nonexistent. This was perhaps one of the chief reasons why the Nazis gave less priority to the elimination of the Afro-Germans. In many ways, class and national differences were more important in determining the character and status of the African and African-descended populations in Germany in the pre-Nazi decades. Along these lines, a number of black organizations, discussed in chapter 3, did emerge that demonstrated that some Blacks in Germany were attempting a race-conscious mobilization, efforts that ultimately could not survive the Nazi onslaught. A countervailing force to the minimized group race consciousness, however, was the globalization of the racial experiences and the racial struggle of African Americans and Caribbean blacks, the anticolonial movements, and Afro-European positionings that informed perceptions of race across the world. I would note particularly, for the purpose of this study, the presence of African Americans in Germany, the influence of African American organizations that by the late 1920s had an international reach, and the popular knowledge of their segregated status in the U.S. South as creating a general awareness globally of racial difference in a black-white framework. I am not arguing here that there was or should have been an African American dominance, but only that the differentiated position and status of black Americans gave them a disproportionate influence in shaping global black issues and perspective.

All of these labels not only embody contests over identity but reflect the deeper core of issues that arise in the effort by oppressed racial and ethnic groups to liberate themselves both internally and externally. The historic transformations and struggles over nomenclature prompt political discourses over identity both between dominant and dominated groups and within dominated groups. This identity yearning has consistently been thwarted by the reality of powerlessness. As Grant and Orr note, "The frustrating search by blacks for a group designation reflects their continued subordination within the American political and economic system."[28] This frustration (and search), I contend, can be applied to other groups in a similar state of subordination.

Thus, for the sake of descriptive clarity and dialogue, "Afro-German" will be used in this work to describe those of African descent who were born and raised and primarily identified themselves as of German nationality, if not necessarily of German culture. For the most part, this cohort is by definition of mixed racial parentage because anyone who was not "Germanic," meaning racially white, could not by themselves become a citizen, although there were exceptions and some nonmixed Africans did become German citizens. The term "Africans" is applied to those from the African continent of a phenotype that ranges from dark to very light, avoiding the complicating though intriguing topic of "Whites" of African descent. The generic term "black" will refer broadly to those of African descent in Germany during the period under discussion whether they were German nationals or not. Please note that this is different from the contemporary "black German," which refers to all Germans of color, citizen or not, who reside in present-day Germany, including those of African, Asian, Middle Eastern, Latin American, and Caribbean heritage.

It is also important to be aware of the difference between "non-Aryan" and "Negrophobia." The former, as employed by the Nazis, could sometimes mean only Jews and at other times include people of African descent, Gypsies, or other non-Germanic people broadly. In fact, as the record shows, the Nazis themselves were sometimes flummoxed by their own policy and political statements regarding mixed-raced peoples and what restrictions applied to them, since in many instances, unlike the Jews or Gypsies, Afro-Germans were not mentioned specifically and only implied. Negrophobia, on the other hand, which I will often use, is specific to people of African descent. I try to make these distinctions clear throughout the text. As for usage, whenever a term is used as a noun to describe a group, it is capitalized, that is, "Black" or "White." When a term is used as an adjective, it is lowercase, as in "black" or "white."

Finally, other than when direct quotes by others are employed, I will not use terms such as "non-Whites," "non-Blacks," or "non-Europeans." At times, this may make the writing cumbersome, but it is critical to make clear the need for a shift in the point of reference employed in the languages of race. No individual or group should be defined by who or what they are not, particularly when the standard has been constructed on racist groundings. As problematic as are all the labels that I described above, from the vantage point of the oppressed, they generally reflect a resistance to being made invisible and dehumanized. My compromise bends in that direction.

The Road Map

Part 1 sets a social and theoretical context for our journey. While this is not primarily a theoretical work or a historical treatise, it is necessary to contextualize and conceptualize the pertinent questions regarding race and racism in Germany and, more generally, present them as social dynamics in modern society.

As it sets a social, political, and theoretical framework for the rest of the study, part 1 problematizes our topic. Chapter 1 focuses on a number of the theoretical concerns that are raised by exploring this relatively uncharted land. The construction of blackness under Nazism and its meaning for a range of discourses is central to our study. The task here is to examine the distinctiveness of the racialization process as it unfolded in Germany for those of African descent. To uncover this uniqueness as it relates to Germany in the first half of the twentieth century requires a deconstructed reading of the relevant concepts employed by German intellectuals, scientists, and state officials. I employ the philosopher Charles Mills's framework of a "racial contract" among Whites as a context by which to examine German and European racial ideas and racial practice.[29] I also look at how this context has been framed by recent theoretical works on black racialization in Germany during the era. The notion of racialization has been perhaps most noted in the work of Michael Omi and Howard Winant and, with qualification, will provide the conceptual platform for the discussion along those lines.[30]

Part 2 focuses on the pre-Nazi era. It was in this era that the black presence made itself qualitatively felt. In particular, in the period from the mid-1880s—when German colonialism in Africa began—to the rise of Hitler, Germany was affected by a complex transformation of modernism and the advances and contradictions of the industrial era that also brought forth "scientific" racism, primarily in the form of eugenics. This, in part, took the form of a discourse by which Whites in Europe and the United States came to define, rationalize, and contain the "other." In Germany and the United States, a confluence of interests and ideas marked a close relationship that flowed between eugenicists in both nations and the racial meanings of their collaborative efforts. Chapter 2 looks at the modern history of contact between the new German nation and people of African descent, both in Africa and in Germany up to World War I. A wide range of black voices emerged, from native-born Afro-Germans to Africans from across the continent to African Americans who sought the intellectual and cultural spirit that characterized Germany during the late nineteenth and early twentieth centuries. This chapter also includes a review of the practice of human exhibits, particularly of Africans, as human or subhuman oddities in Europe and the United States from the mid-1880s until at least the 1930s. Africans as exotica and Africans as scholars, students, and diplomats coexisted in the same space, creating a need for a complicated negotiation of racial signification and understanding.

Chapter 3 analyzes the European-wide discourse and controversy that arose after World War I regarding the placement of black troops in occupied Germany and the children they left behind. France, along with England and the United States, sent troops that included people of African descent, as well as other people of color, to the Rhineland, igniting a regionwide effort to rebuild the unity of Europe along racial lines, an effort that was partly successful. While this controversy has been given some scholarly attention, little discussion has been held on the way in which this particular issue influenced the racial policies and views of Hitler and other emerging leaders of the fledging National Socialist Party in the mid- to late 1920s. I argue that the antiblackness tone of the black troops and Rhineland children debate found its way into the racial ideology of the Nazis and shaped significantly how they would address the black issue. Black resistance of the pre-Nazi period is also examined by a detailed discussion and analysis of the independent black and antiracist organizations that were active in Germany in the 1920s and early 1930s.

Part 3 focuses on the Nazi era itself. Chapter 4 looks at the discourse articulated by Adolph Hitler and other Nazi leaders on the question of Blacks. The transition from the 1920s to the Nazi era constitutes a qualitative change in the fortunes and destinies of Blacks in Germany. As non-Ayrans, Blacks would feel the wrath of Nazism although filtered through the prism of a particular Nazified notion of Negrophobia. There were frequent references to Blacks and Africa in Hitler's seminal and signature work, *Mein Kampf.* Writing in the mid-1920s and advocating the popular consensus on race as a biologically rigid category, Hitler used the controversy of the black troops to elaborate a rambling and often incoherent but nevertheless strong antiblackness and Negrophobic thesis that, while often linked to his anti-Semitism, has its own arguments and character. It becomes clear that the issue of blackness was not to be ignored and was constitutive in the construction of a fluid and contextualized Nazi racial paradigm. The rest of this section focuses on specific areas of encounter between Blacks and the Nazi state and society.

The Nazis, after a serious debate and consideration about whether to exterminate or deport Afro-Germans, decided against these options. After they came to power, one means by which the Nazis attempted to deal with their black "problem" was through sterilization. Informed by the global eugenics movement, German scientists allied with Hitler, in lieu of extermination, determined that Afro-Germans (and some other Blacks) not be allowed to reproduce. Afro-Germans, who were not included among the groups identified when the sterilization law was passed in 1933, were nevertheless targeted for this procedure, and secret, often nighttime visits by the Gestapo spirited a significant number of Blacks to hospitals where they were operated on. Chapter 5 identifies the ideological, political, and organizational links between eugenicists in Germany and the United States from around the turn of the century through the mid-1940s. I show how collaboration between German and American eugenicists was strong and ongoing, and thoroughly imbued with racial meanings and objectives. While this link has been made before, the politics of resistance and connections between Afro-Germans and African Americans has not been explored. This chapter looks at the implementation of sterilization programs in both nations and the politics of resistance that emerged from these campaigns.

Chapter 6 looks at the experiences of Blacks in the many different types of imprisonment camps—internment, labor, concentration, and extermination—created by the Nazis. An unknown number of Blacks suffered and died in the labor and concentration camps. Thousands of captured black colonial troops from France perished in POW camps. In this chapter, a number of case studies are explored, including those of the artist Joseph Nassey, the Congolese resistance fighter Jean Johnny Voste, the entertainer Johnny Williams, the former Senegalese president Leopold Sedar Senghor, and the African American jazz trumpeter Valaida Snow, focusing on the few instances of black camp experiences for which there are some data and knowledge available. It is not possible to generalize this experience because many variables shaped the status and situation of Blacks in the camps, such as nationality, the level of overall brutality, the type of camp, and the period of the war.

Finally, in this chapter, reports of black massacres by German soldiers and civilians are also presented. U.S. Army records and other sources document a large number of credible reports of the slaughter of captured black troops. Just as Jewish American soldiers would be often separated, brutalized, and killed when caught by the Nazis, African Americans too would often face this treatment. Here, the politics of the controversy surrounding the film *Black Liberators,* which contends that Blacks were among the first soldiers to arrive at the concentration camps, is explored.

Chapter 7 notes the manner by which black performativity etched a dualistic text of resistance and collaboration on a social landscape where the threat of death, incarceration, and violence was pervasive and constant. For many Afro-Germans and others of African descent, survival was contingent upon their ability to sing, dance, and act, that is, satisfy the propagandistic and entertainment demands of the Nazis. Their performances capture the contradictory nature of the racial predilections of the Nazis, who were repelled by Blacks as a "race" but, at the same time, wanted to appropriate, exploit, and even enjoy the cultural skills they possessed. Even after Goebbels banned all Blacks from officially performing in public cabarets and shows, black actors were used consistently in Nazi propaganda films. Indeed, the Nazis created their own version of a black cultural presentation with the infamous "German Africa Show," which lasted for a number of years under the authority of Goebbels's Ministry of Culture.

In chapter 8, the even more contradictory Nazi policies toward jazz are investigated. The attacks on jazz by Goebbels and other Nazi officials reflected the Nazi interpretation of jazz as both *black* and *Jewish*, making it totally unacceptable for mass consumption. The war against jazz thus became a means of reifying racial superiority from the perspectives of the Nazis. This was also the case for the Americans. The assault on jazz's racial character was global, and slanders bounced across the seas from Berlin to Birmingham, from Hamburg to Harlem. In Nazi Germany, jazz remained popular and the efforts at banning the music merely sent it underground rather than destroying it. More broadly, even among Nazis themselves, jazz was often condoned and even encouraged with the result that a number of concentration camps had jazz bands. The attempted eradication policies also generated a youth resistance movement, though more social and cultural than political, that objectively challenged the authority and the legitimacy of Nazi leadership. The movement, however, would deliberately eschew any attacks on the fundamental racist foundations upon which the antijazz campaigns were constructed.

Though given only peripheral attention, sports were also a vehicle through which Nazi racial ideology and antiblackness were filtered. Hitler viewed sports training as essential and devoted energy to preparing young Germans physically, especially young men in the boxing skills. He also viewed sports through a racial lens, and German success, at any level, was seen as validation of the all-around superiority of the Aryan race. Afro-Germans discovered that nationalism and who could represent the nation constrained their sports possibilities and opportunities. It is in this context that the challenges presented by boxer Joe Louis, runners Jesse Owens and Ralph Metcalf, and other African American athletes can best be appreciated. The skills of Louis and Owens challenged directly the myth of Aryan physical supremacy. The 1936 Olympics, held in Berlin, was a prism through which a discourse on racial liberalism as differentiated by the "democracies" and German fascism was played out. Chapter 9 also examines how issues of national loyalty and racial loyalty clashed as many Whites in the United States found themselves caught between cheering Blacks, whom they looked upon as otherwise inferior, over German Whites, who were rapidly emerging as the uncomfortable polity of a dominant foreign enemy state. Meanwhile, many Blacks in Germany viewed black sports victory as an absolution and cause for a heretofore-absent racial pride. It is here where perhaps many Afro-Germans faced, for the first time, the dilemma of divided loyalty between race and nation, though with fractured concepts of the former and necessarily ambiguous feelings toward the latter. The racial politics of the Olympics (along with the Louis-Schmeling fights) may be the closest that Nazi-era black Germans came to Du Bois' famous "double-consciousness" psychic quagmire in which African Americans found themselves. Ironically, African Americans and the Nazis highlighted the contradiction of the condemnation of Hitler by the same voices that promoted and defended segregation and racism in the United States.

Also discussed in this chapter is the important Olympics boycott movement that failed. It represented, beyond the critical coalition of Jews and African Americans who sought it, a determined courage to challenge the political interests of the U.S. state, which viewed the Olympics in nationalistic terms.

Chapter 10 looks at the military and nonmilitary means by which Blacks resisted Nazi racism. This includes participation in the formal resistance movements as well as more discursive and individualized forms of defiance. Except in a very few instances, there is very little known about the participation of Afro-Germans and other Blacks in the popular and underground resistance movements in Germany and the occupied lands. This appears to be, in part, the product of both lack of research data and perhaps too rigid a definition of what it meant to fight against the Nazis. The space for political and militant struggle was severely curtailed, and often the only means available were tactical, spontaneous, and small acts. At the same time, feeling perhaps more vulnerable than most, black Germans sought to remain as invisible as possible and understandably avoided any path that would lead to arrest and detention. Outside of Germany, a thriving anti-Nazi resistance movement did exist in other parts of Europe in which Blacks did participate.

Chapter 11 addresses the issue of contemporary racism and race relations in Europe. As Europe is coming together under the auspices of the European Union and other processes, it is also coming apart at the racial seams. From the ethnic wars still humming in Central Europe to the immigration battles in the West to the rise of neo-Nazi organizations in the East (and the rest of Europe), the issue of difference remains salient. Race in Europe is influenced by the past, but also by both internal and external contemporary political and social developments.

Chapter 12 examines the contemporary status of people of African descent in Germany. While comprising several communities, Germany's contemporary black community has increasingly identified itself as such and, unlike in the past, has forged a collective opposition to racism and ethnocentrism. This chapter also looks at the present discourse and politics regarding race and racism in Germany, and the resistance on the part of an estimated 200,000 to 500,000 people of African descent. While racism in Germany and Europe in general has flourished in the post–cold war, globalization era, there is an identifiable antiblack dimension that must be extracted and analyzed. Throughout Germany there persists an antagonism toward Blacks, whether they are Afro-German or other Blacks, that resonates many of the themes of Nazism. Indeed, a relatively tiny but significant neo-Nazi movement has arisen and been strengthened by the unification of the two Germanys while authorities have been slow, if not hesitant, to pursue many of the known guilty parties.

The campaigns for compensation by Afro-Germans and Nambia's Hereros are also examined. As of this writing, there are still a number of Afro-Germans living who survived the Nazi period. Many of them were forced to do slave labor, were in the concentration camps, or were sterilized. In general, under Nazism, Afro-Germans suffered constricted opportunities that theoretically were categories for compensation. Yet, in many cases, they have been denied benefits from the compensation agreements that have been drawn up in the years since the war, the most recent being the U.S.–brokered deal with the German government, German corporations, and the United States in the fall of 1999. Billions of dollars were at stake in the negotiations that sought to compensate somewhere between 1.5 and 3 million slave laborers.[31] Little known outside of Germany, and barely inside, the effort by Afro-Germans to win compensation for their suffering is a telling and significant barometer by which to measure the degree to which Nazism has truly been buried or determine that, as Martin Lee warns, the beast has reawakened.

Finally, it should be noted again that this study is only one voice in a movement of research being done by an increasing variety of scholars and activists inside and outside of Germany. And, I for one, view it is a good sign that a matrix of perspectives and viewpoints—different roads to the same destination—are being expressed as we all discover the undiscovered country of the experiences of Blacks under Nazism.

"Look, a Negro!"

The Structuring of Black Marginality in Nazi Germany

[A]s the material conditions and lived experiences of race are subject to change, so, too are the ways in which race is imagined, represented, and performed.
—*S. Craig Watkins*[1]

Breaking the Contract

In *Black Skins, White Masks*, the late Caribbean psychiatrist and revolutionary theorist Frantz Fanon explores the psychoracial dimensions of social marginality. He is particularly concerned with the ways in which racial experience is mediated and determined through external means and the impact on internal self-conceptions. This process is captured in the defining instant, as Fanon sees it, when white recognition of the black subject—"Look, a Negro!"—manifests as an imposed othering and dehumanization from which there is little escape. The ontological moment for the black "other" is not only denied but aggressively repressed by the nature and state of subjugation in which people of African descent find themselves. Thus, for Fanon, a black-inscribed skin condemns one to a position that requires a mask, a means of simultaneously hiding and existing. Fanon's explication of the colonial encounter from the vantage point of the subaltern astutely illuminates the lived experiences of Afro-Germans and other Blacks in Germany during the Nazi era. This critical slice of black Diasporic history has generally remained unknown and buried even to many Afro-Germans themselves, denying them and us an important appropriation of historical knowledge. The objective of this study, in part, is to reclaim that lost history and integrate it into a larger project that reexamines the phenomenon of Nazism's "antiblackness" during the National Socialist era as it impacted Afro-Germans, Africans, Afro-Europeans, African Americans, and other people of African descent. The delineation of the black experience in the Hitler period is necessary if we are to understand the full arc of the racial paradigm articulated and carried out by the Nazis, and its legacy on the discourses of race that mark modern Europe.

Germany during the Nazi era, similar to South Africa under apartheid and the United States in the Jim Crow period, embodied and manifested the extreme logic of what the philosopher Charles W. Mills refers to as the "racial contract." Using the "social contract" framework associated with Western philosophers such as Rousseau, Locke, Hobbs, and Kant, Mills argues that the racial contract is a set of formal and informal agreements entered into by Whites that sets the parameters of social space for all "others." This exploitive and hierarchical arrangement "is a contract between those categorized as white *over* the nonwhites, who are thus the objects rather than the subjects of the agreement"[2] (emphasis in the original). This dynamic contract is both political and moral in its development and impact. In its political iteration, it "establishes a racial polity, a racial state, and a racial juridical system" that allows for and defends, with full state power, white dominance in daily and social life.[3] Nazi Germany, of course, more than fit this description. But it was not alone, a factor that problematized the critiques raised by other racial states aimed at Nazi Germany as its attacks on Jews and its overtly racialized language drew international attention. Thus, the racial contract is also a globally derived, globally implemented, and globally defended pact. Across Europe and North America and in other enclaves of "white" power a covenant exists that asserts the political, social, and moral authority of Whites. Since the dawn of imperialism and European expansion more than half a millennium ago, racism has been central to the course of global politics, economics, and cultural development. In the first three decades of the twentieth century, the contract held a consensus on the biologically determined necessity of white rule over the world's colored people. Far from being an aberration from this treaty of sorts, Nazi Germany was in the 1930s and early 1940s only its most extreme expression. As Mills writes, "The Nazi project can then be seen in part as the attempt to turn the clock back by rewriting a more exclusivist version of the Racial Contract than was globally acceptable at the time."[4]

The racial contract, however, also should be seen in relation to the social contract theory of the Enlightenment philosophers. As Mills argues, the racial contract is not outside of the social contract, but its ugly underbelly, that is, "The Racial Contract is thus the truth of the Social Contract."[5] The social contract, despite its claim of universality advocated by Rousseau, Locke, and Kant, was meant to be applied racially. While contemporary philosophy ponders the seemingly contradictory character of the racist views of its founders, on the one hand, and their "progressive" calls for an elevated humanity, on the other, Mills contends that there is no inconsistency—if one is willing to blow up the canons.

Mills's racial contract framework is extremely helpful and timely in theorizing the location of Afro-Germans (and others of African descent) within, first, the social structure of pre-Nazi Germany and, second, under Hitler's rule, a transition from a mere hegemonic whiteness or Aryanness to a state of total dominance. The Nazis would appropriate the central tenets of the racial contract even further by isolating and target-ing for extinction many who would otherwise be considered phenotypically white. In effect, the Nazis made the racial argument that while perhaps all Whites are equal, some are more equal than others. As Harold Isaacs contended, Hitler's Germans attempted "to make themselves masters of the master race."[6] In any case, there was no mistaking the first principle that all Whites were certainly superior to all others. The racial con-tract is, therefore, implicated in promoting a discourse of erasure that has removed people of color from German history. Tina Campt notes the conflation of what it means to be German with whiteness when she asserts "the hegemonic discourse of German identity remains a homogenous and homogenizing discourse of whiteness; one that often results in a definition that conflates Germanness with a form of identity —that is, whiteness."[7]

The notion of a racial contract among German Whites also has powerful explanato-ry resonance in addressing the issue of popular support for racist policies implemented with savage force by the Nazis. Some writers, such as Goldhagen, attribute mass acqui-escence to the Nazi racial program to cultural predispositions that were vehemently anti-Semitic and racist. Goldhagen's conclusions are harsh as when he writes, "'During the Nazi period, all of the Germans' policy initiatives and virtually all of their important measures towards Jews, as different in nature and degree as they manifestly appear to be, were in the practical service of, and indeed were symbolically equivalent expressions of, the Germans' desire, the Germans' perceived need, to succeed in the eliminationist enterprise."[8] Note that Goldhagen's language refers to "Germans" and not just "Nazis" as the culprits. While German and European anti-Semitism were very real, his work, however, borders dangerously on the discredited terrain of biological determinism or essentialism that eschews more historicized political, economic, and ideological factors. Others, such as Wilhelm Reich's *The Mass Psychology of Fascism,* have looked at collec-tive psychological factors as central variables that drove the Nazi machine.[9] Here again, there is a lack of concrete grounding in the real political and power dynamics upon which these psychological dimensions rest. The salience of Mills's argument is that it encompasses and explains not only the moral (cultural) and epistemological dimen-sions of popular support but also the political aspects. It is also easier to see the social and cultural ways in which Blacks in Germany were viewed and why they would be oppressed even where they may not have been included in what Goldhagen calls an "exterminationist" consensus in terms of the German people's attitude toward Jews.

The Fabrication of Race:
Philosophical Roots of the German Racial Contract

It should come as no surprise that the first use of the term *race* to distinguish groups of people based on physical and phenotype differences emerged from Europe. In 1670, a rather obscure travel writer, François Bernier, published anonymously *Voyages de Bernier*—known in English as *Travels in the Mogul Empire*—in which he discussed his journeys over twelve years through Egypt, India, and Persia. Writing in immortal prose, Bernier states, "I have remarked that there are four or five species or races of men in particular whose difference is so remarkable that it may be properly made use of as the foundation for a new division of the earth."[10] While other travel writers, of course, had commented on the physical differences between Europeans and those outside of Europe, Bernier elevates the discourse to a planet-level partition with profound implications for the future relations of geographically separated peoples. Neither scholar nor saint, he goes on to discuss in profuse detail the substance of his categories, adding comments on the relative "beauty" of the women of the world. A century later, Bernier's racial vista would be manifest in the works of the first generation of "race scientists" or "race-makers."

In 1776, coincidentally the year that the U.S. Declaration of Independence was written, a German scientist, trying desperately to demonstrate his independence from his mentor and make a name for himself, published *On the Natural Variety of Mankind,* a treatise on racial classifications that prophetically divided the peoples of the world into five groups. Johann Friedrich Blumenbach, a relatively visionary sort, would indeed make his mark upon the world. The groups that he defined were the Caucasians, Mongolians, Ethiopians, (native) Americans, and Malays. Although his mentor Carolus Linnaeus had constructed a taxonomy of four racial groups based on geographic determinants as early as 1758, it would be Blumenbach who would go down in history as the father of the Enlightenment's racial classifications schematic.[11] His geometry of race would forever remap how the world viewed itself, and govern the ongoing debates over race. Blumenbach is also (in)famous for the creation of the designation "Caucasian," which he named after the Caucasus mountain cluster, which lies between Russia and Georgia, because in his eyes it "produces the most beautiful race of men."[12]

For his time, Blumenbach could be considered racially tolerant and perhaps even enlightened. He espoused what was seen by some as a radical view, when he noted that he did not think racial boundaries were impenetrable or different groups were unalterably and permanently unequal. Yet, at the same time, he did not demonstrate a scientific understanding of the fallacy of race. His arbitrary and ultimately racist grouping of peoples into boxes and his creation of an aesthetic hierarchy laid the groundwork for political, scientific, and academic rationalizations for two centuries of global white supremacy. It would be irrelevant to future scholars of racist dogma that Blumenbach did not hold to the notion that intellectual or moral capacities were significantly differentiated or immutable between phenotypically distinct groups of people. These theories of eugenics emerged in the age of imperialist expansion, and the racial boundaries that Blumenbach contrived provided the ideological and moral justification for decades of slavery, colonialism, and mass genocide on an international scale.

Given the subsequent ravages of the slave trade, slavery, and colonialism, racial theories in Germany (and across Europe) had global influence even before the rise of eugenics and Hitlerism. Blumenbach found his place in a long line of pre-Nazi philosophers and intellectuals who would be a whole lot less charitable than he in their views of the possibilities of racial coexistence. At the head of the line rises the name Joseph Arthur de Gobineau, a French nobleman who preferred to be called Count Gobineau, and has been dubbed the "father of modern racist ideology."[13] His two-volume *Essay on the*

Inequality of Human Races (Essai sur l'inegalite des races humaines) was the foundation-
al text, in many ways, for the theoretical movement that saw race in biological and natural terms and, consequently, in social and racist terms. Gobineau wrote, flying in the
face of contradictory evidence, "History shows that all civilization derives from the
white race."[14] He exhibited an extremely distasteful form of Negrophobia, writing, "The
black race is the lowest, and stands at the foot of the ladder."[15] Most critical, he foreshadowed the Nazi mantra when he wrote, "Race dominates all other problems of history and holds the key to them all."

Not to be outdone, the Enlightenment philosophers Kant, Locke, Hegel, and
Rousseau demonstrated a noteworthy lack of enlightenment on the question of race. At
the top of the pecking order is Immanuel Kant, considered by many to be the most significant of the moral theorists of the Enlightenment. In one well-known passage in
which he implicates a fellow philosopher, he wrote,

> The Negroes of Africa have by nature no feeling that rises above the trifling. Mr.
> [David] Hume challenges anyone to cite a single example in which a Negro has
> shown talents, and asserts that among the hundreds of thousands of blacks who
> are transported elsewhere from their countries, although many of them have even
> been set free, still not a single one was ever found who presented anything great in
> art or science or any other praiseworthy quality, even though among the whites
> some continually rise aloft from the lowest rabble and through superior gifts earn
> respect in the world. So fundamental is the difference between these two races of
> man, and it appears to be as great in regard to mental capacities as in color.[16]

Mills contends that far from seeking a greater enrichment of human harmony, Kant
"demarcates and theorizes a color-coded racial hierarchy of Europeans, Asians, Africans, and Native Americans, differentiated by their degree of innate *talent*"[17] (emphasis
in the original).

Other Enlightenment luminaries, such as John Locke, who had profitable invest-
ments from his ties to the notorious slave-trading Royal Africa Company, and Jean-
Jacques Rousseau, who was convinced that the only natural "savages" were peoples
outside of Europe, had more than their share of contradictions and incongruities.
Alongside them strolled the philosopher Georg Wilhelm Friedrich Hegel, who in his
Encyclopedia of the Philosophical Sciences wrote, "Negroes are to be regarded as a race of
children who remain immersed in their state of uninterested naivete. They are sold, and
let themselves be sold, without any reflection on the rights or wrongs of the matter."[18]

These works would inform German thinkers of the late nineteenth century including Houston Stewart Chamberlain. Hitler was influenced greatly by the writings of
Chamberlain, who wrote the seminal *Foundations of the Nineteenth Century* in 1899. An
Englishman by birth and a close friend of Kaiser Wilhelm II, Chamberlain wrote, "Race
lifts a man above himself, it endows him with extraordinary—I might almost say super-
natural—powers, so entirely does it distinguish him from the individual who springs
from the chaotic jumble of peoples drawn form all parts of the world."[19] Hitler would

profusely praise Chamberlain and his work, and the feelings were returned in kind. Joining the Nazi Party in 1923, in its earliest days when it was viewed as an irksome political movement at best, Chamberlain viewed Hitler as destined to lead Germany in its greatest time of need. He wrote, after meeting the future führer, "With one stroke you have transformed the state of my soul. That in the hour of her deepest need Germany gives birth to a Hitler proves her vitality; as do the influences that emanate from him"[20] Prone to believing that his writings were driven by demons that inexplicably possessed him, Chamberlain morphed the theories of Gobineau into the political machinery of the Nazi movement. His zealous anti-Semitism, to the point where he claimed that Jesus Christ was probably an Aryan, bred and fed the Nazis' racial views, in particular, Hitler's.[21] Hitler clearly took to heart Chamberlain's view that "Nothing is so convincing as the consciousness of the possession of race."[22]

Chamberlain matured in a period not only of prolific intellectual energy being devoted to exposing and defending white supremacy and European racial theories, but of virulent and extreme instances of racist violence on a global scale. These theories translated into anti-immigration and segregationist policies in many nations and colonial territories. From Australia and New Zealand to South Africa and the United Kingdom[23] to the United States and Canada, the bluntest racist language was used to argue for and win successful campaigns to exclude and contain people of color. The 1882 Chinese Exclusion Act explicitedly banned Chinese immigrants from entering the United States for the next ten years and denied citizenship to those already here. In Canada, anti-Chinese bias was expressed in the song "White Canada Forever," a line of which went, "We welcome as brothers all white men still, but the shifty yellow race ... must find another place."[24] The fashioning of anti-immigrant sentiments along the lines of a national racial identity took on a global manifestation, but it developed most aggressively, in the still colonial age in Western Europe. Germany, particularly in the post–World War I atmosphere of political bitterness, embraced these notions and was able to marry contemporary discourses on race with traditional national chauvinism emerging, in one iteration, in the formation of the German Worker's Party in January 1919.

For Hitler and the founders of the Nazi Party, the notion of race would be directly linked to the concept of *völkisch*, which translates into a philosophical view that embeds people and nation into one. The concept of *völkisch* would be another ground that anti-Semitism could seed. As one writer noted, "In my view, anti-Semitism is, though a major motive, but part of a more extensive concept of racism underlying the racist Nazi population policy, which in turn is rooted in the specifically German *völkisch* notion of the nation and *Volk*."[25] This popular notion of nation and people was the context that the Nazis could rely on in constructing a more fervent racial state and compelling, deadly anti-Semitism.

German Predisposition on Blackness

It is difficult, if not impossible, to determine the historic point when the English term "black" became primarily negative in connotation and began to be used in a derogatory manner against people of African descent. In a groundbreaking article on the topic, the scholar Alan James elucidates his complex, intense, and ultimately inconclusive search for this answer. He determines that it was "from about 1200 onwards" that offensive connotations of black tied to race grew and that that coincided with increasingly hostile contact between Europeans and Africans, Middle Easterners, and Asians, pretty much guaranteeing a linkage that remains to the present.[26] Although he had neither the time nor the resources to confirm it, James seems to think that this thesis may be applicable to other Germanic languages. In any case, he argues that further research needs to be done to test his hypothesis on the influence of religious and mythical symbolism and ritual in constructing and framing the meaning of "black" and "blackness" in European societies.

Others have written about the importance of images of blackness in the development of the German discourse on race.[27] The point needs to be underscored for a number of reasons. First, in the preliterate era, images were a critical means of socializing of an illiterate population. Truly, one picture was worth one million words in Germany in the eighteenth, nineteenth, and early twentieth centuries. Second, German racists recognized the propaganda and ideological value of images, and long before Hitler and Goebbels came to power, caricatures of Blacks, including African Americans and Africans, were used to unite white Germans and white Europeans under the symbolism of white supremacy.

What was the impact of these images in Germany? Above all, they reinforced the notion of white superiority against the darker races. This took on a political form in Germany in the notion of a *Herrenvolk (master race)* democracy, that is, a democracy for Whites, servitude for everyone else. The state, in other words, would play a critical and enforcing role in the racializing of power and politics. Views toward Blacks were also shaped philosophically by the colonial and postcolonial relationship between Germany and Africa and the popular images that were created through that encounter. Though only tangentially involved with the slave trade, the German people came to know of Africa and Africans in a manner that privileged Germans.

There were German thinkers who specifically addressed the issue of people of African descent. One of the most important early German race scholars and philosopher on race was Christoph Meiners. Writing toward the end of the eighteenth century, he ranted,

> The Americans are unquestionably the most depraved among all human, or human-like creatures of the whole earth, and they are not only much weaker than the Negroes, but also much more inflexible, harder, and lacking in feelings. Despite the fact that this communication contains only a few traits of the terrible portrait of the bodily and moral nature of the Americans, one will nonetheless feel, and be astonished that the inhabitants of a whole continent are so closely related to dumb animals.[28]

Meiners was a strong defender of slavery, and he was a firm believer in racial and sexual inequality. Although relatively obscure, his views were revived by the Nazis.[29] He argued that Blacks were made inferior not only by their skin color but by their entire physical being.[30] Meiners's Negrophobic diatribe was consistent with the racial biology prevalent at the time and later held as gospel by the Nazis.

Autarky vs. Liberal Internationalism:
Depression, Nazi Racism, and the Crisis of Global Capitalism

As powerful as they were, we should be assured that it was not just racist ideas and philosophies that ushered in the era of National Socialism. Following World War I, Germany faced a devastating economic crisis. This was due, in part, to the retribution that the country had to pay following its loss of the war as stipulated in the Treaty of Versailles.[31] Despite a period in the mid-1920s when Berlin and other cities enjoyed a relative prosperity, there was an overall deepening economic crisis, and by the end of the decade a full-blown depression had set in. Following World War I, liberal internationalism reemerged and U.S.-based banks and financial institutions liberally funded Western European nations, particularly Germany, contributing to a growth spurt. This same system, however, would overextend itself and—coupled with domestic monetary policies that let the money supply fall precipitously, collapsing thousands of banks—would begin to eat itself by the end of the 1920s. Autarkyism was the response to the spreading U.S. economic crisis as Germany, England, the Soviet Union, and Japan each attempted to create regional blocs and abandon the international system. Domestically, a strategy of direct intervention, most ruthless in Germany, Italy, and Japan, brought together political extremism and economic extremism. On a global scale, the Great Depression would remap the international economic situation, collapsing economies on every continent. In 1929, the stock market crashed with prices dropping on the New York Stock Exchange by 74 percent. In the United States, between 1929 and 1932, the crisis manifested itself in declines in manufacturing (49 percent), construction (76 percent), nonfarm employment (22 percent), earnings (27 percent), wholesale prices (32 percent), farm prices (54 percent), exports (69 percent), imports (65 percent), and the number of banks (44 percent). These declines resulted in over a millon homes being foreclosed and depositors losing about $10 billion.[32]

Germany was especially hard hit by the international crisis as it not only had large war debts still to pay (100 million pounds annually), but also watched its exports and imports fall by half in a matter of three years. As the historian and Caribbean-born activist C. L. R. James notes, by the middle of 1932, "German production was fifty-five percent of what it had been in 1928. Nearly seventy-five percent of the industry was at a standstill. Between January 1930 and January 1933, imports declined by two-thirds and exports by nearly half ... Tax after tax crippled the workers and poor, crisis tax, occupation tax, head tax, salt tax, turnover tax to the small trader. But on the other hand, the big magnates had been granted financial aid amounting to 144 billion pounds. By this time, the unemployed were nearly seven million and there were 300 suicides per week."[33]

Du Bois would also note the crippling economic situation of Germany, stating that the country has lived through "horrors in living history that no people can experience and remain entirely normal. These are: War; the Treaty of Versailles; Inflation;

Depression, and Revolution."[34] He particularly blamed the decision at Versailles. According to Du Bois,

> The treaty deprived Germany not simply of one-eighth of her territory, popula-
> tion and arable land, but what was far more important, of a fifth of her coke;
> three-fourths of her iron, one-fourth of her blast furnaces, two-thirds of her zinc
> foundries, one-fifth of her livestock, all of her merchant marine, and most of her
> railway equipment. And then saddled her with a debt based on unheard-of princi-
> ples, which no land could or did pay. In other words, in order to establish peace,
> the capitalists of England, France and America made the orderly return of
> Germany to work and self-support impossible without internal revolution.[35]

Employing a class analysis, he continued, "And the people who paid in Germany were the thrifty, the workers, the civil employees—the very classes who had opposed war in the first place ... The accumulated savings of the nation disappeared; pensions, in a land of pensioned civil servants, were stopped; loans were paid in worthless money; property values dropped to nothing; industry was in bankruptcy and labor out of work."[36] Noticeably missing in Du Bois's assessment is a critique of the capitalist class of Germany and its complicity in the deprivations faced by the German masses.

It was this calamity that fed the frustrations the Nazis were able to exploit more effec- tively than any of the other political forces of the time. Neither the liberal parties nor the leftist parties could win sufficient support to stop them. Concessions by the liberals and tactical and strategic errors by the left as well as its in-fighting opened political space for the Nazis' cultural and racial explanations of the crisis and their argument that only an authoritarian hand could bring the situation to a resolution the German and interna- tional bourgeoisie advocated and was willing to finance. It was within this framework of capitalist crisis that a racial paradigm of resolution took hold. The desperation that gen- uinely existed was ripe for exploitation, and the Jewish community that was financially well positioned was a convenient and historically used scapegoat. The logic of an Aryan political economy also meant that other non-Aryan groups as well were not to be included in the racial-economic solutions being proposed. As Solomos and Black note, "For most Germans who were living in conditions of urban poverty the consumption of these images meant their individual misfortune could be lost in the alluring racial fan- tasies of 'heimat' [home] and the promise of a better future."[37]

Hitlerism represented the various strands of German social life. It spoke for the con- servative bourgeoisie who were profoundly antidemocratic and anticommunist. It was a populist banner carrier for much of the impoverished working classes who sought jobs and economic relief. And it stood for the consistently anti-Semitic middle classes who sought social and political stability. It was the necessity of this electoral coalition that required the Nazis to adopt conciliatory and often conflicting public stances as they tactically moved to construct a winning alliance.

To a degree, however, this also explains why the Afro-Germans were of limited inter- est to the Nazis, because they existed neither as a cultural or social community nor as an economic or political community. Other than for strictly racial reasons, or abstract references to the occupation trope, it was impossible to link Afro-Germans to the crisis. While the Nazis, in their drive for power, lost little support in attacking Blacks, they also gained little, so it was simply easier to focus on more pressing political concerns while leaving the assaults to the propagandists and theorists of the party. After coming to power and first addressing the economic and employment crisis, the Nazis would eventually include Blacks in those banned from many occupations, though not all, that were reserved for Aryans. The Nazis argued that Jews had jobs that should belong to Aryans. Unlike Jews, who worked in a number of sectors where their presence was felt economically, Blacks did not and could not dominate any economic area.

The Unimagined Community:
Black Germanness and an Incomplete Racialization

Nazi ideology and practice sought to do at the state level what was impossible at the practical one: identify and codify rigid racial categories. This task necessitated a mammoth bureaucracy that included coercive and propagandistic dimensions in an effort to resolve the contradictions between the state objectives and lived experiences. Given this dissonance, as Susann Samples points out, "[T]he racist state policy of the Third Reich was not always monolithic, but often contradictory. Undeniably, racism permeated German society, but the degree and type of persecution directed toward African Germans (or, for that matter, any of the designated non-Aryan groups) varied greatly."[38] The variance that Samples notes is the localized and personalized nature of race relations and racism often obscured in the macro-level analysis of racial politics.

In grasping the content and forms of Nazism's antiblackness, the most relevant unit of analysis is, in many ways, that of the individual. The micro terrain of experiences—the lived understandings—created conditionalities that determined the nature of the racial life of individual Afro-Germans and other people of African descent. At the same time, the political agency of Afro-Germans, on the one hand, and the attention given by the Nazi state, on the other, demonstrate that a critical mass of Blacks existed such that the specter of blackness under Nazism rises to a level beyond the individual. It is this dialectic that informs the process of black racialization in the pre-Hitler and Hitler periods.

The Samples's insight noted above requires that we seek a more complex understanding of marginality, black marginality in particular, under Nazism. Among the questions to be asked are: (1) Was there objectively and subjectively a black community, that is, did Afro-Germans and other Blacks residing in Germany during the Nazi era regard themselves in a collective manner? (2) Did Nazi policies at the local level toward Afro-Germans and other Blacks contradict the otherwise substantial racial hatred at the core of their ideology? (3) How self-conscious need the notion of an African diaspora be in order to claim its existence? (4) Were Germans predisposed to treat Blacks differently from Jews or other racial or ethnic groups?

An important factor in determining the relationship between Afro-Germans and other Blacks in the periods under consideration is the absence of social or political power. It was this state of powerlessness that conditioned and determined what the experience of Blacks would be under Nazism. What is important here is that the notion of power not be limited simply to the capacity of the state to control the economic and social life of a particular group. The state, in this instance, entirely dominated and managed the discourse on race with little space for a counteroppositional voice or political movement. The hegemonic reification of Aryan superiority was all-encompassing.

Michael Omi and Howard Winant in *Racial Formation,* and elaborated further in Winant's *Racial Conditions,* argue that racialization is an ongoing process in racially stratified societies.[39] Their racial formation theory (RFT) states that in all circumstances where racial groups come into existence, the relationship between them as well as the content of those particular categories cannot be reduced to or explained by ethnicity, class, or "color-blind" frameworks. Instead, they contend correctly that racial categories have their own dynamics in which objective and subjective conflicts between racial groups emerge, are transformed, and are constantly remapped; that is, race is "an unstable and 'decentered' complex of social meanings constantly being transformed by political struggle."[40] This is to say that while the particular social configurations of race relations will vary from society to society, one can still theorize and generalize about racial intercourse by noting and examining the ever-changing political construction and use of race, racial categories, and racial groups. The two writers argue further that racialization is carried out by the creation and institutionalizing of "racial projects," that is, the multitude of ways by which a group identity manifests itself in the social realm. These projects may be cultural, economic, social, or political, and again, may be initiated by the state or the groups themselves.

Poststructuralists have emphasized the role of narrativity in identity construction including that of race. Narratives can be described as the popular stories of community that reflect deeper meanings, understandings, and significance regarding one's role and status in society. As the researchers Margaret Somers and Gloria Gibson explain, "it is through narrativity that we come to know, understand, and make sense of the social world, and it is through narratives and narrativity that we constitute our social identities."[41] Racial identities, according to the paradigm, are constructed and mediated through political struggles that embody contending narratives across overlapping historical and social landscapes. In other words, racial categories are neither fixed nor consistent, but, in fact, are permanently in flux shaped by the transformations in society in any given period. In this sense, racial groups come into existence, exit the historic stage, are expanded or shrunken, and have varying levels of cohesion and identity. Racialization also occurs from a number of concurrent vectors including state-imposed definitions, popular identities, and self-identity, all of which can be in conflict with one another, and are ever changing. Many groups, for example, resist state-defined notions or narratives of who they are, while, at the same time, the state often refuses to acknowledge or accept the racial identity that a particular group seeks. At the individual level, racial identity can range from weak to severe, yet may often again be imposed and resisted from the outside. In particular, racial identities defined by appearance generate numerous and unresolvable contradictions for individuals who may be rejected from a group identity that they seek or be pulled into one they do not. And racial identities exist in relationship to other identities such as class, gender, sexual orientation, nationality, and religion, to name only a few. Moments in which one identity may appear to dominate are transitory at best and more often illusionary and artificial.

In Nazi Germany, state-imposed definitions dominated and set the tone for the structure and nature of the racial society. These definitions, built upon the bogus precepts of racial science, were unforgiving and allowed no space for categorical blur. Unlike in the United States, Brazil, the United Kingdom, or even South Africa, the Germans believed Afro-Germans could not "pass" for Aryans. The massive state bureaucracy established to rigidly identify one's racial background surpassed apartheid South Africa in its intensity and pervasiveness.[42] The effort to seize control and direct the racialization process was the objective of the Nazis from the beginning and was carried out with methodical obsession. According to the historian George Mosse, in Germany, "Racism was a visual ideology based upon stereotypes."[43] This meant that for Afro-Germans, their identity was inscribed upon their bodies. As the Afro-German Holocaust survivor Theodor Michael recalls, "Blacks could not hide." [44]

What appeared to be what I would call a dictatorship of phenotype, however, was tempered by several factors. First, it is unknown how many people of African descent passed for White or Aryan. As has been common in most racialized societies where phenotype serves as a visual means of categorizing, this practice is undermined by the fact that heritage does not determine in all instances a uniformity of appearance. (More than a few, for example, noted that Hitler himself hardly fit the model of a blond-haired, blue-eyed Aryan.) Having a parent of African descent does not guarantee that the offspring will not look phenotypically white, and, in Germany, where most Afro-Germans in the period were of mixed parentage, it would seem clear that at least some *could* and *did* pass for Aryans. This is an unexplored issue, so virtually no information is available on this phenomenon, common in societies as diverse as Brazil, the United States, and South Africa. Of course, a major barrier to being able to pass in Nazi Germany was the vigorous efforts by the state to racially identify every single individual as fully as possible through the creation of a number of state operations and institutions.

Second, people of African descent experienced what can be conceptualized as an "incomplete racialization." While Fanon is useful in explaining the colonial racial encounter and its subjective dimensions, his otherwise valuable insights are limited in their application to the racial situation of those I have referred to as Afro-Germans. At the core of Fanon's work is an assumption of distinguishable and reified racial categories. The imperfect or unfinished racialization experience of Afro-Germans makes it difficult to argue, as Fanon does, that racism created a racial dissonance among people of African descent. In many ways, this thesis presumes a community that, in the case of the Afro-Germans, did not exist.

While the Nazis and other German racial ideologues before them may have viewed Afro-Germans and Africans as a racial group, all indications are that they did not view themselves as such. The idea of an Afro-German did not even exist, although difference was obviously recognized. No black racial community formed during these early periods. What often occurred was the conflation of phenotype, race category, and geography. Whereas from the outside, all people of African descent were seen as one racial group, internally, a clear distinction was made by Blacks determined by nationality, as well as class and social status. Different groups from Cameroon, Togo, Liberia, and other African states congealed into nonracial networks and quasi-communities, while, at the same time, an Afro-German community failed to appear. In this fluid circumstance, identities and locations could transform and blur as Africans interacted with Afro-Germans through marriages and other personal relationships. Fundamentally, there was no social ground on which a racial community of Afro-Germans could be established—culturally, politically, socially, or economically. Even that most trusted distinction—language—did not manifest to differentiate Afro-Germans from other Germans. In other words, to employ the Omi-Winant frame, no racial projects of an Afro-German kind came into being. It is likely that a severe "racial" dissonance was felt by many Afro-Germans who felt and were treated as different but had no means of living that difference.

New Works on Afro-Germans

In the late 1980s and 1990s, a divergent body of literature began to emerge that examines the black presence in Germany and, to a lesser degree, covers the Nazi era. This work took up the challenge of theorizing and well as historicizing the experience of people of African descent and their encounters with Germany. In *Farbe Bekennen: Afro-Deutsche Frauen auf Den Spuren Ihrer Geschichte (Showing Our Colors: Afro-German Women Speak Out)*, an early and important effort to analyze the history and contemporary significance of being black and female in Germany, the three women who edited the collection present a sweeping, often personal view of their subject. In many ways, it has become the standard-bearer for subsequent scholarly research on the subject. While the book does not take up a number of key subjects and gives only brief attention to a number of important ones, its value is immeasurable. The editors make no claim to present a theoretical framework, but they do locate black German history within a sociopolitical context that is essential in moving the discussion beyond the paradigm of individual prejudice and discrimination. At the same time, the authors note and demonstrate in the interviews and other articles that racism is also personal and painful. It is, in fact, the resistance to that pain that animated the authors to write the book in the first place. As black women, they were located at a particular juncture of race and gender that in the German context had real significance on a personal level.

The work accomplishes its mission, which is to tell in broad strokes the story of black Germans, particularly the gendered dimensions of that experience, to a popular audience. It is an unabashedly political effort that arises in the flow of political developments in Germany including the impending crisis of socialism, the growth of domestic racist organizations, and the knowledge of a global tide of resistance against racism in South Africa, the United States, and Western Europe. In the wake of that achievement, there remained a need for more focused approaches to the subject. Both at the theoretical level and at a detailed rendering of particular periods, experiences, incidents, watershed moments, and events, work had to be done. Along these lines, two scholarly works in English came to the fore: Tina Campt's dissertation, "'Afro-German': The Convergence of Race, Sexuality, and Gender in the Formation of a German Ethnic Identity, 1919–1960"; and the edited study *The African-German Experience: Critical Essays.*[45]

Campt's work is a brilliant and rigorous examination of the period after World War I up to the beginning of the 1960s, and how blackness was constructed, deconstructed, and reconstructed, and the strong attempts at destruction. Her approach is sociological with an emphasis on theory. The interviews she conducted with Peter K. and Clara M. (both pseudonyms), the subjects upon which she built much of her understanding of the black experience, are unique and exceptionally well done. Peter K. was born in 1920, and his Algerian father was part of the French occupying forces, while Clara M. was born in 1929 of a Liberian father. Campt not only manages to cull from these sources information that can generally be found nowhere else, such as Peter K.'s membership in the Hitler Youth, but also presents a compelling and ongoing assessment of the interview process itself as a means by which understanding of how racial meanings are differentiated even among Blacks is constructed. For example, she interprets her responses to her subject's response in terms of how racial understandings are informed by our national experiences as well as our racial ones. She also uses the interview process to draw theoretical meaning regarding the language(s) of race.

Her research on the history of Blacks during the Nazi era is brief but critical and well researched. She draws some important conclusions in her dissertation (and other articles she authored or coauthored) on the period. She offers, for example, a theoretically useful framework for understanding the racialization of Afro-Germans in her concept of "textured identities," where she argues that Afro-German identity is not static but out of necessity versatile.[46]

While Campt's work is an indispensable source for understanding the Afro-German experience, she does not link the experiences and interactions of the black diaspora to the cultivation and growth of the black German experience and perhaps identity even in the pre-Nazi and Nazi era.[47] These relationships, I argue, are constitutive of the identities and narratives that informed the era. Further, the link between Nazi leaders and scientists and their U.S. counterparts is also an important variable in the unfolding of the global racial policies, language, discourses, and experiences from the period.

Another important but different work is Hans Massaquoi's 1999 autobiography, *Destined to Witness: Growing Up Black in Nazi Germany*. (The German title is *Neger, Neger, Schornsteinfeger* [*Nigger, Nigger, Chimney Sweep*].) The picture on the cover shows a small boy of about six—clearly of African descent and surrounded by a group of "Aryan" looking youngsters—wearing a sweater with a swastika on it. This photo of Massaquoi was taken in Hamburg, Germany, in 1933, the year that Hitler and National Socialism came to power. Born in 1926 of a Liberian father, the son of the Liberian general counsel, and a white German mother, Massaquoi grew up in and, most remarkably, survived the Hitler years. Like other Afro-Germans, the Massaquois lived in a racial netherland—neither fully accepted by the majority nor able to claim a community among themselves to fall back on. Massaquoi's forte is to provide insight into the ways in which he negotiated the ambiguities of racial identity under the most oppressive circumstances imaginable.

He chronicles with humor, anger, pathos, and, ultimately, steadfast optimism, the survival skills that he developed as he struggled to survive daily living in circumstances that were relentlessly dangerous. At one point, when he was about eight, he was snatched off the street by a Nazi stormtrooper who wanted to hold him up as an exhibit of *Rassenschande* (racial defilement) to a gathering of his drunken comrades, a fate he was rescued from at the last minute by his enraged and protective mother. From this incident and others, he increasingly learned this primal lesson: don't draw attention to yourself. Unfortunately, he was a magnet for attention whether he wanted it or not, such as the time he and his mother visited the zoo and witnessed an exhibit of Africans living in their supposedly "natural" habitat. When the crowd spotted him, he became the objective of their curiosity.

By the time he was six and ready to attend public school in 1932, Massaquoi had endured countless racial taunts, such as being called "*neger*" and "mischeling," and he was already developing the lifesaving skill to know when to fight and when to retreat. After Hitler came to power in January 1933, a sign was put up at his neighborhood park, where he often played, that *Nichtariern* (non-Aryans) were forbidden to use the playground. Although his mother was able to get the park warden to make an exception, Massaquoi decided to never enter the park again.

For Massaquoi, his racial experiences were mixed. Some teachers and principals, generally members of the Nazi Party, treated him with unbridled contempt. His school principal, Heinrich Wriede, who was a "fanatic follower of Hitler," he characterized as "consistently mean-spirited and cruel."[48] Within a very short time, a mutual hatred evolved. And yet Massquoi does not present a picture of unrelieved misery. Other Germans treated him fairly, and at times even protectively. This included a science teacher, Herr Schneider, who admired his "beautiful, smooth brown skin," and Herr Gosau, the school's choir director, who made him a member of the choir. It is not quite so easy to know what to make of such relative acts of kindness, and how one might weigh them in the larger debate on the complicity of ordinary Germans in the genocide of the Jews. Perhaps as the known child of an African diplomat, he may have been spared the most brutal treatment of other Afro-Germans.

One of the most interesting dimensions of Massaquoi's experiences is how he handled the Nazi views against Jews. As a child, he was indoctrinated without opposition to the view that the Jews were the everlasting enemy of the German people and of their leader, Adolf Hitler. Thus, he worshiped Hitler as did all the young people his age. He remembers feeling strongly that the Jews should not be allowed to continue to mistreat Germany. However, his mother's liberal (and, therefore, dangerous) views and eventually his own moral sense influenced by a close friendship that he would develop with a Jewish family that lived in the neighborhood militated against his becoming an anti-Semite. Of course, his own position as a despised mixed-race person certainly eroded whatever tepid affinity he may have had for Nazism by the time he was a teenager. Indeed, far from internalizing the Nazi ideology, he seems to have been led by something akin to race pride to resist the Nazis, albeit in a symbolic fashion.

Massaquoi does not, for the most part, reflect on the larger significance of his life or the broader forces that produced it. Nor does he expand our knowledge of the experiences of other people of African descent who lived and died during the period, a criticism that has echoed through the Afro-German community. Rather, he grapples with the fateful turn of events that destined him to witness and persevere through one of the most tragic eras in human history. After the war, he eventually migrated to the United States where he joined the U.S. Army, served in Korea, and used the GI Bill to receive a university degree in journalism. He eventually found work at *Ebony* magazine, staying for thirty-nine years and rising to managing editor before his retirement.

Destined is very successful in conveying an understanding of the daily negotiations that had to be waged by people of color and those who did not fit the Aryan model. For him, racism was no abstract or temporary or incidental phenomenon. While his youngest days, before Hitler took office, were relatively comfortable and, as far as he can remember, discrimination free, the situation after 1933 worsened rapidly and exponentially. And certainly by the time he was a teenager, roughly in the 1940s, every living moment was tense with racial meaning and a misstep, or simply having the bad luck to run into an individual Nazi who was mean-spirited, could cost you your freedom if not your life. As a black person, Massaquoi had no social hiding space. In *Destined to Witness*, we can witness the maturation of his racial identity that was, initially and for most of the time he was growing up under Hitler, externally imposed and, later, internally reconstructed, as he met African Americans and then actually moved to the United States. In the book, he clearly did not readily accept the wholly negative identity that the Nazis wanted to saddle him with, but the circumstances were not conducive to developing an alternative racial identity that was satisfactory. There was no black community in Hamburg. Ultimately, he was left in a state of racial limbo that did not get resolved until after the war, and then in a manner that shifts the landscape from Germany to the United States. Even today, when asked what identity he embraces, he replies, "Politically, I'm American. I'm acquainted with the life over there. I'm part of the American society."[49]

By summer 2000, *Destined* had become number three on the bestseller list in Germany and more than 100,000 copies had been sold. A part of the book was serialized in a local German newspaper. Why the book became such a popular success is a matter of dispute among Germany's Blacks. Some contend that it raises and resolves satisfactorily for Whites in Germany the issue of the Nazi treatment of Blacks without an indictment of either Germany or the German people. This criticism rests on the fact that *Destined* is the story of a single Afro-German, not of all Afro-Germans. In other words, it satisfies the view that it was, at best, individual Afro-Germans that suffered, but not the group. Another weakness identified is that the book does not address the policies and political nature of antiblackness among the Nazis in a systematic way. Not identifying the role of antiblackness as a political one serves to undermine the the argument for recognition of a collective assault and for compensation.

Afro-Germans and the Black Diaspora

It is useful and necessary to locate Afro-Germans and the construction of a black racial status in Germany within a framework that recognizes the conceptual value of theorizing an African diaspora. The danger of diasporic frameworks is the tendency toward essentializing, that is, attributing characteristics and even values to groups of people across national, social, cultural, and historic timelines on the basis of common geographical and sometimes experiential roots. Many proponents of Afrocentricity, though not all, argue that there is a transhistoric carryover of "African" values and views that are distributed among people of African descent no matter where they are located or what experiences they have had to bear. Those notions aside, the common experience of antiblack racism, the legacy of slavery and colonialism, racialized patterns of migration and immigration, and the conscious outreach between people of African descent contributed to the construction of a descriptive diaspora that demands an assessment and analysis.

The political scientist Ronald Walters argues that the African diaspora was created by several historic and continuing variables including the slave trade and slavery; commerce, war; and immigration.[50] Unlike the black communities that formed in the Americas, Afro-Europeans did not emerge primarily out of the experiences of slavery, but rather as mostly voluntary immigrants from colonial situations. In this sense, the Africans who came to Germany in the latter part of the nineteenth century are more like their counterparts in England, France, Spain, and Portugal. However, in England and, to a lesser degree, in France, black communities and, more critically, a black identity (in addition to a national one) did arise early on that was fed by the knowledge and interaction with other international black communities. In England, for example, not only did Blacks come from Africa and England's Caribbean colonies, but also a significant number of African Americans emigrated to the United Kingdom after the U.S. Revolutionary War. They brought with them the culture and sense of community that had already formed among African Americans in the late 1700s. While there were African Americans who came to Germany in the eighteenth and first half of the nineteenth century, none are known to have stayed permanently and their interactions with Afro-Germans and Africans seem to have been minimal. In other words, they did not qualitatively influence a black identity development or the creation of the imagined black community. This would change in the decades following the middle of the 1800s.

In the immediate pre-Nazi period and during the Hitler era, there were significant contacts between Blacks in Germany and other black communities. These contacts are examined in more detail in chapter 3, but it is important to note here the complex manner by which black Germans fit into the paradigm of an African diaspora. Both objective and subjective factors are entailed in the notion of a functional diaspora. If a black or African descent identity is not embraced, either individually or collectively, then the question must be raised: Under what auspices is inclusion in the diaspora conditioned? The response to this query lies in the construction of the diasporian notion itself. If race is a fiction, can the notion of a racial diaspora not be? While this does not liquidate the social and political value, even the necessity of such a concept, it does put in perspective the difficulty of its realization.

Another dimension of the historic construction of the African diaspora is the centrality and dominance of African Americans. This position is shaped by the size of the African American community, its socioeconomic status, the internationalizing of its culture, and, in general, the hegemonic role of the United States. While, in some instances, this has led to resentment, more often it has led to an expectation and obligation that African Americans would contribute more to the security and well-being of the diaspora and to Africa itself. These expectations have generally been unreal and not appreciative of either the subjective politics of the African American community that has not consistently embraced an international political framework including the interests of other Blacks, especially those in Europe, or the objective economic and political status of African Americans that left little energy and resources for efforts outside of the United States. In addition, ideological and class divisions among African Americans (and, indeed, among all diasporic communities) are factors.

The discourse of an African diaspora, therefore, remains circumstantial, conditioned, and contested. Within contemporary Germany, citizens and residents of African descent vigorously debate their location with the global community of "black" people. While many increasingly view themselves as racially linked to other people of African descent, many do not and will not. No position on race is hegemonic, and the issue continues to problematize itself as each new generation confronts new political and social conditions. Black racial identity in Germany is intricably bound with the histories of Nazism, communism, Western capitialism, and post–cold war reunification.

Summary

The diasporic ordeal of slavery was not the experience or legacy of Afro-Germans or of the Africans who were in Germany at the end of the nineteenth century and in the first three decades of the twentieth. The mostly voluntary migration and journey to Germany as well as the "accident of birth" phenomenon constructed a black presence in Germany that was subject to racial prejudice and discrimination but was, in the main, not systematically victimized by a virulent, state-managed institutionalized racism. Thus blackness was not an internally mobilizing force for resistance against racism as much as it was an externally imposed and irregularly practiced social process that was not the most singular identity for people of African descent in Germany.

At the same time, however, a rich history of racist views and racist practices were not insignificant in shaping the contours of the Blacks who make up the population. All those in the pre-Nazi and Nazi periods who could be called black Germans, that is, biracial persons with one black parent and one white German parent, did not have immediate African heritage, but most did. And, of course, then there were those both of whose parents were Africans who did become citizens. Thus, the story of black Germans begins, in many ways, as the story of the African-German encounters in the era of colonialism and expanding European imperialism. Recovering and contextualizing this history has become essential for Afro-German scholars. In the context of contesting social erasure, history becomes not only a means by which to recapture dignity and identity, it becomes a tool of resistance.

Part II

Blackness before Hitler

Negrophobia
and Nationalism

An Epigrammatic History of
African-German Encounters

*In order to secure the peaceful White settlement against the bad, culturally inept
and predatory native tribe, it is possible that its actual eradication may become
necessary under certain conditions.*

—*Dr. Paul Rohrbach*[1]

*Within the German borders, every Herero, whether armed or unarmed, with or
without cattle, will be shot. I shall not accept any more women or children.*

—*Lieut. Gen. Lother von Trotha,
issuing the extermination order
against the rebelling Herero
in German Southwest Africa*

Germans in Africa

Berlin and the Tarzaning of Africa

Tarzan is an enduring symbol of the racialized imperialist project that characterized
Europe's relationship with Africa from the time of the first sustained encounters until
the most recent presence. The character embodied the dreams of white physical and ideological dominance over the always subjugated natives. As the writer John Newsinger
argues, in the analysis of Tarzan, the character's ideological mission was clear: "Tarzan
provides welcome reassurance of the whiteman's supremacy over both his women and
his blacks, a supremacy that is maintained in any circumstances, no matter how dire,
because it is rooted in the blood."[2] Dark hair and African-tanned skin notwithstanding,

Tarzan's white identity, superiority, and power, buttressed by an imposing physique as popularized in film, television, and literature, is never in question. Tarzan would become one of the iconic figures of the century, popular and commodified decades after his initial introduction to a global audience. In addition to the earlier films and books, there are, into the new millennium, comic books, websites, fan clubs, and other popular expressions of support for the character including a full-length Hollywood cartoon.

Tarzan was created in 1912 by the writer Edgar Rice Burroughs who based his work on the fanciful tales and travelogues of nineteenth century African explorers such as Joseph Conrad, Henry Stanley, and Rudyard Kipling.[3] Burroughs was a hard-core, anti-communist conservative who opposed the New Deal, attacked liberals and organized labor, and opposed the U.S. alliance with the Soviet Union during World War II. He also advocated eugenics as a means of dealing with crime.[4] While Tarzan did not specifically take up these issues in the Burroughs stories, the character did embody his creator's political philosophy. Similar to Daniel Defoe's *Robinson Crusoe*, Tarzan possessed what the critic Edward Said has called an "imperial attitude," and he functioned as a colonial ruler.[5] Tarzan, which means "without dark" or "white," did not impose a formal state structure over the jungle, but he was, in fact, the embodiment of the state, where all decisions were final, where punitive force could and would be applied when and where necessary, and where racial power was absolute.[6] Tarzan, of course, epitomizes anti-modernism and antiprogress, fighting the encroachment of a dangerous "civilization" upon his domain. His strength and organic intelligence had conquered the jungle and all that inhabited it, and that authority had to be maintained. Tarzan's triumphant individualism is more than just the "survival of the fittest," but expressively is the "survival of the whitest," imposing what Catherine Jurca appropriately terms his "intrinsically white identity" over the possessed and controlled territory of Africa.[7] His mission and role in Africa is captured well by Graham Murphy who writes, "Tarzan's domination of Mother Africa extends to everything within that jungle, notably the Africans. Throughout the various stories, native agency and independence is all but evacuated as Tarzan repeatedly assumes the dominant position."[8]

In the films and on the television series, the most enduring Tarzan was former Olympic swimming star Johnny Weissmuller. His character, as fabricated, enjoyed a moral imperative to protect the ancient ways and values of the African jungle—white mystifications that rationalized African disempowerment—even if this meant he had to destroy the people who lived there in order to save them. As "lord" of the jungle, he was, in fact, lord of everything and everyone in it. Another interesting phenomenon occurred as Tarzan made it to the big and little screens: he became an American. Although the story-line remained the same—Tarzan was the lost son of an English lord—he expressed a distinct American attitude and ideological bent. In 1943, during World War II, in *Tarzan Triumphs*, Tarzan successfully fought the Nazis, uttering the immortal words "Now, Tarzan makes war." Ironically, Weissmuller, an Austrian immigrant, was born on 2 June 1904, the month and year that German colonialism, then two decades old, would sink to its lowest and most brutal depth.

European nations, sparked by the industrial revolution, began to expand their global reach for terroritories and colonies with an obsessive intensity by the mid-1800s. As Bennett notes, "The steam engine, quinine for malaria prophylaxis, improved weapons, long-range communications, and a host of other advances made imperialism a cheap, feasible phenomena."[9] The scramble was on. Like schoolchildren fighting over stolen candy, the competition and bickering among European nations (England, France, Germany, Italy, Portugal, Holland, and Belgium) for African lands forced the convening of the infamous Berlin Conference of 1884–1885. Convened by the German chancellor, Otto von Bismarck, the leaders of the major European powers met from November to February to divide up Africa in a manner that would minimize conflicts among themselves and maximize the exploitation of the continent. Bismarck, who in 1871 had unified distinct states into one Germany forming the Second Reich, was the appropriate choice to guide this despoliant task. That the lives and societies of millions of human beings were up for grabs and would suffer some of the most ruthless episodes of genocide in recorded history did not give pause to these proceedings. The relatively recent emancipation of slaves around the world, in no small way by the initiative of those in bondage, had little moral or practical resonance for the participants, and divide Africa they did. Britain would get Rhodesia, France stole Senegal, the Belgians purloined the Congo; to Portugal went Angola, Cape Verde, Mozambique, and Guinea Bissau; and Germany, host of these suppers of thieves, acquired Togo, Cameroon, Southwest Africa (Namibia), and East Africa (Tanzania, Burundi, and Rwanda).

Not the Marrying Kind: German Racial Policies in the Colonies

European incursion into Africa began centuries earlier with religious crusades, explorers and adventurers, and, beginning in the fifteenth century, the slave trade. Germany had played a very minor role in Africa during the slavery era but, like other European nations, understood the value of the land and resources that Africa possessed. Activities would reach a crisis point in the 1880s as England, France, and other European nations sought to resolve their increasing conflicts over territorial control. The Berlin Conference put Germany into the game.

Beginning in 1878, German colonial policy would be set by a number of organizations and government agencies, including the Central Association for Trade Geography and for the Promotion of German Interests Overseas, and the German Colonial Society. In 1890, in an effort to manage Germany's growing multifaceted African operations, the Colonial Office was created. Germany's joining the colonizing wave of Europe was driven by its efforts to recover from a number of economic recessions during the period. The economic gains from their colonial enterprises, particularly the access to European banks and markets, were critical. As the journalist Olayinka Oludipe notes, "Access to the European colonial policy contributed greatly to the transformation of Germany from an agricultural to an industrial society."[10] There were more than eleven million Africans under German rule during its colonial period.

TABLE I   **German Colonial Populations, 1913**

Colony	Year Colonialized	Area in Sq. Miles	European Pop.	Indigenous Pop.
Togo	1884	33,700	368	1,031,978
Cameroon	1884	191,130	1,871	2,648,720
SW. Africa	1884	322,450	14,830	79,556
E. Africa	1885	384,180	5,336	7,645,770
TOTAL		931,460	22,405	11,406,024

Source: Lewis H. Gann and Peter Duignan, *The Rulers of German Africa, 1884–1914* (Stanford, CA: Stanford University Press, 1977)

Racial policies in the colonies unfolded at a rapid pace as Germany turned phenotype difference into a hierarchy of power. Administration of the new territories was contextualized by an awareness and implementation of a racial divide that justified the German presence. Whether through the trope of "betterment" or the troops of the German Army, control of natives was a top priority and was mediated through a discourse of racial dissimilarity. This meant, in the first instance, resolving the issue of commingling. In the early colonial period, while there was no bar to mixed marriages, they were not welcomed with great enthusiasm. By 1890, however, colonial marriage registrars would not officiate at or sanction mixed marriages. Yet, since it was easy to travel to South Africa or areas where the English were in command and did not forbid such couplings, legal marriages between the races could be carried out. The debate escalated, however, and in 1905 the Southwest Africa governor, von Lindequist, issued a decree banning mixed marriages, a prohibition that would be echoed in German East Africa the following year. In 1907, Southwest Africa and Cameroon would pass laws that retroactively annulled mixed marriages that had been legally obtained. Trailing the other colonies, Togo banned mixed marriages in 1908. Finally, in 1908, Article 17 was included in the Colonial Home Rule Act to punish white German husbands who engaged in mixed marriages with an abrogation of their civil rights and disenfranchisement.

The argument for the attacks on mixed marriages foreshadowed similar contentions that would be the hallmark of Nazism's rationalizations: the protection of German blood. A generation before Hitler, the case was being made that racial mixing was to be avoided at all costs if the German nation was to survive. Not only were colonial peoples and *Mischlings* (mixed-race people) to be denied any opportunity or vehicle for citizenship, which, in part, was how the mixed marriages were viewed, they were legally banned in 1913 from even carrying German names.[11] Decrees were also issued, but ridiculously ignored, outlawing sexual liaisons between Germans and Africans. Unless an unprecedented flood of German women was to suddenly decide to come to the colonies, there was little chance that cohabitation and ongoing sexual interaction would slow down, let alone cease.

Given the ferocity of the debate, it is easy to think that at a minimum, thousands of mixed marriages were being sought. In fact, given the millions of Africans under German colonial rule, and the thousands of Germans who served in the colonial service, the number of mixed marriages on record in 1912 for all the colonies was a lowly 166. The panic in some quarters over this paltry amount demonstrates less a concern over a real "racial" threat to Germany and more a hard-line, even maniacal intolerance that would expand in the years ahead.

The Colonial Debate in Germany

In 1905, the German Southwest Africa colonial government proposed an imperial ordinance outlawing interracial marriage. In 1906, a similar ordinance followed for German East Africa, and in 1912, for Samoa. The debate over the Samoa policy in the Reichstag was complicated. The new law stated that marriages that existed before the ordinance would remain legitimate and that the children from those marriages would be classified legally as white (to be known as *Mischlingsliste*) and German citizens. Marriages that happened after the new law went into effect would be automatically annulled, and the children of those relationships would be seen as indigenous, and allowed to obtain German citizenship only after they had submitted an application, demonstrated fluency in German, and displayed an enthusiasm for "European Bildung" (European building).[12]

The discussion in the Reichstag was less a debate than a reaffirmation of the justification of such laws. While the Social Democrats gave soft opposition to the antimarriage laws, they equivocated totally on the issue of racial mixing. Adolf Grober, of the Catholic Center party, in arguing for the ordinances, declared, "Negroes are not fit for Christianity." One significant but no less racist argument was made by the Social Democrat Eduard David, who contended that Samoan women are very beautiful and should not "be thrown into the same pot with negro [*sic*] women." In the end, the Reichstag voted, 202–132, in favor of the law with one abstention and two invalid votes. The arguments presented regarding the humanity (or rather the lack thereof) of Blacks and Samoans, and ultimately anyone who was not seen as Aryan, would surface again and again. The language of race used to describe these groups would easily be extended to Nazi arguments against the Jews and others from the mid-1920s onward. As Helmut Walser Smith notes insightfully, "People who thought in terms of race thought with the future . . . in terms of cultural progress, now of Empire and coming struggles."[13] In a word, they thought of the coming Nazi era.

In the Reichstag, only the Social Democrats, primarily August Bebel, viewed the 1904 Herero uprising as a freedom revolt. Bebel was the parliamentary whip of the German Socialists and he battled with the conservative Graf zu Reventlow over the meaning of and response to the war. Fundamentally, Bebel viewed the Nama and Herero as *Volk*, that is, a people or a nation. While he did not challenge the legitimacy of colonial rule directly, he did attack the manner in which it was carried out against the people who lived there. He called the German attacks on the indigenous population "not just barbaric, but bestial," words that the opposition would deem "a hymn of praise to the Herero." He argued passionately "for humane treatment, for universal human rights, and against the illegitimate domination of one human being over another."[14]

The opposition argued that the Africans were not a nation, and for many not even people. The most vocal supporter of the war was a staunch supporter of the colonial mission, Reventlow, who called the Herero "blood thirsty beasts in the form of humans." Another conservative, Wilhelm Lattmann, stated, "The black race, even when it accepts Christianity, cannot from the standpoint of race be considered to be of equal worth to the white race." Most legislators engaged in the debate—even those who allowed that they were human—believed that they were barbarous. Further, some in the Reichstag felt that the Africans "lacked the capacity to be educated to moral independence." One member, described as a left-liberal, proposed a U.S.-styled solution. Muller-Meiningen asked, "Would it not be possible, much as we have reservations for wild animals, much as we have Indian reservations in North America, to build reservations for the natives in the interest of the native groups whom culture does not really penetrate?"[15] This proposal embodied a contradiction for the liberals because it also signaled an accute failure to acculturalize the natives, the only terms on which liberals and the left, reflecting their times, could justify German colonialism.

Dress Rehearsal for the Coming Holocaust?

> International law becomes phrases if its standards are also applied to barbaric people. To punish a Negro tribe, villages must be burned, and without setting examples of that kind, nothing can be achieved. If the German Reich in such cases applied international law, it would not be humanity or justice but shameful weakness.
>
> —Heinrich von Treitschke, political scientist, 1898[16]

Genocide existed before the invention of the term in 1944 by the Polish jurist Raphael Lemkin.[17] When European imperialism met African, American, and Asian societies, and the latter resisted being conquered, more than just mass murder took place. Conquest required, in many instances, a totalizing eradication of a people, their culture, their legacy, and their memory. As Lemkin wrote, what was necessary was the

> disintegration of political and social institutions, of culture, language, national feelings, religion, and the economic existence of national groups, and the destruction of personal security, liberty, health, dignity, and even the lives of the individuals belonging to such groups. Genocide is directed at the national group as an entity, and the actions involved are directed at individuals, not in their individual capacity, but as members of the national group.[18]

That such butchering would be couched in a language of religious and cultural missionaryism only served to embellish the cruelty of it all. With practices similar to those of the British, French, Spanish, Portuguese, and others, the Germans would leave their legacy of genocide on the African landscape.[19]

Initially, note the authors of Showing Our Colors, the Germans attempted to portray themselves as "civilizing agents"; that is, their mission was to modernize the natives along the lines of white European Christian culture.[20] This mission, to the degree it had any genuine adherents at all, always took a backseat to the establishment and defense of German rule over the indigenous peoples. The civilizing discourse was needed to rationalize and justify the establishment of an authoritarian structure and military presence as the natives relentlessly resisted what the Germans knew was good for them. What the Germans lacked in experience and sophistication in the process of colonialization they made up for in brutality and cruelty. As with every effort at colonialization, they encountered fierce and unyielding opposition from the indigenous peoples. In German East Africa, this meant battles with the Swahili peoples. In German Southwest Africa, the Nama and the Herero peoples fought the conquering ethos of the Germans every step of the way.

German rule was never accepted, and, tensions and wars occurred over the years between the various African groups and the German settlers. The Nama, the Witbois, and other native African groups fought the Germans consistently, forcing the latter to keep a military presence in their colonies at all times. While other massacres and atrocities were carried out, the one that for many epitomized the evil of German colonialization was the slaughter of the Herero peoples in the war of 1904–1907. For more than twenty years, the Herero had attempted to live peacefully with the Germans, repeatedly signing treaties that the Germans repeatedly abrogated. In Southwest Africa, as the nineteenth century came to an end, the Germans ratcheted up their aggressions against the Herero and other peoples in the area, raping women, stealing property and animals, and lynching those who protested against these acts. Finally, determined to take no more abuse, the town of Okahandja became the site for a massive Herero uprising. Reportedly, the native rebels killed all the men—but no women and children—they could grab and captured thousands of cattle. This action would catalyze a new war between the Herero and the Germans that would go on for years.

After a series of skirmishes and victories on the part of the Herero, the Germans decided to get tough and sent in Lieutenant General Lother von Trotha, a butcher of the first order. Displaying callousness and viciousness that would make the Nazis drool, von Trotha was determined to wipe the entire Herero people off the face of the earth. He launched an assault on the badly outnumbered and outgunned Herero accompanied by an extermination order (*Vernichtungsbefehl*) that read, "Within the German borders, every Herero, whether armed or unarmed, with or without cattle, will be shot. I shall not accept any more women or children. I shall drive them back to their people—otherwise, I shall order shots to be fired at them." Feeding a bloodlust, von Trotha forced the retreating Herero into the Omaheke Desert (now the Khalahari), a deathtrap by every measure. His troops were ordered to poison whatever water supplies they could find and, for those who might miraculously survive the desert ordeal, every single one was to be killed mercilessly with bayonets. During the uprising, there were 60,000 Herero killed, 10,000 Nama, and 676 Germans, plus 907 wounded and 97 missing.[21] According to a 1911 census, the Herero had dropped from 80,000 to only 15,000. The near extinction of the Herero people was more than just a military tactic. A broader message was being sent that native life was never to have a value that exceeded the needs and imperatives of empire. The Germans, under the rabid military leadership of von Trotha, felt obligated to display the kind of ruthlessness that they used against the Herero if they were to sustain their colonial power. The French, Portuguese, British, and Spanish carried out similar types of massacres until the very end of the colonial period. Africa, the Americas, and Asia were killing fields in the name of imperialism's self-preservation.

Perhaps simply exhausted from the killings, the Germans let the remaining Herero, down to only a few thousands, surrender only to put them in concentration camps. According to Sven Lindqvist, the phrase "concentration camp" was first used by the Spaniards in their colonializing of Cuba, then was anglicized by the Americans, and employed again by the British during the Boer War.[22] Now, it was the Germans' turn. In the camps, the Herero were subject to medical experiments including sterilization and injections of smallpox, typhus, and tuberculosis. This type of experimentation can be seen as a testing ground for later medical procedures that would be used against Blacks, Jews, Gypsies, and others during the Nazi Holocaust. The Berlin medical historian Christian Pross states, "The scientists and anthropologists who did the research on the skulls and their so-called racial characteristics in the Southwest African colonies became the leading anthropologists and geneticists during the Third Reich."[23] According to one assessment, German concentration camps in Africa had a mortality rate of 45 percent.[24] Many of the women were forced into becoming sex slaves. To this very day, Germany has not atoned for these deeds. In March 1998, the German president, Roman Herzog, visited Namibia. When he was asked if Germany should apologize for what had happened to the Herero people, he stated, "too much time has passed for a formal apology to the Hereros to make sense."[25] Germany refused to confront its legacy of what the writer Hanna Arendt called the destructive nature of colonialism's "administrative massacres."[26]

The German goal of social apartheid would be challenged time and time again by one continuing tendency: the seemingly inability of Germans to cease copulating with African men and women. The long-standing German obsession with racial purity was doubly battered by the inevitable consequences of these sexual liaisons: mixed-race children. How to address the existence of these children (and similar mixed-raced offspring during the Nazi period) would become the career *bête noire*, of one man: Eugen Fischer. In 1908, Fischer conducted a study of 310 mixed-race children from the Southwest Africa colonies that was published in 1913.[27] The study focused on racial characteristics and concluded that these children—known as the "Rehoboth bastards"—were of a "lesser racial quality." Born of Boers and Hottentots, these young people were subjected to racial tests of all kinds, such as head and body measurements, eye and hair examinations, and other ordeals to determine which racial characteristics were dominant. The torments inflicted upon these children were part of a long history of using African bodies for research and experiments. Ficsher's "research" echoed the earlier efforts of German anthropologists who entered African graveyards, stole skeletons and bodies, and took them back to Europe for sale and research.[28] Both Fischer and his study would flower two decades later under Nazism. His research and, more important, his conclusions and recommendations would inform Nazi policy toward the mixed-raced children born in the post–World War I era. Despite its shaky and questionable methods and purpose, "it was used as the principal argument for the scientific substantiation of the Nuremberg laws."[29]

Fischer would fit in snugly with the policies of Nazism as demonstrated when he wrote in his study, "Without exception, each European people that has assimilated the blood of inferior races has paid for this absorption of inferior elements by intellectual, spiritual, and cultural decline."[30] Even more ominous was Fischer's unhesitant advocacy of genocide when he also noted,

> So accord them just the measure of protection they may require as a race which is inferior to us, in order to continue their existence: nothing more, and only as long as they are of use to us. Otherwise survival of the fittest, i.e., to my mind, in this case, extinction. This point of view sounds almost brutally egotistic, but whoever thinks through thoroughly the notion of race, can not arrive at a different conclusion.[31]

Decades before Hitler came to power, the ideological, political, and "scientific" rationale for exterminationist racial policies was already manifest. Fischer would later become director of the Kaiser Wilhelm Institute for Anthropology, Heredity, and Eugenics that would advise and assist the Nazis in their efforts to sterilize the so-called Rhineland bastards (see chapter 5). He would play a critical role in those procedures.

A number of scholars have argued that there was no effective link between the colonial period and Nazism, that is, that Nazism represented a break with the past and that a new and unique expression of the "racial purity" thesis was generated. The argument claims that only a small number of colonial leaders and officials became Nazis and, for the most part, they did not play a central role. Research on the experience of Afro-Germans and Africans reveals a different perspective.

Fischer would not be the only link between colonial administration and Nazi governance. A number of his associates and other scientists who were involved in the colonial effort would surface as racialization proponents and activists during the Nazi period. These included social scientists, physicians, anthropologists, ethnologists, and others from across academic fields. Among those who stood out were the physician Ernst Rodenwaldt, the anthropologist and ethnologist Otto Reche, the physician Philalethes Kuhn, and the physican and anatomist Theodor Mollison, to name a few. Rodenwaldt worked as doctor in Togo from 1910 to 1913, and in the 1930s was at Hamburg Institute where he was seen as an expert on the "*Mischling*" question, doling advice and counsel to the Nazis. Reche conducted anthropological studies in the South Seas in 1908 and 1909, and would later develop an anthropological genetic method that supposedly established paternity, a method that would be used by the Nazis to determine descendancy. Kuhn was directly involved in the wars against the Hottentots and Hereros from 1887 to 1907, and later became involved in the Nazi campaigns against the Gypsy community.[32]

Other than Fischer, Mollison was probably the most renowned. He spent time in German East Africa around 1904, and later became a lecturer and Nazi ideologue at

Munich University. His real contribution to Nazism, however, was the legacy of scientists that he trained. These included the notorious Josef Mengele—known as the "Angel of Death" for his unspeakably cruel and merciless treatment of concentration camp prisoners at Auschwitz—who took his first medical degree under Mollison. Mengele, called appropriately a "medical maniac" by one writer, would maintain professional contact with Mollison throughout his career.[33] Another of Mollison's doctoral pupils was the so-called Gypsy expert, Sophie Ehrhardt. As one critic states, "Those once responsible for committing atrocities in the German colonies were now in charge of governmental health agencies and research institutes."[34]

There were also military leaders—colonial heroes—of the campaigns against the Africans who would become Nazis or strong Nazi supporters. These included Generals Franz von Epp, Karl Astel, Wilhelm Stuckart, Rudolf Hoss, Gerhard Wagner, Paul von Lettow-Vorbeck, and Hermann Ehrhard. They were all members of von Epp's volunteer corps with some holding high positions in the Third Reich. Stuckart, for example, became secretary of state in the Reich Ministry for International Affairs.[35] Interest in Africa was held by more than future Nazis.

Booker T. Washington, German Colonialism, and Black Internationalism

> *Washington's interest in African political development is perhaps explained by his cooperation with European colonial authorities and mercantile interests there.*[36]

On New Year's Day, 1901, three now obscure Tuskegee Institute students and a faculty member, James Nathan Calloway, disembarked from a Hamburg-based freighter that had just arrived in the German colony of Togo, likely in awe of the groundbreaking tasks they had before them in this strange land. They were part of a joint project between Tuskegee and the *Kolonial-Wirtschaftliches Komitee* (KWK)—Colonial Economic Committee—"to train Africans in cotton culture and to experiment with the cloning of local and imported cotton in order to develop a strong commercially successful hybrid."[37] KWK was a German firm involved in the economic exploitation of Germany's African colonies. Tuskegee's founder, the black leader Booker T. Washington, became involved in African affairs for many of the same reasons that he believed were necessary for Blacks in the United States if they were to progress and prosper. This meant that he was willing to collaborate with conservative and even racist whites in furthering the Tuskegee mission of lifting up the black poor through hard work, industrialization, and muted direct resistance to racism. As Harlan notes, "In African colonies and in America, Washington cooperated openly with white authorities and business promoters, while he sought through industrial education to encourage black self-reliance and the work-ethnic."[38]

The pioneering group, along with their African helpers, traveled deep into the country where they would set up the Missahohe experiment station. Because the draft animals they had brought along died, the Tuskegee crew used Africans in their place. To the plows, they hitched four African workers, while thirty-six Africans were used to pull the sweeps that turned the cotton ginning machine. The project sent 25 bales of cotton to Germany after the first year, which grew to 122 bales by 1903.[39] What was working for the Germans was not necessarily working for the black folks who were involved. In addition to the inhumane decision to harness the native peoples to the plows, nearly half of the Tuskegee students, four out of nine, died during the eight-year period (1901–1909) that the Institute was active in Togo. Those deaths, understandably, made other students hesitant to take their place. Although there were no more Tuskegee representatives in Togo after the last student drowned in 1909 in a canoe accident, the agricultural school that trained African farmers in cotton production lasted until the end of the German colonial era in 1919.

Neither the death of his students nor the maltreatment of the African workers seemed to deter Washington from this project and its sanctioning of colonial reign. Harlan notes, "Washington gave German colonialism a sweeping endorsement while passing through Berlin in 1910."[40] The best-known, most influential, and virtually unchallenged leader of black America stated "I have followed with great care the policies and the plans according to which German officials have dealt with the natives of Africa. They do not seek to repress the Africans, but rather to help them that they may be more useful to themselves and to the German people. Their manner of handling Negroes in Africa might be taken as a pattern for other nations."[41] In terms of the mainstream, black American politics toward Africa was being filtered through the Tuskegee leader, who was clearly willing to accommodate himself with one of the most egregious European powers present in Africa during the period. Beyond the distasteful position that Blacks in Africa needed to be "handled," his support for the colonial drive of Europe as a whole was unacceptable and in conflict with the anticolonial resistance movements that raged in all colonial situations.

Fortunately, Washington did not have the last word on how the diaspora felt about the imposition of European and German colonialism on African peoples. Internationalism has always been a constitutive part of African diasporic politics practiced from North, Central, and South America, the Caribbean, and Europe. In the United States, W. E. B. Du Bois, William Trotter, and others had begun to break the grip that Washington had on black American politics. Although the Niagra Movement and later the NAACP did not take up African issues as a priority, they directly confronted Washington's hegemonic position. Across the Atlantic, the Trinidadian lawyer Henry Sylvester Willams organized the 1900 Pan-African Conference, held in London. Although primarily an intellectual endeavor with political ambitions and no power, its value resided in the attempt to critique and discredit imperialism and its racist pretensions. Beyond its noble effort to call into question the legitimacy of colonial rule, the gathering was notable also for being the site where three years before he published it in *The Souls of Black Folks*, Du Bois uttered the classic prophecy, "The problem of the twentieth century [will be] the problem of the color line—the relation of the darker to the lighter races of men in Asia and Africa, in America and the islands of the sea."[42] Ironically, in 1916, arriving too late to work with his idol Washington, who had died,

Marcus Garvey launched his Universal Negro Improvement Association, an even more militant opposition to European colonization in Africa.

Africans in Germany

An Early Black Presence

The racial merging of "white" with being European has little historical (or contemporary) merit. More than a few scholars have identified the presence of peoples from every continent, including Africa, on European soil dating back to antiquity. Of course, this includes the territory that eventually became Germany. An enduring symbol of this diverse habitation is that the oldest skull found in Europe, discovered in Dusseldorf in 1856, was African. Individual Africans appeared in the area dating back to the days of Julius Caesar, and groups of Africans have settled in the region since at least the twelfth century. During their 800-year occupation of southern Europe, the Moors came to Germany from northern Africa during the Middle Ages and a number of them began to achieve prominent positions as poets, scholars, philosophers, religious leaders, and even as part of the royal family. While the black German Roman Catholic patron saint, Saint Maurice, is of African descent and well known, there are numerous religious-oriented statues of Blacks that can be found around the country.[43] As the historian Gustav Jahoda notes, "In the thirteenth century the German emperor Frederick II of Hohenstaufen had Blacks guarding his treasures."[44]

During the global slave era, some Africans were shipped to Germany as "gifts" for the aristocracy. A few became free and even made a name for themselves. William Anthony Amo, for instance, originally arrived in Germany around 1703 as a gift to Count Ulrich Von Wolfenbuttel. After gaining his freedom, he attended the best schools, including the University of Wittenberg at Hale, Saxony, eventually becoming a philosopher. He attained a doctorate degree and was fluent in Greek, Latin, Hebrew, Dutch, French, and German. Unfortunately, as was known to happen during that period, when Amo returned to Ghana in 1743, he was captured and (re)enslaved. He died shortly thereafter in bondage, never again gaining his freedom.[45]

While the instances mentioned above were notable, they involved mostly individual cases and did not necessarily reflect a clash of differences, racial, national, cultural, or otherwise. In the colonial period, a qualitatively altered German-African encounter would also manifest itself in the heart of Germany. While the records are scant, it is known that there were at least a hundred Africans in Berlin alone in the 1890s from a number of walks of life. They included teachers, students, diplomats, traders, ex-soldiers, entertainers, and workers. In the nineteenth century, "Africans began to come to Germany voluntarily to study or to learn a trade. To finance their trip, some had to take up jobs as sailors while others, notably children of African aristocrats, had no such problems. They were meant to be trained in preparation for their future roles in the work force of the colonies."[46] Not only did many Africans want to come to Germany, but also Germans had a desire for specific skills needed to foster the colonial project. African language teachers were encouraged to come to Germany because of the need to train colonial administrators and others in the languages of the natives. Many of these language professors became famous, including the teachers Hassan Taufik, Muhammad Beschir, and Amur bin Nasur bin Amur Ilomeiri. Apparently quite popular, Ilomeiri was originally from Zanzibar in East Africa (now a part of Tanzania) before he became a foreign language teacher at the Friedrich-Wilhelm University, later renamed Humboldt University.[47] While it is unknown whether Ilomeiri came from African royalty or nobility, many others clearly did. There a number of men from the upper crust of Cameroon society, among them Anjo Diek, Rudolf Douala Manga Bell, Theophilus Wonja Michael, Joseph [Boholle], Anton Egiomue, and Thomas Ngambi Ul Kuo.[48] Michael, who was a chieftain, was one of the signers of the treaty between Germany and Cameroon that established the former as colonial ruler.[49]

After the colonial period began, there were African diplomats in Germany from many African countries, signifying a sophisticated and modern relationship between independent and colonialized African states and Europe. Some of these diplomats would achieve renown beyond the German borders. Momolu Massaquoi, for example, was Liberia's counsel general to Hamburg, Germany, arriving in 1922, only a year before Hitler's unsuccessful but pivotal "Beer Hall Putsch" in Munich. Within a very short period, Massaquoi would become "the most visible African personality on the European continent," host to many African American artists, intellectuals, and athletes such as the activist and performer Paul Robeson, the NAACP leader and scholar W. E. B. Du Bois, the Howard University scholar Alain Locke, the boxer Jack Johnson, the jazz great Louis Armstrong, and the poet Langston Hughes, among others.[50] Massaquoi, who also spoke and wrote in English, authored an important book, *The Republic of Liberia,* as well as finding time to teach about African languages at the University of Hamburg.[51]

African women were not as mobile as African men, and the records are limited on the role, status, and experiences of black women in Germany during the late 1800s and the early years of the twentieth century. A consequence of there being so few women was, of course, that single African men often found themselves with little choice for mates other than German women.[52] Michael states that records of these mixed marriages are still on file.[53]

As noted earlier, Germany played only a small role in the slave trade and arrived late in the scramble for Africa, which, in part, accounts for the particular type of black society that formed or rather did not form in the country in the pre-Nazi period. In England and France, black communities, though also exceedingly small, were constructed directly as a consequence of the slave trade and the travel and settlement dynamics arising from it. But "In Germany, unlike in Britain, [the] slave trade was rather a marginal issue, and though the aristocratic class had slaves, no Black enclave emerged."[54]

The peopling of Germany with those from Africa was an unplanned means by which the discourse of "African primitives" could be countered. The fact that African language teachers, for example, learned German in addition to numerous other languages, European and African, challenged the notion of lack of intelligence of African peoples, a key trope in the colonial narrative. Indeed, the visibility of Africans in a wide cross section of occupations and professions should have erased in a concrete way notions of intellectual and human superiority held by European Whites influenced by racist travelogues and sensationalizing journalists. In fact, given the absence of a history of black slavery in Europe, it is highly possible that unlike in the Americas, a notion of race that relegated Africans to the bottom rung of human development might have faded into the back channels of history over the long run. This possibility was forestalled, however, by the spectacle of Africans on display—in Germany as well as on global stages—that reinforced, even in the face of other evidence, the images of the black savage, the uncivilized brute, and barely human creatures.

A Global Shame: Africans on Display

In August 1999, the researcher (and my close friend) Nicola al Laure Samari, who is of Iraqi and German heritage, and I visited the Black Wax Museum in Baltimore, Maryland. The museum is a fascinatingly rich tour de force through black history that uses life-size wax figures and other strong visual arts to provide a three-dimensional flavor to the visit. It is difficult not to be moved by lifelike replicas of the educator Mary McLeod Bethune and the civil rights leader Martin Luther King Jr., as the telling of black oppression and black resistance is chronologically unfolded. In one section of the museum, to our dismay and soon-to-be consternation, we came upon the figure of Ota Benga. Although we are both fairly knowledgeable regarding black U.S. and world history, this was a story that we were not familiar with. In 1906, Benga, who was from the Congo, was put on display at the Bronx Zoo despite vigorous protest and condemnation from the black community and even the *New York Times*. The tragic life of Ota Benga, as described in detail below, is unfortunately neither unique nor limited to the United States. In fact, the exhibition of people from Africa, Asia, Latin America, and the "New World" in the United States and Europe, including Germany, dates back to the earliest days of European imperialism and continued well into the twentieth century. As late as June 2000, the stuffed remains of an African man—known as "El Negro"—from the southern Africa region were finally sent home to Botswana after having been stolen and put on display since 1888 at the Darder Museum of Natural History in the Catalan town of Banyoles, Spain.[55]

It is impossible to grasp the ideological and political means of imperial conquest without an appreciation of the role that these exhibits played in conditioning popular support for the seizure and defending of occupied territories and lands. Even in the face of other encounters with Africans, Asians, and people from other lands, Europeans would take as gospel the racist constructions embedded and exemplified by these outrageous presentations. Germany, led by the zoo keeper Carl Hagenbeck, was a leader in this type of human degradation.

Journalist Olayinka Oludipe argues that the first real contact between Africans or people of African descent and Berliners was through these types of exhibitions and gospel music.[56] In the United States, England, France, and Germany, Africans and peoples from Asia, the Middle East, the Americas, and the Pacific Islands were presented in zoos, carnivals, circuses, and on stage for the entertainment and curiosity of Whites.

From the middle of the nineteenth century to the mid-1940s, the exoticizing of people of African descent, as well as other peoples from Asia, the Americas, and elsewhere, was a profitable business, while, at the same time, it reified notions of racial superiority. These exhibitions, in an urgent manner, were about empire building and consolidating popular support for the imperatives of colonialism and imperialism. By reducing conquered peoples to displays of difference, the empire was able to rationalize and justify the barbarism that was constitutive of colonial conquest. The othering of native peoples as "subhumans" and "savages" allowed for their cold-blooded slaughter.

These exhibitions were also profoundly gendered. While articulating a discourse of racial superiority, they also reinforced both European and colonial notions of gender power and positioning. Women in these displays were sexualized, domesticated, and subservient. Superexoticized, they were viewed through nothing short of a pornographic lens whereby their rumored sexual habits and even body parts were mystified, exploited, and made a central part of the attraction of the exhibit. Prostitution, often forced, was not unheard of, and rapes also frequently occurred. Native men were portrayed as weak and servile in relation to the Europeans, but powerful and commanding in relation to "their" women. Out of context, it was impossible to convey the complex relationship and cultural norms that existed between African women and men in the different societies they represented, nor was that the purpose. These displays were consciously structured to achieve their ideological goal of perpetuating white and male dominance. The gendered and racial proclivities of the exhibitors were never more on stage than in the dreadful and painful saga of one woman from southern Africa.

In Europe, the tragic tale of Saartjie Baartman, who became known as the "Hottentot Venus," epitomized the degree of degradation that society could fall to when dehumanization occurs. Although Baartman's story happened nearly two hundred years ago, it still resonates as symbolic of the gender and racial coding assigned to African peoples as different and perplexing. Baartman, whose original name is unknown, was a member of the South African ethnic group known as the Khoikhoi, who would be called the Hottentots by the Europeans who came to the region. She was living as an orphan as a result of the devastation suffered by the Africans in the area due to the Boer-British war. She was the daughter of a Hottentot who had been killed.[57] She was taken in by a Dutch family, the Baartmans, and given the name Saartjie, which means "little Sarah."[58] It was soon discovered how unique Baartman was. The Khoikhoi women possess, compared with other African people in the region, different body types. Different should not be construed, of course, to mean in any way that a value judgment should be made on one body type being preferred or more attractive than another. She had a body type that has been called "steatopygous," which refers to an accumulation of large amounts of fat in the buttocks.[59] It should be noted that this term itself is loaded with value and meaning. First, it implies a departure from the "norm," a norm that is itself predicated on a biased idealized European physical standard that relatively few Europeans themselves could meet. Second, it also implies an unrealizable and racist aesthetic that is also thoroughly Eurocentric. The Khoikhoi women also had large breasts and what some anthropologists termed "preevolutionary" genitalia. It is believed that the extraordinarily large breasts and posterior were evolutionary necessities that provided needed and extra body fat for a people who may have had long periods of feast and then famine. The shape of Baartman's genitalia was described as being someway similar to that of a man. As one writer describes, "She had a floppy hood or apron of skin over her somewhat large clitoris, and the labia minor, or inner lips, of her vagina were elongated."[60] It is speculated that this shape facilitated female sexual pleasure in a region where rear-entry sexual practice was dominant.

Baartman's physical features came to the attention of the profit-seeking Cezar brothers, Hendrik and Johan. They eventually arranged a deal where Baartman would be brought to England and presented to the public. Lord Caledon, governor of the Cape, gave permission for Saartjie to go, not realizing the purpose of the trip.[61] She was told that her different culture was of great interest to the English and that she would be well paid for singing and dancing in her native ways. She left for Europe in 1810 and would spend the next five years in England and France. Instead of being allowed to present the culture of the Khoikhoi, she herself was presented as an exotic and strange subhuman who constituted the "missing link" between humans (i.e., Europeans) and apes. She was promoted as the so-called Hottentot Venus, a perverse combining of Europe's aesthetic view of the "worst" (the African) and the "best" (the Greek goddess).

At one point, she was "sold" to a Piccadilly circus where she was put on display nearly naked for the paying and curious crowds, although her sexual organs could not be completely seen. According to the biological scientist Stephen Jay Gould, Baartman refused to display her genitalia to the public while she was alive. It was only after she died and was methodically and coldly dissected and then had her body parts displayed at the Museum of Man in Paris that the public rumors about the "uniqueness" of her genitalia were satisfied. Gould makes the important point that "On all accounts (mode of life, physical appearance, and sexual anatomy (London and Paris should have stood in a giant cage while [Baartman] watched."

During Baartman's appearances in England, letters of protest appeared in London papers along with outcries from some Blacks and others about the nature of her exhibition. The attorney-general, speaking on behalf of the African Association, argued that Saartjie's display was "a disgrace to a civilized country" and that the goal of the African Association was to "release her from confinement, put her under proper protection while she remained here, and restore her to her country by the first conveyance that offered." Baartman initially did not consider herself under any formal restraint or illegal commitment. She told a judge that she did the show willingly with the understanding that she was to get half of the profits. She came across as a very intelligent and articulate woman—she spoke Dutch and some English and was learning French at the time of her death—who represented her position well. The court interviewed her for three hours and concluded that she was not in London under duress, and the case was dismissed. Her contract, which confirmed her statement that she would get half the profits from her work, was deemed valid.[62]

After the English public was exhausted and protests and criticisms continued to be leveled against this dehumanizing exhibit, Baartman, rather than being set free, was "sold" to a circus in France. There her already unimaginably cruel treatment would worsen. The renowned French scientist Georges Cuvier, who referred to Africans as "the most degraded of human races, whose form approaches that of the beast," eventually bought her "contract" and kept her at his home.[63] She was often exhibited with animals. Cuvier also allowed his students and colleagues to routinely examine her for ostensibly medical reasons; again she reportedly held her ground and did not allow her sexual organs to be viewed or examined. In 1825, she died, leaving conflicting reports about the cause of her death. One report stated that she succumbed to tuberculosis and probably syphilis, which she had contracted through her frequent and forced sexual encounters. Another said she died of smallpox complicated by alcoholism and medical incompetence.[64] Tragically, her ordeal would not even end with her death. Her breasts, brain, and genitalia were cut off and put on display at the *Musee de L'Homme* (Museum of Man) in Paris, where they would be available for the public to view until 1985, when finally they were taken down. In a visit to the museum in 1998, I inquired about the exhibit. Museum officials, perhaps finally embarrassed by the whole affair, initially denied knowing that the body parts even existed, but later admitted that they had been removed and would never be shown again.

Other women were also brought from the region during the early 1800s. In 1829, for example, a second so-called Hottentot Venus was brought to France. Women in Lesotho and Dahomey, who had the required physical characteristics—large breasts, large buttocks, and preevolutionary genitalia—were captured or "contracted," brought to Europe, and displayed. In 1995, there was a request to the French government by the Khoikhoi to bring Baartman's remains back to South Africa. It was hoped that this would close the circle on a great tragedy that spanned two continents and two centuries.[65] The French refused.

Besides Africans, many others were also brought to Europe and the United States for spectatorship. A number of indigenous people from the Americas, for instance, were brought to Europe as early as the 1490s. During his first misguided voyage to what would become to him a new world, Christopher Columbus captured and brought back to Spain six "Indians" who would be displayed all over Europe. History does not record what happened to them. On his second trip, Columbus returned with 550 captives, of whom 200 died before landing. Columbus and his crew "cast them into the sea."[66]

As noted, the United States was also culpable in this type of exploitation as exemplified in the saga of the Bronx Zoo and Ota Benga. The story of Ota Benga begins far away from New York in the Belgium Congo at the end of the nineteenth century. He was born in 1881, just four years before the Berlin Conference, the European conclave that "gave" Belgium the right to the region where Benga and his people lived. Sometime around 1904, Benga returned home from a hunt and discovered that his entire village, including his wife and children, had been massacred and their bodies mutilated. This unspeakable terrorist act had been carried out by Belgium's infamous Force Publique, which functioned as a murderous guerrilla operation on behalf of Belgium's King Leopold. Apparently wandering in shock, Benga was captured by another tribal group in the area, then eventually sold to the Reverend Samuel Verner for reportedly about five dollars' worth of calico and trinkets.[67]

Verner fit well within the pantheon of what Europeans referred romantically to as "African explorers" along the lines of Livingston, Stanley, and others, who through their travels, adventures, and encounters delivered to the white world an extremely distorted but nontheess popular picture of sub-Saharan Africa as a metaphorically and literally dark and dangerous region inhabited by people they considered subhuman. More accurately, they were the political advance men for colonialism, providing an ideological and narrative basis for the dehumanization and oppression of African peoples while profiting through various trade schemes, con games, theft of valuable items, and crooked land deals. While in the early years these explorers, with their conscripted and indentured African workers, captured and brought back many different kinds of animals, by the late years of the nineteenth century they were bringing back human beings.

In 1903, Verner had been assigned by W. J. McGee, chief of the Anthropology Department of the St. Louis World's Fair, to "secure the voluntary attendance at this Exposition of twelve Pygmies and about six neighboring natives from the Baluba territory in the vicinity of Kasai River."[68] Thus, when Verner met Benga, his contractal obligation to McGee was on his mind. Despite the rhetoric of being "voluntary," Benga had few options and agreed to go to the St. Louis World's Fair with the clear understanding that he would be paid and be brought back home after his work was over. Individuals representing the Ainu and Patagonian peoples, as well as other Pygmies, joined him. Their role at the World's Fair was to present what Verner and McGee argued were "authentic" native cultures. The fair also, cynically, included indigenous peoples from the Americas. The ironic tragedy of having the original peoples of the Americas paraded as a foreign culture was naturally lost on spectators and organizers alike. As the Germans did in their colonial camps and similar to what the Nazi regime would do three decades later, the Pygmies and others were given intelligence tests that were obviously biased, were measured in every part of their anatomies for the purposes of finding comparative inadequacies, and were made to endure physical examinations to find out, for example, "How quickly would they respond to pain?"[69] Similar to the Hereros and the Jews, Benga and company had little recourse but to submit to these horrors.

In spite of a few unanticipated incidents, such as the Africans justifiably attacking overly aggressive and harassing gawkers, the owners of the fair cited the human exhibits as highly successful, and when it was over, Benga did return to the Congo. Misfortune befell him again when his second wife died from snakebite. Reunited with Verner in 1906, in early September Benga traveled with him to New York where the latter was introduced to William Hornaday, director at the Bronx Zoological Gardens. While Hornaday would later claim that the Benga situation was not coerced, the truth was that Benga was set up from the start to be the star attraction at the zoo. Although he was "hired" to look after animals and clean up, Benga was made to live in a monkey cage with an orangutan named Dohong and a parakeet. More blantantly, as the *New York Times* reported on 10 September, a sign was posted that left little doubt as to the zoo's intent:

**The African Pygmy, "Ota Benga," Age
23 years. Height, 4 feet 11 inches.
Weight, 103 pounds. Brought from the
Kasai River, Congo Free State, South
Central Africa by Dr. Samuel P.
Verner, Exhibited each afternoon
During September.**

Source: "Man and Monkey Show Disapproved by Clergy," *New York Times*, 10 September 1906.

Within days of the Benga display opening, several of New York's black clergy, led by the Reverend R. S. MacArthur of the Calvary Baptist Church, protested the exhibit and sought a meeting with Mayor McClennan. Although they were rebuffed by the mayor's cowardly claims that he was too busy to see them and had no jurisdiction over the matter, the protests escalated as a threatened lawsuit, and letters and editorials in the local newspapers demanding that the exhibit be stopped continued. Even an avowed bigot from the South, who claimed that he was not "overfond of the negro [sic]," wrote a letter to the press expressing his disgust at the exhibition.[70] Meanwhile, thousands came to see, as the *New York Evening Post* stated, the "African dwarf," including 40,000 on Sunday, 16 September.[71] In a bow to the protests, Benga was let out of the cage by the third week of September and was able to walk freely around the zoo. However, crowds of zoo patrons would follow him, and, understandably, Benga became irritated and, exhibiting the skills he had learned in his native land, shot arrows at his pursuers, striking at least one in the face. Benga's belligerence, rather than the protests, finally led Hornaday to allow him to leave the zoo, and New York's Howard Colored Orphan Asylum took him in.

While Benga flourished somewhat at the asylum, learning English and gaining some literacy, conflicts arose and, in 1910, he went to live in a black community in Lynchburg, Virginia. He went to school for a while but dropped out and became a day laborer and also looked after the local children on occasion. Though seemingly adjusted at last, he had never given up on his dream of returning home. Allegedly, when he discovered that he would probably never be able to pay the price of sailing back to Africa, severe depression set in, no doubt compounded by years of abuse, alienation, and mistreatment. On 20 March 1916, a decade after his final American sojourn began, he took a gun, walked into the woods near where he lived, and committed suicide. The tortuous path, for Benga, from being victimized by colonialism to zoo display, echoed throughout the world. Germany, however, stands out in one particular: it actually developed a word for the phenomenon.

Germany's Black "Volkschuen"

Volkschuen means the public display of people. As far back as the mid-1800s, this practice began to appear in the land that would become the German nation. A troupe that went to Germany in 1853 was billed the "Zulu Kafirs." Consisting of eleven men, one woman, and one child, they arrived in London in March 1853 from Durban, South Africa. The show, which included drama performances, became extremely popular in England, France, and Germany. The troupe even gave a command performance for Queen Victoria at Buckingham Palace. As with most other such groups, the Africans had agreed to come for a price with the further stipulation that they would be returned to Durban no later than eighteen months after they had left. While wildly popular, the Zulu Kafirs would generate controversy before they got to Germany due to an atrociously racist review written by the novelist Charles Dickens. Referring to the Zulus as "savages" and "extremely ugly," Dickens stunned many by writing that he believed that these people and who they represented should be "civilized off the face of the earth," a view many interpreted to be a call for genocide.[72]

Other Africans to be put on display in Germany were in the Egyptian group, the "Nubians," who were in the country in 1877 and 1878. An estimated 62,000 Germans viewed them. This human display would initiate a continual importation of people from societies outside of Europe who would be paid or forced to perform in circuses or zoos as exotic, strange, and alien subhumans. In June 1905, James Jonathan Harrison, an Englishman who hunted big game in Africa, brought six Pygmies from the Congo to Europe. The four men and two women—Mongonga, Bokani, Mafutiminga, Matuka, Kuarke, and Amuriape—spent a year performing and touring in England and Wales before reaching Germany in July 1906.[73]

In 1907, Africans were shown at the German Army, Marine, and Colonial exhibit. As late as the early 1930s, Africans and American Indians were being put on display at zoos in Germany. The innovative zoo owner Carl Hagenbeck, famous for building the first zoo where wild animals could be seen in their "natural" habitat, displayed humans in his so-called Culture Shows, supposedly showing them in their native surroundings. Both Africans and American Indians were exhibited at his Tierpark (animal park) in Hamburg. As Massaquoi describes the experience in 1930:

> After walking past spectacular exhibits of monkeys, giraffes, lions, elephants, and other African wildlife, we arrived at the "African Village," replete with half a dozen or so thatch-roofed clay huts and peopled, we were told, by "authentic Africans." Like the animal exhibits, the "village" was bordered by a chest-high wooden fence to keep the viewers out and viewees in . . . All of the villagers were barefoot and dressed in tattered rags. Two women, draped in dingy-looking cloths, were rhythmically pounding a heavy wooden stick into a mortar. A guide explained that they were making corn flour in preparation for their dinner. The men were sitting around in small groups, intently watching the spectators while chatting away in an unintelligible language between puffs from short, primitive-looking pipes.[74]

Again there was the contradiction between the presence of well-educated, respected Africans and the display of African peoples in circuses and zoos. This dichotomy can best be explained in two ways. First, ironically, it was in philosophical rather than racial terms that difference was constructed. Race in that period was thought of not only along phenotypical lines in states such as the United States and South Africa, but also through the prism of civilizational development, that is, where on the ladder of humanity one was located. That the former and the latter correlated significantly should not undermine the importance of the space in between where a rationality existed that could see some Africans as more human than others. What were being placed on exhibit, it was contended, were visions of the stages of human development—civilization based on European terms—that while clearly seeing all Europeans as more developed than all Africans could still recognize significant divisions among Africans themselves. The second perspective is the argument advanced by the producers of these shows, on very tentative grounds, that these displays were anthropological, cultural, and scientifically oriented and not meant to be deragotory toward peoples from outside Europe. Many well-known social scientists were indeed complicit in the production of these exhibits as well as in the "examination" of the Africans to determine their level of human development and how they compared with Europeans. One oft-cited point of evidence of the so-called objective and nondiscriminatory nature of these exhibits was that the participants were paid employees who did this work of their own volition. This argument, of course, does not invalidate the criticisms that the shows presented racist stereotypes or that they often employed Africans who were not from the area of Africa that they were suppose to be portraying and, in many instances, had never been in Africa at all.

Images of blackness, nearly always negative and reflective of a Eurocentric position of dominance and control, were pervasive in many ways. Racist advertisements, emerging out of the new science and field of consumer marketing, projected images of Africans and Blacks relentlessly. These images, as well as names, were used to sell everything from candy to shaving creams, such as Chocolates Negerkusse chocolates (Negro kisses) and Mohrendopfe (Moors' heads).[75] There were also popular slurs against Africans and Afro-Germans. As Marilyn Kern-Foxworth, Diane Roberts, Jan Nederveen Pieterse, and and others have documented, racist images, language, and even product names were also used in the United States to sell a wide range of goods from pancakes and soap to rice and peanut butter.[76] Among the products sold were "Nigger Head Brand" canned fruits and vegetables, "Nigger Head" stove polish, "Nigger Head" tees, "Nigger Head" tobacco, and "Nigger Head" oysters, displaying a strange society-wide obsession with one particular racist moniker, in particular.[77]

The African Diaspora in Pre-Nazi Germany

Between the beginning of the twentieth century and World War II, it was not unusual for African Americans to travel to Europe. These travelers included Blacks from many walks of life such as entertainers, athletes, religious leaders, political activists, business people, and scholars. While most went to Western Europe, after Lenin and the Communist Party of the Soviet Union (CPSU) came to power, a significant number of African Americans visited and, in some cases, moved to the newly formed Soviet Union. As Allison Blakey documents in *Russia and the Negro*, several waves of Blacks emigrated to the Soviet Union in the 1920s and 1930s, some joining the CPSU and others being merely strong supporters.[78] Among the well-known African Americans who went to the new promised land were Du Bois, the poet Langston Hughes, the writer Claude McKay, and the performer Paul Robeson, all of whom spoke highly of the Soviet experiment that was in its infancy.

These sojourns indicated the presence of a global perspective held by many African Americans, a perspective that was informed by U.S. racial dynamics. Black travelers invariably did a racial reading of the places they visited, comparing their treatment in these countries as Blacks or the treatment of other local racial minorities with that they received in the United States. While the conceptual basis on which these comparisons were determined may have been flawed and problematic, and lacked empirical verification, there was a highly tuned intuitive sense of racial difference and inequality exercised by African Americans based on the long history of racism in the United States. In virtually none of the visits to Germany by African Americans, however, are there references to either Africans or Afro-Germans, a peculiar omission since most visits were to Berlin, where many of the nation's Blacks resided.

African Americans went to Germany during the decades preceding Nazism, disproportionately but not exclusively as entertainers. Germans demonstrated a keen awareness of the musical talents of African Americans, as did other Europeans. Among the musicians were the classical singer Roland Hayes, who settled in France, the composer and conductor Will Marion Cook, who studied at Berlin's Hochschule fur Tonkunst (College of Music), and his nephew, the actor and dancer Louis Winston Douglas. In 1903, the first African American dance groups came to Berlin and performed the cakewalk. According to one German entertainment weekly, in 1896 alone, more than one hundred black performers visited the country.[79]

Perhaps the best known of the black American entertainers were the Fisk Jubilee Singers of Fisk University who first performed spirituals in Berlin in November 1877.[80] The university was one of the first created for African Americans, and it launched the singing group and tours in 1871 as one means of raising funds. Fisk students represented the emerging post–Civil War black middle class in the United States, although eight of the nine original singers were former slaves. Their performances were very well received and given primarily in front of middle- and upper-class Germans.[81]

The opera singer Marian Anderson, who was denied numerous stages in the United States due to racism and sought friendlier turf in Europe, performed in concert in Berlin in 1931. She had come a year earlier to study German, which was needed by someone preparing for a serious career in opera. The singer and activist Paul Robeson also came to Germany in the 1920s, making an impression on Hitler himself (although it is not clear that the future Führer actually saw him perform). Black intellectuals made the trek to Germany, attracted by its global reputation as a cultural and intellectual center. The writers Langston Hughes and Alaine Locke would both make the pilgrimage. The boxer Jack Johnson, the controversial first black heavyweight champion, visited Europe, including Germany, before World War I.

Black American political leaders, for the most part, did very little international travel, with a few notable exceptions, mostly those on the political left. Marcus Garvey, who was originally from Jamaica and was deported back there in 1927, made his mark organizing in the black communities of the United States. His back-to-Africa campaign mobilized millions of African Americans and black Caribbean immigrants before he was charged with mail fraud and other crimes and his operation shut down. Ironically, he never visited Africa, but did go to Germany in 1928. As he did in Asia, Africa, and the Americas, Garvey had supporters in Germany and went there to meet with them.[82]

W. E. B. Du Bois and the Call of Germany

> When I attended the Friedrich Wilhelm's University in Berlin in 1892 to 1893, the insignia of a student which were absolutely compulsory were gloves and cane. There I acquired the cane habit and have carried one ever since.
>
> —W. E. B. Du Bois[83]

William Edward Burghardt Du Bois remains one of the most astute observers of race relations and race politics ever published. In a number of pivotal and now classic works, including *Souls of Black Folks, Black Reconstruction, The World and Africa, The Philadelphia Negro,* and many, many other books and articles, Du Bois demonstrated a breadth of research interests unmatched to the present. A number of his theoretical insights—"The problem of the twentieth century is the problem of the color line" and the "double-consciousness" of African Americans, to name just two—remain at the center of discussion about the meaning and significant of race many decades after their formulation.

Du Bois said that his third name, Burghardt, was derived from the white Dutch family for whom a direct descent on his mother's side of the family was "either a slave or serf, and in the service of."[84] While he also acknowledged some French ancestry, he was proud to declare that "thank God! No Anglo-Saxon" blood flowed in his veins.[85] At least one Afro-German thinks otherwise. Theodor Michael, a surviving Afro-German from the Nazi era, contends that Burghardt is a German name generally not found outside of Germany.[86] In any case, unique for an African American in terms of our present discussion, Du Bois also had a lifelong interest in the politics and culture of Germany. Given also his lifelong interests in race and, in particular, the experiences and status of people of African descent, it is quite remarkable that as far as the record demonstrates, he had few comments whatsoever on the state of Blacks in Germany. It is difficult to believe that he did not meet some Africans and perhaps even some Afro-Germans in the almost two years he spent in Germany, 1892 to 1894, much of which was in Berlin where Africans were concentrated, highly visible, and many well known, and in his other visits to the country.

While working to complete his graduate studies at Harvard, Du Bois decided that he wanted to spend some time in Europe as he prepared himself for his doctoral studies at the Friedrich Wilhelm University in Berlin. In 1890 and 1891, he wrote three letters unsuccessfully seeking financial assistance from the Slater Fund for the Education of Negroes, chaired by the former president Rutherford B. Hayes. Claiming that he had "no money or property," Du Bois chided the Fund by writing that "the injury you have—unwittingly I trust—done the race I represent, and am not ashamed of, is almost irreparable."[87] Whether motivated by guilt or genuinely concerned with Du Bois's educational goals, the Fund, in April 1892, sent him $750, half of which was a loan that he was expected to pay back.

From the limited experiences he had, Du Bois found Germany to be surprisingly free of racial prejudice. In fact, he would fall in love with a white German woman, Dora Marbach, who even wanted to marry him.[88] As Martin Luther King Jr. would do half a century later, Du Bois determined that in the interest of the work he saw ahead of him, that is, a race agenda in which he would play a leadership role, there was no place for this "blue-eyed stranger."[89] While this ill-fated relationship would somewhat open Du Bois to the notion that all Whites were not irredeemably racist, and he would feel no signs of racism by Germans toward himself, he failed to acknowledge the privileged position he held as both a foreigner and a student, positions that could isolate him from more daily racial incidents. His sanguine view of the Germans would, however, be weakened as he came to recognize the prejudice that was pervasive against Jews. Although he makes no mention of the German treatment of or attitude toward Afro-Germans or Africans, he eventually noted that anti-Semitism was virulent in German society, and would see it as comparable to the views of white Americans toward blacks, that is, "much in common with our own race question."[90]

After beginning his studies in October 1891, he met many of Germany's leading scholars, including the sociologist Max Weber and the political economist Adolph Wagner. Off-campus, he attended political meetings and cultural and social events. In particular, he displayed an interest in the German Social Democratic Party, which Marable describes as "the largest socialist party in the world at the time."[91] Apparently, the only notable negative racial experience that Du Bois recalled was a speech given by Heinrich von Treitschke in which he attacked "mulattoes"—a subject close to the mixed-race Du Bois—as inferior to whites. Germany affected him to the point that he gave his experiences there credit for his becoming a "freethinker," and "[making] him believe in the essential humanity of white folk."[92] Interestingly, Du Bois actually got a taste of anti-Semitism during his visit to Europe. While in Poland, which at the time was controlled by Vienna, he was mistaken repeatedly for being a Jew (and a Gypsy). Both Poles and Germans expressed anti-Semitic remarks and behaviors toward Du Bois.[93]

Yet, despite his affection for the country, Du Bois was no conciliator on German colonialism. In his well-known article linking the initiation of World War I with European imperialism in Africa, "The African Roots of War," he comments on the stealthy manner in which the Germans, during the Berlin Conference itself, had acquired "an area over half as large again as the whole German Empire in Europe."[94] Writing in *The Crisis* in 1914 and commenting on the war, he notes,

> [T]he triumph of Germany means the triumph of every force calculated to subordinate darker peoples. It would mean triumphant militarism, autocratic and centralized government and a studied theory of contempt for everything except

Germany—"Germany above everything in the world." The despair and humiliation of Germany in the eighteenth century has brought this extraordinary rebound of self-exaltation and disdain for mankind. The triumph of this idea would mean a crucifixion of darker peoples unparalleled in history.[95]

Contending that he held no "anti-German bias," Du Bois strongly argued that "The record of Germany as a colonializer toward weaker and darker peoples is the most barbarous of any civilized people and grows worse instead of better."[96] These were his feelings toward a country that he loved.

Summary

Up to this point, the black presence in Germany, while certainly not embraced by all, was generally an accepted fact and within the social parameters of the period viewed relatively moderately in terms of individual and institutional discrimination and prejudice. The chauvinistic exhibition of Africans in zoos and circuses was mediated by the more positive roles played by Africans and Afro-Germans as teachers, diplomats, students, business people, and ex-soldiers. Compared with the United States, where lynchings were far too common, legal segregation was enshrined with an air of permanence, and a black antiracism resistance was growing, Germany could appear almost racially enlightened and harmonious.

Then, on a reportedly blistering summer day on 28 June 1914, an act occurred that would determine the destiny of Blacks in Germany and international relations forever. Gurilo Princip, a member of the Young Bosnia, a secret Serbian nationalist group, had to go and put one bullet each in Austria's Archduke Franz Ferdinand and his wife, Sophie, as they drove alongside the Miljacka River in Sarajevo on their fourteenth wedding anniversary. The First World War was on.

Soldiers of Misfortune, Children of Misfortune

Black Troops and the Race Question in Pre-Nazi Germany

An Franzosen und Neger wird hier nichts verkauft (To Frenchmen and Negroes nothing will be sold here).
        —Signs in shops and elsewhere in Western Germany after the war[1]

It was against blacks, not Jews, that the ominous accusation of "Kulturschande" (rape of culture) was first raised after the war.
                        —George Mosse[2]

Black Soldiers in Germany: A Morel Story

King Leopold's Ghost, the historian Adam Hochschild's 1999 groundbreaking and stunning exposé of the murderous crusade by King Leopold of Belgium around the beginning of the twentieth century in the Congo is, in most respects, an outstanding work.[3] The book's daunting waves of praise—from the *Los Angeles Times, the Guardian* (London), and *the New York Times* to *Foreign Affairs, The Economist,* and *Financial Times*—were overwhelming.[4] The *Boston Globe*'s Richard Taylor declared the book "spellbinding."[5] Among the awards and accolades won by the book is the Lionel Gelber prize that *The Economist* called "now the world's most important award for nonfiction."[6] The book, subtitled "A Story of Greed, Terror, and Heroism in Colonial Africa," was also a finalist for the National Book Critics Circle Award.[7] It also received a Notable Book of the Year declaration from the *New York Times Book Review. Leopold's Ghost* was successful not only in the United States but also globally. The book was published in French and Dutch as well as English. And, unlike most academic or historical works, it became a number one bestseller in France and Belgium, and did exceedingly well in the United States.

Hochschild's literarily inspired detailing of the terror and genocide suffered in the Congo in a brutal campaign waged by Leopold is nothing less than commendable for its scholarly accomplishment and its human rights objectives. Few works have sought, let alone achieved, both. At the epicenter of this turn-of-the century narrative is a conniving and homicidal king who managed to craftily cultivate an image of himself as an international humanitarian and advocate for equal rights. In reality, Leopold set about establishing a rule of terror that would culminate in the deaths of four to eight million indigenous people. While Leopold's evil was revealed in his time, it fell into obscurity and, therefore, has been absent from contemporary discourses on the Congo. For Hochschild, Leopold's grand and scandalous villainy is only matched by what he sees as the journalist Edmund Dene Morel's noble and unimpeachable courage and heroism. Morel not only divulged Leopold's malfeasance in the press of the period but actively campaigned across a number of continents to end the killings and depict Leopold as the brute that he turned out to be. While there are others who took up the cause, such as the African American minister and lawyer George Washington Williams, who "wrote the first full expose of Leopold's reign of terror," it is Morel who receives the lion's share of Hochschild's approbation.[8]

It is, therefore, with the most profound irony that it is Morel who undermines Hochschild's efforts. The failure of Hochschild to fully present Morel's views and politics regarding Africa and Africans reflects, at best, selective research and, at worst, a deliberate effort to hide Morel's ugly and undeniable racism. Hochschild's misguided impulse to heroize Morel represents a formidable crack in his grand and even enviable project.

There is little shame or restraint in Hochschild's admiration for Morel. Indeed, his story opens with Morel at center stage.[9] He gushingly credits Morel with placing human rights on the global agenda. As Hochschild states glowingly in the book, Morel's work ignited "the first great international human rights movement of the twentieth century."[10] This is itself a dubious claim when one considers, for example, the consistent effort by African Americans to win global support for their democratic and human rights, the attempt by many activists in Africa to internationalize their struggle against colonialism, and similar movements in Asia. In speaking of his hero's character, Hochschild sees Morel as "impassioned, eloquent, blessed with brilliant organizing skills and nearly superhuman energy."[11] Beyond his efforts at exposing the murder of millions of Africans and Leopold's hypocrisy, Morel was also an antiwar activist during the First World War, which got him sent to prison for six months in 1918. These activities are also accorded Hochschild's adoration. Referring to Morel as "the greatest British investigative journalist of his time," he lauds his "fiery passion for justice."[12]

Hochschild is not satisfied to claim his idol as a champion for his own time, but states emphatically, in an interview, that "Morel to me is one of the greatest heroes of the century . . . He was one of those people who had the ability to follow his own conscience when everybody else around him was accepting the myths of the day, or else having a few doubts about voicing them. Such men and women are great treasures. He had an internal moral compass that always pointed true North. I wish one like that for us all."[13] Others would pick up on Hochschild's signals. The *Boston Globe's* Taylor, for instance, wrote, "Hochschild's is a morality tale in which light eventually displays darkness, and it has a hero: a Liverpool shipping agent named Edmund Morel."[14]

It is safe to say that without Morel, Hochschild would not have had a book. Given the dependency that the book placed on the role and integrity of Morel, it was even more incumbent that this critical source be thoroughly examined. Unfortunately, Hochschild's construction of Morel, whose full name was Georges Edmond Pierre Achille Morel-de-Ville, as a nearly faultless humanitarian with a stellar record of socially conscious activism is seriously flawed. In 352 pages of text and notes, Hochschild fails to acknowledge, let alone criticize, the fact that Morel obsessively led one of the most racist political campaigns to be launched in the first half of the twentieth century. Paradoxically, Hochschild's efforts at heroizing Morel mirror the hero-creating strategy of Leopold's that he exposed. Beginning in 1919, and lasting until his death in 1924, Morel and his Union of Democratic Control (UDC) led a global effort, using some of the most racist propaganda, tactics, and arguments possible, to campaign against the presence of black French troops stationed in Germany as a consequence of the 1919 Treaty of Versailles.[15]

During World War I, the United States and all the European powers engaged in the conflict used black or colonial troops (African and Asian) in the fighting. The French used Senegalese troops, the Troupes de Couleur, in their military as far back as 1857. France sent soldiers from its famous A.O.F. [Afrique Ouest Française] troops, roughly 77,000 in 1918. The African troops left from Dakar but were not necessarily from Senegal. They were also from other parts of Africa where the French had colonies.[16] There were also troops from Indochina, including Vietnam, Laos, and Cambodia.[17] To a much lesser degree, the United States and Great Britain had Blacks among their soldiers, though for the United States this often meant cleanup duty, not actual combat, and, naturally, serving under the most severe segregation. While the troops of colored included those from northern Africa, sub-Saharan Africa, and Indochina, "black" and "colored" would evolve as inclusive umbrella terms despite distinctions that may have existed internally among the soldiers.

The Germans also had Blacks involved in their African campaigns as the war engulfed the colonies. Germany's African troops numbered about 12,000. Before World War I, Germany created the professional African solders, who were called Askaris, to fight on their behalf and defend colonial territories. These soldiers were recruited from all over colonial Africa including the Manyema peoples from the Congo, the Nyamwezi from East Africa, the Hausa, Grussi, Mossi, Dahomeans, Losso, Kabure, Yoruba, and Wey from Liberia, the Jaunde and Yoki from Cameroon, and Sierra Leonians.[18] After the war, many of these soldiers found their way to Germany, mainly but not exclusively to Berlin. Whether there were black troops among the European German forces is not recorded, although it would have been unusual but not impossible. Hitler argued that Germany would never have used black troops as did the French. He wrote:

The former German colonial policy, like everything we did, was carried out by halves. It neither increased the settlement area of the German Reich, nor did it undertake any attempt — criminal though it would have been — to strengthen the Reich by the use of black blood. The Askaris in German East Africa were a short, hesitant step in this direction. Actually they served only for the defense of the colonies themselves. The idea of bringing black troops into a European battle-field, quite aside from its practical impossiblity during the war, never existed even as a design to be realized under more favorable circumstances, while, on the con-trary, it was always regarded and felt by the French as the basic reason for their colonial activity.[19]

As the war was coming to an end, the Germans, sensing what was coming, lobbied to prevent black troops from being part of the occupation army—to no avail. Reportedly, the always arrogant British had warned the French not to "train big nigger [sic] armies" that would be located in Europe after the war and for the occupation.[20]

Following World War I, France, Belgium, England, and the United States all had Blacks among their occupation troops in Western Germany, with the French send-ing the most. The black French troops that were sent to the Rhineland between 1919 and 1921, depending upon the source, are estimated to have been between 20,000 and 45,000, and were primarily from Senegal, Algeria, Tunisia, Morocco, and Madagas-car.[21] It is not known how many black soldiers represented British and U.S. forces in these forces.

TABLE 2   Number of French Troops in Germany, 1918–1921

December 1, 1918 to May 1, 1919	10,000
May 1, 1919 to March 1, 1920	35,000
March 1, 1920 to June 1, 1920	25,000
June 1, 1920 to January 30, 1921	20,000

Source: J. Ellis Barker, "The Colored French Troops in Germany," Current History, July 1921, p. 597.

The presence of black troops in Germany became an issue that would be debated throughout Europe and even in the United States. The catalyst of this debate and its international character, beyond the apopleptic Germans, was Morel. The historical record shows that Morel felt as deeply about this issue—if not more so—as about the Congo campaign, and fought to keep the issue alive—long after it had been abandoned by others, including the Germans—until his last breath.

This oversight, if you will, by Hochschild concerning Morel's other life's work can-not easily be attributed to inadequate research. In *Leopold's Ghost*, he cites four books (*King Leopold's Rule in Africa*; *Great Britain and the Congo: The Pillage of the Congo Basin*; *Red Rubber: The Story of the Rubber Slave Trade Which Flourished on the Congo for Twenty Years, 1890–1910*; and *E. D. Morel's History of the Congo Reform Movement*)[22] and one article ("At Pentonville: September, 1917–January, 1918") by Morel that span the years from 1904 to 1920.[23] In these works, Morel's liberal credentials are highlighted as he rails against capitalism, imperialism, and Europe's bloody grab of African land. Hochschild also notes that he drew on biographies of Morel written by W. S. Adams, Catherine Cline, F. Seymour Cocks, and A. J. P. Taylor.[24] It is notable that Hochschild chronicles Morel's life after the Congo campaign until his death in 1924.

The prolific Morel, however, wrote a number of other important works that show a different side of his earlier, generally patronizing and sympathetic views of Africa and Africans. Hochschild ignores or fails to cite, for instance, *Africa and the Peace of Europe* (1917), *Black Horror on the Rhine*, a pamphlet published in 1920, or *The Black Man's Burden*, a book one writer called "angry and bitter" that was also published in 1920.[25] This is in addition to dozens of news articles, particularly in liberal and even radical publications, such as the *Daily Herald* and *The Nation*, which he wrote during this time. In these works and others, Morel viciously and unhesitatingly degraded, insulted, and denigrated people of African descent.

Two major themes emerged in Morel's work during this time: Africans are portrayed as less than human, and African men are seen as sexually uncontrollable rapists of European white women. Although Hochschild does not specifically refer to these particular writings, he notes briefly that Morel's "politics also had limitations. Some of these he shared with most other Europeans of his time, from his faith in the magic of free trade to his belief that African men had a higher sexual drive than white men and could pose a danger to white women."[26] This is a mild repudiation at best. Here Hochschild almost dismisses Morel's prejudices, falling back on the oft-used proposition that if one's views are consistent with the dominant ideologies of the time, then they are somehow immune from contemporary harsh criticism. First, this reduces racism and bias to a historical relativism where disapproval is read as imposing contemporary enlightenment on historically situated perspectives. While it is true that one must not judge the past with the wisdom and insights of the present, by no means should one elide unjust, bigoted ideas and behavior. It is no surprise that this view tends always to represent a perspective of the dominant rather than of the subaltern. Second, the notion of representing the conventional ideas of one's time conveniently ignores the voices of dissent that contest the prejudice and hegemonic powers of their era. This can easily become an "only-the-winners" perspective on history and society. Third, in regard to Morel, it was not just his beliefs about the extraordinary sexual drives of African men or the amoral black scourge unleashed on an innocent and virtuous Europe, but the transformation of those beliefs into a conscious and energetic political campaign and social movement.

Black Horror on the Rhine, in particular, became the holy text of his activities. In it, he wrote, referring to the African troops, "their sex-impulse is a more instinctive impulse . . . more spontaneous, fiercer, less controllable impulse than among European peoples hedged in by the complicated paraphernalia of convention and laws."[27] Morel then contended that this fierce, out-of-control impulse "*must be satisfied upon the bodies of white women*"[28] (italics in the original). In this writing (and others), he called the Africans "black savages" and "primitive African barbarians" and deplored what he called the "barely restrainable beastiality of the black troops."[29] The main activity of these troops, according to Morel, was to engage in criminal behavior against Whites. The pamphlet lists eighty cases of alleged rapes and attempted rapes by black soldiers, as well as the spread of venereal diseases. *Black Horror on the Rhine* went through at least eight editions and was translated into German, French, and Italian. The efficiency of his work can be measured in the statement by the British publicist J. Ellis Barker, "It seems by no means impossible that the German campaign against the colored troops of France emanated not so much from the Germans themselves as from Mr. Morel."[30]

For the newspapers and journals, Morel wrote articles with headlines such as "Black Scourge in Europe, Sexual Horror Let Loose by France on Rhine, Disappearance of Young German Girls," "The Prostitution of the Rhineland," "The Employment of Black Troops," and "Horror on the Rhine."[31] On 27 March 1920, in a letter to the London-based *Nation*, Morel made more disparaging remarks about the black troops, calling them "barbarians belonging to a race inspired by Nature . . . with tremendous sexual instincts."[32]

The *Nation* reporter, Lewis S. Gannett, among others, found the rape charges to be mostly tissue paper.[33] While it was found that some rapes had occurred, there were nowhere nearly as many as Morel claimed, white troops also had been involved in rapes, and "the French have inflicted severe punishment upon all soldiers guilty of transgressing against the civil population."[34] In a study by J. Ellis Baker, it was discovered that of the seventy-two crimes that the colored troops were found guilty of, only nine had to do with violations of women. Five of the men found guilty were given more than five years in prison, the rest less. One Senegalese brigade during their entire stay had only one complaint lodged against its troops, and upon investigation there was an acquittal. In the report issued after an investigation conducted by the United States Army and sent to the secretary of state, General Henry T. Allen wrote, "The wholesale atrocities by French negro [sic] Colored [sic] troops alleged in the German press, such as the alleged abductions, followed by rape, mutilations, murder and concealment of the bodies of the victims, are false and intended for political propaganda."[35]

TABLE 3   **Reported Crimes by French Colored Troops**

Total accusations brought for violation of women, crimes of violence, participation in broils, theft, etc.

Number of cases in which accusations were justified	72
Number of cases in which accusations were doubtful	96
Number of unjustified accusations	59
Total	227

Source: J. Ellis Barker, "The Colored French Troops in Germany," *Current History*, July 1921, 597.

Not only did the charges of black troops' sexual aggressions prove mostly false, but counteraccusations were made that the salacious behavior that occurred was initiated elsewhere. According to the respected German journalist Maximilian Harden, "German women were chiefly responsible for the mingling of colored and white blood which has taken place on the Rhine."[36] This view was repeated by Baker, who was in Germany during this period and who writes, "I received numerous complaints from Germans, and especially from elderly ladies, about the attitude of the German women and girls."[37]

These facts notwithstanding, Morel launched his campaign with all the vigor he could muster, to great effect. In Germany, he became a hero, unsurprisingly, leading one observer to note, "The name of Morel is on every man's lips in Germany. In every book-shop there are stacks of his books and pamphlets 'proving' the innocence of Germany and the wickedness of the Allies."[38] The political consequences of his efforts went well beyond the German borders. It was stated that "Mr. Morel's agitation caused Belgium to draw away from England and to incline toward Germany to the great benefit of the lat-ter, and Mr. Morel's propaganda is largely responsible for the admiration of Germany and the distrust of England which were expressed by many leading Belgian diplomats in reports which the German Government published during the war."[39]

The *Daily Herald*, where Morel published many of his stories, had a circulation of 329,000. A free copy of *Black Horror on the Rhine* was given to every delegate attending the 1920 Trades Union Congress.[40] Other liberal and left-oriented publications joined the lynch mob. In the *Commonweal*, they wrote of "Senegalese savages" and deplored the "lust of a black soldiery." In the *Nation* (London), the black troops were trans-formed into "terrorists."[41]

Morel's Negrophobic campaign to rid Europe of Africans did not just settle on the written word. He aggressively campaigned around the world through his organization, the Union of Democratic Control (UDC), to have this "Black horror" eliminated from Europe. In *Ghost*, Hochschild referred benignly to the UDC as a "small, beleaguered group of like-minded men and women [that] quickly became the main voice of antiwar dissent in England."[42] From this perspective, the UDC is read as a tormented band of pacifists whose only goal was to save the world from a great tragedy. In fact, the UDC was Morel's shock troops.

Morel won support for his cause in the Netherlands, Norway, Denmark, Italy, Hungary, Czechoslovakia, Austria, Ireland, Poland, New Zealand, and the United States among other nations. In Sweden, 59,000 women signed a petition on his behalf.[43] Liberal and otherwise progressive women's groups, such as the Women's International League for Peace and Freedom, initially gave strong support to Morel's cause. Although the United States had very little to gain politically in the controversy, racial politics gave Morel a base for his claims in a period of high racial tensions and deadly clashes. Between 1919 (known as "Red Summer") and 1921, there were a number of full-scale race riots, in Texas, Illinois, Arkansas, Tennessee, Mississippi, and Oklahoma, to name a few.[44] Many of these conflicts involved black U.S. soldiers who had returned from the war and were in no mood for immersion back into the racism they had to confront once they came home. U.S. racists, on the other hand, wanted to put these individuals back "in their place" regardless of the service they had shown to the nation. Though enemies in war, a stronger philosophical bond was forged between bigoted Whites in the United States and Germany. Thus, the campaign to clean Europe of its "black men-ace" found fertile ground in the United States that had its own "black menace" to address. Even U.S. President Woodrow Wilson attempted to intercede on behalf of the

Germans to have the African troops removed, expressing his fears about how southern Whites would perceive the black occupation. On 28 February 1921, a rally of 12,000 was held in Madison Square Garden, supported mostly by German and Irish Americans, to endorse the demand to rid Germany of its black troops. There was also a counterrally held a few weeks later, on 18 March, that drew an estimated 25,000 to the same site organized by Commander F. W. Galbraith of the American Legion.[45] In the 1920 U.S. presidential election campaigns, the troops became an issue.

Hochschild notes how Morel inspired such luminaries as the civil rights leader Booker T. Washington and the writer Mark Twain to join his campaign against Leopold. They, along with others, formed the American Congo Reform Association and lobbied Congress and Theodore Roosevelt's White House around the issue.[46] Du Bois spoke highly of Morel, referring to him as someone "who knows his Africa better than most white men."[47] Yet, there were other black leaders and famous writers who would sharply criticize Morel's efforts regarding the black troops.

One point of African American resistance came from the poet and Harlem Renaissance figure and writer Claude McKay. Born of peasant parents in Jamaica, McKay had achieved fame and immortality with his renowned poem "If We Must Die," a call to arms for African Americans to resist racism in the United States. As it happened, McKay was living in London from the end of 1919 through the beginning of 1921, the period when the controversy was at its height. He was working as a reporter; in fact, he was Britain's first black reporter ever.[48]

When Morel's article first appeared in the *Daily Herald*, McKay wrote a letter to the publication refuting Morel's accusations, stating,

> Why all this obscene, maniacal outburst about the sex vitality of black men in a proletarian paper? Black men were no more oversexed than white men; when the latter went among coloured races they did not take their women with them— hence the children of mixed race in the West Indies. If black troops had syphilis, they had been contaminated by the white world. As for German women, they were selling themselves to anyone because of their economic plight. . . . Rape is rape; the color of the skin doesn't make it different. Negroes are no more over-sexed than Caucasians; mulatto children in the West Indies and America were not the result of parthenogenesis.[49]

The Herald rejected McKay's letter. Unperturbed, he published it in the *Worker's Dreadnought*, another left-wing paper of the time. There were also a number of progressive whites who spoke out against Morel's antitroop campaign. The writer George Bernard Shaw, who became an associate of McKay, was one of those who rejected the campaign. Less radical voices, including the *New York Times* and the *Wall Street Journal*, also dismissed Morel's claims as mostly baseless.[50]

Until his dying day, Morel held fast to his beliefs that an evil black peril had invaded Europe with the help of the hated French. As with all historic figures, Morel was complicated and contradictory, a combination that should freeze any impulse to create saintly heroes. In one sense, he was similar to other liberals and even radicals of his time who were not necessarily racially enlightened. It is unknown exactly what was Morel's personal relationship with Blacks. One writer contends, "There is no evidence that Morel actually knew a single Negro except on a master-servant level."[51] Hochschild is critical of Morel's support for British colonialism, but only mildly so. As he notes, Morel found "nothing inherently wrong with colonialism . . . if its administration was fair and just."[52] Certainly, this insight demands far more elucidation. What Hochschild sees as a fault of sorts should raise much larger concerns about the apparently contradictory moral stance of Morel who rejects and embraces African oppression simultaneously. *King Leopold's Ghost* will certainly take its place within the pantheon of works that rewrite the history of Africa and the West and bring a needed balance to the record. Unfortunately, for it to be so anchored to the life and times of Morel prevents it from reaching the height of moral and historic ambition at which it so courageously aimed. A more honest rendering of Morel is needed.

Soldier Stories: Black Troops and the Reconstruction of Blackness

Inside Germany, in the 1920s, the black troop issue would evoke and restructure the national discourses on Germany's place in Europe and its relations with its neighbors and on blackness. These discourses, though embodying their own dynamics, were also interrelated. The former would be central to rebuilding a virulent nationalist movement, never far from the surface in Germany anyway. In particular, the Germans inveighed against the despised French. Loathing their neighbors to the west had always been a favorite pasttime of German leaders, but the French decision to place black troops on German soil elevated the hate to unprecedented levels.

While France would respond somewhat to the criticisms, and secretly withdrew two Senegalese regiments, for the most part, it held its ground and refused to cave in to the pressure. The French position was clear: it was a global power that could mobilize its troops from anywhere, and it was not going to be dictated to by the German losers. It was the French contention that it needed the regular white French troops at home. The German journalist Maximilian Harden wrote, "Clemenceau, Foch, and Millerand have sent colored soldiers to Germany, not in order to humiliate Germany, but for other reasons. France requires the arms of her sons for her agriculture and industry."[53] Piling embarrassment upon the Germans was not the goal of the occupation. As Barker observed, "I did not see any evidence that France wished to humiliate the people."[54] It was also clear that the French were not out to impose undue disgrace upon the Germans, because they sent the best colored troops they had available. Barker notes further, "Far from quartering their worse troops upon the Germans, they have sent to the Rhine their elite."[55]

In 1923, the French occupied Germany a second time in the Ruhr area because the Germans could not pay the reparations they owed. In this occupation, there were no black African troops although there may have been some troops from North Africa such as Algerians. Reportedly, the United States withdrew troops because the French had colored soldiers and it disagreed with the occupation policy of France.

The German media spread stories about the so-called rapes of white German women and even created a monstrous black character that they called "Jumbo" whose main purpose in life was to sexually posses white German women.[56] In the Reichstag, Reichskanzler Friedrich Eben led the call for the withdrawal of the troops.

The opposition to the troops was also manifest across the cultural landscape. The attacks on the black French troops (and Jews) found literary expression. In 1922, *The Black Insult, a Novel of Ravished Germany* (*Die Schwarze Schmach, der Roman des Geschandeten Deutschland*) was published. This novel was about the so-called crimes committed by the black troops in Germany. Count Ernest von Reventlow, who was the leader of an ultranationalist group in the north of Germany and an early Nazi sympathizer, wrote the preface.[57] In 1918, four years before *The Black Insult,* Arthur Dinter published *The Sin against the Blood* (*Die Sünde wieder das Blut*), which attacked Jews as evil threats to the purity of German bloodlines.[58]

Children of Misfortune: The So-Called Rhineland Bastards

For German nationalists, the troop occupation was to become a permanent thorn in their sides when the colored soldiers did what occupation forces have done for centuries: they fathered offspring and left them behind. The German Rhineland region became the seeding ground for the next generation of biracial citizens. Although no one knows with any precision, an impossibility under the circumstances, it is estimated that between five hundred and eight hundred children were born as a result of liaisons between African (and other colored) soldiers and white German women.[59] These mixed children were called "half-breeds," "mulattos," and, most popularly, the "Rhineland bastards." One newspaper blared, at the time, "Are we to tolerate silently the fact that in the future, the light-hearted sons of white, attractive, well-built, intellectually-superior and lively, healthy Germans, are to be replaced by the croaking noise of grey-colored, syphilitic mulattoes?"[60]

While the mere specter of having black troops in Germany was controversial, it was clear that at some point they would be gone. Leaving children behind was a different matter. First, for the ultranationalists, to have mixed-raced children meant a "contamination" of German blood. Second, given that the children were being left behind, they would be a permanent reminder of the occupation and Germany's defeat at the hands of its enemies. A plea issued by the major German political parties of the time states, "For German women and children, men and boys, these primitive are a ghastly danger. Their honor, life and limb, purity and innocence are being destroyed."[61]

In the only major study up to now of the subject, Rainer Pommerin documents that there were 102 children registered in 1920. He also notes that, in 1924, only 78 were registered.[62] The Nazis would exert a great deal of energy attempting to locate the children once they came to power, and enlisted the help of churches, schools, and other institutions.

The issue of the Rhineland children would remain until the end of the Third Reich. From the beginning of the regime, there were advocates for their elimination, including Hitler and other Nazi leaders. In 1933, Dr. Hans Macco, who would later advocate extermination of the so-called black curse through sterilization, wrote the influential book *Racial Problems in the Third Reich*. In the book, he stated, "The mulatto children came about through rape or the white mother was a whore. In both cases, there is not the slightest moral duty or responsibility regarding these offspring of a foreign race."[63]

In the first instance, German leaders hoped to simply get the children out of the country. As permanent reminders of not only the loss of the war and the colonies but the power of Germany's enemies to impose Africans into the heartland of the nation, the Rhineland children symbolized too much of the nation's fall to be welcome. The mulatto children (and other black youth) were originally to be deported to Africa with the help of the Catholic Church.[64] However, the churches were not accommodating, partly because the colonies did not want to accept them. While some children were put in orphanages, most of them stayed with their mothers.

The war had a significant impact on the German attitude toward Blacks, generating a harsher view within some circles abetted by the media and nativist leaders. Yet, while German views on Blacks were certainly as racist as the rest of Europe's prior to the war, it is difficult to argue that a general antiblackness prevailed or that it was dangerous for Blacks to be in Germany in the 1920s. The media campaign against Blacks tapered off after the troops were withdrawn and as Germany began to recover economically. No sustained antiblackness campaign flourished, and foreign Blacks continued to visit the country. Within this morass of relative tolerance arose a new voice manifest in a book that would initially receive little popularity.

Hitler Speaks: Mein Kampf *and the Black Presence*

The black troops and the Rhineland children represented a turning point in black German history. One significance of the black troops' presence was that this became a rallying cry for the small but growing German Workers Party, which became on 1 April 1920 the National Socialist German Workers' Party (NSDDP), more popularly known as the Nazi Party. Eventually, led by the Austrian and former no-account Adolf Hitler, the party within a span of only thirteen years would assume state power and begin its quest for world domination, a Third Reich that would last a thousand years according to the deranged projections of its leader. It would be in the immediate few years after the first war, however, that the Nazis would hone their rhetoric and build a movement based on racial and national chauvinism. Hitler, a war veteran on the side of Germany, viewed Germany's defeat, the French imposition, and the subsequent black troop occupation in personal terms. In reference to the French use of black troops in the war, he wrote, "In these months I felt for the first time the whole malice of Destiny which kept me at the front in a position where every nigger might accidentally shoot me to bits, while elsewhere I would have been able to perform quite different services for the fatherland!"[65]

Unfortunately, Hitler's battlefield fears did not come true. Instead, he would fashion himself a revolutionary patriot of his adopted Germany—though he always claimed that Austria was Germany's land in the first place—and spend the early postwar years building the NSDDP. With moderate success going to his head, he foolishly, but prophetically, attempted the nearly comically infamous and ridiculously unsuccessful

November 1923 "Beer Hall Putsch" and landed in Landsberg prison. Apparently with too much time on his hands, he wrote his masterpiece and the blueprint for the Third Reich. *Mein Kampf* is a rambling, nearly incoherent rant, employing a shrill style in what Shirer terms appropriately "appalling crudity."[66] Much of its meaning, of course, lies not in its coherency and lucidity but in its ability to mobilize a preexisting mass sentiment that was profoundly racist, anti-Semitic, anti-French, and imperialist. While there are other works of racist rampage, none have ever been so popular or successful as *Mein Kampf* would ultimately become. The book's popularity emerged for the most part after Hitler came to power. Between 1925 and 1932, despite the publisher's inflated claims, the book sold only 227,917 copies with over 190,000 of those being sold in the years 1929–1932.[67] In other words, the few thousand copies that were sold when the book first came out were mostly to the hardcore Nazis faithful. Of course, millions would be sold after 1933; indeed, it was dangerous and certainly politically risky to not have a copy at home and office.

In addition to being fervently anti-Semitic, the book is also full of what one writer calls "countless sneering references to Negroes."[68] Although Hitler, in *Mein Kampf*, referred to the Rhineland area as "the hunting ground of African Negro hordes," he blames the presence of Blacks in Europe on the French and on Jews.[69] Feeling no need to provide evidence or reason, he fumes, "It was and it is Jews who bring the Negroes into the Rhineland, always with the same secret thought and clear aim of ruining the hated white race by the necessarily resulting bastardization, throwing it down from its cultural and political height, and himself rising to be its master."[70] The linkage between Jews and Blacks, in Hitler's and the Nazi minds, would be a consistent theme during the Nazi era. Some Nazi "scientists" would argue, for instance, that Jews were the bastardized result of the mating of Africans and Asians.[71] Hitler criticizes France as being in cahoots with this Jewish "aim" of reracializing Europe. As he seethes,

> France is and remains by far the most terrible enemy. This people, which is basically becoming more and more negrified, constitutes in its tie with the aims of Jewish world domination an enduring danger for the existence of the white race in Europe. For the contamination by Negro blood on the Rhine in the heart of Europe is just as much in keeping with the perverted sadistic thirst for vengeance of this hereditary enemy of our people as is the ice-cold calculation of the Jew thus to begin bastardizing the European continent at its core and to deprive the white race of the foundations for a sovereign existence through infection with lower humanity.[72] [He continues:] What France, spurred on by her own thirst for vengeance and systematically led by the Jew, is doing in Europe today is a sin against the existence of white humanity and some day will incite against this people all the avenging spirits of a race which has recognized racial pollution as the original sin of humanity.[73]

Concerned about the potentially changing racial character of Europe, Hitler is pathologically obsessed about what he considers the then foolishness of Germany's policies on citizenship. This was a critical debate among the German elite because of the history of tying the notion of nation to the question of blood linkage and history. The construction of this bond of nation and blood was a pivotal ideological argument employed by the Nazis in building popular support. Similar to the debate that was taking place in the United States regarding the immigration of southern and eastern Europeans during that period, Hitler's view of a racial nation required the identity of parameters by which potential citizens and noncitizens could be distinguished. In reference to who can be "Germanized," he wrote, "But it is a scarcely conceivable fallacy of thought to believe that a Negro or Chinese, let us say, will turn into a German because he learns German and is willing to speak the German language in the future and perhaps even give his vote to a German political party. That any such Germanization is in reality a de-Germanization never became clear to our bourgeois natural world."[74] The so-called de-Germanization that he rails against is a reference to the policy of the German state, similar to that of other European nations at the time, to confer citizenship on those born there. This is upsetting to the future führer: "Today the right of citizenship, as mentioned above, is primarily achieved by birth within the borders of a state. In this, race or nationality play no role whatever. A Negro, who formerly lived in the German protectorates and now has his residence in Germany, gives birth to a 'German citizen' in the person of his child. Likewise every Jewish or Polish, African or Asiatic child can be declared a German citizen without further ado."[75] For Hitler and the Nazis, and millions of Germans, to be a German citizen was conflated with being white, and it irked the Nazi leader no end that, as he saw it, acquiring citizenship was far too easy. "The whole process of acquiring citizenship takes place not far differently than admission into an automobile club," he continues sarcastically, "The man makes his application, it is examined and passed upon, and one day he receives a note informing him that he has become a citizen, and even the form of this is cute and kittenish. The former Zulu Kaffir [*sic*] in question is informed: 'You have hereby become a German.'"[76]

In a telling reference, Hitler notes that there is only one nation that he considers on the right racial path in how it deals with citizenship and immigration: the United States.

> I know that people do not like to hear all this; but anything more thoughtless, more hare-brained than our present-day citizenship laws scarcely exists. There is today one state in which at least weak beginnings toward a better conception are noticeable. Of course, it is not our model German Republic, but the American Union, in which an effort is made to consult reason at least partially. By refusing immigration in principle to elements in poor health, by simply excluding certain races from naturalization, it professes in slow beginnings a view which is peculiar to the folkish state concept.[77]

The Nazis, as we shall see, exploited this essentially on-target assessment of U.S. race politics

Independent of the references and connections to the French and the Jews, Hitler's views on Blacks are patronizing, condescending, and infused with the racist assumptions of the eugenicists. He argues that Blacks are incapable of civilized achievements and are barely above primates. In one extended passage, he expounds upon his views of black potential:

> From time to time illustrated papers bring it to the attention of the German petty-bourgeois that some place or other a Negro has for the first time become a lawyer, teacher, even a pastor, in fact a heroic tenor, or something of the sort. While the idiotic bourgeois looks with amazement at such miracles of education, full of respect for this marvelous result of modern educational skills, the Jew shrewdly draws from it a new proof for the soundness of his theory about the equality of men that he is trying to funnel into the minds of nations. It doesn't dawn on this depraved bourgeois world that this is positively a sin against all reason; that it is criminal lunacy to keep on drilling a born half-ape until people have made a lawyer out of him, while millions of members of the highest culture-race must remain in entirely unworthy positions; that it is a sin against the will of the Eternal Creator if His most gifted beings by the hundreds and hundreds of thousands are allowed to degenerate in the present proletarian morass, while Hottentots and Zulu Kaffirs are trained for intellectual professions. For this is training exactly like that of the poodle, and not scientific "education." The same pains and care employed on intelligent races would a thousand times sooner make every single individual capable of the same achievements.[78]

Ultimately, Hitler's greatest fear of Blacks was linked to blood and the possibility of European "bastardization," brought on by the French in collaboration with Jews. This line of reasoning would be the rationalization by the Nazis for purifying not only Germany of its so-called alien elements but all of Europe. He viewed the area of Germany as too small for the empire that the German nation deserved and needed. In spite of his hatred of France, he was also envious. As he argued,

> From the purely territorial point of view, the area of the German Reich vanishes completely as compared with that of the so-called world powers. Let no one cite England as a proof to the contrary, for England in reality is merely the great capital of the British world empire which calls nearly a quarter of the earth's surface its own. In addition, we must regard as giant states, first of all the American Union, then Russia and China. All are spatial formations having in part an area more than ten times greater than the present German Reich. And even France must be counted among these states. No only that she complements her army to an ever-increasing degree from her enormous empire's reservoir of colored humanity, but racially as well, she is making such great progress in negrification that we can actually speak of an African state arising on European soil. The colonial policy of present-day France cannot be compared with that of Germany in the past. If the development of France in the present style were to be continued for three hundred years, the last remnants of Frankish blood would be submerged in the developing

European-African mulatto state. An immense self-contained area of settlement from the Rhine to the Congo, filled with a lower race gradually produced from continuous bastardization.[79]

Hitler saw "race-mixing" as not only an affront to national identity and culture but a sin against God. Thus, the notion of racial purity is viewed in divine terms that go well beyond the preferences or desires of particular human societies. He wrote, "The result of all racial crossing is therefore in brief always the following: (a) lowering of the level of the higher race; (b) physical and intellectual regression and hence the beginning of a slowly but surely progressing sickness. To bring about this such a development is, then, nothing else but to sin against the will of the eternal creator."[80]

Needless to say, other Nazi leaders and German nationalists also had negative views of Blacks. According to the eugenicist Fritz Lenze, "the Negro is not particularly intelligent in the proper sense of the term, and above all he is devoid of the power of mental creation, is poor in imagination, so that he has not developed any original art and has no elaborate folk myths. He is, however, clever with his hands and is endowed with considerable technical adroitness, so that he can easily be trained in the manual crafts."[81] In the period before the Nazis came to power, this type of rhetoric was not unusual. What is remarkable is that while it is virtually impossible to find a single word of praise from Nazi leaders for people of African descent, antiblackness hyperbole of this type would be muted during most of the time of National Socialism.

Black Resistance in the Weimar Republic

Resistance to antiblackness, though contained, also existed inside of pre-Nazi Germany. While Blacks were small in numbers, this did not stop the organizing efforts of a few race-conscious and politically conscious individuals. Recent historical research has uncovered a number of black or antiracist organizations that functioned during the 1920s and perhaps later underground during the National Socialist era. It should be noted that Blacks in Germany were not uniform in viewing themselves as part of a racial category, although the Nazis and perhaps other Germans certainly saw them as such, so organizations or groups did not necessarily see themselves as "black." There were a number of organizations, for instance, that comprised only or mostly Africans who had more of a continental, regional, or national identity, such as the Colored People in Germany and Africa and West Indian America organization that was founded in the early 1930s.[82] Yet, even for these organizations, it would have been impossible not to feel the homogenizing effects of Nazism's racial views or, even more important, the internationally known situation of Blacks in the United States. The state of apartheid in the United States and the black response in the form of the NAACP, Marcus Garvey, Booker T. Washington, and other organizations were well known, through not only the mass media of the time but also the travels of African Americans in Europe and Germany, in particular. These black-to-black encounters, whether physically or virtual, were part of a racializing atmosphere that would accelerate in a very short time.

While the organizations described below were relatively small and short-lived, their significance lies in their effort to create a counterhegemonic voice to the growing racial rap of Nazism and its followers. All of the black organizing efforts were not necessarily political in nature or self-consciously racial, though they embodied political and social significance. The Aryanization of German politics in the late 1920s and early 1930s was not passively accepted by those who were written out of the equation. The major political battles in Germany during the time involved both the Socialists and Communists on the left in struggle with a wide array of conservatives and reactionaries on the right. In addition to the black organizations described below, Germany's black population was also involved in the leftist parties and movements of the time, sometimes playing a leading role as was the case of the Afro-German Hilarius Gilges, who was a member of the German Communist Party in the Dusseldorf region. (See chapter 10 for more on Gilges.) Finally, there were a number of U.S.-based organizations that also had influence among Blacks in Germany such as Garvey's Universal Negro Improvement Association.

The creation of these organizations, to a significant degree, reflected an effort at constructing community—a racial community at that. As noted in chapter 2, Omi and Winant argue that the building of racial groups and the racialization process are defined, in part, by the initiation of "racial projects." These political projects were not only defense mechanisms against the emerging antagonistic racial state but a counterhegemonic effort at establishing community and moving beyond the individualized circumstances in which many Blacks, particularly Afro-Germans, found themselves.

League for the Defense of the Negro Race

One radical black group was the German chapter of the League for the Defense of the Negro Race (LDNR), an organization that had affiliates in other parts of Europe. The main organization was founded in 1924 and the German chapter five years later by Victor Bell, Thomas Ngambi Ul Kuo, Joseph Bile, Madeline Guber, and other Blacks living in Germany at the time.[83] The League's main headquarters was in France, but it had chapters in various parts of Europe. It even had connections with parts of the diaspora outside of Europe. According to Michael, the African American scholar W. E. B. Du Bois was associated with the League in some manner.[84] As described in chapter 4, the LDNR would attempt to continue its work under National Socialism but find itself under attack and its leaders forced underground or in exile.

African Association for Solidarity

Bell, Bile, and others were involved in another organization during the same period: the African Association for Solidarity. It was primarily composed of Africans from Cameroon, Togo, and other former German colonies but also included Afro-Germans. While it is unknown how long the organization existed, its purposes and goals, or its relationship to the state, it could claim among its membership some of the most prominent Africans in Germany of the period. The accompanying membership list[85] shows that in June 1918, the organization had at least thirty-two dues-paying members from all across Germany including Berlin, Potsdam, Hamburg, and Altona, among others.

Table 4   African Association for Solidarity Membership List, June 1918

Mitgliedsliste fur. Monat Juni 1918	
Hermann Ngange, Tussenhausen/Bayern, Schloß	8.00
Reinhold d'Elong, Zoppot, Gerichstr. 10	60.00
Anjo Dick, Coln, Weinhaus Schubert	10.00
Gregor Kotto, Breslau, Klosterstr. 40	10.20
* Josef Bille, Marggrabowa, Bahnstr. 373	18.00
Conrad Volly, Herne i. W. Sterffens Saalbau	5.00
Gottlieb Kinger, Potsdam, Bertinistr. 16	8.05
Volly, Rotstock, Großherzogl. Palais	5.00
Hermann Kessern, Dulmen Westf, Schloß	8.00
Thomas Sommern, Dulmen Westf, Schloß	6.00
Jakob Mandenge, Dulmen Westf, Schloß	3.00
Albert Jost, Charlottenburg, Knesebeckstr. 16	5.00
Toto bin Hamisi, Charlottenburg, Magazinstr. 9	5.00
Ludwig Mpesa, Berlin, Kurfurstenstr. 40	7.00
David Dipongo, Berlin, Barbarossastr. 14	5.00
Th. Wonja Michael, Berlin, Weißenburgstr. 4	12.00
Victor Bell, Berlin, Driesenerstr. 4	10.00
Mohamed bin Abdullah, Hamburg, Thalstr. 29	5.00
Abo bir. Ali, Hamburg, Seilerstr. 45	5.00
Mukuri Makembe, Hamburg, Dammtorwall 115	10.00
Paul Messi., Hamburg, Laeiszstr. 18	5.00
Ernst Anumu, Hamburg, Koppel, 26	10.00
J. Lawson, Hamburg, Henriettenstr. 25	7.50
Willi Seier., Hamburg, Fruchtallee 121	10.20
David Bismarck, Hamburg, Hansdorferstr. 17	5.00
L. E. Larcheveaut, Hamburg, Neuerwall 54	5.00
Eduard Ramsis, Hamburg, Thalstr. 29	2.00
Rudolf Steinberg, Altona, Bohmkenstr 19	5.00
Hans Nio, Altona, Gr. Muhlenstr 54	5.50
Paul Malapa, Altona, Bohmkenstr 19	10.00
Ambursus de Souza, Altona, Eimsbuttelerstraße 17	5.00
Georg Menzel, Altona, Kl. Prinzenstr	6.00

		275.45
	Mai-Einnahme	54.00
	Bestand	329.45

*The correct spelling is Boholle.

Source: Theodor Michael.

The June 1918 date means that the group likely existed during the war or perhaps as a result of the war. The Afro-German Theodor Michael, from whom a copy of the original list was obtained, knew very little about the organization although his father, according to the list, had been one of its members. The national breadth of the list, the fact that it had a dues-paying structure, and even the existence of the list itself indicates a serious level of organization had evolved.

International Trade Union Committee of Negro Workers/Negro Worker

More radical political efforts involving an international community of Blacks occurred prior to the Nazi era. From 7–9 July 1930, the International Conference of Negro Workers (ICNW) was held in Hamburg. The principal organizer of this gathering was the activist George Padmore. Born Malcolm Ivan Meredith Nurse in 1902 in Arouca, Trinidad, the man who would later change his name to Padmore rose to be one of the foremost leaders of the international communist movement of the 1920s and 1930s and subsequently, after a break with communism, a leader in the African independence movements of the 1940s and 1950s. As a reporter for the Trinidad *Guardian*, he wrote radical and inflammatory articles criticizing Britain's role as a colonial power. To further his education, and to appease his parents' concerns about his safety, Padmore went to the United States around 1924 to attend Fisk University and study sociology and political science. After leading protests against southern segregation and the university's conservative (white) administration, he and Fisk parted, and he ended up at Howard University, enrolling in its law school. He would become even more radicalized in a milieu that featured the nation's top black intellectuals such as the future Nobel Peace Prize winner Ralph Bunche, who became a lifelong friend, and the future president of Trinidad, Eric Williams, among others.[86] Embracing communism, Padmore moved to New York City, became the first Black to attend and graduate from the Communist Party's Workers' School, and, in 1929, went to Moscow, the headquarters of global communism led by the Communist Party of the Soviet Union (CPSU).

In 1929, he was appointed head of the Negro Bureau of the Red International of Labor Unions (RILU), an international alliance of trade unions controlled by the Communist International (COMINTERN) that was directly controlled by the CPSU. In 1930, Padmore was sent to Germany to work on organizing the ICNW. The conference was originally to be held in London, but was refused a venue. At the time, the German communists had a significant amount of influence in Hamburg, even having a number of police officers as members.[87] Also, Russia's relations with Germany were such that Russian ships could move relatively freely in and out of Hamburg's docks, making it an ideal spot for the kind of clandestine activities in which Padmore was involved.

Although Padmore and others would inflate the numbers later, there were only seventeen delegates from throughout the diaspora who actually gathered for the conference.[88] These included delegates from the United States, (among them a woman textile worker), Jamaica, Trinidad, Nigeria, Gambia, Sierra Leone, the Gold Coast (now Ghana), Cameroon, and even a white representative from South Africa.[89] Black representatives from the Portuguese, French, and Belgian colonies were not allowed. According to Michael, there were Blacks in Germany who were involved in the movement.[90]

In January 1930, the International Trade Union Committee of Negro Workers (ITUC-NW), an arm of the RILU, began publication of the monthly *Negro Worker* in Hamburg at 8 Rothesoodstrasse near the waterfront district. Hamburg was chosen as the site for publication not only because it had a relatively friendly city administration, but also because it facilitated contact with the group that would become the principal agents of distribution of the *Negro Worker*: black sailors. The *Negro Worker* functioned underground and the press was concealed in a building that had been turned into a sea-men's club. This property had been initially owned by the German Communist Party (KDP) but later taken over by a missionary society when the party was disallowed and disbanded. Ironically, often the communist *Negro Worker* would be distributed hidden in religious tracts to throw off the police. The newspaper has been called "the very first international journal for the Negro in all continents, which was concerned with his troubles, needs, and pains."[91]

Padmore, after a six-month stint by J. W. Ford of the U.S. Communist Party, became the editor. He was still a member of the U.S. party at the time. Much of the period Padmore served as editor during 1930, he did so from Vienna as Germany increasingly moved toward the Nazi era and it became dangerous to carry out any type of political mobilizing or engaging in non-Nazi or anti-Nazi activism or possessing inflammatory documents. In 1931, he was back in Hamburg running the paper. In addition to the *Negro Worker*, he wrote six pamphlets, including *What Is the International Trade Union Committee of Negro Workers?*; *Life and Struggles of Negro Toilers*; *Negro Workers and the Imperialist War: Intervention in the Soviet Union*; *Forced Labour in Africa*; *American Imperialism Enslaves Liberia*; and *Labour Imperialism and East Africa*.

Political events in Germany began to catch up with Padmore and the *Negro Worker*. By December 1931, the offices of the ITUC-NW (Hamburg) and the League Against Imperialism in Berlin had been raided several times. Despite the growing attacks, a con-ference was held in May 1932 of "dockers and seamen" that involved a number of Blacks. Predictably, 1933 would see an end to the Hamburg-based publishing of the *Negro Worker*. Hitler came to power at the end of January, and by June the *Negro Worker* was being produced and published in Copenhagen, its German offices and files closed, and the leadership that did not manage to get out of Nazified Germany landed in jail—Padmore included, though he was likely jailed more for his political views and nationality than because of his race. His British passport finally got him put on a ship and sent to England. The *Negro Worker*, now publishing in exile, would continue until 1938, which turned out to be four more years than Padmore lasted in the communist movement.

Black Germans who were involved in the ITUC-NW were arrested also when the crackdowns began right before and then under the Nazis regime. In part, they were per-secuted because they were labor organizers and not necessarily or simply because they were black. Michael notes how strong the anti–trade union character of the state had become by the early 1930s and how determined the Nazis were to crush any vestiges of labor mobilization and organizing; a center of that activity still remained in the Hamburg area in 1933.[92]

In August 1933, without consultation, the COMINTERN decided to dissolve the ITUC-NW.[93] In response, Padmore resigned from all his official positions, and, shortly thereafter, there was a bitter parting of the ways. He would spend the rest of his days railing against communism and engaged in the movement to liberate Africa, working closely with the future Ghanaian president Kwame Nkrumah, among other African leaders to emerge in the 1940s and 1950s. Called by no less than the brilliant Caribbean intellectual (and childhood friend) C. L. R. James the "Father of African Emancipation," Padmore died in 1959 in Ghana.[94]

League Against Imperialism

Founded in 1927 in London, the LAI sought the abolition of global racial discrimination. It emerged out of a political conference and included members from around the world. Its founders included prominent radicals and luminaries including Albert Einstein (then from Germany), Sun Yat-sen (China), Lamine Senghor (Senegal), Richard Moore (United States), Upton Sinclair (United States), J. T. Gumede (South Africa), Mohammad Hatta (Indonesia), Messali Hadj (Algeria), Jawaharlal Nehru (India), and Ho Chi Minh (Indochina).[95] In May 1931, the League met in Berlin. Forty-six delegates attended, among them "15 from colonial countries and 15 from the oppressed nations and national minorities."[96] The German chapter took up the issue of racial equality for Blacks, but after Hitler came to power, the Nazi government closed the office down.

Racism and the Black Diaspora During World War I and the 1920s

> That which the Germans represent today spells death to the aspirations of Negroes and all darker races for equality, freedom, and democracy.
>
> —W. E. B. Du Bois[97]

As the war drums beat louder and louder for an expanded theater of war in Europe, the United States geared up to participate. While there were some politically leftist African Americans who opposed U.S. entry into the conflict, viewing it as a war of imperialist grab for land and geostrategic positioning, tens of thousands of Blacks volunteered to go and fight. For many, it would not only be an opportunity to fight on behalf of the nation, but also a means of proving or claiming their American-ness, particularly in a period of high racial tensions and conflicts. Segregation was the law of much of the land and of nearly all the social spaces African Americans occupied, given that the majority of Blacks lived in the Jim Crow South. Campaigns against lynchings and racist violence, the 1909 founding of the National Association for the Advancement of Colored People, and the Garvey movement were only a few of the resistance efforts by African Americans in the prewar period. State and popular responses to these labors were repressive and violent. The Bolshevik victory in Russia in 1917 found a number of African Americans admirers and inspired black participation in socialist and leftist movements within the United

States. This included membership in the Communist Party, the Socialist Party, and the International Workers (Wobblies), as well as independent, all-black formations such as the African Blood Brotherhood and leftist black newspapers such as the *Crusader* and the *Messenger*. Recent historical research has unveiled a persistent and determined effort by several federal and many local agencies to suppress and crush black involvement in these movements. At the federal level, this included the Department of Justice and the young J. Edgar Hoover's Bureau of Investigation, the Treasury Department, and the Military Intelligence Division, among others.[98]

Despite the war at home, there were many African Americans who joined the war abroad and some even fought under the French flag. Among those fighting were the four regiments (369th, 370th, 371st, and 372nd) of the all-black 93rd division.[99] Even under the command of another state, African Americans found themselves in racial conflict with white America. The NAACP leader W. E. B. Du Bois, while researching the history of Blacks in the war, discovered a document issued by the American Expeditionary Forces in May 1919, titled "Secret Information Concerning Black American Troops." In this blantantly racist piece, which the U.S. government attempted to disguise as originating from the French military, the Americans advised the French, "We must not commend too highly the black American troops, particularly in the presence of white Americans. [We must] make a point of keeping the population from 'spoiling' the Negroes. White Americans become greatly incensed at any public expression of intimacy between white women with black men. Military authorities cannot intervene directly on this question, but it can through the civil authorities exercise some influence on the population."[100] The French, upon discovering the existence of this document, confiscated and destroyed all copies they could find.[101]

Given this context, African Americans could identify with the rhetorical attacks on the black troops in Germany in view of the response of white Americans toward black soldiers upon their return. Race riots across the country, and the tragic paradox of black soldiers being lynched while still in uniform, meant that African Americans were hardly in the mood to join any call for actions against Germany's occupying black soldiers.

The pervasive and legal segregation that contextualized life for millions of African Americans foreshadowed the segregation that Jews and racial minorities would face under Nazism. From prohibitions against intermarriage to segregated public facilities, black Americans were legally relegated to second-class status. Similar laws and public policies and practices existed against Latinos, Asians, and Native Americans. The Nazis would take note of these regulations with more than a little bit of admiration and envy.

Du Bois was busy organizing his Pan-African Congresses, while Garvey was calling for Africa for the Africans and end to colonial rule by Europeans. In the aftermath of World War I, black activists from around the world took an aggressive posture toward the new world order and believed that a coordinated collective effort could bring positive change in their circumstances. Du Bois would be central to these efforts. He wrote the platform of the 1919 Pan-African Congress meeting that was to then be presented to those governments meeting at the Peace Congress at Versailles. During this period, Du Bois argued for a black elite—his "Talented Tenth" notion—to lead the black, postcolonialized world. The document took a particularly hard line against Germany's retaining any of its colonial possessions. It stated, "It is clear that at least one of Germany's specific objects in the present war was the extension of her African colonies at the expense of France and Portugal. Their return to Germany is unthinkable." It advised that Germany should not retain its pre-war colonies, nor should they be divided up among the other European powers. By the time this statement was written, the redistribution had already happened (not that the Allied powers would have given any serious attention to the Congress's demands anyway). An even more radical position taken by the Congress was that "The 'decisive voice' in the disposition of the German colonies should be the chiefs and intelligent Negroes among the twelve-and-one-half million natives of German Africa, especially those trained in the government and mission schools."[102]

In the pre-Nazi era, Du Bois would also briefly visit Germany again in 1928 while on his way to the Soviet Union. Due to customs problems, he was forced to stay in Germany for two to three weeks. During that time, to his dismay, he found that his beloved yet "prostrate" Germany was sinking under the weight of its war debt and political chaos. As he noted, "The sight of the German Republic struggling on the ruins of the empire and tottering under a load of poverty, oppression and disorganization made upon me an unfortunate impression."[103]

Little known but certainly the most provocative of Du Bois's visits to his beloved Germany is the trip he took to Nazi Germany in 1936 that lasted between five and six months. This remarkable juxtaposition of one of the twentieth century's most extraordinary thinkers on race and the cauldron of Nazi race hatred, a study in its own right, is detailed in chapter four.

Summary

A black political presence in Germany not only existed, it flourished during the 1920s. The coming of the black troops, the visits and even long-term residence of Blacks from other parts of the world, and the birth of the Rhineland mixed-race children qualitatively changed the black racial equation and the German social scene. The black presence was also political in that resistance to racism and imperialism took on organizational forms that were overwhelmingly radical and leftist, whether in the labor movement, in the Socialist or Communist party, or in independent black and antiracist formations. Though the latter were relatively small, they reflected a global movement for change from the bottom, stirrings of indigenous anticolonial and civil rights movements that, unfortunately, would only bear fruit several decades later.

It can be argued that the popular anger over the occupation provided an additional racial justification along with anti-Semitism that fueled the then small National Socialist Workers Party and contributed significantly to its growth at the end of the 1920s. Fascism in Germany was built along racial lines and hammered this theme home insistently. The construction of an antiblackness discourse with popular support was a new stage in the history of Blacks in Germany with unknown implications for the period ahead. Although the Nazi movement was growing, few would have speculated that it was actually going to come to power, or that its racist rhetoric was more than that. Hitler and the Nazis were opposed by 63 percent of the German electorate in the 1932 elections, yet the divided opposition and a willingness to compromise on the part of leaders of the republic opened the door for a determined and unyielding Nazi movement.[104] If there was any question of whether the Nazis genuinely meant to establish a state that would relentlessly and ruthlessly pursue racial purity and world power, it was resolved when at noon on Monday, 30 January 1933, at the apex of a governmental crisis, President Field Marshal Paul von Hindenberg met with Adolf Hitler in his office at the presidential palace and the latter emerged as the new chancellor of Germany.

Part III

"The Worst That You Can Imagine"

Blacks and Nazism

Hitler's Black Dilemmas

The Face and Fact of Blackness under Nazism

The "Adolph period" was the worst that you can imagine.
—Erika Ngambi ul Kuo[1]

Negroes must be definitely third-class people. Your people are a hopeless lot. I don't hate them. I pity the poor devils.
—Adolf Hitler[2]

Meeting Hitler

The journalist Roi Ottley reports of a dinner meeting in 1932 between Dr. S. J. Wright, an African American in Germany studying at Heidelberg University, and Adolf Hitler. Hitler reportedly spoke favorably of the activist and performer Paul Robeson and the civil rights leader Booker T. Washington. Other than those two, however, he spoke of African Americans in disparaging terms. He confronted Dr. Wright directly regarding his educational ambitions in race-conscious America, asking, "Why do you seek a white man's education, when you know, or should know, that you can never use it—at least as a white man can? This experience in Germany will only serve to make you more miserable when you return to America."[3] While the veracity of this conversation is impossible to determine, even if only partly true, it demonstrates an engagement and concern by the soon-to-be-in-power Nazi leadership with the question of blackness. Hitler's views toward Blacks seemed to oscillate between benevolent pity and downright abhorrence (while never conceding their humanity). According to Ottley, Hitler would later send a delegation of Nazis to the United States to study the policies of racial segregation against African Americans for the purpose of implementing them against German Jews.

Being Black under Hitler

Ottley was among those who claimed that German racial prejudice against Blacks was muted during both the Weimar Republic and Nazism. He wrote, "No stigma was attached to a black skin; the lot of Negroes was pretty much that of Germans. Negro travelers report that they never saw the slightest signs of color prejudice anywhere in Germany."[4] He concludes, "Negroes on the Continent were merely incidental to [Hitler's] program. He could afford a certain back-handed liberalism towards them for propaganda purposes elsewhere."[5] Ottley is speaking primarily, however, of those Blacks who came to Germany as guests or visitors rather than the Afro-Germans. As he correctly states, "Germany always was especially attractive to Negroes who wished to study music, medicine, and philosophy and were unable to gain admittance to universities in the [United States]."[6] In addressing the situation of Afro-Germans, he remains also mostly positive and anecdotal. He speaks favorably of the presence of Blacks in the symphony orchestra and even the German Army. Nude bathing at resorts, he claims, was integrated without any visible problems.

These incidentals, however true, do not begin to tell the story of black life during the Hitler era. The experiences of Blacks under Nazism were multifaceted because there were several categories of Blacks each of whom had a distinct relationship to the facist state and popular sociocultural practices. The black population was divided into Afro-Germans (those who were born in Germany and had citizenship), the African population (students, teachers, workers, business people, diplomats), and those from the diaspora (Afro-Europeans, primarily from England and France, and African Americans) who were mainly entertainers, journalists, educators, and students. Little is known about the experiences of Blacks from other parts of the diaspora, primarily because there is almost no record regarding the presence of people of African descent from Latin America, the Middle East, or Asia. This breakdown is important to understand because of the Nazis' differentiated treatment of the various categories of Blacks. While the Nazis could, in some ways, ignore initially the Africans who were there, at the same time they could launch a program to sterilize the Rhineland youth. While they could brutally murder captured African American soldiers, they could embrace African American and Afro-European singers and performers. While many Afro-Germans could not find work and lived in poverty, according to Samples, "some black colonials led a rather 'bourgeois' existence as shopkeepers or craftsmen."[7] What is being reflected here is the reality of implementing a complicated program of racial hierarchy that had to account for political, economic, and international interests. As Samples states further, "The racist state policy of the Third Reich was not always monolithic, but often contradictory. Undeniably, racism permeated German society, but the degree and type of persecution directed toward the African Germans (or, for that matter, any of the designated non-Aryan groups) varied greatly."[8]

These contradictions, I argue, do not invalidate the pervasiveness and oppressive character of the Nazi racial paradigm but suggest its complications, its nuances, its evolving nature, its pragmatic elements, and its discursive practice. By examining the implementation of the sterilization program, the role of Blacks in the film and entertainment industries, the discourse and policy regarding jazz, the resistance movements in which Blacks participated, the racial uses of sports, and the black prison internment and concentration camp experiences, we can begin to construct a picture of black life under Nazism and what emerged as Hitler's perpetual black dilemmas. Rather than see the period as one unbroken series of consistent politics and policies, we can more usefully construct a periodization that follows critical developments in the Nazi era and their impact on Blacks. The periods can roughly be divided into four distinct but obviously overlapping times: (1) 1933–1935, the Nazi consolidation period; (2) 1935–1937, the Nuremberg laws were passed, including specific policies aimed at mixed-race peoples, and the decision to carry out secret sterilizations against the Rhineland youth was made; (3) 1937–1942, the bulk of (recorded) sterilizations against Afro-Germans and other Blacks are done, passports are confiscated and Afro-Germans are made stateless, and the war to seize Europe is launched; and (4) 1943–1945, the war turns against the Germans, and the "Final Solution" program to exterminate the Jews is begun with implications for Afro-Germans in Germany and other Blacks under the occupation. In each of these periods, national and local variables were important as well as Germany's international situation.

There was no one overall policy, although there was one overall objective. The goal of the Nazi government was to create a pure German "racial state" that did not include Jews, Gypsies, or others who were not Aryan, including Blacks. As can be imagined, after Hitler came to power and the Nazis rapidly began to pass laws that discriminated against Jews, Gypsies, homosexuals, Jehovah's Witnesses, communists, and people of African descent, many Blacks wanted to leave Germany for good. While some were able to escape to France and some went back to parts of Africa, most could not get out. Those who wanted to go back to Southwest Africa were told by the British, who were then the new colonial authorities, that because they had fought on the side of the Germans during World War I they could not emigrate. By the mid-to-late 1930s, the issue of emigration was moot for Afro-Germans because the Nazis had confiscated passports, and it became almost impossible to leave legally. The Nazis, after coming to power, would invoke the *Fremdengesetz* (Foreigner Act) and relegate Blacks and other to the status of "guests," but in reality, they were being made stateless.

No one knows for sure how many Blacks were in Germany in the 1920s and 1930s. The number of Africans in Germany, not including those of African descent from throughout the diaspora, was significantly underestimated in the years from 1885 to 1945. Ottley writes that in the 1920s and early 1930s, before Hitler become chancellor, there were about four to five thousand Blacks in Germany.[9] He is including all people of African descent in his estimation. The researcher Susann Samples states that "a conservative estimate would be that the combined total for all African Germans was about a thousand," but adds that there was "an indeterminate number of black foreign nationals as well as black colonials [who] also resided in Germany during the Third Reich."[10] Hitler himself reportedly stated, "The Jew constitutes only one per cent [*sic*] of the German population, the Negro only one per cent [*sic*] of one per cent, [*sic*] and yet all such homeopathic infusion is placed under the ban."[11] If at the time, there were about 250 million in Germany, this would translate into roughly 2.5 million Jews and 25,000 Blacks. The film *Black Survivors of the Holocaust,* notes that a survey done in Germany in the mid-1920s found that there were 24,000 people of African descent in the country at the time, and that there were about 20,000 during Hitler's first year in office.[12] None of these highly qualified estimations of Blacks disaggregate the different groups that existed. Given the small number involved, it is notable how much attention was given eventually to resolving the dilemma of presence that people of African descent represented.

The number of Africans in Germany and what to do with them also became a debate. Some argued, as several scholars noted, that Blacks from the German colonies should "be given a privileged status" relative to other Blacks residing in Germany during the 1920s.[13] In the 1920s, the colonial administration provided financial welfare to those Africans from the former colonies who were needy and living in Germany as well as some who were repatriated.[14] Even in 1935, two years after the Nazis came to power and had passed the notorious Nuremberg laws that would began the inexorable path toward racial genocide, the policy and political bureaucracies of National Socialism—the Colonial Department of the Foreign Office, Department for Germany of the Foreign Office, Propaganda Ministry, and German Labor Front, Colonial Policy Office of the Nazi Party, and the Racial Policy Office of the Nazi Party—operated to "create a social framework for Africans that would both physically isolate them from the German population and make them useful for colonial administration."[15]

The Nazis were confronted with several choices in addressing their black concern. The easiest and most preferred program (for the Germans) would have been the deportation of Blacks either to Africa or to some other place outside of Europe. A more politically difficult option was to round up all the Blacks and put them in "protective custody," the Nazi euphemism for arrest and indefinite detainment. And, of course, a third, which they planned for Jews and Gypsies, was to include Blacks in the category of those who were to be eliminated. Each alternative had its backers, and depending upon the period and which Blacks were being considered, one had more support than others. In the end, none of these choices would be fully implemented and the preference to address the problem by sterilization of some would be as coherent as the Nazi policies ever got regarding Afro-Germans and Africans. This probably accounts for why the "National Socialist media were virtually silent about the existence of the African Germans."[16] It should not be assumed, however, that if the Nazis had actually won the war or, at least, were in a better position to deal with domestic concerns, Blacks would not have been ultimately exterminated.

The Extermination Option

Afro-Germans, and Blacks in general, were never named as a group to be gathered up and dealt with by physical elimination as only the Nazis could. Although highly visible and obviously of a different hue, Afro-Germans, as a whole, did not feel the total wrath of the German state and, in some instances, were relatively secure, or as secure as one could be under fascism. Afro-Germans were not white, blond, or anything else Aryan and squarely fell within the logic of the Nazi racial discourse of white superiority and black inferiority, yet they were not collectively persecuted and never legally defined as *Auslanders* (foreigners), although many Africans had their passports seized and were declared "stateless." This situation would change somewhat after 1937 as the war loomed and international opinion was less of a factor in shaping the behavior of the Nazi state. But even then, no *general* order was given to arrest, incarcerate, and eliminate Afro-Germans or Africans. In fact, Afro-Germans were consciously incorporated into the broad mobilization of the population on behalf of the war effort, that is, black Germans were employed in military-related industries and at least a few ended up in the military. Like many Germans and those captured during the war, some Blacks were also slave laborers who had no choice but to work where they were told for essentially subsistence benefits.

There were apparently three main reasons why the Nazis did not (initially) go after the Afro-Germans, Africans, and other Blacks en masse. First, the Germans believed that someday they would get their colonial possessions back although it was never clear how this was going to come about since the colonies had been divided up among the victors of the First World War. Nevertheless, in the interest of that objective, it was important that the treatment of Africans or people of African descent not become a factor. The relationship between Germans and Africans who had been under their colonial rule was a complex one involving issues of loyalty and remembrance regarding the defensive role that the latter had played during World War I and after. The patronizing attitude that had accompanied the brutality of colonialization served as a brake of sorts on Nazi aggression against Blacks, more so Africans than Afro-Germans. In 1934, the German Foreign Office issued a statement that read,

> The general mood of the population on the race question has frequently exposed the Negroes to personal offenses and slights . . . That this situation breeds ill-feelings among the Negroes is obvious. These ill-feelings are especially unpleasant for us, as they are not confined to the Negroes living here. Because of the relationships that they naturally have to Africa, they also have an effect there . . . If the question of a German mandate in Africa should suddenly become urgent, these circumstances can have extremely unpleasant repercussions for Germany . . . Thus, if possible, we should try to eliminate the reasons for the ill-feeling of the Negroes living here.[17]

This statement provides an extremely insightful reading into the Nazi politics of Blackness. It is acknowledging, first, that a situation has arisen of Negrophobia that is not acceptable in relation to the goals of the Nazi state. Second, it recognizes a diasporic connection between Germany's Blacks and those elsewhere, a network that could actively work against—"have extremely unpleasant repercussions for"—Germany's interests. Third, the statement notes only "personal offenses and slights," but no overall pattern or structure of antiblack discrimination. In other words, racism against Blacks is not institutionalized (yet). What is clearly being suggested here is an antidiscrimination program of sorts to blunt the admitted racial prejudice that existed against Blacks and the potential resistance that was likely to be generated. War veterans, despite falsified Nazi propaganda, knew that many Africans living in the country had fought valiantly and died in the name of Germany—forced conscription notwithstanding. This experience made it difficult for older Germans to completely accept the annihilation of Blacks or see them in a completely negative light. While Jews had also fought in the German Army, a predisposition toward anti-Semitism was easier to tap into and exploit. The belief from some quarters that Blacks from the German colonies actually had a fierce loyalty to the state was demonstrated in that Africans in Germany were recruited to and participated in protest demonstrations against the perceived excesses of the Treaty of Versailles.[18]

Before 1937, and the start of the European wars, the Nazis were concerned about international opinion toward Germany. The Nazi government was already receiving strong criticism from certain quarters about its treatment of Jews. It is well known, for instance, that during the 1936 Olympics, the Nazis removed signs and other indicators of its discriminatory actions against Jews. The Nazi state did not want also to get criticism about the status and security of Blacks under its rule, including Afro-Germans. This concern about its international image took on an official tone. In November 1933, the Foreign Office stated, "Let us not forget, now that the accusations against Germany over the Jewish question are beginning to abate somewhat, that we must not allow the colored question to provide new substance to the enemy propaganda in the struggle against the new Germany."[19] Here the Foreign Office is not calling for nondiscrimination in its treatment of "coloreds" or the Jews but taking a strategic view toward preserving or creating an image of racial tolerance while the "new Germany" established its real agenda of European and global conquest. The so-called Jewish question was only abated in words because, in fact, the attacks on the Jews during this time were actually escalating. The "enemy propaganda" referred to everyone from Jews outside of Germany to the nation's sworn adversary, France, which was not fooled by the cover-up tactics of the Nazis.

There are other indicators of a calculated tolerance toward Blacks. During the Nazi era, there were Africans teaching at the universities, mainly language studies, who remained employed even after Jews and other "nondesirables" had been fired. Also, although Germany railed stridently against the black French troops, it had included Africans in its own armed forces, many of whom had fought loyally in World War I and some who had returned to Germany to settle and live. Ironically, then, being black was not necessarily a liability in the racial political logic of the Nazis. While Jews and Gypsies were afforded no leniency and would suffer increasingly worse treatment, for those of direct African descent (and even for some of those of mixed heritage), "the very blackness of the black foreign nationals and colonials may have at times 'protected' them somewhat from the worst of the harassment and outright persecution."[20]

It is important to note here that unlike an anticipated African response, it is doubtful that there would have been a great outcry, if any at all, from Western states over the harsh treatment (and even genocide) of Afro-Germans no matter how vicious. The

Nazis knew history well enough to understand that. The overall context is what concerned the fascists and how their enemies would use the issue against them.

A second reason for the reticence on the part of the Nazis to go after Afro-Germans was that they had the larger and more cohesive communities of Jews and Gypsies to deal with. The Afro-Germans were too dispersed, too small in numbers, and too individually situated to pose a political, economic, or cultural threat. Unlike the Jews and Gypsies who formed distinct communities, the Afro-Germans and even the Africans were basically individuals who had come to Germany as diplomats, workers, students, or teachers, or were the children left behind who lived with their white German mothers with few, if any, relatives or friends of color. Separating Afro-German children from their families was a different kind of problem. Hitler stated that it would be a hardship on the mothers of the mixed-raced children to remove them, and it was something he was generally unwilling to do. This again demonstrates a crack in the Nazi racial framework and exposed the problem of trying to address contradictory racial and gender interests: facilitation of the hegemony of the pure Aryan, and upholding the constructed sancity of Aryan womanhood. Though not given as much attention as the racial questions, Nazism was also a very gendered paradigm that embroidered an idealized and pointedly antifeminist notion of womanhood onto a larger map of masculinist Aryanness.

There is some evidence that among the Africans in Berlin, a community of sorts had formed. However, it was tiny, its members did not necessarily see citizenship as a goal, and, again, it was not a threat to the German state. A significant number of those in the African "community" were privileged, especially the diplomat corps. Even though the Nazis had discussed, at one point, sending the Afro-Germans out of the country, there is no evidence that there ever was a move to rid the country of African diplomats.

There is no evidence, however, that political activism on the part of Blacks, after the Nazis came to power, occurred in any independent black organizations. The associations created by Africans were mostly social and cultural with no overt political agenda. Before all internal opposition was crushed completely out of existence, to the degree Blacks were active, it was in communist, socialist, or social democratic movements and organizations.

As many researchers have noted, in the end, people of African descent were "too few."[21] As Samples notes, since there were so few Afro-Germans, it was "much harder for the National Socialist authorities to isolate them as a separate group. Indeed, it is highly questionable whether the African Germans identified themselves as a distinct group or were even aware of others like themselves."[22]

A third reason why the exterminationist option was not employed against Blacks was for political reasons that had to do with the United States. The Germans relatively minimal harshness toward Afro-Germans in the early period could be and was contrasted for propaganda purposes with the treatment of African Americans in the States. In the post–World War I era, from the bloody Red Summer of 1919, when twenty-five race riots and seventy-six lynchings of Blacks occurred, until the 1950s civil rights era,

African Americans continued to live in a state of coercive apartheid, particularly in the U.S. South.[23] The inability of the U.S. government, when it was not complicit, to prevent harm and even murder against African Americans made it vulnerable to criticism from around the globe and gave it little moral authority to criticize others. The Nazis understood the salience of this factor in their response to a growing international rebuke of their internal racial rhetoric and policies. Not only could the Nazis counterpunch with the situation of oppression faced by African Americans, but they would sometimes employ Afro-Germans or the images of Afro-Germans in different propaganda media (film, radio, newsreels, newspapers) to make the point.

African Americans were generally aware of these contradictions. While not embracing fascism in any manner, African Americans could agree strongly that it was hypocritical to highlight the oppression of Jews in Germany when Blacks were facing similar treatment in the United States. Rather than endorse Nazism, however, African Americans used the contradiction to argue before the global community that the United States needed to reform itself to be consistent with the agenda and doctrine of political rights it was attempting to push on other states.[24]

Again, African American leaders and activists were aware that the Nazi reading of U.S. racism had to do with a perceived refusal by the United States to defend its whiteness rather than with any solidarity with Blacks. This can be seen in the determination of the black press to expose all Nazi anti-Negrophobic statements. On 11 August 1936, the *Washington Tribune* reprinted an article by Henrich Krieger titled "How to Wipe Out the American Negro." In the article, first published in a German newspaper, Krieger presented an extended argument railing against the notion of equality that he contended would lead to America's downfall. While he happily acknowledged that the southern states, at the time, boldly ignored the federal laws promoting democracy, he argued that it remained a problem that the principle of equality was still the stated objective of the U.S. government. He suggested three steps that should be taken in order to beat back this drive toward justice: "ideas of racial equality must be given up," "the 14th and 15th Amendments must be removed from the Constitution," and "Lincoln's plan for emigration should be developed and brought into action by degrees."[25] Krieger was calling for deportation, rather than elimination, as the ultimate resolution to the problematic multiracializing and democratizing U.S. society. It is interesting to observe that while he advocated repeal of the Fourteenth and Fifteenth Amendments, which provide for equality and political rights, he hesitated in calling for the revocation of the Thirteenth Amendement, which ended slavery.

This is not to say that a discussion and even internal campaign to move Blacks into the "to be eliminated" category did not happen. At least one researcher believes that at the infamous 20 January 1942 Wannsee conference, where the "final solution" decision to coordinate efforts to exterminate Jews was consolidated, the question of the elimination of the "*mischlinge*" (mixed-raced) was also broached.[26] One participant at a conference sponsored by the U.S. Holocaust Memorial Museum argues that the term "non-Aryan," as then used by the Nazis, was "unprecise" [sic], and that the Nuremberg laws could be applied to Gypsies and Blacks as well.[27] Until the final days of Nazism, a small group of Reich leaders and scientists contended that the "final solution" should be applied to the mixed-raced children and other Blacks under German rule. As noted in a 1993 conference, "To the last days of the Nazi Reich, race scientists continued their debate with Party representatives regarding the 'final solution of the Mischling question,' in other words, the best method by which the Mischling would disappear, either by murder or sterilization, i.e., gradual extinction."[28]

Nazism's Policies and Laws Regarding Blacks

To say, however, that the Nazis did not specifically target Afro-Germans for extermination and were unable to deport them is not the same as saying that Blacks in Germany were not severely and perpetually persecuted. Indeed, the story of the suffering of Afro-Germans and other Blacks has simply not been told and has been located outside of the main discourse on the Holocaust and the Nazi era. It has only been recently that a body of literature has begun to emerge to tell the story of life for Blacks under Hitler. It is notable, for example, that there is only one autobiography or biography, Hans Massaquoi's *Destined to Witness,* concerning an Afro-German who lived through the period.[29] This work and others that are being developed provide insight into the daily lived experiences of Afro-Germans and Africans from an insider's perspective. They demonstrate how common interactions were negotiated through the prism of race, nationality, ideology, and gender. Even further, they pinpoint the contradictory and impossible policing of race that was being attempted at the state level and through individual encounters. Within the broad boundaries of the racial state, individual Afro-Germans or Africans could experience extraordinary and risky acts of human kindness at one moment and the worst form of dehumanization the next. And so it would go on for a dozen—though seemingly a thousand—years.

While the Nazis sought to isolate the Blacks in their midst, at the same time, they tried to find a means by which to use them in the service of Germany's ambition of regaining its colonies, and, later, winning the war. Along these lines, the racial laws and policies of Nazism generated conflicts and contending aims between the objectives of the Nazi state and the institutions of that state including the Colonial Policy Office of the Nazi Party or the Racial Policy Office of the Nazi Party.[30]

People of African descent, especially Afro-Germans, were exposed, as were all Germans, to the dominant positions held by Nazi ideology. In every conceivable way, the Nazi propaganda chief, Goebbels, indoctrinated the nation around the beliefs and precepts of National Socialism and of its leader, Adolph Hitler. As he was presented to the nation as flawless, indeed, as a surrogate father, it was not difficult to see how youth in particular would come to see Hitler as nearly godlike. Schools, churches, community centers, and institutions created by the Nazi government ensured that the image of Hitler was pervasive. It became not only illegal to criticize him, even in the mildest tones, but life threatening. Many people were arrested and imprisoned for the mere act of telling a joke or raising some notions of doubt about the wisdom or veracity of the nation's sole leader. Any criticism of Hitler, National Socialism, or the fascist state could result in a death sentence that was carried out with full prejudice.

On the other side of the coin, as noted above, very few direct attacks on Afro-Germans were printed in Nazi media. Instead, a great deal of attention was given to African Americans. In the *Black Corps* newspaper, the official organ of the Gestapo, much was written about the state of Black-White relations in the United States. One article stated,

> Negroes simply cannot be civilized. Wouldn't it be better to civilize democracy and its ideas of equality? In America, all men are equal. Negroes can even acquire the title of doctor. They go about elegantly clothed in European style. If outraged farmers did not occasionally hang one of them this picture of complete equality would be undisturbed. However a doctor's title and a double-breasted suit prove little. Americans know it, so they are not surprised when Harlem Negroes create a dance [note: swing] which shocks every white man in New York with its obscenity. Such a reckoning does not balance.[31]

Nineteen thirty-five was a turning point in the history and fate of Jews, Gypsies, Blacks, and other racial "enemies" of the German state. It all began on 20 August 1935 with a conference of government ministers held to examine how attacks against the Jews were affecting the economy. There had been increasing verbal and physical attacks by the Nazis and their supporters on Jews and their community in the two and a half years since Hitler had come to power. However, there was little coordination in these assaults or clarity regarding overall policy toward the Jews. The purpose of this meeting was to resolve these concerns. A number of attendees advocated stronger laws and brutal enforcement to address the Jewish question.

Some officials, such as Economics Minister Dr. Hjalmar Schacht, criticized arbitrary and indiscriminate behavior by Nazi Party members and others because it affected rebuilding plans for a German economy that was suffering still. Schacht argued that the entrepreneurial skills of Jews should be used somehow in the economic recovery process rather than squandered by subjecting the Jews to spontaneous and random attacks. Schacht was not, however, calling for the humane or fair treatment of the Jews, only that policy be made that would maximize whatever could be gained by the Nazi state with the smallest amount of cost and confusion. Schacht's concerns were etched into the Nazi legal fabric less than a month later in a hastily drawn set of proposals that became known notoriously as the Nuremberg laws.

The laws were crafted in a rush—reportedly originally written on the back of a menu—on 14 and 15 September at the Congress of the National Socialist Workers' Party. These urgent measures codified what had been ideologically preached since the early days of Nazism and had been in practice since 1933: they were "designed (a) to clarify the requirements of citizenship in the Third Reich, (b) to assure the purity of German blood and German honor and (c) to clarify the position of Jews in the Reich." The Law for the Protection of German Blood and German Honor and the Reich Citizenship Law were aimed specifically at the Jewish community, but would have significant meaning for Blacks in Germany as well. (See Appendices A and B.) A number of auxilliary laws, subsequent orders, and clarifications followed their passage and allowed for the provisions of the laws, in debated interpretations, to be extended to Gypsies, Afro-Germans, Africans, and others. These segregationist laws, resting on an escalating popular consensus of antipathy toward Jews, echoed policies against Blacks that existed in places as dispersed as South Africa, Cuba, Brazil, and the United States. As the Holocaust researcher Ben S. Austin noted, there is an uncomfortable "similarity between these laws and the Jim Crow laws which were passed in the United States following the Compromise of 1877, upheld by the U.S. Supreme Court in *Plessy v. Ferguson* (1896) and remained in effect until the Court reversed the "separate but equal" doctrine in *Brown v. the Board of Education of Topeka* (1954). It is clear that Hitler used the Jim Crow segregation statutes as his model for defining Jews in the Third Reich."[32]

Hitler's response to the laws was emphatic, but also threatening in that he warned that this was only the beginning. Indeed, he informed his listerners that if the laws did not resolve the Jewish question satisfactorily, the National Socialist Party would intervene with stronger measures and produce a "final solution," a phrase that would have horrific meaning a very short time later. In his admonition, Hitler stated,

> This international unrest in the world would unfortunately seem to have given rise to the view amongst the Jews within Germany that the time has come openly to oppose Jewish interests to those of the German nation. From numerous places vigorous complaints have been received of the provocative action of individuals belonging to this people, and the remarkable frequency of these reports and the similarity of their contents point to a certain system of operation. . . . The only way to deal with the problem which remains open is that of legislative action. The German Government is in this controlled by the thought that through a single secular solution it may be possible still to create a level ground [*eine Ebene*] on which the German people may find a tolerable relation towards the Jewish people. Should this hope not be fulfilled and the Jewish agitation both within Germany and in the international sphere should continue, then the position must be examined afresh. The third [law] is an attempt to regulate by law [the Jewish] problem, which, should this attempt fail, must then be handed over by law to the National-Socialist Party for a final solution. Behind all three laws there stands the National-Socialist Party and with it and supporting it stands the German nation.[33]

The Law for the Protection of German Blood and German Honor prohibited marriages and sexual relations between "Jews " and "citizens of Germany or kindred blood." The law also prohibited the employment of "German" females under forty-five in Jewish households implying that older German women were either immune to the possibility of unwanted Jewish sexual advances or were sacrificial. In a bizarre manner that was not untypical of Nazi policy behavior, the law also forbade Jews from displaying either the "Reich or national flag or national colors," although they could, under the protection of the state, display Jewish colors. This provision was a transparent effort to coax Jews into identifying themselves. In any case, this law would formalize the practices of anti-Semitism that were already in full bloom throughout Germany.

The Nazis realized that the first Nuremberg law did not adequately define who was Jewish in full or in part. At what point did one become a "full" Jew or for that matter, stop being one? What about those who were of mixed Jewish-Aryan heritage? On 14 November 1935, these questions prompted the creation of the First Regulation of the Reich Citizenship Law, which was issued by the Reich Ministry of the Interior. (See Appendix B.) A major contradiction in how the Nazis attempted to define who was Jewish was their confluence of the categories of race and religion. While Jews were railed against as an alien race, the Nazis found it necessary to link adherence to the faith as a defining point, thus racializing religious identities. In the addendum to the original law, in Article 2.2, a mixed Jew was defined as "one who is descended from one or two grandparents who were racially full Jews," a Jewish grandparent being someone who was considered "full-blooded if he or she belonged to the Jewish religious community." In Article 5, the classification of "Jew" became even more complicated. A Jew was described as someone who had at least three grandparents who were full Jews, that is, adhered to the Jewish religion, and also had two full Jewish parents regardless if they were married or not. To implement this law legions of biographic and family researchers were designated to investigate allegations of Jewishness.

The Reich Citizenship Law, the second Nuremberg law, took away Jews' citizenship and political rights. In Article 2.1, it was stated that only "German or kindred blood" could become citizens of the Reich, effectively disenfranchising all "others." To make the point crystal clear, in Article 2.3, the law noted, "Only the citizen of the Reich enjoys full political rights in accordance with the provision of the laws." A large number of subsequent orders linked to the Reich Citizenship Law soon followed that step-by-step took away the rest of the political, social, economic, and cultural rights of Jews.[34]

The Nuremberg laws and other laws made reference to *artfremden Blut*, or "persons of alien blood," and explicitly referred to Jews and Gypsies. For those Nazi officials in the Interior Ministry who were concerned about the presence of Blacks in Germany, however, the general nature of this term provided an opening for the initiation of a debate as to whether the Nuremberg laws included people of African descent. In an official commentary on the laws by Drs. Wilhelm Stuckart, who had helped draft the original laws, and Hans Globke, both of the Interior Ministry, they provided an explanation of why Blacks should be included in the prosecution of the Law for the Protection of German Blood and Honor. On 14 November 1935, they issued the First Supplementary Decree to the law. In their argument regarding the limits of certificates of proof of ancestry in determining the certainty of the source of alien blood, they used as an example the case of possible untraceable Negro blood. They wrote, "One might imagine, for example, the situation that an intended husband shows the obvious influence of alien blood, for example, *negro* [*sic*] *blood*, without any indication in his certificates where this influence comes from"[35] (emphasis in the original). They reasoned that in

Europe, in general, "Gypsies, negroes [*sic*], or their bastards" were "carriers of non-German or related blood" as were Jews.[36]

Stuckart and Globke's work had two important consequences for Blacks in Germany. First, it established "Negro blood" definitively as "alien blood." From their perspective, whatever ambiguity may have lingered about the status of Blacks was resolved. References to non-Aryans were generally assumed to be applied to Jews, and the race-specific legislation that evolved in the first year or so did not mention Gypsies, Africans, or people of mixed-raced heritage. Rather than go back and change the laws, the Nazis simply either added clarifying orders or expanded their interpretation of to whom the law applied. Second, their efforts also demonstrated that Black—or rather the location of Blacks in Nazi Germany—commanded some attention and policy concerns. The fact that these assertions were being made by Nazi political operatives rather than just bureaucrats or intellectuals is critical. Stuckart was secretary of state responsible for interpreting and enforcing the constitution and the law, while Globke was the minister in charge of racial name changes. As the Nazis had done on numerous occasions, they would use the general nature of the racial laws to broaden their reach to groups originally not specifically named as targets. In 1935, relatively speaking, both the language of the laws against Jews, Gypsies, and Blacks and their full implementation were muted in view of the international spotlight being focused on Germany by the coming Olympics. The SS aggressively sought to tone down the fervent anti-Semitic assaults and propaganda that it and the Nazi state had so carefully nurtured in the months preceding the Summer 1936 Games.

The Nazis were neither innovators nor the most articulate purveyors and practioners of the pure-blood imperative. A long history in Europe in general and Germany in particular links blood and nation, and such a nation with the oppression of the Jews. With the rise of the nation-state during the middle of the first millennium, nations began to take on the artifice of one race, one blood, one nation. In Spain, in 1449, the Statute of the Purity of Blood was adopted and promoted in the city of Toledo by the Catholic Church.[37] The trope of pure blood was embraced not only by Spain but by Italy, Portugal, and Germany on the European landscape. In the United States, a "one-drop" rule was legally and socially implemented that assigned anyone with a single drop of African or Negro blood to the Black racial category.[38] A corollary of the one-drop rule was a "no-drop" tenet and custom, particularly applied to Jews in many European states, that contended that no matter how much "blood" was mixed in from other races, one's racial being did not change. After several attempts at defining who was a full Jew and who was a half or mixed Jew, the Nazis simply decreed that no one who ever had any Jewish heritage could ever escape the category. In defense of these purification fantasies, the fascist state carried out pogroms, massacres, and human slaughters with mindful determination.

Austin's observation that U.S.-style segregation was likely a model of this Nuremberg law has strong evidentiary support. In 1935, at the time of the passage of the first Nuremberg law, twenty-nine states in the United States—all of those in the South and many in the Southwest—prohibited marriage between Whites and Blacks. Similar to the Nazi law, the law in these states did not recognize such a marriage even if it occurred in a foreign land. Mississippi, Oklahoma, Tennessee, Texas, and Virginia went one step further: someone who married outside of their race could be banished forever from living in those states. And although the northern states of Massachusetts and Vermont allowed mixed marriages, those liaisons could be voided if either state determined that the marriages were done there to avoid southern jurisdictions. Fourteen of the twenty-nine states forbade marriages between Whites and Mongolians, nine between Whites and Malays, six between Whites and Native Americans, two between Whites and West Indians, and one between Whites and Hindus. It should be noted that mixed marriages between various races, excluding Whites, were prohibited in some states. Three states outlawed marriages between Blacks and Native Americans.[39] In Mississippi, always a leader in such matters, it was illegal even to advocate the notion of mixed marriages. The Mississippi law read:

> Any person, firm, or corporation who shall be guilty of printing, publishing, or circulating printed, typewritten or written matter urging or presenting for public acceptance or general information, arguments or suggestions in favor of social equality or of intermarriage between whites and negroes [sic], shall be guilty of a misdemeanor and subject to a fine not exceeding $500 or six months' imprisonment or both.[40]

Necessarily, as the Germans would discover after passing the Nuremberg laws, the issue of racial definition was critical to the implementation of these measures. Conjoined with the laws banning mixed marriages were the statutes that defined who was Black, White, or some other "race." Thus, state definitions of race ranged from Georgia's "white person" who had "no ascertainable trace of either Negro, African, West Indian, Asiatic Indian, Mongolian, Japanese, or Chinese blood in their veins" to Arizona's "Anyone having any Negro blood whatever" to Arkansas's "any person who has in his or her veins any negro [sic] blood whatever."[41] In Louisiana, the five categories of "persons of color" included Negro, Griffe, Mulatto, Quadroon, and Octoroon, each of whom was defined by various combinations of Negro, White, or Mulatto blood.[42] Next door in Mississippi, a White could be defined by the fact that he or she was "reputed to be white."[43]

Yet, as Ian Haney Lopez documents in *White by Law: The Legal Construction of Race,* the flaccid definition of race and, in particular, who was white (and why), was challenged in fifty-two federal cases, two that reached the Supreme Court.[44] The courts consistently ruled in inconsistent and contradictory ways, sometimes claiming that skin color determined "whiteness" and other times citing historical categories and so-called social science data, underscoring that the objective of preserving, as much as possible, the purity of the "White" racial group was paramount to any effort to legally clarify and codify a definition of whiteness.

In defining Jewishness, the Nazis also attempted to protect the category "Aryan" at all costs. In terms of "blackness," no explicit definition was ever determined, but the "one-drop" rule operated in default. The Nuremberg laws would be correctly read as one of the points of no return along the path toward a final solution to the problem of the presence of Jews, Gypsies, Blacks, and others who were not wanted in Hitler's Germany. While the segregation of people of African descent into physical ghettos made little practical sense, and black labor was not present in any appreciable way in any occupation or profession to warrant a prohibition, they would be caught in the broad net of terror and intimidation thrown by the Nazis over Germany social and political life.

Black Daily Life in Nazi Germany

Black participation in German daily life was a minefield of racial traps. This daily existence is what demands exploring because it allows us to view from an entirely different point of view the Nazi racial milieu. This perspective challenges the normative reading of Nazism and the day-to-day implementation and defense of its ideology. An important distinction needs to be made here between Afro-Germans, who had a vested social and cultural interest in being accepted, and Africans and other people of African descent whose roots and potential future lay elsewhere. The latter, as immigrants and visitors, did not necessarily view their presence as long-term or permanent.

Afro-Germans, at most, saw themselves as distinct individually, but generally not as a group and certainly not as a separate community. In other words, no distinct "black" culture or social life emerged. Situated in individualized circumstances, often in small towns or even villages where there were no other people of African descent, they were forced to develop a lifestyle that was both cautionary and at times necessarily assertive.

For young Afro-Germans, slights and insults were a regular daily diet even when protective and interventionist parents were able to stave off the most egregious racial attacks on their mixed-raced children. Massaquoi describes his experience at being denied entry to one of his favorite parks after Hitler came to power and signs went up in public places stating that non-Aryans were not allowed. His mother was able to talk to the park manager and negotiate to let him be allowed to come to the park since he was from the neighborhood and was already known. Massaquoi, however, decided on his own that he was too proud to return where he was not wanted. It is also unlikely that the park manger would have resisted popular pressure to ban this black child if it had arisen. This incident demonstrates how local and neighborhood dynamics, to some degree, were elastic. While one's racial status was generally nonnegotiable—though it is unknown how many, if any, mixed-raced individuals "passed" for white, thus undermining the Nazi theory of immutable racial identity—exceptions could be made if they did not constitute a major threat to the overall racial structure.

Older Afro-Germans faced the fundamental issue of how to make a living. This concern was complicated by both the economic depression facing the nation and the laws that were passed in 1933 and 1934 banning "non-Aryans" from an endless array of occupations and professions in the private and public sectors. The language of non-Aryans was vague enough that employers could safely interpret it to include or exclude Afro-Germans. There is no record of any Afro-Germans in the higher professions of lawyers, physicians, tax auditors, police officers, or other jobs that were high pay, high demand, and high visibility. Needless to say, Afro-Germans were not employed in any occupation where they would hold authority over Aryans. However, many other employment opportunities were available, from laborer and factory worker to chaffeur, maid, and in the entertainment area, that Afro-Germans sought. One professional area where Africans were able to find work was that of teaching. Ironically, this meant filling some of the positions that were made available by the firing of Jews at the universities and lower schools. There was a long tradition of African teachers in Germany, many teaching African languages and studies because of the colonial training needs of the period.

Ironically, Jewish firms employed some Blacks when the latter could not or would not be hired by others. According to Pommerin, "hardly any German entrepreneur hired Negroes, thereby, practically speaking, taking away from them the possibility of [any] livelihood at home. Of course, the 'respectable' elements among the coloreds were the hardest hit."[45] The relationship in Germany between Jews and Blacks, though in need of extensive research, was apparently close and recipriocal in many instances. The surviving Afro-German Gupha Voss observed, "I think we had it easier than the Jews. In fact, when he could, my father helped Jews, by bringing them extra grain rations. But eventually, my father lost his business, and was forced out of the town."[46] Once the war started, as Jews were being gathered and sent to the concentration and death camps, Blacks achieved full employment as they became forced laborers.

Were There Black Nazis?: Race and the Nazi Institutions

One intriguing area is the question of how Afro-Germans related to Nazi institutions. "Applicants for membership in the Nazi party were asked to certify that they had neither Jewish nor 'colored blood' (judische oder farbige Anschlag) in their ancestry. According to a theory popularized in Nazi circles, the Jew and the Negro were in fact related: the Jew was of an 'impure race,' consisting of a 'hybrid' between Negro and Oriental."[47] Given these parameters, it is understandable that Afro-Germans would not be welcomed into the Nazi Party or any of its institutions, nor that many would seek such membership. Yet the record shows that in a very, very few unusual circumstances, Afro-Germans managed to join the Hitler Youth and were part of the German Army.

Hitler gave particular attention to winning youth to his ideas and viewed the future of the nation as embodied in the reorientation of young people to the racial destiny of the Third Reich. To meet these objectives, the Nazis aimed especially at the nation's young boys and girls and created a number of institutions and organizations. For males ten to fourteen, there was the German Young People (DJ), and for those fourteen to eighteen, the notorious Hitler Youth (HJ) organization—officially known as the League of Working German Youth. Although not given the intensity afforded males, there were parallel organizations for girls, the Young Maidens' League for those ten to fourteen and the League of German Maidens (Jungmaedel) for those fourteen to eighteen. The HJ had originally been the Youth League of the NSDAP. By 1935, both of the older groups claimed a collective membership of 1.25 million (17 percent) out of a total of 7.5 million young people in that age range.[48] Neither the 1 December 1936 Law on the Hitler Youth nor the second 25 March 1939 Law on the Hitler Youth explicitly forbade Afro-Germans from joining the organization, but the second law did include a provision that made the exclusion of Blacks easy. Section 2.3 read, in part, "Youths who have conducted themselves well for at least a year in the Hitler Youth, and *whose ancestry fulfills the conditions for admission to the NSDAP* [National Socialist German Workers Party] can be admitted to the regular Hitler Youth"[49] (emphasis added). The latter were criteria that neither Jews nor those of African descent could meet.

How did young Afro-Germans relate to these institutions? Did they desire to be in these organizations? Were they allowed in? Did time and place make a difference in their acceptability? At least in some instances, perhaps in most, it would not have been usual for young Afro-Germans to want to be members of these organizations. The muted rhetoric against Afro-Germans and Africans, at least during the pre-1933 period and early days of Nazi power, coexisted with the concurrent clarion call for building a great German nation. This hype was pervasive and ultimately influential, especially after Hitler came to power and the education system was reorganized in the service of Nazism. The pressure to join these organizations was intense and unrelenting. For Afro-German youth, this was not an illogical choice. First, notwithstanding their "colored" status, young Afro-Germans were German and had been indoctrinated with much of the same ideology as other youth. While it is unknown to what degree the more vicious aspects of Nazism were embraced by young Afro-Germans, the idolization of Hitler and the impressive and overwhelming military symbolism of the Nazis were attractive in many ways. Because the expressed principles of the HJ, at least in its early phase, did not specifically exclude Afro-Germans from membership and did not specifically name Afro-Germans or people of African descent as enemies of the German nation who had to be opposed and eliminated, it was not illogical for Afro-German youth to believe that they could join. At the same time, after Hitler came to power, being a member of the HJ had immense and even lifesaving benefits. Only members of the HJ, for instance, could go on to secondary school after graduating from primary school. Also, although apparently this was unevenly expressed, not being a member of HJ would make someone a target for harassment, at a minimum, or even more extreme punishments and social isolation.

So from the point of view of young Afro-Germans, it was desirable, if not necessary, to be in the HJ. But was it possible? It depends. It seems that it was a question of time and place. The facts show that it was possible, in some instances, for young Afro-Germans to join in the early days of the HJ, although later some who had joined were kicked or driven out of the organization. Research by a number of scholars and filmmakers has uncovered some black survivors of the period who were members of the HJ.

The scholar Tina Campt, in a pivotal set of interviews and exchanges, identifies one Afro-German, whom she referred to as "Peter K.," who had been a member of the HJ from 1933 until 1936, when he turned 15 or 16. Peter K. was sterilized around the time he turned 15, and for him that was an awakening to the reality of what Nazism truly meant for those of mixed heritage. Up to that point, being a member of the HJ, whatever psychological or spiritual value it may have given, had material benefits even for an Afro-German. As he notes, "I was an apprentice with the railroad. Without being in the Hitler Youth, I wouldn't have been allowed to do that."[50] Indeed, Peter K. is insistent, when challenged on the point, that wearing the uniform of the HJ was tantamount to erasing his coloredness. In fact, he states that as a thirteen–year-old, he had "enjoyed the whole Hitler Youth game," referring to the fact that he probably got pleasure from the collectivity and symbolism associated with HJ life.[51] Disillusionment set in, and by the time he was fifteen, his membership was conditioned more on survival and the material benefits—no minor considerations. The uniform did not protect him, however, when the campaign to sterilize the Rhineland children was carried out and he became one of its victims.

The Nazi survivor Werner Egiomue, who is Afro-German and was featured in the documentary *Black Survivors of the Holocaust,* was in the HJ and in the army. In the film, he appears very reluctant to discuss his tenure and activities in the HJ. He does admit, however, that as a young man growing up during the Nazi time he saw himself as a "little führer."[52] He joined the HJ at the age of ten and recalled, "I was one of those who was waving my swastika during the führer's birthday parade through Berlin in 1936."[53]

Afro-German membership in the Hitler Youth, even in the very minimal and extraordinary circumstances in which it arose, raises important questions about the relationship between ideology, nationalism, and racial symbolism. How is Nazi ideology and indoctrination realized in a situation where non-Aryans participate in processes that are expressedly aimed at Aryans only? What did Afro-Germans think of Jews and the anti-Semitic views of Nazism? How did resistance, where it existed, unfold? How was daily life inside the HJ negotiated? This boundary crossing signaled the problematic associated with trying to impose an ideological state that runs against local and regional realities and social practices. While Nazi supporters generally united with the basic tenets of the ideology, personal relationships could not be elided in local situations and upset the smoothness of implementing the total racial state. It would not be surprising if some Afro-Germans embraced anti-Semitic views. They were bombarded with the same propaganda as the rest of society and could focus on the rhetoric of state enemies as opposed to racial enemies to justify their stance. There is no record of black anti-Semitism from the few sources that are available, and, in fact, many black survivors claim strong friendships with Jews during the time. It would have been impossible to avoid the language of anti-Semitism as a member of the HJ, but that would not necessarily translate into an anti-Semitic practice since most Germans overall had no relationships with Jews or the Jewish community.

To this day, there are Afro-Germans who believe that the hardness of the Nazi racial line made it hopeless for a black German to be a member. Massaquoi stated emphatically that on the basis of his experiences and understanding of the Nazis, it was "impossible" for any non-Aryans to be members of the Hitler Youth.[54] He argued that he could not conceive in any way that a person of color would be accepted in the HJ. His own trials concerning the HJ, where his brutally cold disabusal from even thinking that he would ever be qualified as an HJ member was traumatizing, convinced him that no

Black could ever put on an HJ uniform. While his views on this subject are adamant, they counter the research by Campt and others who did discover Afro-Germans who were, at least for a period, in the HJ.

While the image of a black person in the HJ was strange indeed, the presence of Blacks in the German Army during World War II is perhaps not as unusual as it may first appear. Africans had a long history of participation in the German military, although the military under Hilter was obviously not the same service. The Compulsory Service Act of 21 May 1935 technically limited military service to those of Aryan origin with certain exceptions allowed.[55] Yet, some Blacks were able to enlist. Egiomue, who was a member of the German Gliders Sport Association (a flying sports club of sorts) during the National Socialist era, was turned down initially when he first formally tried to join the army. However, he protested, saying, "I'm German. I want to fight." Eventually, he was able to enlist. It is not known what he actually did during the war or how he was received by the rest of the military. Peter K., mentioned above, was also in the military. Although he left the HJ after the trauma of being sterilized, his service to the Third Reich was not finished. In 1942, when the war began to turn against Germany and an all-out effort to mobilize the nation into the conflict was launched, Peter K. was drafted into the German *Wehrmacht* (army) and sent to the dreaded Russian front. Somewhere toward the end of the war, he was captured, and for reasons that are not clear, was held as a prisoner of war from 1945 to 1949, four years after the war ended.[56]

Again, Massaquoi's experiences differed from those of Egiomue and Peter K. Massaquoi argues that the army was not opened to non-Aryans. When he became old enough, he went to the military officials and volunteered to enlist. He wanted to join the army, but not for ideological, political, or patriotic reasons. Quite frankly, he thought the uniform would save him from Nazi harassment, very likely a correct assumption. He was told, of course, that he could not join.

Black membership in the military highlighted the contradiction and dilemma of blackness in Nazi society. Ready, in some cases, to use Blacks when desperate, the Nazis also discouraged Blacks from seeing themselves as Germans and suppressed their efforts to prove their loyalty to the nation. Yet, in another stunning exception to the rule, there was at least one known Nazi espionage agent or spy who was black.

On 11 August 1943, the police apprehended William Marcus "Willy" Baarn in the small Brazilian town of Gargau. According to a front-page story one year later in the 26 August 1944 edition of the New York *Amsterdam News*, when Baarn was put in the same room with another suspect, the Hamburg native Ellhelm Heinrick Koepf, after they had both been arrested, a smile exchanged between the two was witnessed by astute police officers who concluded that they were working together. Reportedly, the thirty-five–year-old Baarn, a former nightclub singer from Dutch Guinea, broke under strenuous questioning and led police to a radio transmitter, a bible used for secret codes, currencies from six different nations, and the rubber life raft that he and Koepf came in on. It was believed that Baarn learned "codes, ship-spotting and radio-telegraphy" at a spy training school established by the Nazis in Paris. Baarn and Koepf had sailed from France on a seventy-five-foot schooner but had been forced to disrupt their plans when the latter got a leg infection that needed care. Once landed, the pair was to make contact with other Nazi agents and operatives. It is not known how the *Amsterdam News* got the story because, as they noted, the arrest was kept hidden for months. As the black newspaper noted, "It marks the first incident in the New World where a Negro has been apprehended on the charge of being a Nazi agent."[57] Although Baarn may have been the only black individual captured outside of Germany, there were many Blacks who were suspected by the victorious Allies and Soviets of having been collaborators merely because they survived either in Germany or in the camps.

Black Women and Nazi Society

Participation in Nazi institutions and society was not only racialized but extremely gendered. The bottom rung location of black women on the social scale was conditioned not only by their racial status but also by their gender. Situated at two intersecting points of social disempowerment, black women possessed virtually no political or social space for realizing an agenda of social equality or justice. Black women, like other women in the society, were imprisoned by a popular conservative view long established in Germany that relegated them, at best, to a supporting role. This Victorian retreat imposed a repressive social structure on women's agency and froze any possibility for women—black, Aryan, Gypsy, or otherwise—to achieve any measure of full inclusion, while, at the same time, generating a benevolent paternalism that afforded some degree of insulation from the excesses of Nazism. Unlike other women, however, black women were viewed with a jaundiced eye that gave them little protection or respect as women. As the bearer of children and a black future, black women were taken and sterilized at a high rate, sent to concentration camps, and allowed little opportunity for educational or professional development.

Despite opposition from some "feminist"-conscious women within the Nazi Party, the male leadership, from Hitler on down, held the view that there were essential and fundamental differences between men and women. The scholar Leila Rupp, who has done extensive research on the impact of Nazi ideology on the status and role of women under Nazism, argues that Hitler held a view of sexual polarity wherein the two sexes functioned best in separate spheres.[58] Women were consigned to the role of child breeder, homemaker, wife, and sacrificer. Motherhood was glorified, and any demand for equal rights or a more prominent role in Nazi society was dismissed as bourgeois liberal thinking. In a 1935 party speech, Hitler defended the Nazi position stating, "When our opponents say: You degrade women by assigning them to no other task than that of childbearing, then I answer that it is not degrading to a woman to be a mother. On the contrary, it is her greatest honor. There is nothing nobler for a woman than to be the mother of the sons and daughters of the people."[59] Hitler's glorification of mothering, of course, served the interest of both the master race and the master gender, further shrinking the access to vehicles of power in the fascist state. Feminist politics had no more chance of public expression and mobilization than did socialist or ethnic ones.

Ironically, the reification of motherhood would actually work in favor, to some degree, of mixed-raced children. Although the Nazis and Germans, in general, saw the children born of sexual liaisons between black soldiers and German women as a reminder of their defeat during World War I, an attack on the children beyond rhetorical flourish was too close to being an assault on German mothers and motherhood. Rather than create a crisis over what was practically and relatively speaking a minor issue, the Nazis did not seize the children from their mothers as some more impatient members of the party advocated.

Some research has been done on the impact of the race-informed, misogynist views of the Nazis regarding black women who were in Germany during that period. The volume, *Showing Our Colors*, discussed in chapter 2, elaborates on the experiences of black women under Nazism. The period is given only minor attention, however, and much more awaits to be done. While it appears that there were many negative images of Afro-German and African women in the popular press, derogatory references were also made about famous black women from other places, such as the entertainer Josephine Baker and the classical opera star Marian Anderson.

There is very little known about the participation or inclusion—or the nature and context of the exclusion—of black females in Nazi institutions such as the Bund Deutscher Madel (BDM) (League of German Maidens) or the military. Black involvement in the BDM was next to impossible because one of the first requirements for membership was German origin and sound heredity, that is, Aryan.[60] Again, local conditions may have created circumstances where in some very isolated cases, a young black girl may have been forced to join, or by some other means was able to join, the BDM. In terms of the military, there are no known instances of black women as members, but black women, as did other Blacks, were made to work in war-related industries—often, but not always, as slave or forced labor.

Outside of military-related employment, most black women who did work found jobs as servants, maids, clerks, or in the entertainment field, such as acting in the colonial films. The former were occupations that few white German women wanted. Further research will undoubtedly discover a broader range of professions, occupations, and jobs held by black women, even if only temporary.

Black Germans and the Diaspora

Activist Afro-Germans and Africans living in Germany were well aware of the black diaspora and viewed themselves as a part of it. Even though a racial community had not formed within Germany, a racial identification of sorts did emerge in relation to Blacks outside of Germany. The visits by African Americans and other Blacks to the country before 1933 and news reports of the racism they faced and their organized resistance reached Germany's Blacks and formed a unity, if only virtual, between the various components of the diaspora. To the degree it was possible, Germany's black population made efforts to maintain contact with and stay abreast of the status of Blacks in other parts of the world.

As the situation deteriorated in Germany, some of the more politically active Blacks found themselves persecuted and forced to flee the country. Joseph Bile, who was originally from Cameroon and secretary of the League for the Defense of the Negro Race

(LDNR), was one of them. He eventually ended up in France. In 1934 and 1935, the International League Against Anti-Semitism (ILAAS), whose honorary president was the scientist Albert Einstein, sent letters on Bile's behalf to black newspapers and journals in the United States including *Opportunity* and the *Norfolk Journal and Guide*. According to the *Opportunity* letter, signed by the ILAAS president Bernard Lecache, Bile was sent as an emissary for the Africans in Germany who had been "discharged from all jobs," "deprived of making a living as musicians, theatrical artists, etc.," and had not been allowed to go "back to their country."[61] The ILAAS and LDNR were writing to African Americans to seek help.[62] Bile had proposed, according to Lecache, going to Africa, specifically Cameroon, to solicit financial and political support from Blacks there. Cameroon, at the time, was under French authority. The letter ended by stating, "We feel certain that the American Negroes, especially those engaged in missionary work in Africa and activities for advancement of their race, will rally to the appeal of their African brothers in the same spirit of racial solidarity which American Jews have shown to the German refugees."[63]

In the letter sent to the *Norfolk Journal and Guide*, and published 20 October 1934, Lecache described the state of oppression of Blacks in Germany. He wrote:

> Although everybody knows of the racial persecution against the Jewish people in Germany, unfortunately it is not so well known that Negroes are also subject to racial terrorism under the Third Reich. The economical and social conditions of these colored people are terrible. Formerly they were permitted to work as theatrical artists and musicians, but today they are deprived of all forms of employment. Those who are married to German women are forced to break up their homes. Neither are they allowed to be on the streets after certain hours. Under such conditions the Negroes are gradually degenerating.[64]

The letters and Bile's appeal indicate that even under Hilter, the LDNR had somehow managed to maintain some level of networking even if it could not formally exist. Hitler outlawed all political organizations except the Nazi Party, and an organization like the LDNR was not going to be tolerated. Bile not only had enough connections to make his case to African Americans but also had contacts in Africa where he could plead his appeal. His letter also demonstrated a level of race consciousness in both its content—the racist attacks on Blacks in Germany both before and during Nazism—and its strategy. The targeting of African Americans was an expression of race consciousness that clearly had at least a foothold in Germany among some Blacks that went beyond just an African identity or even a German one. Bile explicitly called for "racial solidarity" along the lines of what he viewed as a positive solidarity by Jews worldwide in support of their fellow Jews inside of Germany.

It is not completely clear exactly what Bile expected of African Americans in terms of support. He likely wanted African Americans to speak out on behalf of German Blacks and to send whatever financial and material support could be gathered. He did not state directly but implied that there might be a need to assist "refugees" like himself who were able to leave Germany illegally. The fact that the black newspapers even print-ed the letters demonstrated that, to the degree possible, there was support by the African American community. Bile, however, overestimated how much aid the Black American community could actually give. Although many times larger and more coherent and organized, African Americans themselves faced a situation of oppressive segregation, racist violence, and a racial state of its own. There is no indication that any African American groups or leaders were able to give more than vocal solidarity and spread the word about the situation of Germany's black population. It should be noted that, at the same time as Bile made his plea, appeals for help came from other parts of the black world including Africa, the Caribbean, and Western Europe. As Nazism bled across other European borders, more and more Blacks came under its rule with impor-tant consequences for the state of race relations.

Nazism and Blacks in Europe

France, Paris in particular, had been a haven for African Americans who wanted to escape the pervasive racism that existed in the United States prior to the 1940s. The state of terror that characterized the South and the lack of opportunities elsewhere led many entertainers, entrepreneurs, and intellectuals to migrate to a nation that seemed not only to welcome Blacks but, in fact, elevated them to an exalted (though mostly exotic) status. It is little wonder that a significant number of African American musi-cians, among others, would throw off their U.S. national identity, some even their citi-zenship, and become new French patriots. They would also join many others of African descent from the continent and the Caribbean who also came to call France home. In spite of, or in ignorance of, events that were occurring in Germany and the East, Blacks in France continued their idyllic life until June 1940 when Hitler's troops, having turned westward and poured across border after border, entered Paris.

According to Stoval, Nazism and World War II "brought about the end of the com-munity established by African American expatriates in Paris during the 1920s."[65] In October 1939, the U.S. embassy called on all Americans, of all races, to leave the coun-try.[66] Most Americans, including African Americans, caught the first boat or plane they could find back to the United States or some other safe place. The last one to leave fol-lowing that warning was the former black aviator and legionnaire Gene Bullard, who had been manager of the Grand Duc nightclub.[67] Among those who stayed were the jazz trumpeter Arthur Briggs, Charlie Lewis, Edgar Wiggins, and the always flam-boyant Josephine Baker, all of whom viewed themselves as more French than African American.[68] In the following year, things would get considerably worse. On 28 May 1940, the government ordered all men of fighting age to leave the city. Less than a month later, on 14 June, the Germans took Paris, only four days after the government fled.[69]

Unsurprisingly, war brought about dramatic changes in the lives of Blacks. Paris was a war zone, and blackouts meant that the nightlife faded and nightclubs were empty. This, of course, had the hardest impact on those Blacks who were there as entertainers. Most were unable to find consistent or sustained work performing. Beyond the enter-tainers were other African Americans who decided to stay. Charles Anderson, whose profession is unknown, lived in Paris throughout the occupation relatively undisturbed.[70] He was from Illinois and came to Paris in 1884. In all likelihood he was left alone because he was in his early eighties during the occupation years and simply too old to be concerned about.

The Germans, true to form, instituted a number of racist policies once they took over. Jews were banned from most professions and occupations, and had to endure American-style segregation, such as being forbidden to use park benches. Within a relatively short time, the order was given to round up all the Jews and send them to camps in Germany and Poland. The collaborationist French Vichy government of the time generously assisted in the capture and shipment of Jews for the Nazis.[71] According to Stovall, "blacks in occupied Paris did not face the murderous racism that threatened the city's Jewish communities."[72] But "blacks were banned from much French professional life, in particular from performing in the theaters and nightclubs of the city."[73] There was an effort to ban jazz, and Blacks, for a time, had their movements limited such as being unable to travel freely between the occupied and unoccupied zones.[74] Subterfuges, such as changing the names of records, allowed some jazz music to be broadcast. Armstrong's "Saint Louis Blues," for instance, became *"La Tristesse de Saint Louis"* ("The Sadness of Saint Louis").[75]

The nonmilitary black French were more or less allowed to live freely and continue their occupational pursuits. There were some forms of passive resistance on the part of some black intellectuals. The writer Rene Maran, who stayed in Paris, published a 1941 novel, *Les Bêtes de la Brousse* (Beasts of the Bush), that was a subtle criticism of Nazism. Maran also produced a pamphlet criticizing racism against African Americans in the United States.[76]

African Americans and Nazism

> You tell me that [H]itler is a mighty bad man.
> I guess he took lessons from the Ku Klux Klan.
> You tell me [M]ussolini's got an evil heart.
> Well, it must-a been in Beaumont that he got his start.
> Cause everything that [H]itler and [M]ussolini do
> Negroes get the same treatment from you.
> You [J]im crowed me before [H]itler rose to power—
> And you're still [J]im crowing me, right now, this very hour.
> Yet you say we're fighting for democracy
> Then why don't democracy include me?
> I ask you this question cause I want to know,
> How long I got to fight BOTH HITLER—AND JIM CROW.
> —Langston Hughes, "Beaumont to Detroit, 1943."[77]

The African American relationship to Germany during this time is important because it helped to shape and define both blackness and antiblackness under Nazism. The dialectic between African Americans and Blacks in Germany was dynamic and two-way. As noted, not only were Afro-Germans and Africans in Germany in tune with political developments among African Americans, they would eventually appeal on racial grounds for solidarity and support. On the other side, African American newspapers and some black political activists registered the plight of black Germans and called for African Americans to come to their aid. The rub, of course, was that neither group was empowered to effectively give more than moral support to the other. African Americans had more resources and were a relatively stable and established community, yet were themselves engaged in entrenched struggles for civil and political rights while fighting organized quasi-legal racist organizations and the state, in many instances, just for survival. At the same time, the debate on race in Germany by African Americans was complicated by some African Americans' personal experiences in Germany that were plainly distorted in that the situation privileged foreign Blacks. There were a number of African Americans who had been to Germany prior to the 1930s as well as during the Nazi time who praised Germany's reception of Blacks, often to the point of being dangerously naive. The African American jazz pianist John Welch stated, "Before Hitler came into power, the Negro was treated exceptionally well. But even today, just as in any other European country . . . the Negro may [have?] a room in any of the best hotels; he may attend the theaters . . . and be seated in any part of the house; he may go into any bar or visit any restaurant, café or night club and be waited on courteously and attend schools and universities. In short, he may do anything he is big enough to do as long as he carries himself respectably and has the money and means to do it with."[78] Samples correctly notes that Welch was speaking from the vantage point of being "shielded" by his status as an African American.[79] It should be noted that not too long after publishing this piece, Welch was arrested by the Nazi government, accused of being an enemy agent, and sent to a concentration camp, no doubt causing him to reflect critically upon his earlier remarks.

African Americans were concerned about the Nazis' aims toward Africa. European conquest and rape of Africa had always been an issue in black American politics and gave African Americans a jaundiced eye toward Western European nations. The black press, in particular, followed events in Europe related to Africa including Nazi Germany. As *The Voice of Ethiopia* reported, the Germans believed that they would sooner rather than later get their colonies back and had instituted an extensive program of colonial administration training for young men and women.[80]

The events unfolding in Germany would become significantly important to the black community in 1936 as a result of that year's Olympics and the boxing match between the African American Joe Louis and the German Max Schmeling. These two events would catalyze and solidify black opposition to Hitler. While these incidents are discussed fully below, it is important here to note their place in the overall discourse within black America regarding Germany and its treatment of Jews and Afro-Germans. In the black newspapers of the time, a number of critical debates and issues emerged, including a discussion of anti-Semitism among African Americans, the call for a boycott of the Olympic Games on the grounds of German *and* U.S. racism, and expressing solidarity with Blacks in Germany. These concerns crossed ideological, generational, and political lines.

Overall, the black press gave important attention to racial developments in Germany, generally comparing them with racism against African Americans. Hitler and the Nazis were often referred to as the European version of the Ku Klux Klan. As the frequent Nazi critic Kelly Miller wrote in April 1933, only a few months after Hitler came to power, "The racial policy of the Hitler movement is striking similar to that of the neo–Ku Klux Klanism of America."[81] Writing in *Opportunity*, Miller compares the segregationist policies against Jews in Germany with those against African Americans, drawing analogies in terms of marriage prohibitions, separate schools, and discrimination in housing and transportation.[82] The possibility of a Jewish slaughter by the Nazis was commented on soon after January 1933. In a 10 March 1933 news article, the *Washington Tribune* spoke alarmingly of a report in the London *Daily Herald* that "plans are complete for an anti-Jewish program in Germany on a scale as terrible as any instance of Jewish persecution in 2,000 years."[83]

Whenever possible, the black press reported news of the situation of Blacks in Germany and, after the Nazi aggressions in Western Europe, of those under occupation. The *Afro-American*, for instance, reported how the collaborationist Vichy government in France, in 1942, authorized Germany to recruit Blacks under French rule to work in segregated labor camps.[84] Black newspapers were among the first to raise the fear that the Gestapo had marked Germany's Blacks for extermination. The *Afro-American* reported the decision by Gestapo Chief Heinrich Himmler demanding that all people of African descent be registered with the Office of Reich Security, the office that was also responsible for Jewish deportation to the concentration camps.[85]

There was at least one African American living in Germany full-time during the Nazi period: the composer Elmer Spyglass. Born on 1 November 1877 in Springfield, Ohio, and trained at the Toledo Conservatory of Music, Spyglass went to Europe sometime after 1906 to further his craft. It is believed that he visited and worked in London, Liverpool, and Brussels, among other Western European cities. He apparently had a gift for languages and learned to speak French, German, Spanish, Italian, Danish, and even Bavarian. Upon retiring in 1930, he settled in Frankfurt, his favorite city in Germany, and lived there throughout the Nazi era. According to Spyglass, "Perhaps it was because I had lived there off and on since 1907. I knew all of old Frankfurt, from the bank directors down to the police." Unlike many other Afro-Germans and Africans, he did not have his passport confiscated, nor was he harassed. After the war, he began to teach English after being swamped with requests from his neighbors and others who viewed getting those language skills as important to moving up in postwar, Allied-controlled Germany. He died on 16 February 1957 having been made an honorary citizen of Schwalbach three years earlier. Whether it was his American citizenship, the viscissitudes of the local Nazis, or some other factor, Spyglass is another example of Nazism's racial arbitrariness when it came to people of African descent.[86]

An intriguing debate emerged in the black newspapers regarding anti-Semitism in the black community. Most African Americans felt the need to address U.S. racism even while criticizing Hitler. Most did not see themselves as having or advocating antipathy toward Jews. Yet, despite their location at the bottom of the racial well, African Americans were not completely immune to the politics of anti-Semitism that permeated U.S. society. In the well-known jobs campaign in Harlem in the early 1930s, the activist Sufi Abdul Hamid was repeatedly accused of using anti-Semitic rhetoric in his efforts to win jobs for African Americans. Tensions had grown between Harlem's different class communities as poor Blacks found it difficult to find employment with the businesses owned by Whites, including Jews, in the area. Harlem had undergone a dramatic racial and ethnic transformation in the two decades preceding the 1930s. While it had contained about 178,000 Jews during the peak of World War I, that number had declined by 1930 to only 5,000. Almost overnight—actually from the beginning of the twentieth century—it seemed that African Americans had become Harlem's majority. Yet, Jews continued to own a disproportionate number of businesses in Harlem, such as Koch's Department Store and L. M. Blumstein Department Store, some of which did not initially hire African Americans. In October 1934, Hamid, who reportedly referred to himself as the "Black Hitler" and as the "only one fit to carry on the war against the Jews," was brought to court on charges of disorderly conduct stemming from these alleged remarks. The charges that were brought against Hamid by Edgar H. Burman, commander in chief of the Jewish Minutemen of America, were eventually thrown out. In January 1935, Hamid was again brought to court, this time on accusations of producing and disseminating a pamphlet, "The Black Challenge to White Supremacy," making inflammatory remarks, and preaching atheism. He was convicted and sentenced to two concurrent ten–day terms at the local workhouse. While Hamid vehemently stated that he was not anti-Semitic, opposed any such politics, and "could not imagine cooperating with the Nazis," he nevertheless clearly used anti-Jewish histrionics as he tried to mobilize black support.[87]

The journalist L. D. Reddick observed that there was a modicum of sympathy for Hitler's strong-arm tactics and ultraracialism among some Blacks rooted primarily in their ignorance of what Hitler had to say that insulted and disparaged people of African descent. Beyond this tiny anti-Semitism, pro-Hitler trend, he contended that there were some hard-core, scurrilous black anti-Semites such as the publishers of a Chicago-based newsletter, *Dynamite*.[88] That some African Americans would hold these views also reflected the anti-Semitic atmosphere in the United States at the time to which Blacks were just as exposed as everyone else. In the end, black anti-Semitism and tepid endorsement of Hitler did not amount to much politically, given the overall hatred of racism by African Americans. Yet, one individual stands out because be was not only accused of being a leading proponent of Nazism, but he was actually tried in a court of law on charges of treason and sedition. Obscure in black political history and only remembered these days by the far, far right of Holocaust deniers and extreme nativists, it is long past due that the politically complex and geniunely mysterious Lawrence Dennis be examined.

Lawrence Dennis and the Conundrum of Black Anti-Semitism

Perhaps there is no more enigmatic black figure in the period between the two world wars than the writer, diplomat, and lecturer Lonnie Lawrence Dennis. Virtually unknown in the annals of black political history, according to the journalist Justin Raimondo, Dennis was born of an African American mother and a white or mixed-race father.[89] In the United States, the cultural practice of the "one-drop" rule meant that Dennis was by popular definition (and apparently by appearance) a black man. However, not only was the public life he led remarkably divorced from the race question, his prominent position on the U.S. political right made him an even more baffling character. Further, his numerous writings are devoid of any personal racial references. But he would be charged with being an anti-Semite as well as an apologist, if not ally, of Nazism. Reportedly, his closeness to the Nazis was captured dramatically in a picture of Dennis taken with Hitler or near Hitler during the famous 1935 Nuremberg rally.[90]

An inexhaustible though relatively unknown writer and political essayist, he authored a number of articles in major publications, such as *The New Republic*, and books including *Is Capitalism Doomed?*, *The Coming American Fascism*, *The Dynamics of War and Revolution*, *A Trial on Trial* (with Maximilian J. St. George), and *Operational Thinking for Survival*. He was also editor of *The Weekly Foreign Letter* (1939–1942) and *The Appeal to Reason* (1946–1972). These works would appeal to the nativists and, ominously, to others who wanted the United States to stay out of the war between Germany and the rest of the continent. Dennis and his politics would hit prime time when he and several dozen others went on trial in 1944, during the war, and were tried for sedition. Dennis and the others were accused of being Nazis (or supporters of Nazism) and anti-Semites. His writings against U.S. involvement in the war were seen as subversive and an effort to undermine the unity of the military. The government charged that his work was too well received among the U.S.-based antiwar, pro-Nazi movement, viewed as Hitler's fifth columnists within the States. Dennis freely admitted to being an America First isolationist embracing the conservative nativist ideology of nonintervention in international affairs that do not have a direct or immediate U.S. interest. In *The Coming American Fascism*, he had also called for "fascism" as a solution to the crisis that international and particularly American capitalism was heading into, defining it in nationalist semantics and corporatist rhetoric. In one article, reprinted in the 6 July 1939 edition of the pro-Nazi *Weckruf* newspaper, Dennis referred to Hitler as "the greatest political genius since Napoleon" and praised the dictator's "rational" political behavior in obtaining his goals. While accusing the government of conducting a witch-hunt and denying the charges against himself, he pointedly refused to condemn any of the other defendants, who included hard-core Nazis and anti-Semites. The trial lasted seven and a half months before the judge in the case had a heart attack and died. The case was subsequently dismissed in 1947.

Born in Atlanta on Christmas Day, 1893, Dennis was a repository of contradictions. He was of mixed race and was adopted at an early age by what one writer described as a "mulatto couple." He felt the calling at a very young age, and by the time he was five, he had become known as the "mulatto boy evangelist," and traveled across the country and even Europe preaching the gospel. From the time he was eight until he turned twelve, he lived in Europe with his mother and learned several languages including French and German. At the age of ten, he published his autobiography. Dennis was clearly a child destined for a remarkable life.

After returning to the United States, Dennis embarked on an educational path that would propel him into America's most privileged circles. He applied and was somehow accepted at Exeter, one of the top schools for producing the nation's elite. There is no knowledge of how he penetrated this bastion of the U.S. ruling class and managed to survive it financially and academically. Continuing this remarkable rise, from there he entered Harvard in 1915, graduating five years later after a brief stint in World War I. By this time, there was little to stop his ascent into the power networks of diplomats, business and financial leaders, and Ivy League intellectuals. How this black man, who still remains virtually unknown, was able to infiltrate and position himself into these spheres of power in a time when institutionalized racism and racist violence against African Americans was at an all-time high point is a puzzle to this very day.

It is unclear what role race or race consciousness played in his life or that of his adopted parents. Interviews with Dennis over the years yielded little personal information, and, in fact, he seemed highly reluctant to discuss his parents at all. It seems obvious that, at some level. Dennis engaged in "passing," that is, hid his black racial identity. As noted, the so-called one-drop rule usually meant that anyone who had any degree of black or African ancestry in the United States was generally classified as African American and lived a "black" life. There were, however, many individuals who had black ancestry but were phenotypically "white" and crossed over and lived "white" lives. It appears that Dennis would often straddle the fence, as was the case when he was in the U.S. diplomatic corps in Haiti. He discussed in an interview how he was able to move "on both sides of the fence," in dealing with white Americans and with local Haitians.[91]

Dennis was commissioned a second lieutenant in the U.S. Army during World War I and later served with the American Expeditionary Force. These wartime experiences would be very important because when he would later be accused of being a traitor, one of his main arguments was that his war participation proved that he had no antagonism against the army. After the war, he spent six years (1921–1927) working with the U.S. State Department, taking posts in the aforementioned Haiti as well as in Romania and Central America until he resigned in protest over the U.S. intervention in Nicaragua. He would soon begin his next career in the world of high finance. Again, it is unknown how he maneuvered his way into this arena and prevailed. In the late 1920s, he became an investment banker for the New York firms of J. & W. Seligman & Company and, then, E. A. Pierce & Company. This work would put him in a position to meet and befriend some of the nation's top financial and conservative leaders, apparently with little recognition or commentary on his mixed-race heritage.

Dennis's educational path, military experiences, and Wall Street career likely cemented his conservative views. This is speculation because despite being a prolific writer, he wrote very little about how he came to his conservative, isolationist views, and never wrote an autobiography in his adulthood. Yet, it would be his role as an author of a number of controversial books and articles that would bring him to the attention of the political world and the U.S. government. Somewhere along the way, Dennis developed into a true, even classical, American nationalist and isolationist. He argued strenuously that the capitalist era had reached its end and only by developing a state apparatus that fell somewhere between Hitler's facism and a less laissez-faire capitalism could the United States endure. Dennis theorized that old-style capitalism had been a golden age, but was no longer possible. For him, the global future was bleak indeed. At best, he averred, an American nationalism that insulated itself from the rest of the coming political and economic chaos was the only way out. His program included "protective tariffs, antimonopoly legislation, restrictions on credit, and a return to small-scale production for a domestic market."[92] He was a member of the so-called America First political wing of U.S. prewar conservative politics. Tied with the American right and more extremist views, Dennis advocated and supported the call for a noninterventionist U.S. foreign policy and, in the late 1930s, demanded that the United States not enter the war in Europe.

Was Dennis an anti-Semite and a closet Nazi? For the record, Dennis strenuously claimed that he was neither. In his coauthored book on the trial, *A Trial on Trial*, he stated that he could prove by his writings that he had never been anti-Semitic.[93] While the evidence of blatant sedition is unclear, and many of the charges against him must be framed by a political and ideological atmosphere where the right and left freely threw accusations into the air, Dennis made alliances and worked closely with many who were clearly anti-Semites and pro-Nazi. Blinded by his own romanticized conservatism and immature nativism, Dennis offered little coherent critique, let alone rejection, of the racist and fascist right. He certainly did not think that the United States should have gone to war against Hitler on the grounds of stopping the Nazis' murderous domestic and European rage.

Dennis died in obscurity in August 1977. The man *Life* magazine called "America's No. 1 intellectual Fascist ... brain-truster for the forces of appeasement" remained a political enigma to the end. His legacy lies in the hands of some of America's most reactionary forces. While Dennis was undisputedly on the far right, and had embraced Nazism's philosophical, if not ideological and political, tenets, an odder accusation of fascist appeasement was made against one of black America's most stable progressive icons: W. E. B. Du Bois.

Color and Fascism: W. E. B. Du Bois and the Nazis

The political scientist Adolph Reed argues that Du Bois, despite protests and pronouncements to the contrary, embraced a racial philosophy hinged on Eurocentric notions of progress and civilization. Though it was layered under his own often contradictory statements of racial pluralism, Du Bois ultimately rendered a strategy for African Americans that measured the boundaries and heights of civilization to the "universalizing requirements of progress," a measurement that subsumes black development to white, that is, Western European systems of advancement.[94] In 1936, this philosophical grounding would animate Du Bois to make perhaps the most controversial trip of his career. While it is widely known that Du Bois spent two years in Germany (1892–1894) during his graduate student days and that he stopped in Germany during 1928 on his way to visit Russia, few are aware that he spent time there during the early years of the Hitler period.[95] And although Du Bois noted his visit in passing in a few of his writings, the real substance and political significance of the five to six months he spent in Germany during 1936 have only recently been discovered. A series of articles in the *Pittsburgh Courier* in a column titled "A Forum of Fact and Opinion," for which he was paid $100 a month, and an interview given by Du Bois to a New York–based, German-American newspaper, *Staatszeitung und Herold*, published on 29 January 1937, contained most of Du Bois's public reflections on that trip.

That he would even go on this trip was controversial. He had applied for and received a grant of $1,600 for the trip from the Philadelphia-based German-American Oberlaender Trust of the Carl Schurz Society, which was founded by the pro-Nazi Gustav Oberlaender. The trip's purpose, Du Bois wrote, was to update black industrial education by his study of "the way in which popular education for youth and adults in Germany has been made to minister to industrial organization and advance; and how this German experience can be applied so as to help in the reorganization of the American Negro industrial school, and the establishment of other social institutions."[96] Du Bois would also use the trip to travel to other parts of Europe as well as the Far East. U.S. Jewish groups were appalled to discover not only that Du Bois was going to Nazi Germany but also that his contract with Oberlaender prevented him from raising any public criticisms regarding Nazi treatment of Jews or their racial policies overall while he was there.[97] Du Bois indicated to these groups that upon his return, having gotten a firsthand glimpse of German anti-Semitism, he would speak out. Du Bois arrived in Germany shortly after midnight on 1 July 1936, twelve days after Joe Louis had lost to Max Schmeling.[98] This was also the year that Jesse Owens and other African Americans participated in and dominated the Berlin Olympics, although Du Bois was not actually there at the time of the event.

In the *Staatszeitung und Herold* interview, reported anonymously, Du Bois was said to have spoken highly of Hitler's private secretary and party leader, Rudolph Hess. He also apparently praised the Nazis for "constructing apartments and highways, noting that, despite food shortages and a generally depressed national mood, most Germans unconditionally trusted and were grateful to Hitler and his National Socialism."[99] He demonstrated some skepticism about the state of Germany, and felt that war might be on the horizon. The only statement allegedly made by Du Bois in this interview regarding Blacks in Germany was his remark that German attitudes "did not yet show any trace of racial hatred" toward Afro-Germans, Africans, or others of African descent. Du Bois noted that he was distressed by the German treatment and views toward Jews, which he compared with those characterizing the black situation in the United States. But, according to *Staatszeitung und Herold*, Du Bois suggested that the conditions of Blacks were perhaps even more perilous because acts of racism occurred in blatant violation of the nation's laws. The interview concluded with Du Bois's emphasizing, as he did on his earlier stay in Germany as a student, that he had suffered no racial prejudice or overt discrimination.

As Sollors notes, since Du Bois made no reference to the *Staatszeitung und Herold* interview in any of his writings, it is legitimate to question the accuracy and tone of the article and whether it really reflected Du Bois's views on Nazi Germany. One speculation regarding the failure by Du Bois to give this visit any prominence in his own writings may have to do with a subsequent embarrassment at what some construed as a softness for Nazi Germany that he would later find objectionable and be forced to defend. Du Bois's remarks in the interview were so startling that he was forced to respond to a request by the American Jewish Committee to clarify his statements.[100]

In the articles that he wrote for the *Pittsburgh Courier* during and after his stay, a number of themes can be discerned. He noted the status of Jews, criticized the growing loss of political rights and democracy (even as advancements are being made), and addressed his own security. Du Bois acknowledged the horrors that had befallen German Jews and compared them to broader historical tribulations. He wrote, "There has been no tragedy in modern times equal in its awful effects to the fight on the Jew in Germany. It is an attack on civilization, comparable only to such horrors as the Spanish Inquisition and the African slave trade."[101] He added, "There is a campaign of race prejudice carried on, openly, continuously and determinedly against all non-Nordic races, but specifically against the Jews, which surpasses in vindictive cruelty and public insult anything I have ever seen; and I have seen much."[102] Extending his analysis of how various struggles link, he compared German anti-Semitism with U.S. Jim Crowism, the major difference being, from his perspective, that what the Nazis did was "legal," while American racism was mostly carried out in an "illegal" manner, that is, lynchings. While critical, Du Bois's writings seemed to indicate a belief that most Germans simply did not know or care about the persecution of Jews, Gypsies, gays, and other nondesirables targeted by the fascist state, and that the people were fully supportive of Hitler and his (misguided) mission. He softened his criticism by saying, "It is not instinctive prejudice, except in the case of the Jews, and not altogether there."

He saw Nazi Germany as "a state with a mighty police force, a growing army, a host of spies and informers, a secret espionage, backed by swift and cruel punishment, which might vary from loss of job to imprisonment, incommunicado, and without trial, to cold murder."[103] Characterizing the state in the gravest of terms, he wrote, "Germany is silent, nervous, suppressed; it speaks in whispers; there is no public opinion, no opposition, no discussion of anything; there are waves of enthusiasm, but never any protest of the slightest degree."[104]

He explained why he thought the Germans had gotten behind Hitler and, despite the loss of political rights and a democratic state, continued to support the dictator. He argued, "Germany in overwhelming majority stands back of Adolf Hitler today. Germany has food and housing, and is, on the whole, contented and prosperous. Unemployment in four years has been reduced from seven to two million or less. The whole nation is dotted with new homes for the common people, new roads, new public buildings and new public works of all kinds. Food is good, pure and cheap. Public order is perfect, and there is almost no visible crime."[105] He spoke admiringly of the "new roads, new public buildings and new public works" that had blossomed in Hitler's Germany, marking her rise out of economic poverty and desperation.[106] Prosperity for some, of course, masks the terror being felt by many. It is remarkable that Du Bois was not critical of the overt fascist state underpinning the relative and early social and economic successes of the regime. Stunningly, Du Bois also stated that Hitler's dictatorship was "absolutely necessary to put the state in order."[107] He wrote that National Socialism was "wholly illogical" but a "growing and developing body of thought."[108]

Du Bois reflected the central points raised by Reed when he wrote, "Civilization does not center in the United States or in Australia. Despite all our boasting and national pride, we turn continually and repeatedly toward Europe to know and understand the last word of human culture in matters of vital and everyday interest to us."[109] He gave an ominous and undoubtedly truthful explanation of why his criticisms of Germany had seemed muted in his *Courier* articles. He wrote, "I am sure my friends have understood my hesitations and reticence; it simply wasn't safe to attempt anything further."[110] He was well aware that the Nazis as well as their supporters in the United States monitored the press and would have reported any barbs he made against his host country. Still, there was an edge of sympathy returned by Du Bois for the nation that came only second to the United States in influencing his personal life, political career, and intellectual ideas. Writing favorably, he stated, "I have been treated with uniform courtesy and consideration. It would have been impossible for me to have spent a similarly long time in any part of the United States, without some, if not frequent cases of personal insult or discrimination. I cannot record a single instance here."[111] He encountered "complete civic freedom and public courtesy" though "no German woman of good standing would think of marrying a Negro under ordinary circumstances; nor could she do so legally. It is a question if she could legally marry a Japanese."[112]

Du Bois's treatment while in Germany was respectful if not reverent. In fact, he would conclude that ther Germans' behavior toward him was far superior to what he received from white Americans.[113] Lewis erroneously speaks of the "historic absence of nonwhites among the Germans" as a reason for why they could afford to treat Du Bois in a favorable manner.[114]

Upon his return to the United States, Du Bois discovered that his articles in the *Courier* had been disturbing to many Jewish and anti-Nazi groups. They felt that some of his writings, if not most, floated somewhere between ambiguity and appeasement. His 2 January 1937 article, "The German Case against the Jews," which was written after he had left Germany, seemed to share the Nazi view that Jews represented an "alien presence" and a "foreign element" in the nation.[115] As late as 1941, Du Bois was defending himself in the black press. In a 12 April 1941 article in the *Amsterdam News,* he denied an accusation made in Atlanta that he was "pro-Nazi."[116] However, even in this article harshly critical of the German dictator, he couldn't resist making a sympathetic comment about Germany. He wrote, "Hitler's cure is state capitalism and dictatorship of a single political party acting in the name of the so-called master race. *The rationalization of German industry is a splendid accomplishment,* but the utter repudiation of democratic control and the silly worship of race, makes this aspect of Hitlerism one of the most dangerous things in the modern world"[117] (emphasis added).

Lewis's observations on Du Bois's 1936 visit only mildly criticized his stance toward Germany and its handling of the Jewish question. While it is correct to note the inability of Du Bois and others to predict the coming Holocaust against Jews, plenty of evidence existed that the Nazis were not retreating in their discrimination, nor was it minor that anti-Semitism had broad popular appeal. Du Bois's love for Germany seems to have blinded or at least clouded his usually sharp reading of racism. It is also notable that neither Du Bois's nor Lewis's critique of this period acknowledged the presence of Afro-Germans and Africans in Nazi Germany. While not as observable as the attacks against the Jews, discrimination and racist rhetoric toward Blacks in Germany were occurring.

It is highly unlikely and would be inexplicable that Du Bois did not meet Afro-Germans and Africans given both his own lifetime of work and research on Blacks and the black diaspora and the probable effort by Blacks in Germany to reach out to someone with the stature of the world-renowned American. For there to be no comment from Du Bois on black Germans is remarkable in and of itself. Either Du Bois felt these encounters, to the degree they occurred, were too trifling or insignificant to note, or he lived such an extraordinarily isolated and insular life while in Germany that he had no significant recordable interaction with any German Blacks.

Made in America, Perfected in Germany

The Nazi Sterilization Program against Blacks

Shall we silently accept that in the future instead of the beautiful songs of white, pretty, well-informed, intellectually developed, lively, health Germans, we will hear the raucous noise of horrific, broad skulled, flat nosed, ungainly, half-human, syphilitic half-castes on the banks of the Rhine.

—Dr. Rosenberger[1]

If you think that we scientists do not join in the call "Heil Hitler," you are very much mistaken. We, the German scientists, are very much aware of what we owe to Adolf Hitler, not the least the purification of our people from foreign-race elements, whose way of thinking is not the one we have.

—Dr. Theodor Mollison[2]

Racialized Science: The Eugenics Movement as a Global Campaign

One chief means by which the Nazi regime attempted to deal with its "black" problem was through involuntary sterilization. The sterilization program employed under Nazism, which went well beyond just Afro-Germans, had its roots in the global eugenics movement that began in the latter part of the nineteenth century. Eugenics, in essence, is the reduction of society and human relations to biologicalism leading to determinant outcomes in intelligence, behavior, and overall human characteristics. Taking this approach to its logical social and political conclusions, eugenicists advocate perpetuation of supposedly superior genes and the removal of those that in biological terms are physically or mentally unworthy. While eugenics was not always exclusively predicated along racial lines, in most circumstances it became impossible to separate biology and race, particularly in Germany and the United States. The fact that *some*

129

Whites or Aryans fell into the category of the "unfit" did not mitigate the general view that *all* "non-Whites" or "non-Aryans" did.

Eugenics was embedded in modernity and the industrial revolution. With its emphasis on science and "progress," it was easy to propagate the view that races could be not only scientifically measured but also managed and engineered. In an ironic postmodernist way, it was the early racists who truly believed that races could be (re)constructed. Once the biological (and immutable) racial foundation was set by nature, then state support and popular participation could assist science in its goal to simultaneously successfully breed and progressively weed the correct and desirable racial configuration.

Sir Francis Galton, a first cousin of Charles Darwin who wrote a definitive scientific study on fingerprints, left his own originating and decisive fingerprints on the field of eugenics. After reading Darwin's *Origin of Species,* Galton had an epiphany that would take social prejudice to a qualitatively new level. Applying his cousin's insights regarding the evolution of different animal species, he came to believe that science could intervene and alter the human evolutionary process. This British scientist began with the premise that there were worthy populations and individuals and those that were not. He believed not only that the former should be promoted and the latter eliminated but that scientific breeding could accomplish such a deed. In 1907, Galton gave this concept, which had been previously embraced by such prominent figures as Socrates and Thomas Jefferson, the name eugenics.

Racism was at the center of its founder's thinking. He considered Blacks to be at the bottom of the human ladder and argued that they had failed "to sustain the burden of any respectable form of civilization."[3] Galton called for the gradual displacement of Africans, suggesting the Chinese because he did not want Europeans to suffer from the intemperate weather.[4] Galton's followers in the United States would appropriate the link between race and eugenics.

Corn Flakes and Bettering the Race: Eugenics in the United States

The Germans are beating us at our own game.
—Dr. Joseph S. DeJarnette, a leader in the Virginia eugenics movement [5]

For generations, millions have spooned a daily breakfast of Kellogg's Corn Flakes, one of the best-known brand names of any cereal. Will Keith Kellogg founded Kellogg in 1906 in Battle Creek, Michigan. Today, the company sells its cereals and other food products in more than 160 countries. It claims that it is the "world's leading producer of ready-to-eat cereal and a leading producer of grain-based convenience foods, including toaster pastries, frozen waffles and cereal bars." In 1998, it had consolidated net sales of more than $6.7 billion. The cereal that made Will and his brother John millionaires was discovered by accident. John was the physician in chief at the Battle Creek Sanitarium and had spent many unsuccessful years looking for a vegetarian diet—a digestible bread substitute—for his patients. In 1894, according to the company's official history, Will "accidentally left a pot of boiled wheat to stand and become tempered. When it was put through the usual rolling process, each grain of wheat emerged as a large, thin flake. Will persuaded his brother to serve the food in flake form, and it was an immediate favorite among the patients." John left it to Will to eventually package and sell the increasingly popular product, and the company was soon raking in millions.

While Will concentrated on selling corn flakes and other cereals, John became a major player in the eugenics movement. Financed by the fortunes made from the food line, John founded the Race Betterment Foundation in 1911, also in Battle Creek. The foundation sponsored three national conferences on race betterment and eugenics, in 1914, 1915, and 1928. It worked closely with the Eugenics Records Office (ERO) and the man considered to be the heart and soul of the U.S. eugenics movement: Charles Davenport.

A University of Chicago biologist, Charles Davenport was the catalyst for the eugenics movement in the United States. In 1910, he established the ERO, located in Cold Spring Harbor, New York, which over the next thirty years would be the epicenter of U.S. eugenics. The ERO published an influential newsletter, *Eugenical News*, produced monographs and papers, lobbied against immigration, and supported mandatory sterilization. Davenport and other U.S. eugenicists, such as Madison Grant and Harry Hamilton Laughlin, belied their advocacy of so-called positive eugenics—the breeding of "good" genes—by their nearly exclusive focus on the eradication of "negative" traits through breeding and sterilization. Sterilization as a form of social intervention began as a form of punishment specifically aimed at African American men in the 1850s. In 1907, this practice became legal when Indiana passed the first involuntary sterilization law. In 1914, the eugenicist Laughlin proposed a schedule that called for sterilizing fifteen million people in the United States over a twenty–year period.

The political and racial work of the ERO and eugenics organizations such as the American Eugenics Society, American Genetics Association, Human Betterment Association, and Galton Society was buttressed by an intellectual coterie that produced several popular books. This included Davenport's *Heredity in Relation to Eugenics* (1911), Madison Grant's *The Passing of the Great Race* (1923), Thurman B. Rice's *Racial Hygiene* (1929), and Carl C. Brigham's *A Study of American Intelligence* (1923). In all of these works and many others, a discourse presented the argument that the white race was threatened with impurity and even eradication by the breeding habits of lower, that is, colored, races. That some lower breeds of Whites, who carried "undesirable" traits such as mental illness and promiscuity, would also have to be removed did not undermine the view that the main danger rested in the growth and procreation of Blacks, Asians, and others.

It is important to emphasize that eugenicists, whether they advocated "positive" or "negative" eugenics, were fairly united that its social application should be compulsory. A thesis of social engineering at the most fundamental level informed the eugenicist movement from the beginning, and it was understood that the goals of the movement could only be achieved by obligating society to the enforcement of sterilization no matter the personal, social, or democratic costs. The so-called distinction between "positive" and "negative" eugenics in the United States and Germany was a facade. Tucker notes perceptively, "As in the United States, German eugenics tended to pay lip service to the Galtonian ideal of encouraging proliferation of the fit while concentrating in practice on elimination of the unfit."[6]

In the United States, as elsewhere, eugenics was a racialized movement. What made African Americans especially worrisome to the eugenicists was the latter's belief in an extraordinary black tendency of uncontrolled sexual activity. Davenport, echoing the view of fellow eugenicists, wrote that African Americans have "a strong sex instinct, without corresponding self-control."[7] The link between eugenics and sterilization in this discourse was manifest in the manner in which crime was sometimes punished. Black men, in particular, were subject to judicial and extrajudicial castration. As Roberts notes, "The idea of imposing sterilization as a solution for antisocial behavior originated in the castration of black men as a punishment for crime."[8] There are two things to note here about that history. First, crime was completely defined by the white racist social structure. Second, black male castration was a punishment not limited to the crime of rape or attempted rape—those "crimes" also being socially structured in that the rape of black women by white men or black men and the rape of white women by white men were seen in much less severe terms. Laws were advocated that would allow castration if a black male was convicted of being "vicious, disobedient, drunken."[9] Under the rhetoric of stemming the hereditary passing of criminal and antisocial behavior, eugenicists and legislators argued for the compulsory sterilization of prison inmates, and by 1913, "twenty-four states and the District of Columbia had enacted laws forbidding epileptics, imbeciles, paupers, drunkards, criminals, and the feeble-minded," from reproducing.[10] Even President Theodore Roosevelt would endorse the call for sterilization as a means of preventing "racial suicide."[11]

Eugenics-oriented legislation was also linked, in part, to the racializing of the nation's immigration laws. The National Origins Act of 1924, which effectively elimi-nated immigration from southern and eastern Europe, targeted racially undesirable Europeans, a move that had long been in place against people from the developing and colonialized worlds.[12] A critical change occurred in the racial focus of American-style eugenics from the early period to the 1930s. As Robert writes, "The eugenics movement was also energized by issues of race. In the 1930s, it turned its attention from the influx of undesirable immigrants to the black population in the South."[13] Just as Herrnstein and Murray would do in *The Bell Curve* more than seven decades later, eugenicists of the teens and 1920s blended class and racial characteristics, seeing them both as bio-logical and immutable, as when the Harvard geneticist Edward East argued for ending prenatal care for the poor because it prevented the "natural elimination of the unfit."[14] Thurman B. Rice, a prominent eugenicist and author of *Racial Hygiene,* wrote, "the colored races are pressing the white race most urgently and this pressure may be expect-ed to increase."[15]

Besides advocacy aimed at policymakers, eugenicists would also become engaged in political and social movements that were often baldly racist in nature, such as forming alliances and providing "scientific" discourses to the Ku Klux Klan and the birth control movement during the first half of the twentieth century. The most disturbing national collaboration, however, would happen between eugenicists in the United States and Germany.

The Eugenics Brotherhood of Nazis and Americans

Germany is the first of all the great nations of the world to make direct practical use of eugenics.[16]

Working in tandem, eugenicists from the United States and Germany dominated the global movement. Although they would generally deny the accusation, eugenicists from the two nations were more bonded by their racial views than any genuine scholarship. The U.S. movement cheered the work of their German counterparts even as many of the latter began working in the service of Nazism. There was plenty of evidence to support the contention that eugenics was profoundly linked to questions of race and racism. In 1921, at the Second International Congress of Eugenics, where U.S. and German representatives dominated, papers were presented with titles such as "Some Notes on the Negro Problem," "The Problem of Negro-White Intermixture," and "Intermarriage with the Slave Race." Eugenicists and their supporters in the United States hailed the publication of *Human Heredity*, the first part of a two-volume series written by three of Germany's most prominent eugenicists, Erwin Baur, Eugen Fischer, and Fritz Lenz. Despite its ominous intonations, the book was called a "masterpiece of objective research."[17] This work would elevate the status of German eugenicists in the eyes of those in the United States who envisioned the eugenics movement as a global calling.

In 1933, in celebration of the passage of the new Nazi sterilization law, the *Eugenical News*, a leading U.S. publication on the eugenics movement, wrote, "It is probable that the sterilization statutes of the several American states and the national sterilization statute of Germany will, in legal history, constitute a milestone which marks the control by the most advanced nations of the world of a major aspect of controlling human reproduction, comparable in importance only with the states [*sic*] legal control of marriage."[18] It was even suggested by a staff member of the Eugenics Record Office that Adolf Hitler himself should be made an "honorary member" of the organization.[19] Given the politics of the Eugenics Office, it could be argued that he already was.

Reflecting a core view of the Nazis, many U.S. eugenicists were also anti-Semitic and, like the Nazis, would sometimes view Jews as more dangerous and horrid than African Americans or Blacks. The sociologist and eugenicist Edward Alsworth Ross, for example, commenting without evidence in the early days of Nazism, wrote that even Blacks would leave for "a more spotless environment" when Jews moved into the neighborhood. Like the Germans, American eugenicists also tended to view Jews as a racial group rather than a religious one.

The relationship between American and German eugenicists was one of mutual admiration. The Nazis not only envied the proposed ideas and programs of their U.S. counterparts but also coveted the policy initiatives that had been implemented. As

Tucker notes, "German scientists saw the United States with its antimiscegenation statutes leading the way."[20] Unlike the southern United States, with its Jim Crow segregation laws in full force in the first half of the century, Germany at the beginning of the National Socialist era did not have explicit laws that segregated different racial, ethnic, or religious groups. Until Hitler, the practice of racism and anti-Semitism operated mostly de facto rather than de jure. Praise for the eugenics movement in the United States came from many quarters in Germany, but especially from the race scientists.

There was not only ideological unity between eugenicists in the United States and Germany but a direct and ongoing relationship from the turn of the century through the Nazi era. Key eugenicists in the United States, such as Charles Davenport, Harry Laughlin, superintendent of the Eugenics Records Office, and their corporate and academic supporters closely allied themselves with Eugen Fischer, Fritz Lenz, and other leading German eugenicists. U.S. and German eugenicists worked together through the International Society for Racial Hygiene. Laughlin, who successfully lobbied the U.S. Congress to pass the 1924 anti-immigrant National Origins Act, would later receive an honorary degree from the University of Heidelberg, in 1936. In 1934, the California eugenics movement organized an exhibit of the German eugenics program, showing it during the American Public Health Association annual meeting. Five years later, American eugenicists met with Fischer, then director of the Kaiser Wilhelm Institute for Anthropology, Human Heredity, and Eugenics, and with Wolfgang Abel, the SS anthropologist who had been in charge of the sterilization campaigns against the Gypsies, the Afro-Germans, and the Africans under German colonial rule.

Nazi Sterilization of Afro-Germans

> We want to prevent . . . poisoning the entire bloodstream of the race.
> —Counselor of the Reich Ministry of the Interior[21]

Hitler subscribed to the so-called *Entmischung* thesis, which rejected those eugenicist supporters who argued that eugenics led to a betterment of the superior race. *Entmischung* proponents believed that after many generations something akin to pure racial types would reemerge out of mixed-race people. However, these people would still be inferior, disproving the "betterment" goal of so-called positive eugenics. Only in the most exceptional of cases, it was argued, would betterment occur.[22] The most direct implication for Blacks in Germany (as well as other racial groups) was another rationalization for stopping their reproduction, if not their existence altogether. Race mixture, in other words, left a permanent contamination that could only be arrested, short of genocide, by sterilization. Although the Nuremberg laws and other statutes forbade the sexual liaison between Aryans and other races, the Nazis wanted to guarantee that the generation of mixed African and German children living under National Socialism would be the last. The racial science attack on the Rhineland children and the use of a discourse on race driven by biology did not begin with the Nazi period in Germany. In the three decades leading up to the time of Hitler, a thriving eugenics movement existed that produced a number of the key race doctors who would emerge in the 1930s. It is telling that the largest figure in Germany's pantheon of eugenicists was trained in the United States.

Alfred Ploetz, the acknowledged founder of German eugenics, spent time in the United States where undoubtedly he solidified his admiration for the South's segregation laws and popular practice.[23] In Germany, he would also be credited with coining the term *Rassenhygiene* (racial hygiene), whose deadly meaning would leave its bloodstain on the Nazi era.[24] He founded the first German eugenics journal in 1904, *Archiv fur Rassen- und Gesellschaftsbiologie (Journal of Racial and Social Biology)*, and, a year later, organized the *Gesellschaft fur Rassenhygiene* (Society for Racial Hygiene).[25] In 1907, the influence of the Society for Racial Hygiene would lead to a major debate within the Reichstag regarding a proposed sterilization bill that would eventually be rejected. The issue and its advocates would not die, however. Increasingly, eugenicists found support from the Weimar government. Many proponents of eugenics were employed at state-funded *Rassenhygiene* institutes and clinics. A decade before Hitler came to power, eugenics had migrated from a theoretical discourse to an applied science and effort at social engineering.

Some have argued that anti-Semitism did not play a strong role in the pre-Hitler eugenics movement or that at least it was contested by a number of leading proponents who even considered the Jews to be Aryan.[26] In fact, German eugenicists were race conscious in their actions throughout. The Society for Racial Hygiene began performing sterilizations for "eugenic reasons," that is, eliminating "racial diseases," as early as 1919.[27] German eugenicists did not necessarily want initially to jump into the political fray, that is, take responsibility for the policy implications (and implementation) of their ideas. At first, they rejected the policy of mandatory government intervention. In October 1921, the Society for Race Hygiene adopted a twenty-one–point eugenics program that, inter alia, strongly opposed compulsory sterilization. Within a very short time, however, this attitude would change.

The German eugenics movement was strongly influenced by the work of the American eugenicists Ezra Gosney and Paul Popenoe. Gosney was a wealthy philanthropist who became obsessed with eugenics, and Popenoe was the editor of the *Journal of Heredity*. In 1929, Gosney and Popenoe published *Sterilization for Human Betterment*, a study of work and efficacy under the 1922 California sterilization law. A number of German eugenicists would claim that this book was the singular inspiration for the 1933 law enacted by the Nazis. As Dorothy Roberts notes, "the Nazis modeled their compulsory sterilization law after the one enacted in California."[28] That California statute and the Model Eugenic Sterilization Law developed by Harry Laughlin in 1922 had global impact. Notably, the Nazi law was more moderate than the one proposed by their American counterparts. The Laughlin model, which influenced the California and other state laws, called for sterilizing the mentally retarded, insane, criminal, people who were habitually drunk, blind, deaf, deformed, and economically dependent. In the United States, between 1929 and 1941, more than 70,000 people had been involuntarily sterilized. Under the California law twice as many Blacks as Whites were sterilized. The law allowed for sterilization based on "hereditary diseases" including weakmindedness, schizophrenia, insanity, epilepsy, blindness, deafness, bodily deformities, and alcoholism."[29] Even with all of these stipulations, there were, from the beginning, complaints that the law was not broad enough because it did not address hidden "defects" such as race or other traits that were not visible to the naked eye, a complaint that would be echoed in Nazi Germany.

The link between Nazism and the pre-1933 eugenics movement was strong. The anti-Semitic rantings of Ploetz and others informed the theoretical basis of Nazi thinking. Tucker contends that "while Hitler was still imprisoned in Landsberg am Lech fortress and just beginning *Mein Kampf*, renowned university scholars like [Fritz] Lenz and [Eugen] Fischer and cruder race theoristd like [Hans] Gunther had already provided the intellectual and scientific foundation for much of what would become the Nazi program."[30] In 1931, at the conference of the National Socialist Pharmacists and Physicians, it was proposed that the Aryan or Nordic part of the German population be nurtured, a middle group that was near Aryan be tolerated, and the lowest, most unfit, and non-Aryan sector be sterilized.[31]

As this brief history demonstrates, eugenics was well established in Germany long before Hitler came to power, and before the fascist state turned its attention to the Afro-German young people and other Blacks. Although in 1927, addressing the issue of the mixed-race Rhineland children, an "official of the Bavarian Ministry of the Interior recommended sterilization, but the suggestion was turned down at Reich level because of the demoralizing effects upon the children's German mothers."[32] Six years later, on 14 July 1933, the Law for the Prevention of Genetically Defective Progeny passed and became the legal justification for the Nazis' euthanasia and sterilization programs. The German law passed, in part, due to the appropriation of legal and medical arguments that had been used to pass similar laws in the United States. The objective of the law was to prevent or stop the spreading of so-called negative and impure hereditary diseases and illnesses.

The Nazi sterilization law went into effect on 1 January 1934. (See accompanying Table 1.) According to Kevles, about 225,000 were sterilized in the first three years of the program.[33] Beginning on the effective date, medical professionals had to report all "unfit" individuals to the Hereditary Health Courts that had been created by the hundreds across Germany. According to the law, each court had a jurist and two physicians. This body would make a determination whether an individual was to be sterilized or not. There are no official or trustworthy figures on how many sterilizations were done overall after that time. Campt gives a figure of 300,00–400,000 individuals between 1934 and 1945.[34] She goes on to note, however, that those figures "exclude countless *illegal* sterilizations carried out in secret on the basis of racial/racist, rather than 'hereditary' or 'biological' grounds"[35] (emphasis in the original). These included, of course, Afro-Germans and others of African descent in addition to Gypsies and Jews. Finally, Muller-Hill estimates that 350,000–400,000 sterilizations were performed between 1934 and 1939, and then were effectively ended after the passage of new laws.[36]

TABLE I   **Law for the Protection of Hereditary Health:**
The Attempt to Improve the German Aryan Breed
(July 14, 1933)

Article I.

(1.) Anyone who suffers from an inheritable disease may be surgically sterilized if, in the judgment of medical science, it could be expected that his descendants will suffer from serious inherited mental or physical defects.

(2.) Anyone who suffers from one of the following is to be regarded as inheritably diseased within the meaning of this law:

    1. congenital feeble-mindedness
    2. schizophrenia
    3. manic-depression
    4. congenital epilepsy
    5. inheritable St. Vitus dance (Huntington's Chorea)
    6. hereditary blindness
    7. hereditary deafness
    8. serious inheritable malformations

(3.) In addition, anyone suffering from chronic alcoholism may also be sterilized.

Article II.

(1.) Anyone who requests sterilization is entitled to it. If he be incapacitated or under a guardian because of low state of mental health or not yet 18 years of age, his legal guardian is empowered to make the request. In other cases of limited capacity the request must receive the approval of the legal representative. If a person be of age and has a nurse, the latter's consent is required.

(2.) The request must be accompanied by a certificate from a citizen who is accredited by the German Reich stating that the person to be sterilized has been informed about the nature and consequence of sterilization.

(3.) The request for sterilization can be recalled.

Article III.

Sterilization may also be recommended by:
(1.) the official physician
(2.) the official in charge of a hospital, sanitarium, or prison.

Article IV.

The request for sterilization must be presented in writing to, or placed in writing by, the office of the Health Inheritance Court. The statement concerning the request must be certified by a medical document or authenticated in some other way. The business office of the court must notify the official physician.

Article VII. The proceedings of the Health Inheritance Court are secret.

Article X. The Supreme Health Insurance Court retains final jurisdiction.

Source: *The Holocaust\Shoah Page.*

Other relevant laws included the 26 June 1935 Law for the Alteration of the Law for the Prevention of Hereditarily Disease Progeny and the 18 October 1935 Law for the Protection of Hereditary Health of the German People. The former sanctioned compulsory abortion (for up to six months!), while the latter required that all those who sought to get married carry a "certificate of fitness to marry."[37] Also, the Nazi eugenics racial program was one of "weed" and "breed." The SS chief, Heinrich Himmler, instituted the *Lebensborn* (The Well of Life) program that consisted of encouraging SS members to impregnate as many racially suitable women as they could who would then be given the best prenatal care possible in spalike resorts set up across Germany. Moral issues notwithstanding, these women were both married and unmarried.

On 13 April 1933, three months after Hitler came to power, Hermann Göring, the Prussian minister of the interior and one of Hitler's most loyal henchman, ordered data to be collected on the Rhineland children from the local authorities in Dusseldorf, Cologne, Koblenz, and Aachen. Dr. William Abel of the Kaiser Wilhelm Institute for Anthropology, Heredity, and Eugenics used the information collected from 145 children to conclude that these children were racially inferior and something should be done to "prevent their reproducing."[38] Around the same time, Dr. Hans Macco, who produced a pamphlet, *Racial Problems in the Third Reich,* that also called for the sterilization of mixed-raced children as well as Gypsies, echoed these conclusions.[39] And in that same year, Hitler's minister of agriculture Richard-Walther Darre, made the case that for the future of the German nation, the Rhineland children had to be taken care of. In the harshest terms possible, he wrote:

> It is essential to exterminate the leftovers from the black Shame on the Rhine.
> These mulatto children were created either through rape or by white mothers who
> were whores. In any case, there exists not the slightest moral obligation toward
> these racially foreign offspring. . . . Thus, as a Rhinelander I demand: sterilization
> of all mulattoes with whom we were saddled by the black Shame at the Rhine.
> This measure has to be carried out within the next two years. Otherwise it is too
> late, with the results that hundreds of years later this racial deterioration will still
> be felt. [40]

Since the 1933 sterilization law did not allow for sterilization based solely on race, the Nazis were aware that they had to rewrite or amend the law, create a new law, or operate outside their own regulations. In the end, the Nazis simple choose to carry on in secret and in violation of the ordinance, usually employing the mask of "parental" consent. Applying a formal reading of the statute, as Friedlander noted, "The sterilization law did not, however, permit sterilization of children whose only hereditary disease was their race. The ministry decided to sterilize them secretly."[41] The counselor of the Reich Ministry of the Interior, responsible for the enforcement of the sterilization law, made it clear what the Nazi objectives were with the law when he stated, "We want to prevent . . . poisoning the entire bloodstream of the race."[42] Perhaps few outside the Nazi leadership saw this as the first step in a diabolical plan eventually to physically eliminate the "racially" unsuitable. The complete dominance of the Nazi state over the political and social life of the nation ensured that legal recourse was closed and popular resistance, to the degree it existed, was muted and brutally repressed. Although initially, about half of those sterilized were labeled as "feebleminded," this charade would soon be dropped. It is also evident that feeblemindedness itself was a cover that could be used to target any group, especially given the racial hierarchy that informed Nazi and, more generally, German thinking.

The decision to sterilize the Rhineland children was explicit. On 11 March 1935, a group that was part of the Committee of Experts for Population and Racial Policy met to address "ways to solve the question of [the Rhineland] Bastards." The children who had been born during the occupation were about to reach childbearing age, an unacceptable danger to the Nazis. It was suggested by one attendee, Dr. Walter Gross, and agreed upon by the group that the way to handle the situation was by sterilization of the children. First doing an anthropological investigation was mere window dressing for a policy of slow genocide. For unknown reasons, it took another two years to decide that there would be no pretense of a legal cover—such as extending or amending the 1933 law—and that the parent(s) or guardian(s) would be forced to sign consent statements initiating sterilization procedures.

Rather than have the process go through the Hereditary Health Courts that had been created by the 1933 law, the Gestapo created Special Commission No. 3, whose task was to locate, identify, and implement "the discrete sterilization of the Rhineland bastards."[43] The members of Special Commission No. 3 included Eugen Fischer, Wilhelm Abel, and Heinrich Schade.[44] Abel was in charge of the Department on Race at the Wilhelm Institute run by Fischer.[45] Among the characteristics that were attributed to the *Mischlings* by the Nazi leadership and Reich scientists were "biological inferiority," "disharmonies in the phenotypic appearance," "preponderantly negative character traits," and "torn by inner conflicts."[46] The medical attacks on the young Afro-Germans and other Blacks, as were all national racial policies, were sanctioned by Hitler himself.

Between 1935 and 1937, at least 385 Rhineland children were sterilized, according to available documents. These were mostly done in open secret. Hitler's race experts collected data on 385 of the Rhineland children in the Bonn and Cologne areas with the collaboration of churches, schools, and other institutions. Once identified, the youths were taken from their schools or homes, usually with the coerced signature of their parent or legal guardian, and brought before a special commission and tried. In nearly every instance, it was determined that the person on trial should be sterilized; the person was then taken away and the procedure performed.[47] The Bonn University Women's Clinic and the Evangelical Hospital in Cologne-Sulz were among the sites used for the sterilizations.[48] Besides the young people, black men who had been sterilized had to carry certificates showing that they had had a vasectomy.

While information concerning black sterilization exists about Afro-German and African men, there were also a significant number of sterilizations of black women athough exactly how many were done is unknown. Nazi romanticizing of German womanhood did not extend to women of African descent. This is an open arena of research and likely to demonstrate some important differences in rationale and argument. It is known that in at least one instance, a young black girl was saved at the last minute. Doris Reiprich, whose Cameroonian father bought German citizenship for fifty gold marks in 1896 and eventually married a white German woman, was taken to the clinic to be sterilized in 1943. Extremely distraught, she cried and apparently aroused the sympathy of a man at the clinic who let her go. She eventually married and had two children, including one daughter with blue eyes and blonde hair.[49]

The ritual of an examination generated a report that served as the legal document authorizing sterilization. A typical report or finding noted the undesirable racial traits possessed by Blacks. The 2 June 1937 report from Frankfurt on Marianne Braun, who was born 16 May 1925, describes how she was driven to the hospital and questioned, with the inevitable conclusion:

> According to statements by the mother and the anthropological opinion it was established that Marianne Braun is a German citizen who, as the descendent of colored occupation forces, has characteristics alien to her race. The father of the child was then informed about the results of the examination, and it was pointed out to him that the descendents of the child would retain the colored blood alien to the race, and that for this reason propagation by the child is undesirable. He was thoroughly informed about the character and the consequences of sterlization.[50]

A similar report was issued regarding Cacilie Borinski, who was born on 7 April 1922. The 17 June 1937 report from Bonn notes that her father was an American soldier. As with Marianne Braun, it is noted that Borinski is a German citizen. The document states:

> The Commission has reached the following conclusion: The German citizen Cacilie Borinski . . . is the descendent of a member of the former colored occupation troops and distinctly has the corresponding characteristics. Therefore she is to be sterilized. [51]

A third example is the report done on Josef Feck. His report was issued on 19 June 1937 in Frankfurt. Again, the language is chillingly clinical and strikingly similar to those already noted:

> The German citizen Josef Feck, born 26 September 1920, and residing in Mainz is a descendent of the former colonial occupation troops (North Africa) and distinctly displays the corresponding anthropological characteristics. For that reason he is to be sterilized. His mother consents to the sterilization.[52]

More than fifty years later, victims of these torturous operations would speak in cold bitterness of the psychological, let alone physical, destruction they felt. The Afro-German Hans Hauck, who was featured in the film *Black Survivors of the Holocaust,* tells sourly of how the Gestapo came and got him and his grandmother into a car and took them to the Health Office, where he was examined and measured. A decision was made to sterilize him without the benefit of anesthesia. After it was over, Hauck was given a vasectomy certificate and warned not to have sexual relations with white German women. He also had to sign papers stating that he would commit to that agreement and that his sterilization was not forced.[53] Another Afro-German shown in *Black Survivors*, Thomas Holzhauzer, is also resentful about being operated on by the Nazis. He was picked up along with his sister and taken to the Elizabeth Hospital in Darmstadt. He remembers distinctly that the doctor, who was wearing a Nazi uniform, "made two cuts around my testicles" during the procedure. There is more than a little anger when he tells the filmmakers, "Sometimes I'm glad I could not have any children."

The deleterious impact of these sterilizations on Black Germans cannot be overstated. This slow holocaust terrorized an entire generation of Blacks. While there is no evidence that any of the U.S. eugenicists were aware of the secret sterilizations that had been carried out against Afro-Germans, the threat of sterilization had been addressed fairly early in the Nazi era and was even discussed in U.S. black newspapers of the time.

Although a number of American eugenicists would begin to break with and criticize the fascist tendencies of the movement as early as the early 1930s, it was not until the early 1940s that the discrediting was full and that nearly all involved in the U.S.-based movement would denounce the policies of the Nazis, policies that they had championed only a short time before. Without rejecting eugenics as a "science," many contended that the violent and unrelenting execution of the Jews of Europe was not what they had been advocating. Instead, they argued, they wanted to pursue a course of "positive" and noncoercive encouragement to breed a better racial stock for the nation. There were others, of course, who continued to embrace the Nazis long after they had been exposed for the medical terrors that were being unleashed against German citizens. In 1936, upon receiving a University of Heidelberg honorary doctorate award, the Eugenics Record Office's Laughlin stated that the award was "evidence of a common understanding of German and American scientists of the nature of eugenics."[54]

African Americans, Afro-Germans, and the Response to Sterilization

As early as 1934, a year before the Nazis officially met and decided to carry out their program of slow extermination of German Blacks, the issue of the sterilization of Afro-Germans and other Blacks in Germany was being raised in the U.S. black press. On 17 February 1934, the *Washington Afro-American*, in a page-one story, warned about a "new Nazi plan is to sterilize all children born as a result of affairs between French African troops and German women during the after-war occupation."[55] The report of the plan came from a black Republican representative, Oscar Stanton DePriest, who was the first African American elected to Congress in the twentieth century and the only Black in the U.S. Congress at the time. Although elected from a black enclave of Chicago, DePriest (as would others to follow) saw himself and was seen as a voice of black interests nationally and internationally. Though powerless to affect the status of black America and the broader black world, DePriest used his congressional platform to articulate a politics of resistance. He was far from being a radical, but in Jim Crow America, he had little choice but to become a "race" man, if only by default, and articulate the real, perceived, and threatened grievances of black people.[56]

The black movement against sterilization was addressed at the intersection of race, class, and gender. Roberts points out the contradictory relationship that many African Americans, including a number of leading intellectuals and civil rights leaders, had with the eugenics movement. Criticism of the so-called immoral behavior of lower-class African Americans by Du Bois, parts of the black press, and other black leaders led them to support the birth control movement that overlapped substantially with the eugenics movement. Their arguments reflected many of the same claims of "betterment" spoken by more racist elements. This debate was also a gendered discourse in a number of ways. Black women, held responsible for the socialization of their children, were principally held accountable for the "irresponsible" behavior that was manifest in the black community. As a class, they were also chastised for having children out of wedlock, promiscuity, and attempts at gaining equal footing with men, black men in particular. The responsibility of black men in these instances was elided and simply not a part of the debate. Neither was a contextualized framework that recognized the socially driven forces that determined under what circumstances poor blacks, women, and, especially, poor black women could exercise the agency necessary to control any of these factors. A (black-white) matrix of power from any number of vantage points always resulted with white men at the top, followed by white women, trailed by black men and, last, black women.

While white men could freely exercise sexual power over white and black women, and racial power over black men, white women were circumscribed to exhibit only racial power, still a very significant force nevertheless. Black men, trumped by the racial power of white women and the totalizing power of white men, were then left with only a limited gender power whose boundaries were thrown over the political and social spaces of black women. Thus, black women were doubly vulnerable due not only to the direct assault upon their physical and psychological being by white men, black men, and white women, but also to the explanatory race-sex discourse that then justified their exclusion, marginalization, and oppression in the first instance.

Though real and expressive of the diasporic solidarity tendencies always present in black political life, the alarm sounded by some black newspapers about the sterilization threat to Afro-Germans and Africans was compromised by the political frame and behavior of black male leaders and intellectuals of the period regarding eugenics-driven birth control in the black community. Beyond the fact that there was precious little that African Americans could do to prevent the attacks on Afro-Germans, little had been concretely done to stop the profoundly racialized eugenics and sterilization campaigns that operated in the United States. It is not known if Blacks who were sterilized by the Nazis ever knew that their kinfolk of sorts had raised the issue, but no direct action of prevention was possible and none was forthcoming.

Conclusion

Sterilization was perhaps the worst action that could be taken by the Nazis against Blacks in Germany short of mass execution. It not only destroyed the future of individual Blacks but also sought to erase any future blackness on German soil. At the same time, the sterilization option reflected the complicated relationship that the Nazis had toward its black population. Unable to win consensus on extermination, yet compelled to address the "otherness" of Blacks, they used sterilization as a gradual, but inexorable death, long-term erasure that, in part, solved some of Germany's black dilemma. Hitler and other Nazi leaders made it clear that Blacks were not desired in the Third Reich, but a number of factors out of their control such as the international situation forced them to compromise.

Yet sterilization was not the end of the story. While the efforts at sterilization were an initial means by which the Nazis attempted to address one of their black dilemmas, at least as it concerned young Afro-Germans, a more evil and fatal destiny awaited many more. In the period leading up to the war and during the war, the Nazis would initiate a hurricane of brutality and death that swept all in its path. One of the most tragic legacies of Nazism was the construction, peopling, and administration of those earthbound abysses of hell known as concentration camps. For millions of those who did not die on the spot at the hands of the Nazi onslaught from the East and the West, as well as their enemies within Germany, the last stop in this life was in the thousands of death, concentration, labor, transition, and prisoner of war camps. Many of the black victims of sterilization would end up in the camps as well as other Blacks who were unlucky enough to be caught. It is to their stories that we turn next.

6

Behind the Wire

Black Captives of Nazism

My name is Clifford Pepperidge and I am in trouble.
—The opening line of John A. Williams's novel, Clifford's Blues[1]

From *The Great Escape* to *Schindler's List,* Nazi concentration camps and prisons have been Hollywoodized as film producers have seized upon one of the most horrifying moments in the history of humanity, a true "Heart of Darkness" manifestation when the unimaginable would come to pass. On film and television, concentration camp narratives have been created in every genre including adventure, drama, comedy, and fantasy. For many in the United States, a television program, *Hogan's Heroes,* for six years (1965–1971), provided a comedic spin on the relationship between Allied prisoners of war (POWs) and the Nazis who held them captive. Colonel Hogan (Bob Crane) led his men to carry out sabotage, escapes, and secret missions against the incompetent and inept Nazis who ran Stalag 13. Tellingly, race, whether in the form of antiblackness or anti-Semitism, was not generally an issue that the show dealt with. In fact, one could watch the show and never have a clue as to what the Nazis were trying to accomplish either in terms of their war goals or their broad political or racial agenda. In this sense, the show was a grand distortion of the meaning and significance of World War II and served to reduce history to a narrative homage of the cunning and military supremacy of the Allies, in particular, the Americans. As is often the case in the commercializing of history, *Hogan's Heroes* was more about the politics of the times, the late 1960s, than a cogent rendering of the war or POW experience.

Though never given any special attention, one of the notable elements of the show was that it had a black character, Sergeant Ivan Kinchloe (Ivan Dixon), the unit's radio and technology expert. When Dixon left after the fifth season to pursue other career options, another black actor, Kenneth Washington, replaced him and also played the role of a radio operator. *Hogan's Heroes* was one of the first network programs to put an

African American in a role that essentially was on a par with that of whites. Kinchloe had brains and brashness and, extremely unusual for the situation comedies of the period, was never reduced to a racial foil or minstrelsy. In fact, Dixon's role was seen as so important to the black community that, in 1967, the executive producer, Ed Feldman, won the NAACP Image Award for the program. This acclaim was given despite the historical reality that the racial segregation of the U.S. armed forces of the World War II period actually limited the number of African Americans who would even have been in a POW camp in the first place.

I would guess that most, if not all, of the audience was not inspired to reflect too much on whether Dixon and Washington's roles were simply a bow to the black political demands of the period—occurring in the intersecting moment between the civil rights and Black Power movements—for representation even in the seemingly unlikely circumstance of a Nazi prison camp. Nor was the audience likely to wonder whether there was a larger but generally unknown story regarding the presence of people of African descent in the wide variety of prisons, detention centers, internment camps, labor camps, concentration camps, and death camps established by the Nazis from the early months of their coming to power in 1933 until the last days of the war in 1945. Indeed, there is a larger and heretofore generally unknown story to tell about the black presence in the camps, and the racial significance of those experiences for our understanding of the Holocaust, Nazism, black diasporan relations and racism more generally. Furthermore, the experiences of people of African descent in the various camps exposed not only the complicated antiblack racism of the Nazis but also the racist views of white U.S. military officials, which the Nazis would seek to exploit. In a peculiar though perhaps not all that unfamiliar manner, Smith's "racial contract" played itself out behind the wires.

The Body and Soul of the Condemned

The philosopher Michel Foucault, in his incisive history of the development of prisons, *Discipline & Punishment*, contends metaphorically that the soul is the prison, the body the prisoner. In tracing the evolution of the uses of punishment in the construction of the European carceral system, he demonstrates that the spectacle of public executions and torture gave way by the end of the eighteenth century under a barrage of criticism of the incongruity between principles and practiced barbarity. While the imprisoned body was still "caught up in a system of constraints and privations, obligations and prohibitions," it was no longer the site of the most severe penalties and pain.[2] As the body-punishment relationship became more hidden, from the public and as a point of fact, an even more dangerous objective grew. The purpose of penal punishment, at its most callous and unforgiving, became not simply the destruction of the body but the penalizing and, ultimately, the annihilation of the soul.[3]

Murdering the soul was profoundly at the heart of the Nazis' system of concentration camps and prisons. Although the physical elimination of the Jews and other opponents—the "final solution" thesis—was the most immediate means of doing so, Hitler sought the obliteration of any legacy or memory of Jews in the cruelest ways possible.

Enemies of the state were not to be just executed, but a matrix of tortures, extremely public and frightful, was to be visited upon the community body. Every effort was to be made to break down the soul before death was achieved. In this sense, the merciless methods of killing were as much meant for the victim(s) as for the living witnesses and soon-to-be victims. In the maniacal atmosphere of the camps, this element of total condemnation separated, in general, the treatment of Jews and, to a strong degree, the Gypsies from that of others, including Blacks. This is not say that the murder of Blacks, Russians, Slavs, and others did not have a vicious and evil drive behind them, nor that the general application of death techniques was just to particular groups. The body of the black condemned was exoticized and could receive special fixation, negative or positive, that was determined by nationality, time period, and individual vissicitudes.

Caught: Black POWs and Nazi Racism

Perhaps the greatest and certainly the most obvious irony of black military participation in the war against the Nazis was that Blacks, whether from the United States, Great Britain, France, or the colonies, did not experience and enjoy the equality and inclusion that was propagated by the Allies as the moral imperative for stopping Hitler. The racial state sought by National Socialism was the logical extension of much of the racial policies in place in the nations that went to war against Germany. The trope of democracy found little reception among those who lived at the bottom of the social barrel. In every instance, Blacks in the military, especially those from the United States, found themselves fighting a war on two fronts. Their participation, voluntary in most instances, was predicated on two hopes. One, that their expression of national loyalty would speed up the process of civil and political rights that was being fought for before, during, and after the war. While white resistance to black democratic rights was mostly unyielding and popular, it was believed by many that cross-racial national participation in the war would melt white hatred. Two, the specter of Nazis in power and the spread of fascism was clearly more frightening than the present state of affairs, as unacceptable as that might have been. Although some would be conflicted by the racist discourse employed to mobilize the nation against the Japanese after the December 1941 attack on Pearl Harbor, the strong strain of democratic inclusiveness prevalent in the African American community supported the war against the retrogression that Hitler represented. Ironically, these fears and hopes would manifest in the POW experiences that some Blacks endured where not only would they suffer excessively at the hands of the Nazis, but also feel a supreme sense of abandonment and racism from their superior officers who made it clear that white POWs mattered more than colored ones.

The experience of black POWs is one of the least-researched areas of World War II. One obstacle to the research is that very little has been written by those actually held prisoner. All of the Allied powers—the United States, England, Canada, and France— had black soldiers and military personnel operating in the war theater. While the POW focus here is on Blacks that were captured and held prisoner by the Nazis, and the experiences of Afro-Germans who were caught by either the Allies or the Soviet Union, it should be noted that a broader black POW experience of combatants and noncombatants in the campaigns in Africa and the Pacific also remains mostly undocumented and unacknowledged.[4] As far as is known, the Soviet Union did not have any Blacks among their military forces, although there were Africans and African Americans residing there at the time, some of whom had become citizens and were loyal to their hosts.[5] Between 1939 and 1945, perhaps as many as thirty-five million combatants fell into enemy hands. All sides captured large numbers of prisoners and held them, in some cases, for over five years.[6] One study found that 130,201 American troops were captured and interned during the war with about 11 percent (14,072) dying while being held.[7] The researcher Paulette Reed-Anderson estimates "there were about three to four thousand African American POWs in Germany."[8]

This estimate and other evidence contradict the official data held by the United States. According to the records of the Office of the Provost Marshal General, specifically the World War II Prisoners of War Punchcards database, out of 143,360 records of POWs and civilian internees, only 153 are listed as "Negro," one of the categories of race.[9] The other categories were "White," "Chinese," "Japanese," "Filipino," "Puerto Rican," and "Others." A check of the "Others" category revealed 212 names, most of which appeared to be either Hispanic or perhaps Filipino-"sounding." Some of the individuals in the "Others" list may have been persons of African or mixed-race descent who were, in part, black. The database gives the name, rank, branch of service, the date of their capture/date of their entrance to the camp, in what country or region the camp was located, the name of the camp, the date they were released, and their final status (returned or died). Technically, the coding for the camps included concentration camps also, but in the records for the Negro POWs, no concentration camps were listed. The small number of offical black POWs, 153, can somewhat be accounted for in a few ways. First, the National Archives and Records Administration (NARA), where the database was produced and is held, concedes that it has only 98 percent of the data that were known from paper and card records because about 2 percent were damaged or otherwise unreadable. Second, the original data required information not only from those who had been POWs but also from the German authorities who were either unable or unwilling to provide full information in the closing and immediate aftermath of the war. Third, some people simply got lost in the system. There are too many credible reports of individual Blacks—POWs or civilian internees—who do not show up on the official list to be dismissed as data collection mistakes. Clearly, there were many people for whom no records were kept at all.

The NARA database appears to include a number of women who were civilian internees. With the database lacking a breakdown by women and men, this conclusion is based on the qualified assumption that some first names are gendered. While there are names on the list that have been popularly used by both women and men, such as "Robin" or "Marion," most are traditional female and male names such as Margaret and Kathryn and Robert and William. If this assumption is employed, there are five women on the list—Kathleen Gonyou, Marjorie H. Gunnison, Mrs. Marie Halsema, Kathryn Kuhn, and Ethel Robinson—all of whom were civilian internees and were held in

Japan, with the exception of Robinson, for whom no information other than her name is included.[10]

Eventually, the Nazis established 119 POW camps (*Stalags*) and civilian internment camps in Germany and the occupied territories. Some camps were just for officers, while others held both officers and enlisted men. There are virtually no records available on the number of women who were captured or where they may have been held, and little demographic data on them.

As in other areas, the treatment of black POWs was inconsistent and contradictory. In May 1940, General Heinz Guderian, commander of Germany's notorious Panzer troops, had his chief of staff issue a disingenuous statement that "colonial soldiers have mutilated in bestial fashion our German wounded."[11] This lie was to justify the merciless treatment that was to be the official policy toward captured black French solders. The statement order by Guderian went on, " . . . all kindness [toward these troops] would be an error. It is rigorously forbidden to send these prisoners towards the rear without a guard. They are to be treated with the greatest rigour."[12] In many instances, "they were segregated from white prisoners, denied food, and made to do the most difficult jobs."[13] Yet the policy as it was actually carried out was paradoxical and "a mixture of indifference and downright malevolence by the Germans towards their non-white captives."[14] In some camps Africans or other black soldiers were segregated and in others they were not. Similarly, in some instances, black POWs were given better food and treated more kindly than white soldiers, and in other circumstances, they were treated much, much worse.

Hans Haber, who was a prisoner of war, was a witness to this unpredictable behavior. He reports that in his camp Blacks were treated initially with extreme cruelty. According to Haber, "They were executed at random, denied water on long marches, and starved until many fell ill. No white man was allowed to converse with a Black." Then, "suddenly flogging was replaced by pampering. Negroes alone among the prisoners were permitted weekly walks in the nearby village. They were given one cake of soap for every four men, a privilege never granted white prisoners. Their food was improved, princely compared with that allotted whites, and they were permitted to attend the daily reading of news reports, from which they had been previously excluded."[15] Haber gives no reason for the dramatic change in behavior by the Nazis, and most likely he did not know.

The conflicting policies of the Nazis were likely due to a number of factors, from the tactic of divide and conquer to the predilections of individual camp guards and commanders. Even the Nazis' most generous pampering, however, did not rise to the level of benevolence and kindness or acceptance of Blacks as equals. And certainly by the time the war began, concerns about international criticism were not a very relevant factor. Nationality, however, may have played a role in the treatment of black prisoners from Africa. The German hatred of France and memories of the black troops from the occupation period doubtless reflected themselves in the attitudes manifest toward African captives from the French colonies. In the end, Blacks from the different allied nations found themselves abandoned, for the most part, once captured, and the lucky few, only by a miracle, survived. Blacks from France, the United Kingdom, the United States, and a number of countries in Africa became POWs and opened up a new chapter in diasporic encounters.

France

In September 1939, when war broke out between Germany and France, the latter had seven divisions in Europe, out of eighty total, that consisted solely of Africans; less than one year later, when an armistice was reached, these troops numbered about 100,000.[16] They constituted about 10 percent of the whole French Army and hailed from Martinique, Guadeloupe, Algeria, Senegal, and other African nations. Nearly half of these soldiers—as many as 48,000—would be declared missing and assumed killed. An additional 15,000 to 16,000 would become POWs, with only half of them surviving.[17] In other words, states Killingray, somewhere between 55,000 and 65,000 African soldiers may have been killed or died at the hands of the Nazis either as prisoners or in combat situations. Some estimates of the number of Africans who were captured are much higher. According to Bechhause-Gerst, "During the war some 80,000 French African prisoners of war were sent to camps in Bordeaux on orders from Hitler. Some Africans were held in Luckenwalde where they were used for research in tropical medicine or for language study by so-called African specialists."[18]

Many of the Africans received extreme treatment as captives, including arbitrary and wanton murder. On 18 March 1945, in Moosburg, Germany, at Stalag VII-A, an SS guard was alleged to have executed a black South African with the excuse that he was trying to escape.[19] French African prisoners were usually segregated from other prisoners and even put in separate camps located primarily in northeastern France, but also in Germany. They were held at camps at Mirecourt, Morasse, Reims, Romilly-sur-Seine, Troyes, Amiens, Poitiers, and dozens of locations, some serving as many as four years.[20] Callous winters, ghastly food, hard labor, and persistent illness characterized daily existence for many Africans. In many instances, if not most, the once-a-day meal consisted of "a small piece of vegetable chopped up in hot water, a little bit of potato, and some grass."[21] Malnutrition, dysentery, and other sicknesses were epidemic. These conditions bred both comradeship and ruthless competition. Few would attempt to escape, not only because it was difficult and punishment was a nonnegotiable death sentence, but because their blackness made it impossible for them to hide among the local population.

In many ways, these conditions echoed the experience of the slave trade where culturally and socially distinct African peoples were forced into a coexistence by outside oppressors. For African captives, the horrors of the slave ship can be seen as a metaphor for the unknown terrors that awaited them in the camps.

The United States

The United States enlisted over 1.15 million African American women and men into the military by 1945, although segregation would leave most far from the front lines and generally not likely to be captured as POWs.[22] The United States sent more than 200,000 black soldiers to France alone, with more than 30,000 of them engaged in direct combat.[23] The all-black Tuskeegee Airmen were an exception to the back line role as they flew missions directly over the enemy's territory risking life and limb. Some would be shot down and either captured or, in some instances, shot on the spot. Those captured were sent off to the POW camps. While mostly given a subservient role and manual tasks, such as burying the dead, Black troops would occasionally get a fighting role and, in part, played a role in the liberation of some of the concentration camps in late 1944 and 1945 as the Allies began the final assault on the Nazis, driving them further and further back into Germany.[24]

In the United States, a war against racism was also being waged. From the beginning of the World War II to the end, African Americans raised the issue of hypocrisy, citing the contradictory position of the nation fighting a war for democracy abroad while ignoring, indeed, obstructing the democratic rights of African Americans back home. The war became an opportunity to put the issue of racism, including its role in the U.S. armed forces, on the front burner. The radical civil rights leader A. Philip Randolph's threatened 1941 march on Washington protesting segregation in the armed services and military industries sent chills down the back of President Franklin Roosevelt who was attempting to win broad support for U.S. involvement in the war. On 25 June 1941, in response to Randolph's protest, Roosevelt issued Executive Order 8802 requiring all employers, unions, and government offices and agencies to "provide for the full and equitable participation of all workers in defense industries without discrimination because of race, creed, color, or national origin," and creating the Fair Employment Practices Committee to enforce the new order.[25] The threatened march was called off.

While the defense industries would be legally desegregated, the military was still divided by race. Despite this continuing insult, black civil rights and political leaders did not call for a boycott against joining the military. On the left, those Blacks in the Communist Party followed the Soviet line and, initially, opposed the war on the grounds that it was a battle among imperialists; later, when Hitler broke the 1939 nonaggression treaty between Germany and the Soviet Union, they joined with the call by the party to build a Popular Front of the political left and center in support of the Allies. Other black socialists and leftists, particularly those who were Trotskyite, remained against the war throughout. In the end, African Americans would join the fight and would, in some cases, just like Sergeant Kinchlow, end up in Nazi prison camps.

Although the records on black POWs are scant, it is clear that the already desperate situation for black prisoners was compounded by the racism they experienced from their Allied fellow white soldiers and white officers. Furthermore, the U.S. military was thought to be more interested in helping white POWs. This appeared to be the situation at Frontstalag No. 122, in Compiegnes, France, where a number of African Americans were being held. In a letter dated 16 January 1942, a Dr. Lowrie suggests that there was "a good deal of disension [sic]" between the white and black American soldiers, perhaps because, Dr. Lowrie notes, there had been only "attempts to obtain whites [sic] release from the camp."[26]

One internment camp that was used to hold captured U.S. and British citizens was at Vittel, also known as Ilag Vittel and Frontstalag No. 194. Many of the U.S. internees at the camp were black. Vittel has been described as "a relatively comfortable camp and detention center."[27] The camp was set up in 1940, and the Germans used it to keep prisoners they thought they could use in exchange for German citizens who had been arrested by the Allies. In addition to some African American soldiers, there were Senegalese prisoners of war at Vittel and they were used to do the manual labor at the camp. It is unknown what relationship developed between the African Americans and the Africans at the camp. Given the description of the camp as "relatively comfortable," it is likely that the prisoners were able to associate freely and that the two groups, notwithstanding language concerns, interacted regularly. The journalist Ottley, whose writings about the period provide much of the contemporary documentation available regarding Blacks under Nazism, notes that there were black POWs and Afro-Germans at the Dieuze concentration camp in the Department of Moselle.[28]

On the other side of the ocean, African American soldiers had to address other indignities. In many instances, black soldiers had the duty of transporting or guarding white German POWs. To their dismay, they found that racial segregation triumphed over national identity. White prisoners were allowed to use the white side of segregated facilities and entertainment. The civil rights lawyer Charles Houston laments that "there was one drinking fountain for white guards and German prisoners, and a segregated fountain for Negro soldiers" at one camp in the South.[29] In January 1945, correctly reading the racial fault lines in the South and the possibility of a white united front, German POWs working as kitchen help at the MacDill Field Base Hospital in Tampa demanded and achieved the segregation of black military patients so that they would not be allowed to eat in the same mess hall as Whites.[30] The fight against German racism took place in Europe and the United States as the global racial contract of white supremacy was once again enacted.

It was not only German POWs who were vexing black soldiers in their quest for a victory over domestic racial justice. Black soldiers guarded Italian POWs who were also sent to the United States. The complaints made regarding the Germans were echoed in the feelings toward the Italians. Harold Lawrence, one of those guarding the Italians in the South, wrote an angry letter to the *Pittsburgh Courier*: "[L]ast night I went to one of my Army Post Theatres, No. 4, Fort Knox, Kentucky, and because of color, I was forced to sit on the right of the theatre. The Italian internees are free to sit any place they please. Gee! How do they think we Colored soldiers feel about things like that? Is this what they call democracy?"[31] Gee is right.

The United Kingdom and the Caribbean

The British also recruited Blacks, mainly from the Caribbean, to join the war effort. A large number of men and women volunteered.[32] The racial politics of the U.S. military would run into conflict with the more liberal British position of integrated troops. Numerous incidences of clashes occurred between white American officers and their British counterparts over treatment of U.S. black troops.[33] Britain had permanently ended segregation in its military in 1939 and included Blacks among their officers.[34]

Several of these individuals were pilots and their crews who were shot down by the Germans and sent to POW camps.

Similar to African Americans, many of the black British soldiers did not engage in combat. For the British, however, this had less to do with U.S.-style segregation policies and more with the nature of the war. Blacks, however, were in all branches of the British armed forces and suffered losses as well as imprisonment with their white counterparts. Many of the black British POWs have written about their experiences, among them racist encounters with white U.S. soldiers who viewed all Blacks, whether they were African American or not, as inferior. The Guyanese RAF officer Cy Grant was imprisoned for two years at a POW camp after being shot down near Arnhem, Holland, in 1943. Grant stated, "The only racism that I encountered [there] was from an American . . . a corporal or something who happened to be in this holding camp. And he called me a nigger [sic] one or two times, but I got nothing from the Germans. They didn't single me out for any special treatment."[35] Some Blacks who were in the British Navy also found themselves under Nazi rule. In December 1939, Ransford Boi, a seaman in the British merchant fleet was caught by the Nazis and sent to the Stalag XB at Sandbostel between the towns of Bremen and Hanover.[36]

In the Killing Fields: The Massacres of Black Soldiers

As horrific as the POW experience could be for many captured Blacks, more than a few never survived to even make it that far. A number of massacres against people of African descent occurred that were never acknowledged until after the war had ended, and many were never fully investigated nor the perpetrators brought to justice. Credible evidence of the killing of downed black pilots or captured soldiers who were separated from other troops and shot has been uncovered. This evidence gives a graphic and detailed picture of the antiblack racism that informed the treatment of Blacks by the Nazis as well as by German citizens. These killings belie the notion that ordinary German citizens and regular army soldiers did not hold racist views in line with the Nazi leadership. In fact, the idea of a marauding black invasion force, as sold by Goebbels and other Nazi culturalists, resonated with the broad German masses and fed a sense of racial desperation that would rationalize the unnecessary murder of thousands of black soldiers. As Solomos and Black state, "Nazi propaganda combined anti-Semitic images with references to the 'black Allied soldier.' The propagandists deployed images of black soldiers to stand as a measure of Allied racial decay and a symptom of the mongrelization of American society. The presence of the black soldier was thus turned into a corrosive threat to European civilization."[37] Although the Germans had used black soldiers during World War I and even a few during the Nazi era, the construction of a black racial danger was privileged over losing to a military composed of only Whites. Being conquered by white troops was an acceptable outcome; defeat at black hands was not.

A number of investigations were held after the war into specific massacres and killings of black soldiers. Many of these cases were closed without any conclusive

rendering due in large part to the near impossibility of securing evidence in the circumstances of war and the disorganization of the postwar situation. Many witnesses and
suspects simply could not be located and the postwar chaos militated against efficiency
and rigor in carrying out criminal investigations. In 1944 and 1945, when Allied soldiers, which included African American troops, began to penetrate German-occupied
territories and Germany itself, the number of allegations skyrocketed. In most instances,
the unwarranted murders of black soldiers were not in dispute; the identity of the perpetrators of these war crimes was the issue at stake. Individual German soldiers, units of
soldiers, and even German civilians were all alleged to have committed heinous slaughter of black soldiers. While each instance of a battlefield homicide was obviously not
ordered from Berlin or by higher-ups, a clear message had been sent that African
American and Jewish captives could be disposed of in the most expedient way possible
without repercussions. The following chronological list compiled by the U.S. Holocaust
Memorial Museum researcher Robert Kesting, covering roughly the last fifteen months
of the war, gives some indication of the racial nature of the ground war by its end:

- February 20, 1944: In Salzburg, Austria, a Dr. Prima, who may have been in the SS,
  was accused of coming upon wounded African American airmen and summarily
  executing them.

- May 5, 1944: In Budapest, Hungary, near a local prison, the Gestapo hanged three
  African American pilots to death.

- (On or about) September 1, 1944: Near Merzig, Germany, black American soldiers
  were ordered to dig their own graves and then shot. It is also alleged that perhaps
  another 20 black American soldiers were taken to a nearby forest and executed there.

- December 17, 1944: Near Wereth, Belgium, 11 African American solders of the 33rd
  Field Artillery Battalion were murdered, allegedly by members of the 1st and/or 2nd
  Panzer Division. Among the killed were Curtise Adams, Mager Bradley, George
  Davis, Thomas Forte, Rob Green, Jim Leatherwood, Nathaniel Moss, George
  Motten, and William Pritchett.

- December 18, 1944: In Sopron, Hungary, at a local jail, a black American pilot was
  executed without cause or explanation.

- (On or about) December 18, 1944: Near Muehlberg, Germany, while being marched
  to Stalag IV-B, a black American soldier was singled out and killed by the SS.

- April 1, 1945: In Moosburg, Germany, at Stalag VII-A, a SS guard was alleged to have
  executed a black American, with no excuse being given.[38]

While there were killings of white U.S. soldiers during the same period, the allegations were far fewer, and the racial dimension element was not present except in the
case of Jews. The black executions demonstrated a predisposition against black soldiers
that was especially egregious in that they occurred, in effect, after the war was lost. The

war had turned against the Nazis by 1944, and there was little to gain from the wanton murder of black troops.

African captives suffered as well. One notorious case involved a thousand black Senegalese soldiers who were being held at a slave labor camp in Fritzlar, Germany. It was reported on 16 July 1945 by four surviving inmates that the SS member Alfred Moretao had carried out the execution of these African troops because they allegedly were stealing potatoes. This case was eventually turned over to French authorities who ultimately closed it without any resolution, as would happen with many of the charges of homicide and war crimes brought against individual Nazis.[39] There were other large massacres carried out during the war. On 10 June 1940, 400 to 500 black prisoners were lined up and killed at the French town of Erquinvillers. Around the same time, another 250 African soldiers were murdered in the little village of Chasselay-Montluzin.[40]

Blacks in the Concentration and Labor Camps

Evidence and documentation on the number of Afro-Germans and others of African descent in the concentration and labor camps and their experiences are almost nonexistent. Despite the extensive research done on concentration camps, this has been a large area of neglect and only recently, primarily through the work of the researcher Paulette Anderson, has this area been given some attention. For a number of reasons, collecting accurate and reliable data is difficult. First, it is believed that many of the Afro-Germans who went to the camps died there and no records remain. Second, although some records were found in many of the camps, the SS began to destroy evidence of their crimes as the war was ending and for most of the camps there simply are no official records available. For example, more than 77,000 records were missing from the Ravensbruck concentration camp that housed women, destroyed in spring 1945. Third, even at the former camp sites where records were discovered, there is no certainty that even if there were Blacks in the camp, they were identified as such. In many instances, if not most, skin color was not recorded and only nationality was noted, and even that could be misleading. The letter "A," for instance, may have been used in a shorthand manner under nationality, but "A" could have stood for Albanian, Algerian, or simple African. Finally, those Blacks who did survive the camps have not, for the most part, written or spoken extensively about those experiences, information that would give insight into not only their experience but that of others.

No one knows for sure how many people of African descent were actually in the camps or how many perished. Toward the end of the war, the Nazis made every effort to bury and destroy all evidence and records of their murderous rampage. While many of the larger camps have been turned into memorial sites with some documentation on who the inmates were, for the most part, those data are unavailable. On the basis of her research, the German-based scholar Anderson, who is African American, estimates that about two thousand Blacks died in the concentration camps. She has been contacting the former camps directly and seeking any information that could yield clues about the presence of Afro-Germans and other Blacks who were interned and likely died.

Documents available at the U.S. Holocaust Memorial Museum support the assertion that Blacks were used as slave laborers in some of the concentration camps. According to a report submitted to the United Nations War Crimes Commission on 1 June 1945 by the U.S. 21st Army Group, "Negroes" were used as slave labor at the Neuengamme concentration camp.[41]

While there were literally hundreds of camps and subcamps established by the Nazis in Germany and the occupied lands, there was an extremely organized system that created several layers of operations and functions. The Category I camps were the killing centers of which there were four: Chelmno, Belzec, Sobibor, and Treblinka. The purpose of these horrors was clear and simple: to kill as fast and as efficiently as possible as many people as possible who had the misfortune to end up there. All four centers were located in Poland. Category II-A camps were combination labor and extermination complexes. These two camps, Auschwitz/Birkenau and Majdanek, were also located in Poland. Mass exterminations also occurred at these sites. Category II-B camps were the "official" concentration camps sanctioned by the SS and the Gestapo chief, Heinrich Himmler. These eleven camps were Dachau, Sachsenhausen, Ravensbruck, Buchenwald, Flossenburg, Neuengamme, Gross-Rosen, Natzweiler, Mauthausen, Stutthof, and Dora/Nordhausen, most of which were located in Germany. In Category III was Bergen-Belsen, which was primarily a reception, holding, and transfer camp. And finally, in Category IV, was Theresienstadt, an entire town that functioned as a prison. The difference between Category I and the other categories was in the method and systemization of the killings. In every camp run by the Nazis, death was a constant and there was a relentless, obsessive search for more efficacious and quicker means of slaughter. The thousands of other camps established by the Nazis revolved around the ones noted and were designated as mainly subcamps.[42] The Nazis set up other means by which to mass-murder Jews, Russians, Gypsies, and others—most notably the Einsatzgruppen (Security Police) and Einsatzkommandos (Security Commandos), killing teams that roamed through the East. It would be in the camps, however, where the real systematic slaughter would take place.

Colored badges were used in the concentration camps to identify categories of inmates. Yellow badges were used for Jews, red for political prisoners and communists, pink for homosexuals, violet for Jehovah's Witnesses, black for asocials, brown for Gypsies, blue for immigrants, and green for habitual criminals. Often prisoners wore two overlapping triangle badges or a patch over the triangle with a letter on it that further identified their "crime" or status. What is notable here is that there was no badge that specifically designated people of African descent in the camps. In one sense, of course, for Blacks, their skin was their badge. For historical research, however, not having a badge has made it difficult to identify black inmates because the records based on the distribution of badges do not classify them by a specific category. Blacks in the camps could be and were labeled asocial, communist, homosexual, or Jehovah's Witness along with others. Further complicating matters, asocials included prostitutes, vagrants, murderers, pimps, beggars, thieves, lesbians, and race defilers, all "crimes" that Blacks were accused of frequently. Also, many of the smaller camps were destroyed, or there are no records available. Given that there were Afro-Germans in small towns all over Germany, especially in the West, it is likely that there were Blacks in the camps situated in those areas and that data is forever gone.

It has also been extremely difficult to find information on black women who were in the concentration camps. The suffering and degradation that women faced in the camps were, in many ways, much more severe than that faced by men. While a critical component of control for the Nazis was to strip inmates of all shades of human dignity, women were deprived additionally of every possible vestige of womanness and feminity. Women had to endure being sheared of all body hair, the loss of their menstruation cycle driven by extreme stress (or lack of sanitation if they did menstruate), rape, forced prostitution (what one victim termed "organized rape"), brutal abortions, and sterilization either by poison chemicals in their food or through X-rays that literally burned their insides. Extreme humiliation before death was the object of these methods.

In some cases, only sketches of information about black women inmates are available, and much more investigation must be done. For instance, it is known that there were Afro-German women at Ravensbruck, a concentration camp for women. Records from the camp received by Anderson identified only three for sure: Erica Ngando, Bolau J., and Johanna Peters. Ngando, who was born 5 July 1915, was recorded as a "negroid [sic] half-breed" who had been arrested as an "asocial." She entered the camp on 12 October 1940. Bolau J., born 7 September 1901, was listed as a "Protection prisoner," that is, political arrestee, and her nationality was listed as "Afr.," meaning African. It is unknown whether either survived. Further research by Anderson discovered one other black woman at the camp, Johanna Peters, but no other information was available about her. In addition, according to a 1998 BBC Channel 4 documentary on Jehovah's Witnesses in the camps, including Ravensbruck, there was at least one unknown black woman who was in the camp as a Jehovah's Witness.[43]

Even prominent Blacks who were well known in Germany were not protected. The Boholle family, who were originally from Cameroon and had been active in a number of black political and social groups during the 1920s, were sent to the Stutthof camp in Poland near Danzig. Before they were arrested, members of the family had been involved in the infamous "Africa Show" touring performing company and acted in Nazi propaganda and entertainment films about Africa. Although it is believed that most of the family died in the camps, Josef Boholle and Josefa Boholle both lived to see the end of Hitlerism.[44] Lesser-known and thought to be black or African camp prisoners for whom there are some official records include Charlie or Charly Mano, Abdulla Ben-Moosa, and Guillermito Ster, all interned in Sachsenhausen. There is little information on them other than their date of birth, when they arrived at the camp, and their prisoner status. It appears that Mano was released at some point, but that is impossible to verify.[45]

In addition to the Afro-Germans and Africans residing in Germany at the time, a number of unlucky African Americans and other Blacks were in the concentration camps. Sources for these data include some camp records, media reports, and official government documents. Notably, there are few autobiographies or first-person accounts available. Many of these individuals were entertainers who had refused to leave as warnings about Nazi invasion to the West grew. Either they did not believe the alarms or thought they would be exempt from the Nazi terror, and, indeed, many were for a while. However, even some of those who were initially left alone were eventually interned, even if only for a short time. Among them were the Paris-based jazz trumpet player Arthur Briggs who was sent to Saint-Denis on 17 October 1940. Records from Sachsenhausen also list Robert Demys, an African American. Demys is recorded as entering the camp on 22 June 1940 and given prisoner number 026019. His date of birth is listed, 20 May 1908, but no further details are available.[46] Lionel Romney, a black merchant marine fireman on the SS Makis, was captured by the Italians and turned over to the Germans after the ship was sunk on 17 June 1940. He was sent to Mauthausen where he was forced to do lumberjack work, which apparently got him extra food rations. Mauthausen was opened on 8 August 1938, near the city of Linz, Austria, with forty-nine subcamps. It is believed that more than 150,000 died there. It mostly functioned as a slave labor camp. Mauthausen was classified as a so-called category three camp, meaning that prisoners there were not to be returned (Rückkehr unerwünscht) and worked to death (Vernichtung durch arbeit). It is unknown whether Romney survived.[47] There were also Blacks at the Lodz concentration camp.[48]

Many of the African Americans who were interned were later traded for Germans. In March 1944, the Swedish ship SS Gripsholm arrived in New York carrying twelve black men and one black woman who had been in either internment or concentration camps. The men included a number of musicians including the pianist John Welch, the guitarist John Mitchell, and the horn player Freddy Johnson. The other men, some of whom were also musicians, included Henry Crowder, Maceo Jefferson, Reginald Berry, Jack Taylor, William Bowman, and George Welch (no relation). Mitchell had been in the Willie Lewis band and was arrested in Amsterdam on 11 December 1941, the day that Germany declared war on the United States. After being held in Holland for about a month, he was put on a train, along with Taylor, Johnson, and Bob Young, all African Americans, and sent to Germany. Visits to the unnamed camp from the Red Cross and the YMCA brought "cans of corn beef, pork meat, sardines, butter, condensed milk, coffee, cocoa, and prunes, orange powder, hard tack, cheese, three packages of cigarettes and smoking tobacco."[49] George Welch, who was arrested in Brussels, was sixty-two at the time of his arrival back in New York and had been out of the country for more than forty years. He had left the United States in 1901 to "travel the world."[50] Welch was sent to the Tittmorning concentration camp, which was located near Hitler's Bavarian retreat.

The one black woman who was on the ship was Evelyn Anderson Hayman. She had first gone to Europe in 1925 as part of the Josephine Baker revue. Hayman was held in a concentration camp near Liebenau, Germany. Through the Red Cross, she was able to get access not only to food and coffee, but also female items such as "lipstick, perfume, and face powder."[51]

In all the instances cited above, for the Afro-Germans, the Africans, and the African Americans, very few details are available on why these individuals were arrested in the first place, how they were treated while incarcerated, how they related to other prisoners, and what they ultimately thought about their imprisonment time. The authentic voices are few, and, of course, many of those who even made it out of the camps have since passed on. While a general history of Blacks in the concentration camps has yet to be written, there are fortunately, a number of instances where quite a bit of information is known on what happened to individual Blacks. These experiences vary from the unyielding cruelness of the worst concentration camps to the relatively benign imprisonment of the transition and civilian camps. Among those whose stories must be told are Bayume Muhammed Hussein (also known as Mohamed Husen), the Belgian Jean Johnny Voste, the Surinamese painter Joseph Nassy, the poet and political leader Leopold Sedar Senghor, the singer Johnny Williams (also known as Armand Huss), and the African American entertainer Valaida Snow. These cases provide evidence not only of how Blacks were treated in the camps but also of the tenacious will on the part of black victims to fight and often survive the Nazi death machine. All of these individuals suffered to different degrees at the hands of the Nazis, and their stories provide critical and previously unknown insights into the intersection of Negrophobia and fascism in the camps.

Bayume Muhammed Hussein (Also Known as Mohamed Husen)

Under National Socialism, "racial pollution" was a criminal charge, a pretext, of course, on which Afro-Germans, Africans, Jews, Gypsies, and others could be—and were— arrested and sent to the camps. As time passed, interracial or interethnic social intercourse of any nature could generate state repression; sexual intercourse, that is, racial pollution, would especially guarantee the harshest response and treatment from the Nazis. One black victim of this "crime" of racial defilement was Mohamed Husen, who was born Bayume Muhammed Hussein. Originally from German East Africa (Tanzania), he came to Germany in 1929 at the age of twenty-five. This was after his service during World War I on behalf of the Germans. As a soldier, Husen stood out and was awarded a number of war medals.[52] But, according to Michael, he felt that he had not gotten all that he deserved and sometime later, after Hitler had come to power, he demanded from the government a medal that he felt was due. Apparently, again states Michael, he had also brought a lawsuit of some sort against one of his German employers. These incidents, and perhaps other issues, won him a reputation as a "troublemaker," the last designation anyone would want in Nazi Germany.[53]

Husen was also upset that he and his wife had had their passports taken away from them in June 1933, a practice of creating "stateless" people that had happened to all the Africans who were in Germany during the period. While most, left with little democratic recourse, accommodated themselves to the situation this was another area of Nazi power that Husen rebelled against.

His troubles were perhaps tied to the desperate economic woes that he and most other Africans faced with their labor becoming less and less wanted as National Socialism marched forward. He held a number of jobs including those of waiter, barman, and even lecturer at a seminar for oriental languages at one of the universities in Berlin, this last postion reflecting a long history of employing African instructors. His luck would pick up, however, as the technological advances in moviemaking and the emergence of a vast German propaganda operation helped to create a Nazi film industry in which he and many other Africans and Afro-Germans would find lucrative employment. Work in the films generated not only a source of income but also a site of refuge for Husen. He appeared in a number of films, including *Knights of German East Africa,* which Michael characterized as "the first in the long row of colonial films" that the Nazis hoped would build their case for reclaiming their former colonies.[54] This film and others served the propaganda interests of the Nazis who used them to construct a narrative of colonialization in which the Germans are heroes, the Blacks are willing servants, and other imperialist states, such as England and France, are the enemy of both the Africans and the Germans.

While this film work provided Husen with a generally safe existence, and a reprieve of sorts, he continued to voice his complaints and thus was not able to escape the inevitable wrath of the Nazis. In August 1941, he was arrested and prosecuted on the racial pollution—*Rassenschande*—charge. The Gestapo's animosity toward him was clear in notes from a secret report on his arrest that read, "The charge 'racial pollution' was not sustained; no date set for his release."[55] The Nazis had fabricated a reason to arrest Husen, and now that they had him, they were not about to let him go. He was not given a trial and, instead, was turned over to the Gestapo. He was sent to the infamous Sachsenhausen concentration camp where he would die on 24 November 1944.[56] His twelve–year-old son Bodo would later be given his father's ashes. Bodo died during a 1945 bombing attack.

On 24 November 1999, a ceremony that included a visit to his gravesite was held in Germany commemorating Husen's life and his symbolic significance for those unknown and forgotten Blacks who died at the hands of the Nazis in concentration camps and elsewhere. Organized by Paulette Anderson and others, the event was attended by Husen's family members, Black activists, and even a government official.[57]

Jean Johnny Voste

Jean Johnny Voste, who was born in the Belgian Congo, was a prisoner at Dachau, one of the most infamous of all the concentration camps. Dachau was the setting for John A. Williams's novel, *Clifford's Blues,* the saga of a homosexual African American musician, Clifford Pepperidge, who is caught by the Nazis soon after Hitler comes to power in 1933, taken into "protective custody," and sent to the camp. In the novel, Pepperidge is in a constant battle of wits as he tries to survive the capricious and arbitrary nature of the Nazis and daily life in the camp where good and evil are in ever-changing form.

Voste had been active in the Belgium resistance movement.[58] Eventually, he was caught and arrested in May 1942 for acts of sabotage that he and others had been accused of commiting near Antwerp. The Nazis decided to send him to Dachau where he stayed until the end of the war. In the film *Black Survivors of the Holocaust,* a former camp prisoner, Willy Sel, remembers Voste fondly. He recalls that although he is not sure where he got them, Voste shared vitamins with his fellow inmates.

Amazingly, Voste managed to survive Dachau. On 29 April 1945, when soldiers from divisions of the 7th U.S. Army arrived, he was still breathing. There is a photo of Voste

Manoli Spiru and Jean Johnny Voste at the time of the liberation of the Dachau concentration camp. Frank Manucci, courtesy of USHMM Photo Archives.

and another inmate, the Greek Manoli Spiru, preparing some scraps of food after the Allies had liberated the camp. Written on the photo are the words "Liberation Feast." Although he lived through the experience, there is very little information on what life was like for Voste during his capture. In the picture, he looks very thin but relatively healthy compared with the usual image of gauntness and near-death fragility that dominates so much of our visual reading of what concentration camp inmates looked like at the time of being rescued. Voste is wearing a hat and shoes and sitting near Spiru, who has neither. It is not clear whether he received the shoes and hat just before the picture was taken, but his ability even to search for food is indicative of a will to live that was not broken by the Nazis.

Joseph Nassy

One of the more remarkable camp stories of the period is that of Josef Johan Cosmo Nassy who defied the odds and not only survived Nazi imprisonment but managed in his own unique way to chronicle a part of it through art. Nassy may have been the only black Jew—certainly the only known one—captured by the Germans during the war. Here you had, in one individual, the embodiment of two of the most despised and hated groups the Nazi racial hierarchy could possible conceive. The very existence of Nassy disrupted the racial boundaries established by the Nazis, some of whom believed that Jews were the "bastard" offsprings of Negroes and Asians.[59] Yet Nassy, for a number of reasons described below, survived to tell and display his remarkable tale. The road to internment at three German civilian prison camps for this prisoner-artist began in Suriname.

Nassy, a black Surinamese whose family was of Jewish religious background, was born in 1904 in Paramaribo into a prominent family in what was then Dutch Guiana. His father, ironically named Adolph, was a member of the national parliament and a descendant of Spanish Jews. Although his son and other family members were not practicing Jews, Adolph did retain his Jewish identity and did practice the ancient traditions of Judaism. There is little else known on the Black Jews of Suriname or, more generally, the practice of Judaism in the country. It is also possible that Adolph's religious practices may have been heavily influenced by his frequent trips to New York City.

By 1919, Adolph lived pretty much full-time in Brooklyn, and had two of his sons, Henri and Joseph, living with him. His wife, Caroline, never left the island and did not even attend her husband's June 1926 funeral in Brooklyn. Joseph and his siblings would eventually scatter to many different parts of the world: Percy and Jettie (Suriname), Henri (Aruba), Alwin (New York), Heidy (Holland), and Joseph (Belgium).[60] According to the Nassy researcher Monica Rothschild-Boros, Joseph never returned to Suriname.[61] To further his education, he studied electrical engineering at the well-known Pratt Institute. After graduation, he worked for the Melotone Corporation installing sound systems for the new talking pictures that were the emerging cultural rage. Soon, the company, which was a subsidiary of the Warner Brothers film studio, wanted Nassy to travel to Europe and work for them there.

On 29 July 1929, Nassy would unknowingly make a decision that would save his life years later when he was arrested and imprisoned by the Nazis. In applying for a passport to travel to Europe, he filled out the application for a "Native Citizen." For some unknown reason, he changed his name from "Joseph Johan Cosmo Nassy" to "Josef John Nassy." It is known, however, why he changed his birthdate from 19 January 1904 to 19 January 1899, and the place of his birth to San Francisco. The "great" earthquake of 1906 had destroyed nearly all the city's official records, and it was impossible to determine if someone had actually been born in the city prior to that time. Not only did Nassy claim American citizenship, his brother Alwin signed an affidavit stating that Nassy and their father were both born in San Francisco. His passport was issued on 30 July 1929, and he set sail the next day for Europe where he would spend the rest of his life.

Arriving in England, he began doing sound installations for Melotone. The following summer, he was sent to Paris to do the same type of work.[62] One year later, he was on his way to Belgium, which would become his home, for similar employment, now for the Gesco Company, a subsidiary of Melotone. Belgium would be good for Nassy. In 1935, he met Rosine van Aerschot, whom he married four years later.[63] She would be his lifeline to the outside world while he was incarcerated.

It was a measure of his character that Nassy was not satisfied with just being on the innovative edge of new technologies that were revolutionizing the global film and mass media industries: he also sought to fulfill his artistic inclinations. From 1938 to 1940, again finding the love for painting he had had when younger, Nassy enrolled at and attended the Academie de Beaux Arts in Brussels.[64] Though never to achieve the status of a great technical or brilliantly creative artist, he would become extremely competent and committed to his work.

With his refusal to heed the warning signs of the coming Nazi war machine and with Rosine's unwillingness to leave Belgium, the times caught up with Nassy. On 14 April 1942, Nassy was arrested by the Nazis, who had seized Belgium in spring 1940. He was initially sent to the Beverloo prison in Leopoldsburg, Belgium—which he apparently preferred—that functioned as a transit camp where prisoners captured in the occupied territories were held for a short time before being sent east to the more secure and hostile concentration camps. Later, he was transferred to Laufen and Tittmoning camps in southern Bavaria in Germany. At those camps, Nassy joined about two thousand U.S. citizens, some of whom were Black or Jewish. Although by no stretch were these country clubs, the internment camps were qualitatively different from the torturous and deadly concentration and death camps that the Nazis established in other parts of the conquered territories. In some of the civilian internment camps, prisoners would often be more under house arrest than being held in a regular prison. In these camps some prisoners were able to practice their artistic or musical talents while incarcerated. Nassy, for example, was able to get art supplies from the International Red Cross and the Swiss YWCA, both of which visited the camps regularly. This one act of self-interested rationality—the principle of committing no harm to U.S. and other Allied non-military captives—coming from an otherwise irrational regime was the basis for the relatively moderate treatment accorded arrested U.S. citizens. This was largely driven by the Nazi's need to have their own soldiers and nationals treated fairly and with minimum harshness. Nassy's documented evidence that he was "American" was a stroke of luck. He was fortunate in another equally important way. When he registered in Belgium as an American national with the U.S. Embassy, he did not list a religious affiliation. So, when arrested by the Nazis, he was not seen as a Jew, which likely would have been fatal no matter what national allegiance he claimed.

In the camp, he was tasked to teach art, and having relatively free time on his hands, Nassy painted portraits of his fellow inmates and everyday scenes of prison life. At Laufen, in addition to Nassy, there were about a dozen Blacks and about fifty Jews out of the five hundred men interned. The nationalities of the Blacks are not clear, but most were from Africa rather than being African American or Afro-European. There were other prisoners from Poland, Czechoslavkia, and other parts of Europe as well as the United States. At that camp, the prisoners were allowed to send three letters and four postcards a month, which Nassy did to his wife who was still in Brussels.

From 1942 to 1945, when he was freed, Nassy completed 277 sketches, drawings, and paintings. The images that dominate Nassy's work convey the despair and pain of being imprisoned with no end in sight. One art expert called Nassy's drawings a "visual diary." Susan Bachrach, who curated the collection, says, "We use these works not as examples of great art, but as artifacts which document an era." Nassy painted in vivid colors as well as sketching in black and white. His scenes consisted mostly of other inmates, black and white, doing ordinary daily activities such as reading a book, sitting at a table, or just walking around. Although the faces in most of his work do not look happy in the least, they also do not bear the demeanor of complete despair.

Fortunately, the commanders at the camps where Nassy was incarcerated were art lovers. Nassy and his artwork would survive the war. Since that time, it has been on display in Europe and the United States at various times. In 1992, the whole collection was donated to the U.S. Holocaust Historical Museum, which displayed the works in January 1998.[65]

Johnny Williams

In a 1999 interview in *New African*, Johnny Williams, who was held in Neuengamme and survived, stated that "There were six of us and as soon as we were taken there, we were separated from the white deportees. They considered us to be subhuman, like animals, chimpanzees."[66] The man who started life as Ernest Armand Huss would find his voice, in more ways than one, while a prisoner of the Nazis.

Williams was of mixed racial and national heritage. His mother was from the Ivory Coast and his father from Alsace, France, where he would go to live in 1922. He worked at the Sagem factory at Montlucon that became a target of the resistance movement after the Nazi takeover in 1940. The destruction of machines and other acts of sabotage created a dangerous situation for the young man of twenty-two. In fact, after the attacks began, he was warned not to return to the place because of the possibility of being accused of the acts. However, he did come back, and, in 1944, he and other workers were arrested, tortured, and forced to dig up unexploded bombs in a suburb of Paris. In May, he and the others were deported to the camps where many of them died. He was sent to Neunengamme, which contained, among others, many Senegalese.

Williams was told upon his arrival, "From now on you are not people, you are numbers."[67] Williams's life and the lives of some other Blacks were saved by the arbitrariness that characterized Nazi behavior. Initially, when most Blacks arrived at the camp they were separated by the camp guards and then sent to the showers that meant certain and immediate death. At the particular moment when Williams and some other Blacks came, the SS showed up and ordered them brought back. The SS men found the Blacks to be a curiosity, even rubbing their skins to see if the color would come off. One of the SS men said that Blacks were good athletes and, for whatever that meant to the SS officers, they decided that Williams and the others should not be killed. Williams believes that black victories in the 1936 Olympics and the Joe Louis fights against the German Max Schmeling in 1936 and 1938, somehow earned him and the others enough respect, even if indirectly, to rescue them from a terrible death. As a skilled machinist, Williams was tasked to work in the Walther arms factory.

Neunengamme was originally a regular prison. When it became a concentration camp, one of the largest and harshest, the criminals were made capos and put in charge of all the inmates. They were exceptionally brutal. In an atmosphere of betrayals and constant cruelties, Williams remembers daily killings by gassing, shootings, and hangings. He recalls the reduction of life down to its most basic needs, stating, "At Neuengamme, like in all other death camps, we satisfied ourselves with what we had . . . by necessity. Here it is the ultimate voice of wisdom to be satisfied by a simple life on every level, not to dream of the impossible."

While simply trying to make it to the next hour alive, Williams began to sing as a way to uplift his and his fellow captives' spirit. That "splendid voice," as one Italian voice teacher would later call it, would salve the pain of the camp inmates up until the time of liberation and freedom. Many of those survivors and other friends would strongly encourage Williams to pursue a singing career after the war, which he did to great success. As he would say later, "I didn't know of my vocal talents. I discovered them in prison where my companions constantly asked me to sing."

When the Germans evacuated the camp, they first made the prisoners walk for miles and then turned them over to the German Navy, who then passed them on to the Red Cross. They were put on three boats that unfortunately carried the German insignia, and two of them were sunk by Allied bombers. Williams was on the third and survived.

He believes that he drew many important lessons about life from his camp experiences. "The deportation taught me a great lesson," Williams recalls, "that man should be measured by the goodness of his heart and spirit, and not by the tag which he or others have posted on his back. Out there, we were all naked. Man revealed himself just as he is, strong or pathetic. The tragedy that we were living in stripped us to the bone." Meeting years later, Williams and some of the individuals he suffered with in Neuengamme shared their thoughts and feelings. According to Williams, "We concluded that we could not hate the officers who delivered all these massacres because they were only following orders." In 1983, he returned to the camp, now a memorial site, and even sang at a ceremony honoring those who were incarcerated and died there.

He later published a book of memories, *Si Toi Aussi Tu M'abandonnes* (*If You Also Abandon Me*), that became quite popular in France. Although he was able to rebuild his life after his camp experiences—he even receives a pension from the German government that was given to French deportees—and, in significant ways through the book and other interviews, he released many of the hard feelings, much of the pain remains. As he pointedly notes, "I will never get out of Neuengamme."

Valaida Snow

The life of Valaida Snow is imperfectly known.[68]

The mysteries of the jazz trumpeter Valaida Snow, who was captured, tortured, and eventually released by the Nazis, have only grown with time. Amazingly, not only have journalistic articles contained contradictory information, but even the spate of "well-researched" scholarly articles that have appeared in recent years conflict with one another in important ways. Questions regarding her year of birth, who her father was, whether she was mixed-race, and even her name are debated as fiercely as the issues surrounding her horrific experiences during the war. When did the Nazis capture her? Where was she detained and for how long? Was she in an internment camp or a concentration camp? Why was she released? What actually happened to her during her detainment? More than a half century after her incarceration and then release, there are as many questions as answers.

What is equally remarkable is the fact that so few have heard of Snow, let alone her tragic and compelling story. Despite the many areas of dispute regarding this remarkable but generally unknown black woman, there is a general consensus that by the time of the events that would be a watershed in her life, she was one of the best swing jazz trumpet players in the world. This was only one of many talents that would never be fully recovered in the time from her release to her death in 1956. Unfortunately, she did not leave a written or much of an oral record behind. In addition, many were skeptical about what she did have to say or write, so that much of her life has been cobbled together through anecdotes, journalistic articles, and even hearsay, as well as several scholarly articles. Even the scholarly pieces published about her life have major points of disagreement over critical details. There are a number of web sites devoted to her or to black women jazz artists in which she is included. These sites provide little detail about her life in general and virtually nothing regarding her experiences with the Nazis or in the camp. Fortunately, at the same time, they reflect a growing interest and desire to know more about her.

Female jazz instrumentalists, especially in the pre–World War II period, were rarely given the exposure, recording opportunities, and popular press that their male counterparts received. From the beginning of jazz, however, women players have participated in the music's creation and performance in every period, in every form, and in every style on every instrument. In the early 1900s, women pianists in New Orleans, such as Dolly Adams and Emma Barrett, and in Chicago, such as Lil Hardin Armstrong and Lovie Austin, made important contributions to jazz's development. In the first half of the twentieth century, all-women jazz groups formed although they were often segregated by race. In the 1920s, there were Bobbie Howell's American Syncopators and Bobbie Grice's Fourteen Bricktops, both white groups, as well as black groups such as the Harlem Playgirls and the renowned International Sweethearts of Rhythm. Besides Snow, other horn players of the pre-1950 era included the trumpet-playing mother and daughter team of Dyer and Dolly Jones; the trumpet players Billie Rogers, who performed with Woody Herman, and Jean Starr of the Benny Carter band; and saxophonists Elsie Smith of the Lionel Hampton band, Vi Burnside, and Margaret Backstrom.[69]

The exact year of Snow's birth is in dispute. By her own account, she gave different years, including 1900, 1903, and 1909.[70] At least one researcher has suggested 1905. Most do agree that she was likely born in Chattanooga, Tennessee, on 2 June of whatever year may be correct. Snow was probably biracial; her father, John V. Snow, was believed to be white, and her mother, Etta, was black.[71] Though this is not known definitively, Valaida's own words claim that she was mixed and also give some insight into her views on miscegenation. In 1934, she wrote in an article that appeared in the *Chicago Defender,* (having been originally published in the *London Daily Mirror*), "As it happens I am strongly against marriage between the two races, despite the fact that I myself am the result of such a fusion."[72]

Although John Snow was somehow involved in the entertainment field, very little is known about him, and he appears not to have played a large role in Valaida's life. For certain, her musical training came from her mother. Etta Snow, a graduate in music from Howard University, taught her children to play a wide number of instruments including the "cello, bass, violin, guitar, banjo, mandolin, harp, accordion, clarinet, and saxophone."[73] Here again, there is puzzlement about how many siblings Valaida had and even their gender. Reed writes that Valaida had a "sister and brother, Lavaida and Arvada," as well as an adopted brother, J. Gould Snow, whom she performed with as a child in a group billed as "Snow's Gold Dust Twins."[74] Mario Charles contends that Valaida had two sisters, "Alvaida and Lavaida," with whom she performed, and a brother, "Arthur Bush."[75] Rosetta Reitz, a well-known Snow researcher, adds another sister, Hattie, to the already confusing story.[76] It is clear, however, that she did have a sister named Alvaida whom some researchers have confused with Valaida. In any case, she apparently did not maintain the strongest ties with her sister(s) and brother(s), but did stay close to her mother.

Maturing as a performer in the early 1920s, she quickly rose to acclaim and found herself working with the great ones of the period including Ethel Waters, Louis Armstrong, Josephine Baker, Earl "Fatha" Hines, and William "Count" Basie, among others. Valaida began her serious adult career around 1920 in Philadelphia and Atlantic City, then went on to New York in 1922 with Barron Wilkin's Harlem cabaret. She was later in the program "Chocolate Dandies" as well as the legendary "Will Masten's Revue." She would soon take her talents to the rest of the world. From 1926 to 1928, she was in the Far East heading Jack Carter's band; she sang, danced, and played the trumpet. In 1929, she went to Russia, the Middle East, and then back to Europe. From then on, her career would zigzag between the United States and, primarily, Europe. In 1933, she was in a group with Earl "Fatha" Hines that played at Chicago's Grand Terrace Ballroom. She then returned to London where she conducted the "Blackbirds of 1934" revue band.[77] In 1936, she headlined a show at the Apollo in Harlem. Snow also played with the legendary Gypsy guitarist Django Reinhardt. She settled that year in Europe, mainly in Paris and the Scandinavian countries.

As befell other black women jazz musicians of the time, Snow faced a number of obstacles. Race was already a factor in the production, distribution, and consumption of jazz where an emergent white appropriation was occurring that sought not only to whiten the music to make it more accessible, but also to whiten the historiography of jazz, claiming its creation and perpetuation. Black jazz musicians, in the post–World War I period, found it increasingly difficult to get paying gigs, recording contracts, and radio time. In a sense, they were not seen as legitimate by the domineering forces in the music business. Even more so, there were efforts to separate the black musicians from their natural audience through the segregationist policies of major clubs in New York, Chicago, Philadelphia, and elsewhere. Despite these roadblocks, black jazz artists continued to create and persevere. For Snow, a woman in a male-dominated art who played a male-inscribed instrument, the trumpet, the situation was compounded.

Her talent, and the emerging popularity of swing, was too big to be contained inside the borders of the United States, and soon she was headed to Europe and other far-flung destinations. In Europe, Snow was called "Little Louis," a reference to the great jazz trumpeter Louis Armstrong.[78] This, as is always the case, is an unfair and sexist comparison that dismisses the capabilities that Snow demonstrated on her own without the unnecessary comparison to Armstrong. Other writers have also compared her to the New Orleans great; the jazz scholar Krin Gabbard, for example, refers to Snow's "distinctly Armstrongian style."[79] Will Friedwald is less charitable, opining that Snow "mimicked Armstrong" and was not that talented.[80] He does, however, concede that "Valaida broke down traditional notions of what male instrumentalists and female canaries are supposed to do" when one listens to her "exciting records."[81] That she could appropriate the Armstrong style and then create her own is important to recognize.

In order to make it, Snow not only played trumpet but also sang and danced, which, in most instances, was how bandleaders wanted to view her. She was sometimes unfairly criticized for making this choice. According to the entertainer Mary Lou Williams, "Snow's fame was due as much to her showmanship as to her playing abilities . . . She would have been a great trumpet player if she had dropped the singing and concentrated on the trumpet." Williams ignores the limited choices that Snow and other women had if they wanted to have a chance to play their instruments at all.

Snow also has very few published recordings. A search of music sites on the Internet reveals only two collections of her work.[82] These are compilations of her work from 1935–1940 and include standards such as "Minnie the Moocher," "Tiger Rag," "I Got Rhythm," "Swing Low, Sweet Chariot," "St. Louis Blues," "It Had to Be You," and "Singing in the Rain." Snow also tried her hand at some movie work. She sang the title song for two film shorts, *If You Only Knew* and *Patience and Fortitude,* in Los Angeles during this time.[83] Snow is also known to have claimed that she appeared in two Hollywood films, *Take It from Me* and *Irresistible You,* but neither film is known to have actually existed, according to Reed.[84] In France, where she was highly popular before the war, she did appear in *L'Alibi* (also known as *Snares*) in 1936 and *Pieges* (also known as *Personal Column*) in 1939.[85]

As an entertainer of growing fame, Snow lived an extravagant and ostentatious life. According to the pianist Bobby Short, she "traveled in an orchid-colored Mercedes-Benz, dressed in an orchid suit, her pet monkey rigged out in an orchid-jacket and cap, with the chauffeur in orchid as well."[86]

An Arresting Experience.   In late 1939, according to Reed, Snow was in Paris and became worried about the possible invasion and capture of France by the Germans. By then, it was clear that the Nazis' intentions toward Jews, Gypsies, and perhaps Blacks were harmful if not completely murderous. While it is not known how she expected Blacks or African Americans to fare under Nazi rule, self-preservation seemed to warn her that it was time to go. She decided to leave Paris, but instead of returning to the relative safety of the United States as many black musicians and entertainers in Europe had done, she went to Holland. Within a very short time, however, it became certain that

Holland would also fall soon to the Nazis, so she beat a retreat to Denmark. Unfortunately, as again Reed notes, "Snow had called all the shots wrong."[87] Like a fuming tidal wave across Europe, the Nazi war machine continued to roll westward. Having initially seized Austria in March 1938, then Czechoslovakia (March 1939) and Poland (September 1939), the Germans turned their attention to their western flanks. At exactly 4:20 A.M. on the morning of 9 April 1940, the governments of Denmark and Norway were informed that they were now under the "protection of the Reich," a perverse Nazi euphemism declaring their conquered status.[88] German troops, fighter airplanes, and warships were there to back up this assertion. While the Norwegians offered some resistance but would not be able to hold out, the Danes virtually surrendered on the spot. Ironically, France was not seized until June. If Snow had remained there, she might have had time to escape.

Morten Clausen notes that Snow performed in Copenhagen and other areas of Denmark throughout much of 1940. Then in early 1941, she reportedly became involved in some illegal drug activities, got into trouble with the authorities, and had her work permit revoked. Clausen claims that she then spent a little time in Sweden but was sent back to Denmark, where she was unable to work. This is where her life and destiny would be forever transformed.

Most accounts contend that the Nazis arrested Snow soon after they seized Denmark, and, at some point, she was sent to the Wester-Faengle internment camp in Copenhagen.[89] This is one of the most hotly debated areas of Snow's story. She was clearly not in a concentration camp, though this is reported in many accounts. It is possible that she may have also spent time in Westerbork, near Copenhagen. Westerbork was a transition camp that was initially established to house Jews who were then sent to concentration camps in the East. The camp grew rapidly, and many others besides Jews were placed there. It is notable that Snow is not listed in the U.S. National Archives database of POWs and civilian internees.[90] Dahl and others also note that there are conflicting reports about whether Snow was under house arrest or in a more serious category of incarceration, and how long she was kept.[91]

The liner notes of Snow's two-volume CD collection from Harlequin Records, written by Howard Rye (Volume I), and Morton Clausen (Volume II) do not mention her being in either a concentration camp or an interment camp as chronicled by nearly every other Snow researcher. According to Clausen, Snow was in a situation of "enforced idleness" for four months during early 1941, but was able to get permission to go and perform in Sweden for a few months. In November 1941, she was sent back to Sweden, where she could no longer make a living. At this point, Clausen does not say whether Snow was incarcerated or held by the Nazis or other authorities, where she was possibly held, and for how long. He notes next that she left Scandinavia on 28 May 1942 from Goteborg on a Swedish ship chartered by the U.S. government. Perhaps he felt there were too many unanswered questions about Snow's time of incarceration that he would rather avoid. Perhaps the producers of the CDs did not want to "politicize" the notes. In any case, the absence of any perspective on Snow's pivotal time under Nazi authority leaves in question a crucial time in her life.[92]

There is little doubt, however, that she was for a significant time in the clutches of the Nazis, who had little reason to treat her humanely or fairly. The basis on which she was arrested is unknown although, as already noted, Clausen cites illicit drugs as one possible basis. Under any number of laws passed by the Third Reich—or no laws at all—Snow could have been detained and put in "protective custody." The Nazis had no reason to justify or explain their behavior, and any explanation was meaningless. Many people were simply picked up and gone. Since Snow never fully discussed the experience for the record, little is known about the terrible ordeals she went through while in the hands of the Nazis for as much as eighteen months. According to one report, she was relieved of all her possessions, which was the usual practice, including "$7,000 in traveler's checks, all her jewelry and expensive clothes, and the gold trumpet that had been awarded her by Queen Wilhelmina of the Netherlands."[93]

Although she was an American, and was not placed in the worst of the camps, she was, as an African American and a black foreigner, potentially subject to excessive brutality. Reitz details one incident that was supposed to have occurred during her detainment. One day, while using her body in an attempt to protect a child who was being abused by prison guards, she fired up the wrath of the always sadistic camp guards. The guards turned on her and started to beat her badly and "split her head open causing blood to gush."[94] This incident would scar her for the rest of her days and be a permanent reminder of the horror she endured and survived. It was reported that after she tried years later to revive her career, she would attempt to comb her hair over the scar "in order to hide it."[95] In one of her very few statements on her detainment experiences, Snow writes in an article titled "I Came Back from the Dead," that beatings and lashings of prisoners, presumably including herself, were routine.[96] Prisoners were also nearly starved, according to Snow, and given "a single potato, three times a day," a diet reported by others who were imprisoned during the war.[97]

She finally surfaced in New York somewhere near the end of 1942 as a result of a prisoner exchange and the fact that she was a famous jazz musician. It is said that the Copenhagen police chief was a jazz fan and his fondness for Snow or for her music led him to arrange for her to be released through a prisoner exchange. One reason the Nazis were less barbaric toward Allied prisoners and citizens was that they wanted to be in a position to swap for important captured Germans. One report notes that Snow was swapped for Ann Hoffman, a manicurist on the SS *Bremen* and an infamous German spy. Under the watchful eye of the Gestapo, Snow was put on the SS *Gripsholm* in Portugal and returned to the United States in extremely poor health.

Overall, the ordeal had a devastating physical and psychological impact on Snow, leading a number of her old acquaintances in New York and the entertainment field to state that they did not recognize her upon her return. The experience also apparently led to her despondent mother's death from the stress. Reitz writes, "The rumor of Valaida's death in the camp literally killed her mother before she returned."[98] It is unknown if there was correspondence between Snow and her family during her internment. In a number of camps, prisoners could and did write and receive letters. Under the circumstances, letters were a lifeline to the world closed out by the camp's walls.

However, by the early 1940s, when Snow was imprisoned, the escalated war situation, in addition to Nazi reluctance, may have prevented any form of communication from occurring. In any case, Snow returned to New York having to face not only her own recovery but the knowledge and pain of her beloved mother's passing most likely due to the stress and anxiety associated with her arrest and detainment. After her return, she later married her manager, Earle Edwards, who helped nurse her back to health. As early as 1943, she tried valiantly to restart her career. She performed at least once that year at the Apollo in Harlem, and could sometimes be seen hanging out with other famous celebrities, such as the heavyweight champion boxer Joe Louis.[99]

Those who performed with her during this period recalled someone who was still very talented but clearly and permanently scarred by her ordeal. Clora Bryant, who performed with her, states, "There was Valaida Snow. She was playin' at a theater in town when I saw her—they put on real good shows there—and she was *good*." [100] The trombonist Melba Liston was less charitable in her remembrance. She states,

> I worked on a show with Valaida Snow. Now, there was something about her, the way she acted, that saddened me and that I never forgot. This was right there at the Lincoln Theatre. I said, 'Boy, when I get her age I'm not going to let that happen to me—whatever it was. She was so talented, so beautiful and so sweet. But she was so unhappy. She was like hurt all the time. In my youth I didn't understand. But I felt the pain from her all the time. I figure she must have been forty-something, and she didn't last much longer. I loved that lady! There was that confusion there that I couldn't understand in my youth, but I promised myself—when I get old, I'm not gonna be onstage with my trombone and let nobody do that to me. [101]

Snow's life would end doing what she loved best. On 9 May 1956, after performing at New York's Palace Theater, she suffered a massive stroke caused by a cerebral hemorrhage. Perhaps the strain of trying to return was too much, although it had been more than a dozen years since her war experience. She lingered on for twenty-one days in Kings County Hospital, finally succumbing on 30 May. She was buried on 2 June, her birthday, in Brooklyn's Evergreen Cemetery.

In recent years, a number of scholars and artists have rediscovered Snow. Research on her life continues, and there was even a play about her. In 1999, the University of Georgia's Black Theatrical Ensemble presented a musical drama, *Valaida*, based on her life and music. Professor Freda Scott Giles, who is a specialist in African American theatre, directing, and acting, wrote the play.

Snow and countless other women jazz musicians have been the orphans of the genre. While vocalists from Bessie Smith, Ella Fitzgerald, Sarah Vaughn, Billie Holiday to the modernists such as Cassandra Wilson, Anita Baker, Diane Reeves, and Rachel Farrell, to name only a few, are rightfully celebrated, women jazz instrumentalists have been ignored. Contemporary jazz, however, can be proud of the rich music and unstoppable talents of great players such as the jazz violinist Regina Carter, the flutist Bobbi Hutchinson, the guitarist Mimi Fox, and the pianist Keiko Matsui, to name only a very few. Fortunately, it has been increasingly recognized that no history or contemporary understanding of the significance of jazz is complete without appreciation of the pivotal contributions of women who committed themselves to the art despite all the obstacles in their way. Snow's story is particularly compelling because she embodied so much potential that was tragically thwarted by political forces beyond her control. It will never be known how much she would have influenced the trumpet and jazz in general if given the opportunity. As the journalist Bill Reed notes, Snow was "a jazz trumpeter who didn't merely 'play well for a woman,' but was tops in her field."[102]

The writer Carmen Moore perhaps best captures the meaning of Snow when she writes, "She was black, outspoken in seven languages and good-looking and smart rather than beautiful and dumb, so it's perhaps a tribute to her ingenuity and iron will (lightly-veiled behind a panther-taming smile), that she was not chained down and jailed in the U.S."[103] Despite her confinement, Snow prevailed and remains a symbol of the tenacity and unyielding spirit of jazz women who refuse to submit and who live their choices uncompromisingly.

Leopold Sedar Senghor

The prison camps also held a future African president: Leopold Sedar Senghor (1906–2001), who in 1961 would become the first president of an independent Senegal. In many ways, it was in the camps that Senghor found his negritude voice that later resonated as one of the most influential discourses of liberation rising out of and through the Africa continent and her diaspora. Negritude was the political-cultural movement and ideology, rooted in the cultural notions of the Harlem Renaissance writers Claude McKay, Langston Hughes, and Sterling Brown, that blossomed in the late 1940s and 1950s led by writers and intellectuals such as Aime Cesaire, Leon Damas, and Senghor.[104] Criticized as fostering a black bourgeois expression, negritudists contended that all people of African descent shared a common African way of thinking and being, and that that essence should form the basis for the construction of a liberated Africa. In the 1960s and 1970s, a major debate emerged in Africa between those who advocated negritude, such as Senghor, and Marxists and leftist political leaders, such as Guinea's Sékou Touré, Guinea Bissau and Cape Verde's Amilcar Cabral, and Mozambique's Samora Machel. For Senghor, it was the fulcrum of his camp experiences that helped to shape both his politics and his cultural philosophy.[105]

He achieved critical acclaim as a poet in his native country and abroad, and if there is any substance to the truism that suffering breeds imagination and inspiration, then being held captive by the guardians of National Socialism was Senghor's rite of artistic passage. Senghor was in a number of camps, and many of his most famous poems were written during his sojourn in Nazi hell. Before entering the French colonial forces, he had been a teacher and intellectual, but camp life and its demands were a leveler, and Senghor constructed bonds with peasants and working-class compatriots that would stimulate his political and cultural ideas for decades to come.[106]

Senghor was first called up to serve in 1939 but failed the physical examination because of poor eyesight and was sent home. Less than a year later, as the French situation became more and more perilous, he was called up again and enrolled along with thousands of other Africans. Senghor was a member of the legendary Tirailleurs Senegalais, the military unit that fought on behalf of the French in World Wars I and II. These troops, after their service to France, were given citizenship rights and privileges.

On 20 June 1940, Senghor was taken prisoner while defending the bridge at La Charité-sur-Loire.[107] He would eventually spend time in seven different camps including Poiters at Frontstalag 230, Charité-sur-Loire, Romilly-sur-Seine, Troyes, and Amiens, among others.[108] In many instances, the camps that held the African POWs were more like labor camps with prisoners tasked to a wide range of duties. Some African prisoners found themselves working on farms as hired prison labor, while others were domestic and personal servants for German officers. The type of work assigned to the Africans embodied the difference in how the Nazis viewed them as opposed to Jews and Gypsies. The visceral hatred for the latter two groups meant few, if any, would hold positions as personal servants to any Germans.

Life for Senghor in the camps was far from ideal, but ultimately it was a crucial transitional period for him. First and foremost, a leveling occurred and he found himself peered with peasants and working-class Africans who re-created their cultural life from the many villages that were represented there. He experienced a cultural reawakening that included telling stories, music played on a makeshift kora (a traditional Senegalese instrument), and writing poems. Many of his prisoner poems would end up in his second published collection, *Hosties Noires* (*Black Hosts or Black Victims*).[109] *Hosties Noires* is primarily concerned with the themes of service, sacrifice, and loyalty to France by black soldiers from Africa.

In spite of the sacrifices made by African troops, there were often conflicts and at least one serious massacre of Senegalese soldiers by the French. On 1 December 1944 at Thiaroye, a reparation center where Senegalese who had fought in the war waited before being shipped home, a now obscure provocation ended with twenty-four Senegalese troops being killed, eleven seriously wounded, and another thirty-four put into detention. This incident would be one of many that angered the entire colony and fed a growing anticolonial sentiment. It reflected the French determination to demonstrate that after the war France would still be in command, while, at the same time, it foreshadowed the will of blacks to no longer see themselves as subjects, especially given the years of military duty that thousands had performed. The fact that the French initially attempted to cover up the incident only furthered exacerbated the feelings of resentment and militancy spreading among the younger generation of Senegalese. Senghor wrote a poem expressing his strong feelings about the killings and his incipient disillusionment with France. In the poem, which he called "Tyaroye," he lamented, "Is it true that France is no longer France?"[110] He was expressing his recognition that what he had perhaps perceived as the ideal France was contradicted by the reality of French power.

In other poems, he praises soldiers, women, and others who fight and gave their lives in the name of justice, freedom, and peace. The last poem in the volume is titled "Priere de paix" ("A Prayer for Peace"). While the poem calls for peace in regard to bringing a just end to the European war and forgiveness on the part of Africans for their maltreatment by the French colonial authority, it should not be read as a statement of conciliation. In fact, it appears to be more of a warning of the rising tide of dissatisfaction that colonial subjects had toward their colonial status. It is especially notable that privileged and middle-class Blacks, who like Senghor were given opportunities and a chance at assimilation, emerged as a new leadership class to guide the independence movement a few short years after the war. This leadership would embody the conflicting tendencies between desiring political freedom and seeing oneself as culturally French. Senghor attempted to address this contradiction with his famous statement that the goal of the African was "to assimilate, not to be assimilated."[111] He also argued through his poetry that Africans did not die in vain.

> No you did not die for nothing you who are dead!
> This body is not lukewarm water.
> Thickly it waters our hopes which ill blossom at twilight.
> It is our thirst, our hunger for honour, those great princes
> No you did not die for nothing. You are witnesses of undying Africa
> You are witnesses of the new world that will be tomorrow
> Sleep O Dead, and let my voice cradle you, my voice of anger cradled by hope.[112]

The camps were an opportunity for tremendous intellectual and political growth for Senghor. While in captivity, he learned German well enough to read literature and philosophy including Goethe.[113] Yet he recognized and argued that the emerging African leadership, in prison and out, must also learn as much about African traditions, languages, and cultural practices as it could, and that they should take advantage of the opportunity to learn from and associate with Africans from all classes.

In February 1942, Senghor was finally able to have a French doctor in the camp at Poitiers declare him afflicted with some unknown "colonial disease," and he was released back to Paris.[114] While the diagnosis made by the doctor may have been manufactured, Senghor's physical deterioration was not, and it took him some time to heal from his experience. After recovering, he found himself in a France that was at war with itself as the Vichy government became less and less legitimate while the Nazis in charge turned more brutal and desperate. Senghor ostensibly went back to teaching, the work he had done before the war. In fact, like hundreds, if not thousands, of the Africans in France, he participated in the underground resistance movement. He became an active member of the Front National Universitaire, for which he received the coveted French Franco-Alliee medal after the war.

After the war, Senghor became a global leader in the Negritude movement and his writings were central to the debate over the nature of blackness and what strategies would unite and move Africa (and the diaspora) forward. In 1961, he became president of Senegal, a post he held until he left voluntarily in 1980. He was generally seen as representative of bourgeois class interests though devoid of the brutality and crude despotic characteristics of some other African leaders of the period.

Black Liberators

One controversy regarding the role of black U.S. soldiers during the war has to do with their participation in the liberation of the concentration camps. The Allies stated that their goal, as the war was coming to an end, was first and foremost to destroy the Nazis and capture Berlin. The liberation of the camps was secondary and left to the troops who were in the back lines, where the black troops were disproportionately positioned. In this role, two divisions of black troops, the 183rd Engineer Combat Battalion and the 761st Tank Battalion, were situated to help in the liberation of some of the camps in 1945. According to the documentary and accompanying book *Liberators,* soldiers from these divisions were among the first troops to enter the Dachau and Buchenwald camps.

Controversy arose after the documentary was broadcast on Boston public television station WGBH on 11 November 1992. A number of veterans' organizations and conservative publications declared that the video was based on falsehoods and misrepresentations. This reaction included articles by Jeffrey Goldberg in *The New Republic* (8 February 1993, titled "The Exaggerators"), Christopher Ruddy in the *New York Guardian* of December 1992, and Eric Breindel in the *New York Post* on 6 February 1993. The critics charged that the divisions in question were nowhere near the camps and were not in a position to participate in their liberation. As proof of their claim, they note truthfully that there are no army records showing that either the 183rd or 761st were officially in the areas of Buchenwald and Dachau at the time of their liberation. However, they then made a giant leap in logic and, despite the testimony and statements of black soldiers and camp survivors, concluded that the film was simply lying. They ignored the fact that at that stage of the war everything was chaotic and divisions and battalions were breaking up and regrouping on a continual basis. It was impossible to know accurately who was anywhere. In fact, there are missing and misleading army records concerning the entire last stage of the war. The protests were effective, however, and several local public television stations and the national PBS network refused to rebroadcast the film.

There was also an important report, *The Liberators: A Background Report,* done for the American Jewish Committee by Kenneth Stern, that was in many ways critical of the film but also positive on many points.[115] Overall, the Stern report acknowledged the immense difficulty of attempting to document what was a muddled and frenzied time and that probably most of the controversial issues will never be fully solved. Opponents of the film, who used the negative statements in the report to bolster their case, ignored perhaps the most significant passage of all:

> It should be understood that there is no claim here that either the survivors or the veterans of the 761st have lied about their recollections . . . After talking with survivors, archival experts, and members of the black units in question and meeting with the film's producers . . . *it is clear to me that the message of the film—that black soldiers were among the liberators of concentration camps—is absolutely true*[116] [emphasis added].

The producers of the film refuted their critics' allegations and offered an abundance of evidence to back up their case. First, there is the testimony of a number of former concentration camp inmates who vividly remember seeing black soldiers among the troops that initially rescued them. The Buchenwald survivor Gunter Jacobs stated, "The first black people I ever saw in my life were the black soldiers who liberated us on April 11, 1945. I don't even have to close my eyes to see those people in front of me. There's no mistake in my mind, no doubt whatsoever. If ever I was 100 percent sure of anything, this would be it."[117] Another survivor who has strongly supported the film's producers is Ben Bender. He simply stated, "I was seeing black soldiers for the first time in my life, crying like babies, carrying the dead and the starved and trying to help everybody. That's the way it was."[118] The Nobel Laureate Elie Wiesel made no bones about what occurred on the morning of 11 April 1945 at Buchenwald. He wrote passionately, "I will always remember with love a big black soldier. He was crying like a child—tears of all the pain in the world and all the rage. Everyone who was there that day will forever feel a sentiment of gratitude to the American soldiers who liberated us."[119]

Then, of course, there is the testimony of the black soldiers who were there on the spot. The tank driver William McBurney, who crashed through the gates of Dachau, stated, "I thought I had come into a prisoner-of-war camp. It looked like the land of the living dead. They were nothing but walking skeletons. We carried food on the backs of our tanks because our food kitchens couldn't keep up with us. We gave some people food but that was the worst thing we could have done. They just weren't used to real food. Some of them got sick."[120] Other black soldiers describe graphically how shocked they were to come upon freshly murdered bodies. Preston McNeil, of the 761st, stated, "I walked to the back of the building where this doctor had just put people to give them showers and gas them. And I just cried and cried. I said, 'I can't believe what I see.' No one in my life span can tell me it's propaganda because I really saw it."[121]

It took almost fifty years, but the black troops finally won recognition. In 1992, the Anti-Defamation League honored the 761st Tank Battalion as being part of the first contingent to enter the Buchenwald and Dachau camps.[122] Black troops that were part of the 761st were also involved in the liberation of Gunskirchen, a subunit of the Mauthausen concentration camp in Austria, where 15,000 Hungarian Jews were being held.[123]

Neither the documentary, the book, nor any interviewees mentioned the presence of Blacks in the concentration camps they entered. As noted earlier in this chapter, the Afro-Belgium Johnny Voste was at Dachau at the time of liberation. There had been at least one Black, Johnny Nicholas, at Buchenwald, although he was gone by the time the camp was liberated. More broadly, the film and book did not acknowledge the presence of Blacks in Germany or as captives of the Nazis at all.

Summary

African captives who were liberated by Western forces fared better than some of their counterparts who were in camps captured by the Soviets. Inexplicably, a small number of black French soldiers ended up as forced laborers under Soviet authority and, reportedly, were treated more harshly than they had been under the Nazis. The Soviets held them, and apparently some black Germans, for three to four years after hostilities had ended.[124]

While this chapter addresses only Blacks in the camps in Germany and the occupied European terroritories, there were black captives across the theater of war. In the Pacific and in Africa, the Japanese and the Italians held Blacks, on the Axis side, and, in Africa, the British and French detained those Africans who fought on behalf of the Italians, Germans, or Vichy government. In addition, South Africa recruited more than 200,000 Coloureds and Blacks for the Non-European Army Service (NEAS) who saw military action in Africa and the Middle East, and many were captured and sent to German POW and concentration camps.[125] Many of the NEAS prisoners were incarcerated at the infamous and brutal Babenhausen (Germany) and Chartres (France) POW camps.[126] Others were sent to Stalag 17A in Austria.[127]

For those Blacks in Germany who were not in the camps and were trying desperately to maintain that status, they found themselves in service to the Nazi state in other ways that were not always necessarily objectionable, given the circumstances. If a person could sing, dance, act, or in some other manner meet the entertainment-propaganda proclivities and needs of the Third Reich, there was more than a good chance for survival.

Imagining Blackness

Negrophobia and the Nazi Propaganda Machine

In order to pursue a policy of German culture, it is necessary to gather together the creative artists in all spheres into a unified organization under the leadership of the Reich. The Reich must not only determine the lines of progress, mental and spiritual, but also lead and organize the professions.
    —*The law establishing the purpose of the Reich Chamber of Culture*[1]

Within Nazi Germany, cultural management would play a significant and dual role in articulating the racial and political agenda of the Third Reich. First, control of the cultural superstructure allowed the Nazis to manage the popular construction of national identity and purpose. No arena of culture was left to chance, and artistic creativity was only acceptable within the framework of National Socialism. Second, the distracting role of mass entertainment—filtered through state-mediated institutions—became increasingly necessary for a nation at war both within and without. The Nazis made Blacks and blackness critical elements of the cultural discourse and performances of the period. Afro-German and African performances in theater shows and films paradoxically provided a sanctuary for these performers from an antagonistic state while, at the same time, furthering the propaganda imperatives of Nazism that advocated, among other objectives, the subjugation, degradation, and elimination of those of African descent. Whether it was the "German Africa Show" or the African colonial films, the black presence in the Nazi cultural machinery functioned through this duality in an interdependent fashion creating simultaneously survivors and subversives. As unwilling propagandists for the Nazi state, some black survivors would harbor deep conflicts and guilt over the role they were forced to play, to save their lives, for the rest of their lives.

The Nazi state recognized early the pivotal role that mass and popular culture could play in the consolidation and reification of Nazism. Immediately after seizing power, the Ministry of Culture was created and Paul Joseph Goebbels, whose model approaches to propaganda and cultural hegemony would influence these areas for decades to follow, was placed in charge. A failed writer, Goebbels's force of personality would be nearly as strong as Hitler's in its reach and breadth in shaping the image and consumption of the Third Reich. All of the arts were Nazified, while works by Jewish artists, painters, musicians, and other cultural workers and artists who were not Aryan were expressively *verboten*. Non-Nazi cultural works were systematically discredited and, where possible, destroyed. The book burnings that began on 10 May 1933, only four months after Hitler came to power, in a number of cities across Germany symbolized dramatically the suppression and destruction of any independent, creative, tolerant, and critical cultural production for the next dozen years.[2] Goebbels's Reich Chamber of Culture created seven divisions under which it would control and manipulate Germany's cultural life: fine arts, music, theater, literature, press, radio, and films. This would be the grandest and most ambitious effort at cultural control by a state in modern history. Of course, it would be impossible to conceive of a fascist order that did not acknowledge and attempt to take charge of the nation's cultural life. The political scientist Murray Edelman notes, "The Nuremberg festivals and other celebrations of Nazi power constructed a mythical paradise of heroes and a mythical hell for their enemies that diverted attention from everyday struggles and problems and created general enthusiasm for the Nazi leaders and their policies, no matter how difficult or odious they would have seemed without the cynical translation of repressive government operations into spectacle."[3]

Germany during the 1920s was alive with foreign entertainers, especially African Americans. Recovering from war's devastation, wealth generated from industrialization and a solid and sizable middle class with lots of disposable income led to an explosion of clubs and cabarets. In the mid-1920s, Germans were ready to enjoy life again and Berlin became the epicenter of the revival. And although the United States had been a decisive part of the alliance that defeated Germany, anatagonism against Americans was muted and U.S. musicians, including African Americans, found wide (though not universal) acceptance by their hosts. Indeed, there were German agencies specifically focused on bringing black talent to the continent. According to the researcher Paulette Anderson, the Martinell entertainment agency was the main booking company in Europe responsible for getting black acts from the United States. The agency was able to exploit a push-pull situation. The pervasive segregation that existed in the States pushed many African American performers to seek more friendly places to develop and perform their art. At the same time, they were pulled by the desire of Europeans who craved black entertainment.

Germany had been very hospitable to black entertainment, particularly from the United States, since the end of the nineteenth century. As noted earlier, from the Fisk Jubilee Singers to Josephine Baker, Germans had been exposed to African American cultural expressions. Among the black entertainers who came to Germany in the pre-Nazi period were the Bohee Brothers, Seth Weeks, Belle Davis, Hampton and Bowman, the Musical Spillers, Edgar Jones, the Black Troubadours, the Louisiana Troupes, Will Garland, Arabella Fields, the Black Diamonds, and Louis Douglas. All of these artists are featured in Rainer E. Lotz's book *Black People: Entertainers of African Descent in Europe, and Germany.*[4] In the years preceding Hitler's Germany, many black performers from around the world made their mark in Berlin and other major and even small cities.

Among the Blacks who made their success in Europe, and Berlin in particular, were the dancers Louis Douglas, Dora Dean Johnson, and Charles Johnson. Douglas was born in Philadelphia on 14 May 1889. He began his entertainment career as a child juggling plates and dancing. In 1903, Douglas first came to Europe with the singer Belle Davis at the age of fourteen (though listed officially as eleven). It is unclear whether Davis's troupe made it to Germany then, having disembarked initially in England, but a year later, in 1904, the group spent the whole summer in Germany. In the following years, Douglas would spend a great deal of time in Hanover, Berlin, and other major German cities. Although framed by a racist language and environment of white supremacy, he became extremely popular in Germany, generally referred to as the "king of nigger [*sic*] dancers."[5] In 1927, he performed with the great Josephine Baker, who referred to him as "a rubber man."[6] Douglas last performed in Germany in October 1931.[7]

The Nazis had sought to ban black performances as soon as they came to power. Even prior to Hitler, a backlash had begun against black performers. In 1931, a law was passed that outlawed the employment of foreign musicians except for concert soloists. This legislation would have a disproportionate impact on African American entertainers. Yet the Nazis would soon find themselves employing Blacks to serve the interests of the fascist state.

Blackness and Nazi Propaganda

The Nazi use of blackness and Blacks in their propaganda went through several stages with different points of emphasis. Prior to the Nazis' coming to power, Blacks were vilified by the Nazi leadership as exemplified throughout Hitler's *Mein Kampf.* This rhetoric would retreat somewhat after Hitler came to power when the foreign policy objectives of the state dictated a more moderate tone. The Nazis explicitly decided, at one point, to warn against any harsh or undue treatment of Blacks, particularly African natives. This new dispensation had more to do with the strategic objectives of Nazism than with a new morality or racial tolerance. In fact, once the state decided that the Africans and Afro-Germans were not to be collectively eliminated or sent immediately to concentration camps, it discerned a variety of propaganda means by which they and discourses on blackness could be used to further the Nazi cause. This included juxtaposing Nazi treatment of Afro-Germans and Africans with the racist indignities and violence that African Americans had to endure in the United States; the use of black actors in documentary and entertainment films; the state-controlled "Africa Show," an entertainment vehicle with clear political purposes; and, as the war was being lost, the dissemination of leaflets and flyers warning Europe of a black takeover should the Germans be defeated. Nazi propaganda was aimed first and foremost at the German people. The objective was to convince and to reinforce the authority of Hitler's vision of Aryan world dominance. In criticizing other states, a backhanded strategy was employed that sought to demonstrate approvingly the racist nature of other Western European nations and the United States. The Nazis were actually arguing that it was O.K. to be racist and that other (white) states should take responsibility for their role in furthering the racial contract of white supremacy. For this task, all branches of Nazism and the state were employed, as well as many different media.

Cartoons were one major form of media that was employed. They were used to simultaneously justify Nazi treatment of Jews and demonstrate the practice of racism in the United States. In the 24 November 1938 issue of *Das Schwarze Korps* (*The Black Corps*, newspaper of the SS), there is a cartoon that illustrates the racial propaganda war being waged against the United States. (See figure 1.) A white man wearing a T-shirt with both "USA" and a Star of David on it, is ranting against the "barbarism" of the Nazi state in its conduct toward Jews. The man is made to appear to have stereotypical Jewish "features." Behind him are two black men. The one on the left is being executed in an electric chair, while the one on the right is hanging from a noose with a sign pinned on him that reads, in English, "Lynch."[8] The cartoon seeks to expose a contradiction where the U.S. government (or its Jewish citizens) raises criticism of Germany's treatment of Jews while failing to address its own racial problems and issues, that is, the public and private executions of African Americans. This cartoon was printed in Germany, so it did not and was not intended to reach a U.S. public. It can be assumed that the target audience was the larger German public that needed to be reassured that its views and practices toward Jews were valid and perhaps not that different from how other states treated their minority or marginalized populations. To a certain degree, it can be assumed that Blacks in Germany at the time were being targeted and were also being told that life in the United States was not that receptive for people of African descent. The point is also being made that Jews control the debate about race and policies in the United States. This politics of race that the Nazis ascribed to the United States, which did not differ from many of the same criticisms and hypocrisies raised by some African American leaders and media, demonstrated a sophisticated and close reading of U.S. race dynamics.

Hypocrisy, of course, was two-way in this instance. The Nazi treatment of Jews was barbaric. The Nazis did not argue that they were treating the Jews any better than African Americans were being treated, only that it was hypocritical for the United States not to acknowledge its own complicity in racist practices. By 1938, when the cartoon appeared, the Nazis had not only passed laws against the Jews and attacked them physically, as occurred in that same year on 9 November, also known as *Kristallnacht*, the infamous "night of the broken glass," but had begun to round them up and send them to the concentration camps. The Germans had also begun massive sterilization of Afro-Germans and some Africans, as well as other groups. And for all of their patronizing rhetoric regarding the plight of African Americans, the Nazis still considered Blacks as well as Jews to be less than human.

Der letzte Schrei

Zeichnung: Bogner

„... und so protestieren wir im Namen der Menschlichkeit
gegen die barbarischen Methoden Deutschlands!"

Figure 1. Das Schwartz Korps (the Black Corps), newspaper of the SS, cartoon showing black men being executed and lynched while a Jewish man criticizes Nazi treatment of the Jews in Germany.

In a similar cartoon (see figure 2), also produced in November 1938, *Das Schwarze Korps* has a comic strip of a white man talking to his fellow Jewish passenger—his name is "Mr. Cohn" and he has a stereotypically large nose—on a New York subway. The first man is telling the second about how nonracist life is in the United States. The former, bragging in light of the black victories in the 1936 Olympics and the 1938 Joe Louis fight with Max Schmeling, is noting how "our best track star, our world champion boxer, comes from the ranks of the . . . " when he is interrupted by a black man who sits down beside him. The white man gets up and punches the black man and drives him away. He resumes his conversation saying, "These Niggers are always getting fresher! This imprudent one thinks he can sit down in the compartment for whites! Oh well.

Figure 2. Das Schwartz Korps (the Black Corps), newpaper of the SS, cartoon criticizing the hypocrisy of white Americans.

Where was I? Oh yes, we Americans are against racism, we ... " As with the previously mentioned cartoon, the Nazis are again targeting contradictions between what is exposed as a loudly articulated principle of equality and the reality of hard-core discrimination. This cartoon focuses on the ordinary white American rather than the state. The white man in the cartoon is oblivious to the incongruity between his words and his actions. The Nazis' familiarity with the Jim Crow segregation laws regarding public transportation is also evident although New York did not have formal laws or social practice against Blacks and Whites sitting together on the subway. In fact, in New York City, despite normal racial tensions, white, black, Asian, and Hispanic coexistence was the norm, including the shared use of public facilities. What is also insightful here is the recognition of how often the cultural and athletic talents of African Americans are embraced even by those with hardened racist views who would, at the same time, vehemently and physically deny all Blacks political and civil rights. The attack on the black man is unprovoked other than that his attempt to sit down is an affront to the racial construction of white power as expressed in the racist legal and social doctrine of "sep-

arate, but equal." It is also important that the Jewish passenger does not come to the rescue of the black man, sending a message that Blacks cannot count on Jews to assist them
in their battle against racism.

The theme of U.S. hypocrisy regarding black American oppression was repeated in
many German newspapers. The *Preussiche Zeitung*, in 1937, published an article titled
"The 'Cruel German Racial Theory' and Its Comparison Abroad," and, in 1939, the
Nationalsozialistische Partei Korrespondenz published the article "Double Standard in
the U.S."; both pointed to the fact that the United States had Jim Crow laws in place
long before the Nazis came to power.[9] Again, comparisons between African Americans
and Jews emerge as when the *Berliner Borsenzeitung* wrote, "The Nigger would well be
surprised that the white American becomes outraged at the elimination of Jews from
German universities, while they do not even consider the exclusion of Negroes from
many American universities."[10] This statement is interesting from several lights. First,
African Americans would not be shocked at the disconnect between support for human
rights externally and denial of rights for Blacks. Second, a racist slur is used at the
beginning of the sentence, but a formal reference is used at the end. Again, I would
underscore that the Nazis are not exactly advocating the opening up of higher education for African Americans.

Blackness for the Nazis became a useful instrument of propaganda and ideology. It
afforded an opportunity to counterattack one of its enemies on the same grounds on
which it was being accused. Interestingly, there is no evidence that the Germans ever
charged the United States with practicing anti-Semitism. This was due, in part, to the
fact that they did not oppose such practices, and also because they believed that the
United States government was unduly influenced, if not totally controlled, by Jewish
forces. Naturally, this logic overlooked the strong strain of anti-Semitism that did exist
in the United States. Anti-Semitism was rampantly manifest in covenants against selling
properties to Jews, stereotypes in the media, and even in physical attacks. At the same
time, of course, racism against African Americans (and Hispanics, Arabs, Indians, and
Asians) was unrelenting and obvious, and the fact that it operated primarily through
state-sanctioned segregation made it an easy target for the Nazi propaganda cannon
fire. In fact, separate-but-unequal policies against Blacks and Jews were practiced in
both the United States and Germany during this period. Visual racism did not stop with
cartoons and drawings but expanded in more complicated and popular ways through
the magic of cinema.

Blacks and the Nazi Film Industry

Since the emergence of cinema as a major arena of popular culture, researchers have
examined the negative image of Blacks in films made in Hollywood and elsewhere.[11] In
the United States, from Griffith's 1915 *Birth of a Nation* to Spike Lee's 2000 *Bamboozle*, a
vigorous debate has persisted over the representation of blackness on the screen and the
uses of popular film to reinforce or challenge structures of racial power. Hollywood has
been the epicenter of global film making, but Blacks have also always been present in
films from Germany, Italy, England, and other countries. While African Americans have

been able to mount a community and collective response to racism in the movies, most notably beginning with the NAACP-led campaign against *Birth of a Nation* in 1915, German Blacks had little capacity to respond either before Nazism or during the Hitler period. The lack of a black "community" limited any type of collective reaction to racist images, and the repression of National Socialism squelched any popular or individual opposition. This is not to say that Blacks in Germany did not resist racist images, but that response was not in the form of a countercinema expression. In contrast, African Americans were able to develop an incipient independent black film culture as a number of black films, filmmakers, and film companies emerged as early as 1912—beginning with William Foster's short *The Railroad Porter*—that could formally and structurally, if not always thematically and substantially, challenge Hollywood's racist images.[12] Not only did Blacks in Germany not have the resources to make their own films, any protest of the Negrophobia that characterized the films of the Nazi era was tantamount to treason and would lead to severe and even fatal repercussions.

The debate over Germany's former colonies, the central discourse in films that featured Blacks under Hitler, preceded the Nazi takeover. Following the end of World War I and the draconian measures of the Versailles Treaty, the loss of Germany's colonial possessions remained a theme in domestic politics. At the popular level, the Deutsche Kolonialgesellschaft (German Colonial Service) and similar procolonial forces and organizations led the arguments for recapturing the lost empire, which harmonized with the fascist state's imperial and continental objectives.

Under National Socialism, an ironic relationship evolved in which the image of Blacks consistently and unequivocally was presented in the most racist manner while, at the same time, those very Blacks who carried those images to the screen were protected from Nazism's worse treatment and often lived better than most other people of African descent then in Germany. This dichotomy reflected a confluence of interests wherein the ideological need to make the case for the return of Germany's former colonies merged with the imperatives of black survival. Blacks appeared in a wide range of German film media including documentaries, features, newsreels, propaganda, and shorts. The (anti)blackness in Nazi films was expressed in two trends: antiblack images that were used to argue against the integration of people of African descent in German society, and the colonial films that averred the correctness and legitimacy of Germany during the colonial period. While Blacks appeared in other German movies, it was the colonial films that set the racial tone of black image representation. These films were mostly made between 1938 and 1943. The dynamics appeared over and over in films such as *Kongo Express, Quax in Africa, Carl Peters, Auntie Wanda from Uganda, The Wilderness Dies, People in the Bush, Longing to Africa, The Sunbathe-Country Southwest-Africa, With the German Colonists in South-west-Africa, German Planters at the Cameroon-Mountain, German's Country in Africa, Secretary of State Dr. Solf Visits Togo, In the German Sudan, Ohm Krüger, In the Unknown Cameroon, Our Cameroon, Cruise over Africa, Bananas, Bantu Knows Nothing of Europe, Monga Ma Loba,* and *With the Fisher Wambo.* In all of these movies, Blacks in Germany were used as proxies for African natives.

Africa, in the German imagination, signified a time of global conquest and control, the displacement of national and racial power, identity, and meaning. The colonial films were the effort to recapture that lost idealized and never fully realized moment. Alain Patrice Nganang, a perceptive critic of German film, astutely terms the discourse embedded in these movies a "colonial longing."[13] The ideological nature of these films took place on the contested terrain of the political relationship between Africa and Europe. As Edward Said insightfully notes, "To represent Africa is to enter the battle over Africa, inevitably connected to later resistance, decolonialization, and so forth."[14] These works were multipurpose, serving a range of international and national political interests. The films were used not only to glorify the German time in Africa with a self-serving argument on its "civilizing" role, but also to criticize its adversaries in France and Britain. The so-called rabid conspiracy between the French and the Jews or the British and the Jews against Germany is also a thematic drive of the multirhetorical nature of these films. As Hake notes, "German films about the colonies partook not in 'the battle over Africa,' but in the battle over Europe."[15] Although the Nazis gave lip service to the demand for the return of the colonies, when given the chance they retreated. In 1938, as Hitler threatened Czechoslovakia, he was offered the African colonies as appeasement but clearly showed his priorities when he went for continental expansion.[16] The films would also provide space for displacement of attacks by the British. In the film *Ohm Kruger* (*Uncle Kruger*), the plot, in part, shows the British as the creators of concentration camps, thus displacing a major criticism hurled at the Nazis.[17]

Finally, the films were also about domestic politics. The efforts to resolve the conflicts of colonial settlement, as presented in the films, were generally a metaphor for internal conflicts and concerns in Germany. Sabine Hake argues that, for example, in German colonial films, natives were stand-ins for Jews.[18] I would add, however, that "natives" were also presented as a literal representation of indigenous people for whom the Nazis articulated an independent racial narrative. She goes on to say,

> Several factors contributed to the transformation of Africa into a projection screen for domestic concerns: the rediscovery of colonialsim as a political program and paradigm of empire; the fascination with the 'dark continent' and its primordial nature in the cultural film; the discovery of Africa as an attractive setting for adventure films; the proliferation of newsreels about German military operations in North Africa under Rommel; and, last, but not least, the enlistment of the colonial imagination in seemingly unrelated discourses and contexts.[19]

Thus, in one sense, Africa and Africans were not so much "othered" as they were politically expedient in a wide range of areas.

In these films, the dialectic between the backgrounding and foregrounding of black performers was critical and essential. The presentation of "Africans" as context served the ideological purpose of locating Blacks in their "natural" setting, reinforcing European views of Africa as the Dark Continent. The unspoken native, backgrounded in servile and domesticated positions, functions on a lower human and social scale than the Germans, and thus rationalizes on observable racial grounds the legitimacy of German control. This positioning underscores the centrality of the colonializer's point of view where action and narrative progress operate through German agency. When voiced or otherwise foregrounded, Blacks verbalize and support the dominance of Germany, shifting, importantly, the point of view from the hegemonic to the subaltern, but with the same message. This variety of forms generates a more creative and politically strategic presentation of Nganang's colonial longing, embodying both oppressor and oppressed. This multifaceted, raciopolitical mission is manifest in all of the films from the period. Ideologically, the case was being made that not only did Germany need its colonies back, but the racial superiority of the German people meant that it deserved them. "The claims to colonies in Africa," states Hake, "are presented not by means of political or economic arguments, but via categories of race, biology, and nature."[20]

Samples gives a rich example from *Carl Peters* of the racial and ideological use of the African image in these films. Dr. Carl Peters, the former head of the Society for German Colonialization and the German East African Society who was placed in charge of German colonial territories in East Africa, was a national hero. Hake refers to the real Peters as "a sadistic psychopath" with the reputation of the "man with the bloody hands," who was ultimately relieved of his duties because of his brutal and cruel manner toward the colonialized population.[21] In examining the black image in *Carl Peters,* Samples writes, "The one native who manages from time to time to assume a more distinct personality is the guide-interpreter. He represents the changing social institutions brought about by colonialization. Having attended a mission school, he has already been assimilated. This phenomena is readily evidenced by his Western clothing."[22] The foregrounded guide-interpreter visualizes the argument that only by Europeanizing can natives emerge from their primitive state. One review of *Carl Peters* stated, "The natives are deferential—indeed almost subservient—to the Europeans, who have assumed the position of chiefs; that is, they are superior. The Germans are thus always depicted leading the safari—even though they presumably did not know the land."[23] Samples also points out that *Carl Peters* is a "decidedly masculine film" and that "black African women are almost entirely invisible, appearing only in quick shots. It is possible that this phenomena could also be explained by a more mundane reason, namely, the dearth of black female actresses."[24] Of course, even if there had been more black women available, their image and role would have been consistent with the stereotyped images of African women expressed in other areas of German popular culture.

As job opportunities shrunk for Afro-Germans and Africans under National Socialism, more and more began to look toward the film industry for employment. It was rumored that there was one booking agent in Berlin who had the names of all the Afro-Germans and Africans in Germany who could be called to make films. According to John Welch, an African American journalist who was in Germany during the early years of the Hitler regime, the Afro-Germans and Africans who worked in the film industry actually did quite well financially. He states, "They earn 40 marks a day during such a filming. In normal times a single man can live comfortably on fifty marks a week and as the shooting of such a film lasts anywhere from three to eight weeks they often earn enough in one picture to live easily for a year. I was sometimes tempted to 'get in on the gravy,' but my studies prevented me from doing so."[25] Other researchers have echoed Welch's assessment. Samples states, "A small number of Africans as well as black foreign nationals and colonials were able to have fairly lucrative and successful film careers."[26] Ironically, some Afro-Germans were only able to work in the films by wearing blackface.

Films were shot in Germany (Grunewald Studios of Tobis Filmkunst GmbH near Berlin, and Ufa Studios near Babelsberg), Poland (Barrandov Studios), and Italy (Cinecittà near Rome).[27] The provision of black actors came from several sources. In addition to the Blacks in Germany, Italy also provided black film extras. According to one source, "The Italian Ministry of Popular Culture has been extremely accommodating in making enough Negroes available."[28] It was unclear whether these performers were forced into these roles or did them voluntarily.

Another source of black actors was prisoners of war. It is known that some African POWs were also used as extras to act in Nazi films."[29] For these Africans, participating in Nazi filmmaking was a hazardous, periodically deadly enterprise. In August 1940, according to David Irving's *The Trail of the Fox,* Field Marshal Erwin Rommel and Goebbels involved black French troops in the making of a film. The film, released as *Victory in the West,* sought to re-create the German victory over France, and a whole battalion of black French troops was employed to play the part of surrendering solders. Rommel "told the blacks to come out toward the tanks with their hands up and looking scared; but the men overreacted, rolled the whites of their eyes and screamed with terror."[30] The tanks, apparently in the name of realism, used lived ammunition and fired directly at the troops. Apparently, things got too real and out of hand, and a number of the "actors" were killed. Several more battle scenes cost several more lives before it was all over. While it is unknown how the Africans felt about their movie experience, Rommel was jubilant with the results. He wrote paternalistically, "No expense has been spared to show it as it really was. There were blacks in it again today. The fellows had a whale of a time and thoroughly enjoyed putting up their hands all over again."[31] It probably is safe to say that Rommel's assessment was not shared universally.

According to a report by the Afro-German survivor Erika Ngambi ul Kuo—though never verified—even African American POWs were used as extras in Nazi propaganda films.[32] Some scholars have picked up and perpetuated this unfounded rumor.[33] It is possible that some African American POWs were mixed in with the African troops, but that is unknown.[34]

Many of the Blacks who worked in these films speak less about the quality and content of these films and more about the benefits of working at the studios as opposed to not having any work at all and being left to the mercy of an intolerant fascist state. The survivor Werner Egiomue worked in a number of films at the Ufa Studios. For him, it boiled down to basic survival. He states, "Outside you could be arrested. Inside, was as safe as in a bank."[35] In fact, work in the films during this period helped to form a community of Blacks that did not exist before. This sense of building community is also reflected in the recollections of Doris Reiprich, another surviving Afro-German from

the Nazi time, who along with her sister Erika Ngambi ul Kuo worked in the film industry. Doris states with warm reminiscence, "Yes, as of 1938 I came to Berlin for the
movies. That's where I met the home folks—home folks—that's what we still call each
other today. Before that I didn't know any."[36] "Home folks" is a significant phrase, for it
unites the past—and clearly the positive feelings that that conjures—with a recognition
of race and continental commonality in the present. This is a powerful statement of
identity discovery and community construction. Doris goes on to say, "During the filming we had a lot of fun. On our breaks the Africans would often get their drums and
we'd sing in front of the studios. People would come running from all the productions.
They loved to listen to us."[37] This almost idyllic description of life for a specific group of
Africans under fascism must be seen in the context of a desperately small social space
for any public expression of attitudes, opinions, views, or artistry that did not meet
Nazi standards. This remarkably complex and contradictory scene—Africans performing traditional music in a nonstereotypical manner before an appreciative white audience on their break from making pro-Nazi and racist colonial films—is all the more
extraordinary for having been repeated for a number of years.

It should be noted that the use of Blacks in propaganda films occurred on both sides
of the ocean. Several branches of the U.S. armed forces made films that sought to
address the race question. These films included *Negro Colleges in Wartime* (1943), *The
Negro Soldier* (1944), and *The Negro Sailor* (1945). While the Germans did not specifically seek to gain Afro-German support for the war, though many were forced into war-
related work, the U.S. government was very concerned about winning and maintaining
black backing, particularly in a period when race relations were at a low following the
blood-drenched race riots in 1943 in Harlem and Detroit. The objectives of these films,
aimed at both black and white audiences, were to downplay the nation's racial discord
and the issue of segregation and to promote cooperation and patriotism. A sermon by a
black minister is the narrative vehicle by which a history of black participation in past
wars and conflicts is presented in *The Negro Soldier,* which was produced by the War
Department. As one critic noted, the film "overlooked numerous historical contradictions and completely ignored the discrimination in the forces in the 1940s."[38] The film
was most clearly meant to salve white anxiety about black loyalty, but it echoed more
the delusionary slave faithfulness of *Gone With the Wind. The Negro Sailor,* made one
year later by the Navy, reflected similar themes of racial togetherness and devotion to a
national mission of defeating fascism. By the time the film was done, however, the war
was over and it was not shown publicly until February 1946.

While *The Negro Soldier* and *The Negro Sailor* created fictional discourses of black
and white unity, *Negro Colleges in Wartime* attempted to document the admirable effort
by black colleges to transform those institutions into training grounds for black war
input. Only nine minutes long, the documentary film visits Tuskegee, Prairie View,
Howard, and Hampton to display the training that young black women and men were
undergoing as their contributions to the war effort. This included being trained as engineers, mechanics, chemists, and nurses and for other professions. In spite of the welcome benefits from the government funding to increase the skill level of these college

students, issues of economic, educational, and social segregation and employment discrimination are as unaddressed on film as they were in reality.

Both the Germans and the Americans demonstrated a willingness to exploit blackness through the miracle of film. While evading real issues of equality and justice, narrative texts of black loyalty to states that practiced and sanctioned racism, in general,
and Negrophobia, in particular, are consistent themes of the era's state-produced films.
In none of these films does the notion of antiracist resistance appear as very calculated
discourses of power are shielded behind the rhetoric of unity, devotion, commitment,
and nationalism. The Nazis (and the Americans) soon discovered that control of image
is a lot easier than control of reality, and circumscribing their black residents was nearly
impossible.

Showing Our Africans: The "German Africa Show"

The Nazis continuingly sought ways to control the position and place of Blacks in
Germany. One grand effort that was to serve political, entertainment, and ideological
purposes was the Nazi takeover and management of the Afrika Schau (Africa Show).
This traveling road show of "African" cultural performances, craft displays, and talks,
originally called the "Negro Show," was started in 1936 and run by Juliette Tipner,
whose mother was from Liberia, and Adolph Hillerkus, Juliette's white husband. Their
goal was to display African talent to the German public. In 1940, the SS and Goebbels
took over the show, putting the Nazi hack Wilhelm Stock in charge and hoping that it
would become useful not only for propaganda and ideological purposes but also as a
way to gather all the Blacks in the country under one tent. Theatrical agents had the
names and addresses of every Black who they knew was looking for work, all of whom
could be called upon to be extras in the entertainment industry. Nevertheless, it was
harder for many mixed-race Afro-Germans to get this work because their light skin
phenotype made them look less "African" than the popular image in most Germans'
imagination. The fact that many of those who did play the role of Africans either in the
Africa Show or in films had never been to Africa and had little idea of what being
"African" meant had little influence on the selection of participants.

The show went to fairs, festivals, and similar events throughout Germany. Once
Goebbels took control, it became "a combination of Nazi colonial propaganda and
racist, stereotypical African cultural presentations including medicine men, prayer cere-
monies, and a war dance."[39] The impact on the members of the troupe was stark, and
they were forced to wear swatiskas and give the Hitler salute. The overt ideological component of the show was in the form of a slideshow that presented the German perspective on the history and role of Germany in the colonial period. The slideshow also
expressed the German view regarding the loss of her colonies following the World War I.

As noted, the Germans hoped that all the Blacks in Germany could be placed in the
Africa Show, thus simultaneously removing them from society and using them for
propaganda purposes. However, Campt et al. contend that there were never more than
thirty Blacks in the show at any given time. They argue that by the time the show was
finally closed down, the Nazis had shifted their position on what to do with their black

problem and decided to try to expatriate all Blacks back to somewhere in Africa. This objective also went unrealized.[40]

For Goebbels, the disaster of the Africa Show was multifold. The show not only failed in its containment, propaganda, ideological, and entertainment missions, but had the opposite effect in one major area that the Nazis sought to control: sexual relations between the Africans and German women. While the directors of the troupe were given explicit orders "to ensure that the members of the Negro show do not engage in sexual activity with whites," by 1939, Friedrich von Lindequist, executive director of the Colonial Office, would conclude, "The social isolation of the Natives and their supervision was frequently insufficient and led to intimate relations with German girls and women."[41] There was an explicit command to keep the Africans away from the German population and especially white German women and girls. Also, some of the members of the show were married to white women and even had children by them who also appeared in the program.

For these reasons, Goebbels decided to shut down the show. While it is not completely known what happened to all of the performers, there are indications that they were not sent en masse to the concentration camps or otherwise immediately threatened. In fact, at least two of the Blacks who had been a part of the show at its very end were performing in a special operetta two weeks later. Goebbels not only attended but praised their performances afterwards.[42]

The End Game: Preparing for a United White Post-War Europe

One last use of blackness (or antiblackness) by the Nazis occurred as the war began to shift decisively against Germany. Using a theme of a "Coming Black Invasion," the Nazis propagandists hoped to stave off defeat by uniting white Europe against the specter of Blacks occupying the region (à la post–World War I), or, in the event of losing, build a consensus that these troops should not be employed in any postwar situation. In 1944, the Germans began to circulate leaflets and pamphlets that warned of a black takeover of Europe should they be defeated. Produced by Goebbels's Ministry for People's Enlightenment and Propaganda, one pamphlet in particular sought to convince white non-Germans of the dangerous presence of Blacks in Europe (see figure 3). The document, written in Dutch and distributed in Holland, was titled *Groeten Uit Engeland: De Komende Invasie* ("Greetings from England: The Coming Invasion.) It read, in part,

> From the beginning of the year, more than half a million Negroes have been brought from America to Scotland, where they get a special training in parachute jumping. An interesting detail is that their parachutes are made from dark-grey silk. As the clouded skies above Holland are usually dark-grey as well, this handy camouflage makes it pretty much impossible for the Germans to shoot the parachute legion. It will be an enormous humiliation for Hitler, the prophet of racial theories, when his warriors will be driven from western Europe by the black race. Dutchmen, your cooperation will be counted upon when the black legion is coming. Make your old jazz-records ready, because at the celebration of liberation

your daughters and wives will be dancing in the arms of real Negroes . . . Dutch girls and women. A beautiful and pleasant task lies ahead of you, to which you will have to give yourself completely and without any restraint, in order to contradict the racial nonsense of Hitler.[43]

While satirical in nature and even parodying Hitler himself, the pamphlet sought to win the Dutch to the idea that while Nazism might appear problematic, it was a better alternative to a future of Negro domination, sexual seduction, and unrestrained debauchery. Race-mixing and rape, never seen as separate, were platforms upon which the Nazis hoped to construct white European unity in the face of their coming defeat. This document was presented not so much to change the course of the war but to lay the basis for Germany's postwar situation. A chief concern was, of course, not to have a repeat of black occupation forces that had been stationed at the end of World War I. On the front cover of this document was a picture of a broadly grinning and clearly happy black man. The sarcastic "beautiful and pleasant task" that white women could expect was, of course, a reference to the supposedly ugly and brutal sexual liaison that would be anticipated and forced by the black soldiers. To the white women of Europe, Goebbels was saying that if you believe that Hitler's racial politics are wrong, then by all means embrace the black legion that is coming. The rhetoric, of course, was primarily aimed at Western European men and the assumption of the threat to gender power. A second picture on the same page had dozens of men, presumably black, parachuting down against a darkened sky—the "invasion."

An even more complex and multilayered propaganda piece was created and distributed by the Nazis. A poster produced in English that was also distributed in Holland in 1944 contained the whole kitchen sink of racial signifiers and codes. In this one poster, we see markers for the Ku Klux Klan, the Jewish financier, jazz records, the Star of David, Miss America with a Indian headdress, a noose for lynching, the Statue of Liberty, and boxing gloves all tied to a large monsterlike figure with dark skin and bulging muscles. In the center of this creature was an exaggerated and negative image of a black woman and a black man in a cage dancing with a sign reading, "Jitterbug— Triumph of Civilization" in English. This monster, more intense and complicated than the Jumbo character used in the aftermath of World War I, was also clutching two white women in his massive arms. These jubilant were clearly not meant to represent images of German women. The creature, which had four arms and hands, also carried a machine gun in one hand and a hand grenade in another. It represented the black invading soldier. The graphic made a strong connection between jazz, sex, Jews, and African Americans. The Nazis saw blackness as embedded in jazz and Blacks celebrating jazz in the form of dancing, swing music, and interracial (potentially sexual) relations.

Summary

Black perfomativity was appropriated by the Nazi state for ideological and political reasons. Rather than simply remove Blacks from German society, a doable possibility given the high visibility factor of people of African descent, the Nazis found more devious means by which to exploit blackness. There was a perverse, evil brilliance with which they used cartoons, films, traveling shows, and flyers to connect building a white European united front with the Aryanizing objectives of the fascist state. The unwanted complicity of Afro-Germans and Africans in these ideological plots and programs was conditioned by the coercive nature of the Nazis and the survival instincts of individual Blacks. The luxury to think about the long-term consequences of their work did not present itself in the cauldron of fire that had to be immediately and daily addressed.

Goebbels was intent on using blackness and black culture wherever possible to advance the Nazi cause. Whether this meant promoting African dance or displaying arts and crafts, he was eager to demonstrate that blackness could be accommodated albeit under terms established by the Nazi hierarchy. However, in one area he would ignite (or rather enjoin) a cultural war that rivaled the Nazi states' battle with the Allies. For twelve years, Goebbels and the Nazis sought, in a variety of ways, to defeat the one U.S. black-rooted export that would not easily go away: jazz.

8

"Nigger Music Must Disappear"

Jazz and the Disruption of Cultural Purity

Oh! Silver tree!
Oh, shining rivers of the soul!
In a Harlem cabaret
Six long-headed jazzers play.
A dancing girl whose eyes are bold
Lifts high a dress of silken gold
Oh! Shining tree!
Oh, shining river of the soul.
　　　　　　—"Jazzonia" by Langston Hughes[1]

We have no sympathy for fools who want to transplant jungle music to Germany.
. . . Nigger music must disappear.
　　　　　　—Quote from 6 November 1938 German newspaper[2]

Jazz and Race

Whether in Germany, the United States, France, Cuba, or other venues, jazz has always been seen in racial terms—it could not be any other way. Given the U.S. racial structure of power in the formative years of jazz, roughly around the first and second decades of the twentieth century, the black-rooted music became a vehicle for the cultural articulation and global marketing of a resistance discourse by (initially) the southern and urban working-class sector of the black community, and later the disaffected voices of the black middle class. It also became a source of social irritation, cultural challenge and appropriation, and financial exploitiation for Whites. For nearly a century, the relevance, sophistication, and significance of jazz have been hotly contested in the public sphere. Yet while musicologists and musicians, music magazines and music critics duked it out over issues of form and content, and popular appeal versus art, in the final analysis, the debate about jazz, whether in the United States or Germany, was a debate about inclusion, democracy, freedom, and race.

As jazz migrated from the musical epicenter of black culture to the edges of white society in the United States in the 1920s and 1930s, it came under attack from many sources: white music critics, white musicians, and white racists generally. In the United States, the discourse against jazz flourished in the 1920s and would continue for several decades to come. Though, for the most part, criticism was anchored by the racism permeating the white music industry that included producers, musicians, writers, radio owners, and critics, there were also voices in the black community who viewed the emergence of jazz as negative and fought its spread. There were basically three arguments proffered by African American critics. Civil rights leaders contended that jazz and the jazz culture were linked to "low-class" behavioral norms that only harmed the full integration of African Americans into the U.S. mainstream. Black religious leaders saw jazz as too sensual, secular, and uncontrolled, and opposed it on those grounds. Intellectual and cultural voices, from music critics to writers, reflecting the growing middle-class–working-class schism in the black community, joined the chorus of condemnation citing the untrained and primitive nature of the music (and musicians).

At the turn of the twentieth century, many in the black community, across class lines, viewed blues and then later jazz as a retreat from black spiritual life. Transitional figures, such as Jelly Roll Morton, W. C. Handy, and Eubie Blake, all encountered various sanctions from family and community for their excursions into musical worlds that bridged spirituals and gospel with blues and jazz. As African Americans became more urban and more northern, these criticisms began to take shape along class lines as blues and early jazz were identified as southern, rural, and low-class. This explained, in part, why many black intellectuals and leaders—W. E. B. Du Bois, the writers James Weldon Johnson and Charles Johnson, and the NAACP leader Walter White—denounced or denigrated jazz initially. Musically, Du Bois preferred German classical music—such as Beethoven and Wagner, and the spirituals that he liked immensely—to jazz. His qualified opposition to blues and jazz was also shaped by an elitist morality that viewed these music genres as hopelessly linked to the most criminal and immoral sectors of the black community.

However, many black intellectuals came to embrace the music. The historian Joel A. Rogers, the writers Alan Locke, Zora Neale Hurston, and Claude McKay, and the writer/poet Langston Hughes became great defenders of jazz. They not only viewed the roots of the music in the struggle by African Americans for equality and freedom, but also noted, as the jazz scholar Kathy Ogren writes, "the participatory qualities of jazz performance."[3] Jazz conveyed racial pride and solidarity, they contended, in what amounted to an intellectual class struggle carried out, paradoxically, within the corridors of the black middle class. Jazz, as an organic artististic African American creation, reached high popularity within the black community, which, in part, accounted for the antagonism that emanated from a number of voices among white intellectuals and social critics, who viewed jazz in another light. Often in crude racial terms, jazz was dismissed as unsophisticated and unworthy of serious consideration as music—and maybe even dangerous.

The most developed voice along these lines was that of Theodor Adorno, a German intellectual who had actually escaped from Nazism in its early years. His criticism went to the heart of the music itself. He charged that jazz was "static," and he expressed deep frustration at not understanding how "millions of people seem never to tire of its monotonous attraction."[4] Indeed, he thought that jazz was profoundly undemocratic, what he called a "musical dictatorship over the masses." Although much of his antijazz writings occurred after World War II, he resonated the feelings of the antijazz diatribe that emerged in the 1920s, 1930s, and 1940s from music purists. In his famous broadside against jazz, "Perennial Fashion—Jazz," in which he was hysterical in his denunciations, he embodied the less articulate but no less passionate distaste held by the gatekeepers of American popular music. With not an ounce of compromise, he wrote, "Jazz has shown itself to be utterly impoverished."[5] The philosopher Lee B. Brown countered with a stinging critique of Adorno's diatribe. In analyzing Adorno's leveling of the music, Brown charges "by simply taking jazz as just one more instance of popular music, he smooths [sic] out and ignores features that differentiate the popular music landscape."[6] Brown believes, most fundamentally, that Adorno did not understand the music at its most organic level. He argues, "Adorno's Eurocentrism inclines him to understand this musical inevitably almost entirely in terms of tonality and harmony."[7] There is also an idealism behind Adorno's critique that jazz is not truly spontaneous. As Brown finally notes, "Adorno . . . will settle for nothing less than a form of pure improvisation that comes, literally, from *nowhere*. Such an ideal is an empty dream"[8] (emphasis in the original).

In much less high-tone terms than Adorno's, jazz was debated in raciocultural terms as to its racial origins and cultural importance. Inexorably, however, jazz continued to grow as a popular music form and to reach acceptability with white America. A reflection of that shift was the increasing participation and fame of white jazz musicians, such as the saccharine Paul Whiteman, in the 1920s, and later, in the 1930s, the swing bandleaders such as Artie Shaw, Benny Goodman, and Tommy Dorsey, the three most well known from the period. Although early black jazz groups, such as the Original Dixieland Jazz Band, became popular with the hip, as Baraka states, "Whiteman got rich; the O.D.J.B. never did."[9] As Michael Bernard-Donais notes, "jazz moved from the margins to a kind of transitional position in the movement from marginality into the canon: it became popular."[10] The political economy of jazz in the period was also fully racialized. This was reflected in the dichotomous access to the radio airwaves, the ability to get recording contracts, and the opportunities and benefits from live performances.

In the 1920s, these racial fault lines were inpenetrable in many ways and black jazz musicians found that they had little choice for advancement, prosperity, or respect—in the United States. But what was racially and culturally repulsive to many in the States was more than welcomed in other parts of the world, especially Europe. After World

War I, as the first great wave of black migration north took place, reconfiguring the political, social, and musical character of the nation's major cities, many a jazz player, if at all possible, set sail for Europe and the opportunities available there, including Germany under the Weimar Republic.

I Got It Bad and That Ain't Good: Jazz in Pre-Nazi Germany

"Negro tribes do not march."
—*German quote.*[11]

Jazz came to Germany seriously after World War I, although it had already been flour-ishing in other parts of Western Europe. Its popularity in Berlin and other major German cities was tied significantly to the postwar dance craze. Kater argues that, unlike in Germany, not only was jazz accepted in France and England, so were its African American practioners. This also meant that the music was accepted as much, if not more, for its musical qualities than for its danceability. In Germany, jazz's populari-ty was tied to its danceability. The first American jazz records appeared in Germany in 1921. Jazz in the pre-Nazi era brought many African Americans to Germany, including the flamboyant Josephine Baker, the horn player Sidney Bechet, and numerous other performers. Contradicting Kater's assertion, these non-German Blacks were given star status. Baker played in Berlin and other cities on numerous occasions, always making a big splash and performing there in 1925 with a band that included the clarinetist Bechet. She also came back in 1927.[12] Bechet studied music as well as performed in Germany, becoming a composer, conductor, and even an actor in a number of German films. Other black performers during the pre-Nazi period were the "Chocolate Kiddies," a jazz revue show, the trumpeter Arthur Briggs, the entertainer Samuel Wooding, and the dancer/singer Louis Douglas.

In addition to live acts, jazz was heard on the radio being first broadcast on 24 May 1924.[13] This would bend toward the likes of Paul Whiteman, who billed himself as the "King of Jazz," and his more acceptable, muted, and understated form of the genre. In fact, many musicians did not consider the music played by Whiteman's band to be jazz at all, despite the band's including some of the best white jazz musicians to emerge from the period. At various points, Whiteman's band included Red Nichols, Tommy Dorsey, Frankie Trumbauer, Joe Venuti, Eddie Lang, and Bix Beiderbecke. Just as in the United States, Whiteman was an entry point for more rigorous and challenging forms of the music, and for black artists whose records would not become available until the end of the 1920s and early 1930s. Then Germany got to hear the premier black jazz musicians of the period. Among the black Americans who were heard and who would become even more popular than Whiteman were Duke Ellington, James Johnson, Sidney Bechet, Fletcher Henderson, Coleman Hawkins, and Louis Armstrong.

While African Americans were ubiquitous, Afro-Germans were rare on the jazz scene and, in many instances, were mainly used as background dancers in the clubs and caberets. This should not be surprising, however, given the undoubtedly limited access isolated Afro-Germans would have to the music, let alone to a music community that favored and encouraged jazz and their participation. Jazz in Germany was concentrated in Berlin and a few other major cities, while many Afro-Germans were located in smaller cities and towns disproportionately in the western parts of the nation. Even with these limits, there were some Afro-Germans who did take up the call. One pivotal individual was the black jazz musician and trombonist Herb Flemming. Born Niccolaih El Michelle on 5 April 1898, he performed regularly in a Berlin club owned by Mustafa El Sherbini, a prominent Egyptian businessman.[14] He also spent a great deal of time outside of Germany working with world-class jazz artists. From the early 1920s on, he played and recorded with a number of African American musicians such as Mamie Smith's Jazz Hounds, James Reese Europe, Noble Sissle, Fats Waller, and Fern "Jelly Roll" Morton, among others. Flemming, who died in 1976, also wrote his memoirs covering much of the pre-Nazi period.

Another prominent Afro-German jazz performer was Wilhelm Panzer also known as William MacAllen (1909–1969). MacAllen's father was a black banjo player from Somalia and his mother, Emmi Panzer, was a white German and also a musician. MacAllen began to play music at the age of four but reached national fame as the advertising image for Sarotti chocolates where he was pictured in "Turkish" dress in a display of naked racism. The ad, as did similar ones in the United States, tied dark skin in a mocking manner to a product that had little to do with race other than to exploit it. As a child and teenager, he also appeared in a number of silent movies, including *Der Kleine Muck* (*The Baby Muck*), *Meine Tante—Deine Tante* (*My Aunt—Your Aunt*), and *Rheinparade* (*Rhine-Parade*).[15] By the late 1920s, MacAllen, who was a drummer, had formed his own jazz band in Berlin at the Wild West Bar that, at one point, included Sidney Bechet. The band was promoted as "The MacAllen Blackband, Saxophon Virtuoso Sidney Bechet," and performed with other jazz groups such as the Tom Bill Nigger Band and the New Yorkers.[16] It is unclear if MacAllen actually performed in Germany during the Nazi era, although he did spend some time there. For the most part, he was outside the country playing in Switzerland, Hungary, Italy, Turkey, and elsewhere, not returning until after the war. In the early 1960s, the German government gave MacAllen a pension of 60,000 DM annually as compensation for racial discrimination he suffered during the Nazi time. It is unknown what specific instances of racism MacAllen had had to endure. He died on 22 December 1969 while in semiretirement in Berlin.

The notion of disaporic discursions is also relevant here. Although the views of Flemming and MacAllen (the names they are best known by as opposed to their German names) on racism are not known to any great extent, it is logical to believe that their consistent encounters and interactions with African Americans likely raised their racial consciousness in ways that would have been impossible if they had just stayed in Germany. The racial tensions in the United States, which in many instances pushed black artists out, not only inspired many of the songs of the period and the names of groups and revues, but almost certainly provided the content of the ongoing informal discourses between musicians. Flemming and MacAllen would have been privy to and participants in these conversations.

Lotz argues that an indigenous black German music was developing but was effectively arrested and ended when the Nazis came to power.[17] As an associate of Bechet and other well-known jazz greats, Lotz speculated that if MacAllen had not been driven out of Germany, he would have been a leader on a stellar German jazz scene.[18] In any case, this did not happen, and any semblance of an indigenous black music was qualitatively squashed during the 1930s and early 1940s. By the late 1920s, a rising German nationalism, along with a deteriorating economic situation, would begin to be felt in the cultural realm. Both factors meant an increasing intolerance and dwindling opportunities for foreign and black musicians. Other variables also came into play such as the invention of the sound film that put most orchestra pit players out of work. Competition from foreign musicians was increasingly problematic, and nationalists, especially the National Socialist Party, took advantage of the souring mood. Many foreign musicians could read the handwriting on the wall, and by 1930–1931, most British and American jazz players had left the country or were resistant to going there. Meanwhile, things would take a racial turn.

Even before Hitler came to power, black musicians, domestic and foreign, were under assault. In 1932, with the growing fascist movement railing against all foreign elements and non-Aryans, the Papen regime that preceded Hitler banned the hiring of "colored" musicians.[19] Although the decree, in many instances, was brazenly contravened, it was a sign of things to come. In this context, a strong campaign by music critics, conservative intellectuals, Nazi party leaders, and a chorus of musicians was launched against "Neger music," meaning jazz. Ideology became policy as the Nazis began to creep toward power. In 1930, when the Nazis took over the state government in Thuringia, they passed an ordinance that prohibited "jazz band and drum music, Negro dances, Negro songs, Negro plays."[20] One music historian, Alfred Einstein, called jazz "the invention of a Nigger in Chicago."[21] As early as 1920, German music critics were denouncing jazz. Alfred Heuss railed against the "orgies of Negro jazz," and he would expand his rant when he later became editor of *Zeitschrift fur Musik* (*Music Magazine*), an influential, pro-Hitler music journal.[22] Many of these critics were open or secret followers of the Nazi Party. By the mid-30s, all black jazz artists were banned from performing in Germany including Duke Ellington, Coleman Hawkins, Louis Armstrong and even the classical singer Marian Anderson, not that any of these artists were clamoring to entertain in the country anyway. According to Kater, Anderson was not allowed to perform in Germany during her celebrated European tour of 1935–1936 because of "the color of her skin as a Negress."[23]

What had been skirmishes against jazz during the Weimar Republic and the short-lived Papen administration became an all-out crusade. The ideological attacks on jazz were a necessary correlate in the attempt to build the racial state, and in turn in racializing Jews. The freedom found in jazz, Adorno notwithstanding, also had to be crushed if the facist state was to be satisfactorily established and consolidated. On moral, political, and racial grounds, jazz and its black and Jewish practioners would find themselves at war with the incoming regime. The general in this battle was the Nazi leader turned cultural czar, Joseph Goebbels.

Killer Joe: The Nazi War Against Jazz

Now you can go packing with all your jazz.
—The director of the Berlin conservatory, on the day that Hitler came to power

The Nazi Party leadership, especially Minister of Culture Joseph Goebbels, would target jazz early as a source of alien cultural racial disease. Goebbels, in one of his most charitable statements, notes, "Everyone knows, America's contribution to the music world consists merely of jazzed up Nigger music, not worthy of a single mention."[24] He also referred to it as "alien nigger music from the Hottentots"[25] and "Negrodom, the art of the subhuman."[26] There was no mistaking the connection between jazz and Negrophobia by the Nazis. Goebbels's approach to the problem was multifold and even contradictory as he tried to resolve an impossible contradiction. On the one hand, the black and Jewish role in jazz was indisputable and thus made the music unacceptable on fundamental principles. On the other hand, the music was popular not only among a significant number of the population but among German soldiers and even Nazi members themselves. Given this paradox, with its local variations of celebration and repulsion, Goebbels tried unsuccessfully to ban jazz-related activities and create a Nazi version of jazz time and time again. The attacks on jazz—officially labeled *Entartete* ("degenerate") and called "uncouth and tasteless music"—were part of a larger agenda of cultural control implemented by the Nazis after coming to power. The Nazi attacks on jazz received exposure and critique even in the United States. In a series of articles, the *New York Times* reported that the Nazis sought to ban jazz to protect "the foundations of our entire culture."[27]

The principal government instrument for controlling the politics of music was the Reichsmusikkammer (RMK), or Reich Music Chamber. The RMK was one of the seven chambers of Goebbels's Reichskulturkammer (RKK) or Reich Culture Chamber. The RMK would eventually be headed by the fervent anti-Semite and talent-challenged conductor Peter Raabe. He would put in place a system that attempted to register and control all of the musicians under the Reich as well as the content of the nation's music. Both tasks would prove unpopular and unachievable. Eventually, between 86,000 and 94,000 musicians would be examined and registered, a process that allowed for the weeding out of undesirables such as jazz players. Frequently, however, officials were bribed or otherwise convinced to let untrained or otherwise problematic players pass the tests. Foreign players, increasingly under pressure, were also forced to register. In furthering the domestic-foreign divide, a law was passed that German musicians could not use foreign names. In part, this was also an effort to identify "alien" parties, especially Jews, inside of Germany. Of course, many respondents lied without compunction. Nevertheless, by fall 1938, after the Nuremberg blood laws three years earlier and the 1937 *Kristallnacht* attack, very few Jewish musicians were either left in the country or working in their profession.[28]

Driving Jews out of the performing business, however, did not resolve the Nazi dilemma of foreign music, especially swing jazz and its influence and penetration into the Third Reich. From sheet music and records to live performances and the radio airwaves, the jazz just kept on coming. In addition, Germans all over the country received foreign broadcasts of jazz, which would increase significantly after the war started. A swell of antijazz policies and ordinances emerged in Frankfurt, Cologne, Saxony, Franconia, Stuttgart, and many other cities and towns. These local campaigns, however, contradicted the approach preferred by Goebbels and Raabe, who sought to win by persuasion rather than edict. Thus, the RKK was hesitant to issue sweeping restrictions banning jazz outright and, despite a healthy rhetoric, never did.

German jazz, however, was destined for a mugging with the coming Hitler regime. Unlike any other cultural expression of the period, jazz was viewed by the Nazis as both black *and* Jewish. It was viewed as black because of its origins in the U.S. African American community, and as Jewish because it was Jews who disproportionately played and promoted the music in Germany. Given that pedigree, jazz would appear to have had little future in Hitler's era. The music and the musicians were held in suspicion and murderous contempt. On 14 December 1937, Goebbels declared all foreign, non-Aryan music, including jazz, banned. It became illegal even to tune into shortwave broadcasts of foreign music. In 1941, the struggle over jazz was so serious that the SS/Gestapo held a national seminar in Berlin on jazz whose chief purpose was to effectively and permanently eliminate the music. The Gestapo wanted to be more ruthless and tenacious in the war against jazz and jazz musicians.[29]

Jazz was clearly against the ropes, and Goebbels had plenty to say regarding the significance of the music. His statement on banning jazz from German radio, for example, demonstrated how completely he dismissed it even as he offered a musical critique of it. He wrote, "Now I speak quite openly on the question of whether German radio should broadcast so-called jazz music. If by jazz we mean music that is based on rhythm and entirely ignores or even shows contempt for melody, music in which rhythm is indicated primarily by the ugly sounds of whining instruments so insulting to the soul, why, then we can only reply to the question entirely in the negative."[30]

Goebbels tried on several occasions to create a Nazi version of jazz, but failed. The term "Nazi jazz," of course, is oxymoronic. First, the RKK, in an act of desperation to address the popularity of jazz among purists, who viewed the music as art, and those who enjoyed the danceability of swing, attempted to construct its own jazz bands who would limit the form and content of what was official jazz. In practice, what this meant was that Goebbels was forced to allow some jazz to be played on Nazi airwaves and to create a "jazz" combo that was ideologically, racially, and musically acceptable. That band was the Golden Seven. Its tenure would be relatively short, however, lasting from December 1934 to the summer of 1935. The complaint that the combo sounded too much like jazz was its downfall. Predictably, this effort and others failed. Next, in October 1935, Goebbels's deputies hit upon a scheme to have a radio-sponsored jazz contest as another means of creating a tolerable form of the music. The contest and the whole wacky idea came to an end in March 1936 when the Nazis were forced to cheat the expected winner, the hot jazz band of Fritz Weber, out of the first-place prize, choosing instead the mediocre and unknown Willy Burkart group, which maintained that status after the charade was over. Weber, on the other hand, became more popular than ever.[31]

According to Zwerin, a Luftwaffe pilot named Werner Molders, who loved swing music, was able to influence Hitler who then pressured Goebbels to make German radio music more swinging. Goebbels attempted to co-opt the jazz swing mode with his own Berlin radio band that would broadcast to the German people. The band was called Charly and His Orchestra. It would not last long.[32] One last stab at creating Nazi jazz occurred in 1942. Goebbels formed the German Dance and Entertainment Orchestra (DTU); its goal was to satisfy the military's jazz longings as well as compete with the British broadcasts.

Goebbels and the RMK also went after the record industry. The regime was initially reluctant to try to ban the sale of foreign jazz because it needed to be able to sell its own music internationally. On 14 December 1937, however, Goebbels issued an order that stated, "All records created through the efforts of non-Aryan authors or artists shall be prohibited from sale in Germany, effective 1 April 1938."[33] For Blacks and jazz, this order would become problematic in its implementation for two reasons. The term "non-Aryan" sometimes was meant to target Jews and at other times to be inclusive of other groups including Blacks. In this instance, it was mostly interpreted to mean all those who were not Aryan, thus generally including Blacks but with some wiggle room—although well-known black jazz artists, such as Louis Armstrong, Duke Ellington, and Count Basie, were banned.[34] The second problem was that the Nazi censors were rather ignorant of exactly who and what was black. While the work of well-known artists such as Ellington and Armstrong could be easily identified as such, many lesser-known black musicians were allowed to be sold simply because no one knew their race with any certainty. After the war started, it became easier for the RMK to justify—though no easier to enforce—the banning of foreign music. In February 1942, Goebbels prohibited all records from enemy states including the United States, as well as live performances. The effort to stop the records was a dismal failure because "even during the war, German swing bands continued to issue jazz-oriented recordings."[35]

The Nazis, in 1941, created an antijazz propaganda film, *Around the Statue of Liberty*, a movie about U.S. swing bands that included many black musicians. As did many of the antijazz efforts, this one also famously backfired. The film actually attracted jazz afficionados who flocked to see some real American jazz being played by real American players, albeit within the context of its being vilified. Rather than educate the German masses to the horrors and dangers of American culture, the film drew a cult following of jazz fans that were able to view what was impossible for them to obtain otherwise. It had a *Reefer Madness* type of effect where official ridicule was transformable and appropriated for popular and oppositional purposes.

Despite the Nazi official opposition, jazz, particularly swing, remained popular and played because of "its popularity with the listening public and . . . its protection by Nazi functionaries themselves."[36] Critical to its popularity was the dancing associated with swing, also appropriated from African American cultural styles. The most popular dance imitated by the German jazzers was the Lindy Hop. The Lindy Hop, a wild, free-wheeling, and energetic dance style, surfaced in Harlem in the late 1920s at house parties and the Savoy Ballroom. It did not become national and famous, however, until it burst onto the dance floor of the Cotton Club around 1935. Frankie "Musclehead" Manning and Herbert "Whitey" White put together dance groups of top dancers who began to perform around the country, in Hollywood films such as the Marx Brothers' *A Day at the Races* and Olsen and Johnson's *Hellzapoppin,'* and even internationally. In Germany, dance was a form of release, a relief that became increasingly necessary as the repressive and oppressive nature of the Nazi state expanded. As Solomos and Black note, "Jazz dancing allowed for counter-hegemonic forms of bodily expression and individuality that was so emphatically repressed within Nazi popular culture, music, and dance."[37] Goebbels's concession to the presence of jazz, in fact, was an oblique acknowledgment of this mass need. In this sense, the needs being met by jazz dancing in Germany served a similar purpose to the music and dance for African Americans. Yet, for the Nazi fanatics, even this would become a battleground.

On 4 September 1939, public dancing was banned in the Reich, but the ban was modified less than a month later to apply only before 7:00 P.M. This would later be made more liberal, and then a full ban was again attempted in August 1940, and that new ban was again changed.[38] These back-and-forths were shaped by the inability of the Nazi regime to legislate and enforce an alternative and acceptable form of public pleasure. From soldiers to citizens, dancing was a functional means of cultural identity and release from the growing deprivations and consequences of the war.

It Don't Mean a Thing If It Ain't Got That Swing: Resisters Fight Back

Resistance to the antijazz campaign of the Nazis took popular form not only in covert listening and playing but also in a quasi-organized manner through the Swing-Heines movement that was centered in Hamburg. As captured in the Hollywood film *Swing Kids,* Swing-Heinis—also called Swing Boys and Swing Babies—were young people, male and female, who boldly resisted the ban on jazz music and dancing. The movement was nonideological in that it was not united by any overriding political viewpoint or political objective. In fact, given that most were involved because they wanted to dance to the music, expert or even well-informed knowledge about jazz itself was lacking. The movement was more aware of the big band swing leaders, such as Benny Goodman, than nondance jazz players such as Louis Armstrong. A schism was created between the purists, who were knowledgeable about the music but mostly remained inactive, and the youth who wanted to dance the Lindy Hop and be left alone by the Nazis and the Hitler Youth. Many of the young men involved in the Swings were resistant to the compulsory membership of the Hitler Youth, which also led to physical confrontations.

The debate over the direction of jazz took place on different terrains in the United States and Germany. In the United States, a three-way struggle was unfolding between swing, Dixieland, and bebop. The ascendancy of bebop in the mid-1940s, expressed in the music and musicianship of Charlie Parker, Dizzy Gillespie, Bud Powell, and the young Miles Davis, challenged the dominance of swing, was already responding to the antimodernist proponents of so-called classical and original jazz referring to the New Orleans styles of the 1920s. In Germany, the Nazi battle against jazz effectively arrested the penetration of bebop into the debate and essentially constructed a dichotomous situation that pitted the swing of Benny Goodman, Tommy Dorsey, Glenn Miller, and Duke Ellington, who were already losing favor in the States, against the music of Louis Armstrong, Earl Hines, and Bix Beiderbecke. The Swing Boys campaign reflected this struggle. Politically, then, while swing represented a radical motion in the music in Germany, it embodied the opposite tendency in the United States. In addition, given that nearly all of the beboppers were African American, who within and outside of the music were being swept up in the ever-growing anti–Jim Crow ethos of the black community, the U.S. jazz discourse was being reracialized along the lines of modernist versus antimodernist. In Germany, modernism as swing gave the music a different racial and political function.

Only in one known instance was an Afro-German part of the swing movement. Hans Massaquoi, profiled in chapter 1, grew up around Hamburg, a center of the movement. As he recalls, the movement was properly called the Swing Boys movement, although there were young women involved. He says that he only heard the term "Swing Kids" after the Hollywood movie came out.[39] In retrospect, he views the Swing Boys movement as comparable to the contemporary punkers. It had "no organization and no political agenda," and mainly sought to "express its disdain of authority and regimentation."[40] He remembers vividly that the boys grew their hair long, dressed in what they considered jazz styles, and performed what they believed was swing dancing. Some of his favorite memories involved listening as a youngster with his friends to recorded jazz including African American greats such as Louis Armstrong, Duke Ellington, and Count Basie. All of these artists were included on the Nazi list of forbidden musicians who were not to be listened to by Germans. As a "member" of the Swing Boys, he did not receive any special treatment one way or the other from the other Swings because he was black—he did not, he says, play (trumpet/sax) well enough to be special, but being black did not get him ostracized or denied association.[41] In Massaquoi's case, jazz was a leveler, bringing together those whom the state wanted to promote as racial enemies and uniting them in cultural and personal appreciation of a music rooted in the experiences and resistance of African Americans.

While the Nazis persecuted the Swing-Heines movement in Hamburg, similar proswing campaigns in other parts of the country were virtually left untouched. An all-out suppression of the Swings was muted by the lack of a clear anti-Nazi politics on their part. As Solomos and Black contend, "The Swing subculture was not a self-consciously radical movement, despite the vicious suppression meted out to them by the Gestapo and the Hitler Youth. It was estimated that from 1942 to 1944, seventy-five Swing youth were sent to concentration camps by the SS, who classified them as political prisoners."[42] The repression by the Nazis was often very severe. It included beatings, arrests, and, as noted, being sent to the concentration or labor camps.

Jazz fans organized what became other forms of resistance. In a number of cities, "clubs" were created that were centers of jazz celebration and, of course, illicit jazz activities. In Frankfurt, the Harlem Club was formed during the first years of the war and gathered at a bar called Rokoko-Diele. They brazenly flouted the law and listened not only to jazz illegally on the BBC but also the equally illegal news. They, like the young people in Hamburg, also avoided joining the Hitler Youth.[43] The Hot Club of Frankfurt was formed in 1941 and fought the HJ while a Berlin Hot Club was formed in 1934.[44] Club members frequented jazz spots in Berlin such as the Ciro, Quartier Latin, Carlton, and Patria.

'Round Midnight: Jazz, Jews and Race

One road to the obliteration of jazz was anti-Semitism. By linking Jews to jazz, a strategy employed from the beginning, a campaign against one was a campaign against the other. Jewish support, financing, and participation in jazz, in the United States as well as Germany, had existed early on. The music reached deep into the spirit of resistance against persecution that African Americans and Jews shared. Early Jewish jazz artists, most notably the swing leader Benny Goodman, often expressed this common heritage that resonated up to the contemporary period.

As attacks on the Jewish community escalated, including the area of culture, many Jewish artists left Germany. By 1938, most Jewish musicians (who could) had left the country. Most others were in the concentration camps, or making a living in some other non-music-related occupation. Having been banned from performing any type of music, they certainly were not playing jazz. The removal of Jewish musicians from the jazz scene was important because, according to Kater, they were the majority of the leaders and constituted a significant number of players.[45] Jewish jazz players, of course, found little solidarity with other German musicians or music leaders. The German classical musical elite of composers, players, and critics played a chief role in the Judaizing of jazz. The operetta composer Joseph Snaga bragged that he used only Aryan talent as his protest against "Jewish music and Nigger songs."[46] It should come as no surprise that many of these individuals, such as Snaga, both before and after 1933, were either open or secret members and supporters of the Nazi Party.

Nazi organizations across the board attacked jazz on anti-Semitic grounds, referring to the "Judeo-Negroid" essence of jazz.[47] The Hitler Youth, in particular, was concerned about the influence jazz had over the youth and the so-called machinations of Jews in exploiting the music. One HJ leader stated, "The Nigger has a very pronounced feeling for rhythm, and his 'art' is perhaps indigenous but nevertheless offensive to our sentiments. Surely, such stuff belongs among the Hottentots and not in a German dance hall. The Jew, on the other hand, has cooked these aberrations up on purpose."[48] In other words, the Nazis fell back on the trope of "naturalness" regarding black musicians who simply could not help themselves. However, according to this logic, the Jews were more conniving and this was part of the master plan of cultural and social control they were implementing.

The link between Blacks, Jews, and jazz (and homosexuals) was made graphically in 1938 when a now infamous poster was developed advertising an exposition in Dusseldorf of so-called "degenerate music." On the poster is a dark-skinned black man in a tuxedo and high top hat. He has extra large lips that are white, and an excessively wide nose. He is leaning over and playing a twisted saxophone. On his right lapel, he is

1938 anti-jazz poster against Entartete Musik (Degenerate Music).

wearing a Star of David, and in his right ear, a large, looping earring. Written in large letters across the bottom quarter of the poster are the words *Entartete Musik* ("degenerate music"). The image demonstrated an inseparable bond between Blacks, Jews, and jazz, though not an equal one. The dominant line among the Nazis was that it was Blacks who performed the music while it was Jews who functioned as composers, arrangers, publicists, financiers, and agents. In other words, Jews manipulated the musical genius or talents of Blacks and it was Jews, therefore, who were mostly responsible for the spread of jazz and its contamination of German culture.

Not in a Sentimental Mood: Jazz under Occupation

The failed campaign to eradicate jazz in Germany became even more complicated after the war started and lands were occupied or under attack. To the East and West, jazz was being played and loved by both local and international artists including many African Americans. Even after 1940, American jazz musicians were still performing in Europe, being among those who had been unwilling or unable to leave. In a number of instances, black, Gypsy, and Jewish jazz musicians were harassed, arrested, and imprisoned. In other cases, these musicians were left alone, at least initially.

There were several reasons why the Nazis occupiers made a relative peace with jazz outside of Germany. First, the Germans wanted to win over the citizens of these states, and after capturing them, they laid down somewhat tolerable rules. After the first stage of occupation, the Germans preferred a minimum amount of resistance, so they attempted to maintain a facade of normalcy. They also needed local cooperation in their rounding up of Jews and others they meant to destroy. Second, the Nazi leadership needed to please the Germany army troops and, despite what military law did not allow officially, conceded pleasures desired by the soldiers including listening to jazz or going to clubs where the music was played. Third, the Nazis also made profits from jazz by allowing it to be recorded and then sold on the international market. In several of the occupied nations, jazz records were a profitable business that the Nazis wanted to and did get in on. France, Belgium, Denmark, and the Netherlands were all hosts to jazz bands and a jazz culture at the time of the Nazi takeover.

France was the scene of a relatively vibrant and passionate jazz culture. The legendary Gypsy guitarist Django Reinhardt held forth in Paris during this time. Reinhardt and the France-based Quintet du Hot Club were considered by many to be the most important non-American jazz artists in Europe during the late 1930s and 1940s.[49] They generated a brand of swing that combined small combo rhythm with overlapping strings of guitar, violin, and bass. Although he had lost the use of two of his fingers on one hand, Reinhardt was viewed as a virtuoso and innovator, and by the time the war broke out, world famous. It was said that "Gypsies in concentration camps tried to save themselves by claiming to be Django Reinhardt."[50] Reinhardt was left virtually untouched by the Nazis after they seized Paris. He shared the spotlight and played with a number of black American jazz musicians who were in France during this time, including "Dixie" Lewis, Maisie Withers, and Palmer Jones, and the trumpet players

Bobby Jones, Gut Bucket, and Arthur Briggs.[51] The black musicians were banned from playing, most of the time, by the Nazi rulers.

In Amsterdam, jazz was quite popular before the Nazi takeover. Freddy Johnson was one of the African Americans who played there with a trio that consisted of a drummer, a tenor player, and himself on piano.[52] Johnson had played with the bandleader and composer Benny Carter, and the sax man Coleman Hawkins, among others. Johnson and the others had played all over Holland before the war, performing in Amsterdam, the Hague, and Rotterdam. Local jazz groups also existed including Het Ramblers Band, De Moochers, Boyd Bachmann, and Pim Maas Band.

In Copenhagen, the Willie Lewis Band, another African American jazz group, sought unsuccessfully to escape the Nazi dragnet and leave the continent.[53] Fats Waller and his band had managed to get out in time. Other Blacks in Denmark included the pianists Sammy Richardson and Jonny and Jimmy Campbell, and the Harlem Kiddies.[54] It is likely that many of these same groups played all over Belgium as well. It is known that Nazi soldiers went to Brussels, Antwerp, and Luttich to hear and dance to the music. At various points, when the Nazis attempted to crack down on jazz in the occupied lands, they ran into resistance. In France and Belgium, the "Zazous" who were the equivalent of the Swing Boys, formed.[55]

Mercy, Mercy, Mercy: Jazz in the Camps

The purgatory of the concentration camps was eerily filled with music of all sorts from classical and Yiddish folk songs to opera and jazz. Inmates were not only forced to play for the entertainment of the camp guards and officials and parties, but were also made to accompany shootings, hangings, executions, and marches to the gas chambers. In the torturous effort to survive another day, prisoners used every skill at their disposal including composing and performing music. While the release and pleasure that playing music gives may have been present, playing in the service of fascist captors certainly diminished any satisfaction the musicians could have felt. The always present threat of death, for the most arbitrary reasons, hung in the air.

Black and Jewish jazz artists were among those in the camps. Some of the black musicians were able or forced to play music while being held. The jazz trumpeter Briggs was arrested in 1940 during the war and sent to the Saint-Denis internment camp in France. Briggs's musical talents were put to use and may possibly have saved his life. He reportedly played jazz in the camp with a trio and conducted a twenty-five–piece classical orchestra. According to reports, there were two thousand internees at the camp of whom fifty were black.[56] Briggs was freed on 25 August 1944.[57] He would later claim that he was not mistreated nor did he witness any race prejudice.[58] After the Japanese bombed Pearl Harbor, which formally brought the United States into the war, the pianist Freddy Johnson was arrested by the Gestapo in Amsterdam and sent to a prisoner-of-war camp in late December 1941. He would be exchanged for some German prisoners in 1944 and allowed to return to the States.[59] The Nazis also arrested the black American jazz pianist John Welch, who had initially praised Germany under Hitler, and sent him to a camp. [60] Another African American musician imprisoned by the Nazis was the pianist Charlie Lewis.[61] One last example is an unnamed black American musician interred at the Kassel concentration camp in the north of Germany after being arrested in Paris. He was made to conduct the camp's fifty-person symphony orchestra composed of white prisoners.[62]

In some of these instances, Jewish and black jazz musicians played together. Many of the Jewish jazz artists had learned about the American jazz scene through records, the radio, and jazz magazines, particularly *Downbeat*. Primarily through these means they came to "know" African American jazz culture and styles. For many Jewish players, the camps provided the first chance to meet, let alone play with, black musicians. Unfortunately, there is little historical record from either side on this musical bonding under tragic circumstances.

There were also ethical and moral issues that plagued those who survived while so many others around them died. In the camps to be privileged with life always went with the painful acknowledgment that others were not. Capriciousness, luck, and unpredictability more often than heroism or individual will power determined who lived and who died on a daily basis. Yet this understanding did not diminish the immediate and long-term guilt that many surviving musicians would harbor for decades.

It is unknown how widespread the playing of jazz was at the various concentration and labor camps. However, there is documented evidence and testimony that jazz was performed at three of the most notorious and dreadful concentration camps: Auschwitz, Flossenburg, and Theresienstadt.[63] In these camps, where millions were murdered in the most horrific ways imaginable, musical groups were created to perform a genre, jazz, despised by Hilter and most of the leading Nazis. Jazz was also performed at some POW camps. There was a jazz combo, for instance, at Stalag 8–A at Gorlitz in Saxony. The band consisted of drums, sax, trumpet, accordian, and triangle.

Auschwitz

Auschwitz holds a hallowed place in the pantheon of concentration camps. For many, Auschwitz is the Holocaust, the best-known symbol of the systemized depravity of Nazism and the forging of Jewish memories of an era of unmitigated anti-Semitic hate. Though popularly seen as one camp, it was actually a network of three main camps— Auschwitz-I, Auschwitz-II (Auschwitz-Birkenau), and Auschwitz-III (Auschwitz-Monowitz)—and about forty satellite camps. It was mostly at Auschwitz II where 900,000 or so Jews were gassed.[64] The Auschwitz camps, which used slave labor, also held and murdered Poles, Russians, and Gypsies by the tens of thousands.

In this nightmare existence, this commune of unyielding suffering, there were symphonies, operas, and other forms of music played, including jazz. An all-woman orchestra was created that played as the gassing and shootings were taking place. Fania Fenelon, an orchestra member who survived, wrote a memoir of the experience, *Playing for Time*, whose title captures the anxiety that drove the music. Fenelon, a Jewish cabaret singer in prewar France, had participated in the Resistance and was eventually caught. Within a day of her arrival, someone recognized her as a musician and songstress and she was put into the orchestra. Often, Fenelon's orchestra and other bands would be forced to play for twelve hours a day.[65] Her story was made into a controversial 1980 television movie, *Playing for Time*. It starred the radical actress Vanessa Redgrave in the title role. Redgrave was known to be pro-Palestinian, and many Jewish groups, in addition to Fenelon, protested her selection. Not only did the film get made, but Redgrave also won an Emmy for her portrayal.

As noted, jazz also made an appearance at Auschwitz. A jazz band was formed and led by the Polish trumpeter and accordian player Bronislaw Stasiak.[66] Before the occupation, Poland had a relatively dynamic jazz life that somehow continued even after the Nazis took over and banned dancing. Even under fascism, a number of jazz groups, including one led by Stasiak, flourished, performing at Warsaw's Butterfly Theater and the Golden Seven. There was also a combo led by George Scott, who was mixed-race. Reportedly, the Auschwitz band lasted for only a short while and included Marciej Dobrzynsky, a well-known Polish jazz drummer.[67]

Flossenbürg

Jazz was also played at the Flossenbürg Concentration Camp.[68] In May 1938, Flossenbürg, located near Bayreuth, Germany, became the fourth concentration camp to be established, after Dachau, Buchenwald, and Sachsenhausen, with more than ninety-three subcamps. Flossenbürg was a camp that even the SS considered harsh. It had crematories and other places where executions and killings were carried out. By estimates, more than 111,000 prisoners passed through Flossenbürg and more than 73,000 died inside its gates and the electrified barbed wire fence that surrounded the place. According to the camp survivor Wieslaw Machan, inmates were killed so quickly that the Nazis did not even bother to mark them with numbers.

Machan describes how the jazz band there came into being. When captives first arrived, they were separated into those who could be useful in some kind of way and those who would die immediately such as lawyers, engineers, and teachers. One category that was selected for at least temporary survival was that of musicians. Machan, who came to the camp in 1944, intially played piano but later switched to violin. He first performed in the quasi-symphony orchestra, but at some point a six-piece jazz band was started. In that group, he played double bass. Although musicians had double duty in that they had to work during the day, they did get extra rations such as "a half a loaf of bread, some marmalade, and a few cigarettes."[69]

Theresienstadt

In 1941, the Nazis created Terezín (*Theresienstadt* in German), located north of Prague, Czechoslovakia, as an entire town cum concentration camp for Jews. It was a political sleight of hand to try to convince the international community that Jews were not being persecuted and slaughtered as rumors of the gruesomeness of the concentration camps started to spread. The Nazis even made a film, *The Fuehrer Gives Jews a City*, to sell this deception. The town at its peak held over 140,000 people, that is, prisoners. Ultimately, fewer than 20,000 survived, most being shipped to Auschwitz and other camps where they died. Terezin was unique among concentration camps in that the prisoners were allowed to express themselves culturally and music of all kinds was permitted, although the instruments were makeshift or used.

In a now classic cover article the 7 December 1961 issue of *Downbeat* magazine, the jazz trumpeter Eric Vogel wrote about his 1939 arrest by the Nazis in Brno, Czechoslovakia, and the eventual command he received to organize a jazz course and teach classes in theory and history in the Jewish ghetto. Out of this course came the jazz combo the Kille Dillers that played in the Benny Goodman swing style. The name came from an article in *Downbeat* read by Vogel that used the term "killer diller," meaning something of high quality. Vogel did not know what the phrase meant, but he liked the sound of it. He dropped the "r," and "killer" became "Kille," which ironically was the name of the Jewish community (from the Hebrew word *kehilah*).[70] The group's existence was short-lived, however, because the transports to the concentration camps escalated and on 25 March 1942, Vogel got his order to go. He was sent to Theresienstadt.

Several jazz bands were created in the town. The first was a band led by the clarinetist Bedrich Weiss that began in December 1941 in the Sudeten Barracks. Weiss apparently made a deal with a guard to get music and instruments. The quintet fell apart in the late summer of 1944 after Weiss left with his father on a transport to Auschwitz, and they both died there. The best-known jazz band to emerge was the Ghetto Swingers, founded by Vogel in 1943. Some of its members overlapped with Weiss's group. The band grew as large as thirteen members. Jewish members came from Germany, Holland, Denmark, and Czechoslovakia. Unfortunately, with the exception of a very few Danish and Dutch band members, all the other players were deported to Auschwitz and other camps when Theresienstadt was closed in 1944.

All Blues: The African American Reponse to the Nazi Jazz Attack

Black American newspapers were diligent in following the developments in Germany under Hitler that related to racism. That sophistication was demonstrated in their even getting and reproducing copies of articles in German newspapers and magazines that addressed these issues. On 21 December 1935, the *Norfolk Journal and Guide* reprinted part of an article that had appeared in the virulently racist German newspaper *Stuermer*, which charged that jazz was a creation of Jewish composers. The indignant headline of the *Journal and Guide* was "Nazis 'Clear' Us of Jazz, Blame Jews." The headline sarcastically made the point that the Nazis would not credit African Americans with development of even the despised jazz phenomenon. The quoted article stated,

> Jazz music hails from the brains of Jewish curb composers, invented at a time when the Jews reigned over the Fatherland and triumphed over German folk songs with their dirty Jewish jokes and ditties. It is quite wrong when people say that jazz hails from the Negroes. The Negro race has nothing to do with jazz, since Africans don't know any jazz music. It's the Jewish race that invented jazz, and made it fit the Jewish idea of life with its disharmony and distortion.

> The gigantic contrast between German and Nordic music and jazz is the same as the gigantic contrast between a man of nordic [*sic*] race and a Jew. A later period will fail to understand how it was possible for the Jews to make German people accept their jazz tunes and jazz dancing. The German people created the biggest composers of all times such as Johann Strauss, Mozart, Schubert, Haydn, Franz Liszt, Beethoven, Bach, Richard Wagner, and many more, and it's a shame that the German nation during the two decades had to stand this abominable jazz craze.[71]

African Americans took it very personally when Goebbels stated, "Everyone knows America's contribution to the music of the world consists merely of jazzed-up Nigger music, not worthy of a single mention."[72] The defense of jazz, in particular the roots of its genesis, by African Americans was seen as the equivalent of defending the race as a whole. Just as white American criticism of jazz was viewed through a racial lens, Nazi critiques, shorn of any pretense of racial comity, were read for the racist diabtribes that they were.

Body and Soul: Summary

In the two major works on jazz under Nazism, Michael H. Kater's *Different Drummers: Jazz in the Culture of Nazi Germany* and Mike Zwerin's *La Tristesse de Saint Louis: Jazz under the Nazis,* Nazi antiblackness is viewed somewhat differently. Zwerin tends to reduce or dismiss racism as a central motivator of the regime's antijazz campaign. Kater, on the other hand, accumulates a great deal of evidence of the critical energy that the Nazis gave to denouncing the black and especially African American character of the music. He attempts to locate that discourse within a framework that views Negrophobia as an element of Nazi social thought and practice.

Both authors are correct not to see antiblackness as the sole motivation for the attacks on jazz, but neither was it secondary. Although I agree that the perceived "democratic" nature of the music was the chief target of the antijazz campaign, the democracy in jazz is not racially neutral but organic to the music's history and its political meaning. Their antiblackness was not limited because the Nazis had only fragmentary contact with real African Americans. In fact, a consciousness about Blacks and blackness existing a priori that contact only subjectively reinforced but, in the end, was unnecessary. Although the Nazis and Germans generally could (and would) go from racial romanticism of African Americans to virulent viciousness and back again, at the core was a deeply embraced sense of superiority. In 1936 and 1938, this sense would be tested and bested in the arena of arenas.

9

Punched Out and Overrun

Black Athleticism
Meets Nazi Racism

> *German sport has only one task: to strengthen the character of the German people, imbuing it with the fighting spirit and steadfast camaraderie necessary in the struggle for its existence.*
>
> —*Joseph Goebbels, minister of propaganda, 23 April 1933*

Gupha Voss is an Afro-German survivor from the Hitler times. In an interview, she recalled how the second historic fight between the African American boxer Joe Louis and the German fighter Max Schmeling in 1938 was received in Nazi Germany. Her father, who was black, had watched the fight in a public bar. When it was over, and Louis had unceremoniously dispatched Schmeling in less time than it took to announce the two pugilists, Voss's father was asked what he thought of the fight. Clearly thinking diplomatically (and doubtless with his personal security in mind), but also with an edge of diasporic pride, he replied, "In sports, the best man wins." Suddenly, he was hit in the head from behind with an iron chair, requiring him to go to the hospital emergency room. Unfortunately, his suffering did not end there. He was stitched up by a doctor who refused to give him any anesthesia. The doctor, likely a Schmeling fan, certainly one of Hitler's, racially rationalized this "medical" decision by stating, "People from the jungle can take it."[1] The acknowledgment or acceptance of black athletic superiority, domestic or foreign, was intolerable under Nazism.

Hitler's Athletes: The Racialization of Sports under Nazism

Nineteen thirty-six was a decisive year in the history of Nazism. It was probably the last opportunity for the international community to isolate Hitler and to support whatever opposition might have arisen in a unified stand against the fascist state. Although the

Germans had already established concentration camps and were implementing and facilitating attacks on their perceived internal enemies, they were still cautious about how far they could go with regard to international considerations. On 7 March 1936, however, Hitler escalated the tensions when German troops invaded the Rhineland and seized it back in the name of German nationalism and in direct and bold violation of the Treaty of Versailles. This was a critical test of wills between Nazi Germany and the Western European powers, a test that the latter failed.

A further test of the big powers' commitment to challenging Hitler came in the contest over whether to hold the 1936 Olympics in Germany. Although the decision to have the games there had been made prior to Hitler's coming to power, an international movement against the German Games did arise. But with representatives from the United States leading the way, the movement was unsuccessful in stopping the Olympics and denying Hitler at least a symbolic upper hand in legitimizing the Nazi state. Increasingly, the debate regarding the legitimacy of Germany in the family of nations pivoted on its theories and policies regarding race. An organized global Jewish community continued to expose the rising attacks on German Jews and the racist proclamations emanating from all quarters of Nazi leadership. African Americans would also engage in these debates as news about the treatment of Jews and people of African descent reached black newspapers and civil rights leaders. It became clear that no area of social life would escape the racial discussion including that of sports.

In many ways, the notion of athletic superiority tied to race invoked a debate that ran on the turf of biological determinism. The argument of physical superiority was problematic on all sides. To link race to athletics was to enjoin the notion that physical attributes were racially determined. It was unavoidable, however, in an atmosphere both in the United States and Germany that racialized every human activity. The problem of racializing athletics was framed and exacerbated by the reality of segregation that not only constricted the social spaces of Blacks in both societies but promoted black heroes almost solely in the area of sports. Unfortunately, this led to a disproportionate emphasis on the achievements of black athletes as advances for the black race as a whole. Beyond the problematic cultural acceptance of a racially gifted body, many in the U.S. black community embraced white racist notions of black physical supremacy that was a trade-off for beliefs in black intellectual inferiority. The social structure of racial power that limited (barely) acceptable black victories in the public sphere to sports, at best, needed to be challenged on the embedded assumptions of racial differences.

Sports were also viewed racially in another manner. For many, sports were seen as the magic bullet of racial unity. Though segregation persisted, common loyalty to home teams signaled cross-racial bonding that had the potential of translating into broader social arenas. This perspective was articulated by civil rights leaders, white liberals, and, most strongly, by athletes themselves.

The racializing of sports in Germany, the United States, and elsewhere, of course, did not begin with the black community but emerged from a worldview that needed difference in order to build, consolidate, and perpetuate power. At every juncture of the European encounter with people of African descent, the notion of superiority was necessary and the black body was always viewed as less than that of Whites. The embrace of the black athlete by Blacks, even to the present, is a response to the racist notions of black inferiority that characterize the fears of white defeat. For a subjugated community (globally), winning sports figures represent the claiming of ideological territory against racism. That these atlethes themselves often represent less than a stellar antiracist posture or that few vestiges of power are actually opposed or destroyed in this celebration has little damped the embrace or dissipated the debate. The contemporary black community discourse over the racial status of the multiracial golfer Tiger Woods and his own controversial contribution to the discussion by his creative racial term "Cablinasian" reflects more than a century of arguments over the relationship between race and sports.

The racialization of sports under Nazism extended a discourse that existed globally regarding the relationship between race and athletics. Since slavery and colonialism, and the physical interaction between the oppressed and the oppressing, myths and tropes about the racialized black body abounded. On the one hand, the black body was seen as inferior in all aspects, underdeveloped, weak, separated from the mind. Yet, on the other hand, a discourse that saw colonialized and enslaved peoples as beasts and subhuman often attributed to them an animalistic strength and aggression that was natural and afforded a physical (though never mental) advantage. This inferior-superior dichotomy was boosted by the so-called rigorous investigations of the science of eugenics. Nazi arguments about the physical and athletic reign of Whites echoed elite and popular beliefs held in much of North America and Europe. In Germany and the United States, in particular, these notions were manifest in segregating sports as much as possible. The Nazis excluded Jews from German sports associations, for example, the amateur boxing champion Eric Seelig, the top tennis player Daniel Press, and world-class high jumper Gretel Bergmann, among others. Gypsies were also expelled, such as the Sinti boxer Johann "Rukelie" Trollmann who had been the middleweight boxing champion.

Despite the inveighing against the participation of Blacks (and Jews) in German sports events, there was, in fact, participation from both groups, at least in the early years of the Nazi era. There was at least one Black who was involved in German athletics at the national level. Louis Brody-Alcolson was a heavyweight wrestler on a national wrestling team that included a large number of Nazi Party members. Born Louis M'bele Mpessa, he was on the Circus Crown team in 1936 and perhaps even longer. In a picture of the team competing at the Internationale Ringkampf-Konkurrenz im Schwergewicht (Ring-fight-competition in the Heavyweight division), in which seven members are wearing swaztikas including one sitting next to Brody-Alcolson, he is right up front with the rest. His inclusion in the picture indicates not only his acceptance on the team but a willingness to let it be known to a broad audience. It is possible that the picture was taken and released for propaganda purposes in a year when Germany was trying to maintain friendly international ties. Unfortunately, there is little biographical information available regarding Brody-Alcolson. It is not known how he got on the team, how he was treated by the team, what he achieved, or any personal details, that is, was he married and to whom, did he have children, and how did the state respond to him and his family? It is known that he died in 1951 at the age of fifty-nine, meaning that he did not die during the war.[2] More research is needed to know what his fortunes were during the war, that is, whether he was in the army, war-related industries, a concentration camp, or lived as professional athlete.

As we know from Massaquoi's memoirs, there was also black sports participation at the local level. Massaquoi discusses how he trained as a boxer and became pretty proficient. He was actually approached by a local trainer, Rudi, around the age of twelve and soon became very proficient, often whipping boys older and larger. However, as good as he was, he was not able to go further than his local Hamburg gym. After a couple of years of training, Rudi submitted an application to the Reichssportverband (Reich Sports Association)—which naturally included a question on racial heritage—on Massquoi's behalf for participation in a national tournament. The application was rejected because of his race.[3]

An important dimension of Massaquoi's discussion of the impact of Joe Louis and the African American Olympic participants is the raciomasculinist nature of their sports. He notes that he "felt a surge of pride" from the victories and renown of Louis, Jesse Owens, and other black sports figures and that pride sustained him throughout his challenging childhood years. Boxing, in particular, was a male-accessible sport (in those days) and a means of masculinist expression that was not available, except by proxy, to women. While Afro-German and African women in Germany likely also embraced the emotions that went with Louis's loss and victory, and the black Olympic wins, there were also limits to their opportunities to participate in the celebration, anguish, and popular interpretation of the events. Many, if not most, black men felt a loss or diminished manhood as a result of Louis's defeat by Schmeling, while, conversely, his 1938 revenge was also a regaining of male dignity. Unfortunately, there is no record of the views of black German women on their reading of the Louis fights and the racial and gender politics of the Olympics.

While the Nazis may have opportunistically tolerated Brody-Alcolson and a few other Africans and Afro-Germans on some of their sports teams, they vehemently rejected any notion that Blacks were physically capable of competing with Aryans, particularly Germans. African Americans were seen as the epitome of this inadequacy thesis. Nazi theories of racial athletic superiority over African Americans would be tested twice in 1936 (and again in 1938), in the first Joe Louis–Max Schmeling heavyweight nontitle bout and the Berlin Olympics games.

And the Beat Goes On: Race, Nation, and the Louis-Schmeling Fights

> And here one sport in particular must not be forgotten, which in the eyes of many 'folkish' minded people is considered vulgar and undignified: boxing. . . . There is no sport that so much as this one promotes the spirits of attack, demands lightning decisions, and trains the body in steel dexterity. It is no more vulgar for two young men to fight out a difference of opinion with their fists than with a piece of whetted iron.
>
> —Adolf Hitler[4]

In the mid-1930s, professional boxing was among the few integrated sports in the United States. Professional teams in baseball, football, basketball, and hockey were Jim Crowed and had no black figures. Boxing, known as the "sweet" science where accomplishment and success were completely rooted in individual heroics, had not necessarily handled integration with honor, however. Since the first African American heavyweight champion, Jack Johnson, and the racist persecution that he had to endure including fleeing the country to avoid charges of interracial sexual congress across state lines, black boxers were always fighting at the crossroads of race and sports. The film critic Donald Bogle notes how film clips of Johnson's 1908 championship victory over his white opponent, Tommy Burns, were banned in theaters around the United States because it was feared that race riots would occur if Whites actually saw a black man plummeling a white champion.[5] It did not help ease white anxieties that Johnson was self-confident, flamboyant, and considered racially arrogant, that is, not subservient.

By the mid-1930s, the prizefighter Joe Louis was a hero to American Blacks. Each of his victories generated exhilaration and racial pride, creating, if only temporarily, a liberation zone of racial accomplishment. That his conquests occurred in the face of racists of all sorts made them that much tastier. Called the "Zooming Zulu" and the "Tan Tarzan" by white commentators, Louis had to endure endless insults and slurs. At one bout, he was introduced by, "Although colored. . . . " Known affectionately by the black community as the "Brown Bomber" for his string of knockouts, Louis viewed himself not just as a skilled black man who rose up from Alabama and Detroit but as a race ambassador. Contrary to Johnson, Louis's response to the racial environment he found himself in was to accommodate rather than directly challenge it. He embraced a "role model" paradigm in which he felt his public face had to be one of subdued presentation and he limited the opportunities of racists to transfer to him indictments of the whole race. Louis would not even eat watermelon, which he loved, in public because he was conscious of showing a positive image of Blacks.

In 1936, as Depression raged and tensions in Europe grew, Louis, the top contender for the championship against the titleholder, James Braddock, scheduled a fight between himself and the relatively underappreciated former champion from Germany, Max Schmeling. As a boxer, Schmeling was so-so, having lost his 1930 championship only two years after winning it. As a German of international fame, however, he was more complicated. He represented the Nazi state on the world stage, although he never formally joined the Nazi Party. During the war, he became a paratrooper in the Germany military, but, going against the racial grain, he had a Jewish manager/trainer throughout his boxing career. In the end, Schmeling never reconciled these contradictions and maintained a soiled legacy of contributions to Nazism at its most critical hour in the prewar years. Allowing himself to be used by Hitler, whether for career or country, ultimately worked in the service of fascism and racism.

Despite some early hype, the Germans had little hope that Schmeling would beat Louis in their first encounter, and, therefore, they did little to promote the fight. In fact, they were preparing to lay the anticipated Schmeling defeat to Louis's supposed brute character. On 19 June 1936, after rain postponed the fight a day, it was held in Yankee

Stadium. To the world's shock, in the twelfth round, Schmeling knocked Louis to the canvas where he remained for the decisive count of ten. Louis had not properly trained and prepared for the fight and was not in very good shape. Schmeling was able to endure Louis's relatively weak punches and seize the opportunities when they came. According to boxing experts, Schmeling saw Louis drop his left hand repeatedly and would consistently tag Louis with powerful right-hand punches.

Louis's own views on the fight were somewhat muted though precise. He stated insightfully, "White Americans—even while some of them still were lynching black people in the South—were depending on me to K.O. Germany."[6] I have some doubts about the split-consciousness theory of Louis because there were a great number of Whites who recognized that the defeat of the white German did mean more than one nation besting another, or democracy beating fascism. Many Whites would likely have preferred no fight at all because it was a no-win situation: either national loss or racial loss. Certainly, anticipation of a postfight celebration by millions of African Americans brought more than a little racial stress. However, Louis was correct in seeing the contradictory aspect of being cheered by a nation that wanted a victory even if it was achieved by a black man.

The black community was itself knocked out by Louis's loss. In the United States, black newspapers wailed in the wake of the fight. Plans for dancing in the streets and all-night victory parties were shelved as the mourning and even embarrassment began. If Massaquoi's disappointment and shock were representative, Blacks in Germany felt the same way. He provides some perspective into how the German branch of the diaspora tree dealt with the fight and Louis's loss. As a ten-year-old mixed-race child who looked a helluva lot more like Louis than Schmeling, Massaquoi switched loyalties from the nation's hero to the Braune Bomber while also becoming the center of attention in his crowd of friends as the fight loomed. It was one of the few times in his childhood when he felt pride in his African heritage and black status. The impossibility of a black hero in Germany was abridged by the relentless racialization of Louis and the fight by the Nazis. Massaquoi's smugness was bursting not only because Louis was such a good fighter but also because he was about to beat the stuffings out of the highly promoted German national idol. After getting up at 2 A.M. to catch the fight that started an hour later German time, he would spend the night mourning with millions of other Blacks in the United States (and probably elsewhere), also anticipating correctly the harassment to come. He got into a fight when he went to school over the teasing by his classmates. In the end, although his hero was defeated, Massaquoi's prefight respect seemed to survive as some recognized that Louis had lost honorably.[7]

Needless to say, once Schmeling won, he was heralded as the greatest boxer in German history. Additionally, he had defeated not only an American but a black one at that. For the Nazis, this was a double reinforcement of the superiority of Aryans and of the German people. He was flown back on the *Hindenburg* and treated as a conquering hero. The Nazi weekly journal *Das Schwarze Korps* (*The Black Corps*) commented, "Schmeling's victory was not only sport. It was a question of prestige for our race." The

German minister of propaganda, Joseph Goebbels, proclaimed Schmeling's victory a triumph for Germany and Hitlerism and turned his victory into one of the most successful Nazi films ever made. *Max Schmeling's Sieg—Ein Deutscher* (*Max Schmeling's Victory, A German Victory*) reached millions and offset the Olympic defeats the Germans would experience later that year.

Feeling vindicated, the Nazis believed that the fight supported their claims of racial superiority. One article, reprinted in the U.S. black press, argued that the victory should be embraced not only by Germany, but also by England, France, and "white North America." *Der Weltkampf* wrote, "The Negro is of a slave nature, but woe unto us if this slave nature is unbridled, for then arrogance and cruelty show themselves in the most bestial way . . . these three countries—France, England, and white North America—cannot thank Schmeling enough for his victory, for he checked the arrogance of the Negro and clearly demonstrated to them the superiority of white intelligence."[8] This rhetorical effort at building a white united front against the Negro shielded the real master plan of the Nazis that was unfolding. Within two short years, German aggression against its neighbors and the threat of a second multinational war in less than twenty years would put the second Louis-Schmeling clash in an even more intense global light.

There would be a different outcome in 1938 in the rematch. Louis was well prepared as the growing war mood in the United States and the breaking waves of war in Europe formed the backdrop for a fight whose racial overtones were intense and transparent. Louis had been brought to the White House and given a pep talk by President Roosevelt.[9] Many boxing and nonboxing fans saw the fight as a symbolic showdown between American democracy and German dictatorship. Germany was no longer attempting to mollify its European opponents and dismissed critiques of its racial and political policies toward Jews, who were now being gathered in large numbers and sent to the concentration camps. Though given no international attention, harsher policies toward Blacks, including sterilization and forced labor, had also grown. The Louis-Schmeling fight no longer was simply about national or racial pride; it was the opening shot in a battle for world domination.

In the rematch, Louis defeated Schmeling in 124 seconds of the first round. Louis would frame this battle in political terms, stating, "To the world Schmeling's defeat foretold of things to come for Nazi Germany."[10] This time there was celebrations in the streets of black America, particularly in Harlem where Blacks by the tens of thousands rejoiced over Louis's triumph—again, over not just Germany and Hitler but white America's hesitancy to accept African Americans as full citizens capable of representing the nation on a global scale. This victory was, of course, unacceptable to the Nazis who reportedly pulled the plug on the international broadcast of the fight and banned newspapers from printing details of Schmeling's trouncing.

Two years earlier, Nazi celebration of Schmeling's 1936 win had been short-lived. Only two months later, with the whole world watching, African American athletes would outrun, outjump, and outlast the best that the Nazis could throw at them in the Eleventh Olympiad.

Run, Jesse, Run: The 1936 Olympics

Occurring in the middle of the Depression, the Olympics provided the opportunity for national assertion and a means by which states could divert attention from the poverty and suffering of their citizens. Although only forty-nine nations participated, the Olympics drew international attention and focus. For much of the world, it was the first glimpse of Hitler on the world stage. The dictator and the Nazi state received premium exposure and hoped to use the Games to validate its notions of Aryan and German superiority. To Hitler's everlasting displeasure, not only was Germany defeated in numerous events, its most high-profile losses came at the hands and feet of African Americans. These victories would be read as achievements for people of African descent everywhere. The 1936 Olympics stood out for Blacks for several reasons: the spectular wins by black athletes; the slanderous language used by Nazi leaders about African Americans; and the "snub" incident. Some would credit the Olympic triumphs and the controversial Nazi response as the final push in solidifying the black community against fascism.

That the Games happened at all was not a given. Lost in the popular history of the historic 1936 Olympics are the international boycott movements that sought to prevent the Games from being held on German soil, movements against facism, racism, and anti-Semitism that included African Americans, Jews, communists, trade unionists, and religious leaders from around the world.

The Boycott

On 13 May 1931, two years before Hitler came to power, the International Olympic Committee (IOC), headed by Count Henri Baillet-Latour of Belgium, awarded the 1936 Summer Olympics to Berlin. It did not take long after the Nazis assumed power for a protest movement to emerge against having the upcoming Olympics in Germany because of the fascist state's discriminatory views and policies toward Jews. Though initially hesitant about having the Games, Hitler soon realized the unprecendented public relations bonanza he had been given. He placed Hans von Tschammer und Osten, who headed the Reich Sports Office, in charge of the German Olympic Committee that was to plan the Games. This hard-core Nazi had supervised the segregation and expulsion of Jews, Gypsies, and Blacks, among others, from participation in German athletic events. His selection and escalating evidence of Nazi anti-Semitism led many to believe that it was hypocritical and immoral to hold the Games in Germany. The early protests led some of the Olympic officials, including Avery Brundage, president of the American Olympic Committee, to consider moving the Games. Reiterating the principles of inclusion and antiracism, Brundage stated, "The very foundation of the modern Olympic revival will be undermined if individual countries are allowed to restrict participation by reason of class, creed, or race."[11] The Nazi response to this threat was to invite Olympic officials to a tour of Germany and the proposed facilities to assuage concerns that Jews were under attack and that Jewish athletes were being treated unfairly. The sham worked, and Brundage and others concluded that the Games should be held in Nazi Germany. Brundage was not an objective and disinterested observer. He reportedly was close to Karl Ritter von Halt, the German representative to the International

Olympic Committee and a loyal member of the Nazi Party. It was von Halt who escort-
ed Brundage and the others during the 1935 inspection.

The capitulation by the IOC did not stop the momentum of the boycott movement.
Indeed, the movement expanded to include a wide range of non-Jewish groups. A
number of African American leaders and publications joined with Jewish activists and
leaders in calling for the United States to boycott the Games on the grounds that
Germany under the Nazis was a racist state. Some of these activists were also attempting to point a finger back home at the United States. The *Baltimore Afro-American*
wrote an editorial as early as 1934 unambiguously titled "Boycott the Olympics."[12] The
NAACP's *Crisis* also called early for a boycott for the same reasons, stating, "Keep
American athletes at home in 1936. In the meantime, if we just have to work up a lath-
er over discrimination in sports, let us address ourselves to the color line in our own
backyard."[13] These and other calls by African Americans for the United States to stay
out were due not only to objections to the Nazi racial policies and statements that were
already well known in black America, but also to the anticipation of how black
American athletes would be treated in Germany. While there were some African
Americans who argued that indigenous Blacks in Germany and other people of African
descent were being treated well, most felt that Hitler's treatment of the Jews was a short
step away from how he viewed Blacks. The black press meanwhile wrote numerous editorials denouncing the Games and Hitler and loudly urged that the United States not
go. Comparisons with the treatment of African Americans in the United States were
offered as another reason to stay away. The segregation that was being imposed on
Germany's Jews mirrored the segregation that African Americans lived under not only
in the South, where de jure discrimination prevailed, but also in other parts of the
country de facto.

However, the boycott momentum in the black community was dissipated when the
Nazi-influenced IOC, after its 1935 visit, concluded that it was safe for African American athletes to participate in the Games. Also, in December 1935, the *Chicago Defender*
reported that the black track and field stars Jesse Owens, Ralph Metcalfe, and Eulace
Peacock (who was ultimately unable to go due to injuries) favored participating
because they felt that their potential victories would serve to repudiate Nazi racial theories.[14] With the IOC stamp of approval and leading black athletes eager to go, most
African American newspapers that had initially supported the boycott now opposed it.
In defending their new position, some Black journalists and newspapers pointed out
truthfully that the leading advocates of the boycott had not spoken out previously
about the problem of discrimination against Black athletes in the United States. The
Philadelphia Tribune stated, "The AAU shouts against the cruelties of the other nations
and the brutalities in foreign climates, but conveniently forgets the things that sit on its
own doorstep."[15]

Failure to support the boycott was problematic politically. Belief that the Nazi movement and, by extrapolation, racism in the United States would be undermined by black
victories was illusionary. Much of this was rooted in faith that demonstration of
black national pride would convince racists that African Americans deserved full civil

and political rights. This view failed to see that there were many Whites who held perspectives quite similar to Hitler and even more who did not accept Blacks as equals. Also, while black newspapers were now willing to casually drop or soften their revulsion for Nazi anti-Semitism, they also did not address the issue of Afro-Germans and their participation opportunities or, more broadly, their safety and status. A critical opportunity for solidarity that could have demonstrated a united front opposing racism across group boundaries that faced similar systems of oppression was squandered.

Yet the campaign grew internationally. Efforts emerged in Great Britain, France, Sweden, Czechoslovakia, and the Netherlands, although none would last long. Some Germans in exile would lead many of these campaigns. One group of German socialists and communists living outside Germany published a newspaper, *Arbeiter Illustrierte Zeitung (The Worker Illustrated Newspaper)*, that supported the boycott movement.

Not only was there support for a counter-Olympics, the "People's Olympiad" that was planned for summer 1936 in Barcelona, but it was actually in the process of being staged when the Spanish Civil War forced it to close down. Thousands of athletes had actually traveled to Barcelona in July 1936 to participate. Many Jewish athletes from some European countries and elsewhere chose to boycott the Berlin Olympics whether their country did or not. These campaigns became even more intense after the 1935 Nuremberg laws stripping Jews of all political and civil rights were enacted.

The boycott and protest movement against the Games manifested itself among Olympic officials with the American Ernest Lee Jahncke, representing the United States on the IOC, strenuously arguing against going to Germany. In a 25 November 1935 letter to IOC President Baillet-Latour, he wrote, "Neither Americans nor the representatives of other countries can take part in the Games in Nazi Germany without at least acquiescing in the contempt of the Nazis for fair play and their sordid exploitation of the Games."[16] Jahncke, a former assistant secretary of the U.S. Navy and actually of German descent, fought Brundage and others over the issue. Ultimately, Jahncke was expelled from the IOC and cynically replaced by Brundage. Reportedly, he is the only member in the history of the modern IOC to be ousted.

In November 1935, trade unionists in New York City held a rally in support of the Olympics boycott. Also, in the same month, the Committee on Fair Play in Sports came out in favor of the boycott. In a statement, it noted, " . . . sport is prostituted when sport loses its independent and democratic character and becomes a political institution . . . Nazi Germany is endeavoring to use the Eleventh Olympiad to serve the necessities and interests of the Nazi Regime rather than the Olympic ideals."[17] Jeremiah Mahoney, president of the AAU, the most important sports organization for those athletes who wanted to participate in the Games, recommended against going to Germany. At the AAU, a critical and decisive vote was held to decide whether a U.S. team would be sent to Berlin. Brundage operated behind the scenes to pressure the vote in support of the Germans. On 8 December 1935, in an extremely close vote, the AAU defeated the proposal to boycott the Olympics by only two and a half votes. Having survived all the protests, the IOC moved forward with the Games.

Image Management and the Olympics

In 1936, the Nazis were still concerned about their image. It is well known, for instance, that Hitler ordered signs taken down that discriminated against Jews. On 16 July 1936, in a move to "clean up" Berlin before the Olympics, the German Ministry of Interior authorized the Berlin police chief to arrest all Gypsies prior to the Games, and more than 800 Gypsies were held under police guard in a special Gypsy camp in Marzahn, a Berlin suburb.

Goebbels's office issued a number of press statements or rather orders as to how the Olympics should be covered. While the Nazis did not exclude initially two women of partial Jewish heritage from the Games, hoping to win medals for the nation and appear less anti-Semitic, the Reich Press Chamber made it ominously clear that their racial heritage was not to be mentioned. In an edict issued 19 February 1936, it commanded, "No comments should be made regarding Helene Mayer's non-Aryan ancestry or her expectations for a gold medal at the Olympics." Another statement, on 16 July 1936, was issued just before the Games commenced reemphasizing the point. It stated, "Press coverage should not mention that there are two non-Aryans among the women: Helene Mayer (fencing) and Gretel Bergmann (high jump and all-around track and field competition)."

Ultimately, the Nazis could not tolerate having a full Jew represent the nation. Mayer, in the racial ranking of Nazism, was somewhat marginally acceptable because she was mixed, her father being Jewish and her mother Christian. Bergmann, on the other hand, had no racially redeeming qualities according to the Nazis. On the same day that the 16 July statement was released, Bergmann received a letter notifying her that she had not qualified for the high-jump team even though she had tied a world record in pregame trials and the Germans had filled only two of three slots available.

Contradictory messages emanated from the Nazi leadership regarding how black athletes were to be covered in the press. On the one hand, the reference to African Americans as "auxiliaries" and other slanderous remarks by Hitler, other Nazi leaders, and German newspapers reflected genuinely the racial lens through which Blacks were seen.[18] The racial and racist boasting that had occurred after the Schmeling win in June left little room for doubt about Nazism's prejorative ideas about black people. Yet the imperative of appearing to be pluralistic and forbearing led Goebbels's office to direct the press not to print any disparaging remarks about Blacks. On 3 August 1936, a press directive was issued that read, "The racial point of view should not be used in any way in reporting sports results; above all Negroes should not be insensitively reported. . . . Negroes are American citizens and must be treated with respect as Americans."[19] This statement reflects a couple of interesting points. One, it implies that the Nazis are aware of what "insensitively reported" means, that is, they claim to know what is insulting to African Americans. Two, the racial status of African Americans is pointedly tied to their national identity as Americans. Ironically, the Nazis call for a respect for African Americans that they did not receive at home. The reference to Negroes as "American citizens" without the qualifier "second-class" as so many Blacks viewed it is striking. It would take almost twenty years before legal segregation was outlawed and real first-class citizenship status, at least formally, was achieved. Third, it would also seem, though it was not explicitly stated, that Afro-Germans and Africans were not to be insulted and maligned although there were none representing Germany in the Games. The Nazis likely recognized that a diasporic connection existed among Blacks, especially if the Nazis monitored African American newspapers that reported on Nazi treatment of people of African descent. While some of the most racist and rabid German papers, such as *Der Stumer*, did continue Negrophobic discourses, it appears that most followed orders and toned down or eliminated anti-Black harangues.

"Auxiliaries" and Achievements

The most celebrated African American figure was James Cleveland Owens, better known as Jesse. Born on 12 September 1913 in Oakville, Alabama, and raised in Cleveland, James would become Jesse when one of his teachers misunderstood him when he told her that his name was "JC," his initials. The teacher heard "Jesse," as would everyone else from then on.[20] By 1929, when he was in East Technical High School, which was less than 5 percent black, he was considered one of the best track athletes in the nation. After finishing high school, as Ashe notes importantly, "not a single black college made an attempt to recruit him," and he ended up at Ohio State, which, at the time, barred black students from living on campus and would not serve them in university eating establishments.[21] As Owens began to shine in his sophomore year, the black press lavished unrestrained praise upon his remarkable achievements. The *Norfolk Journal and Guide* reflected the view of many in the black community when it wrote, "Owens . . . is without doubt the greatest individual performer the world has ever known."[22] Other black track and field athletes of outstanding talent were also emerging at this time, including Willis Ward, who had actually beaten Owens in hurdles, Eulace Peacock, who had beaten him in the 100–meter dash and the long jump, and Ralph Metcalfe, who, along with Owens, would make the 1936 Olympics memorable.

The Jewish community sought to have U.S. Jewish athletes boycott the games. Despite the protests, two Jewish runners, Marty Glickman and Sam Stoller, did join the team. A controversy arose at the Games when both Glickman and Stoller were taken off the 400–meter relay team, which won a gold medal, at the last minute. The coaches had stated earlier that they would be on the relay team, along with Mack Robinson and Foy Draper. Owens, Frank Wykoff, and Metcalfe replaced Glickman, Stoller, and Robinson even though Glickman and Stoller had outrun Wykoff in a trial race, and Owens already had three gold medals. Reportedly, Owens protested Glickman's and Stoller's exclusion, stating "Coach, let Marty and Sam run. I've had enough. I've won three gold medals. Let them run."[23] The coaches told Owens to do as he was told, and the Jewish runners were left off the team. While a bias toward University of Southern California athletes—Draper and Wycoff—was perhaps involved in the incident, it was also clear that the coaches failed to take the opportunity to challenge Germany's anti-Semitism. Glickman and Stoller had different views about what motivated head coach Dean B. Cromwell to pull them from the race. Glickman believed until his dying day that

Cromwell and Brundage were probably members of the conservative America First Committee and anti-Semites who cared more about mollifying Hitler than racial justice or fairness.[24] While Stoller was more charitable and did not impeach their motivations, he was extremely bitter about what happened and described it as the "most humiliating espisode" in his life.

In addition to Owens, other blacks on the U.S. Olympic team included the sprinters Metcalfe and Mack Robinson (brother of baseball's Jackie Robinson), the high jumpers David Albritton and Cornelius Johnson, and the long runners Archie Williams, James Luvalle, John Woodruff, Fritz Pollard Jr., and John Brooks.[25] Black women on the team included the sprinter Louise Stokes and the hurdler Tydie Pickett. Howard King, a black boxer, arrived with the team on the SS *Manhattan* on 24 July 1936, but never got to compete. He was accused by the Germans of stealing a camera at a local shop and was subsequently banned from the Games.

It should not be assumed that because there were African American athletes on the U.S. team that racist views were not prevalent among the coaches and other officials. Cromwell, for instance, later wrote an influential book on track and field, *Championship Technique in Track and Field.* In it he wrote, "The Negro excels in the events he does because he is closer to the primitive than the white man. It was not so long ago that his ability to sprint and jump was a life-and-death matter to him in the jungle. His muscles are pliable, and his easy-going disposition is a valuable aid to the mental and physical relaxation that a runner and jumper must have."[26]

While the Nazis and many Whites in the United States subscribed to theories of physical differences between the races as an explanation of black athletic victories, the physical anthropologist William Montague Cobb refuted these arguments in a number of important articles. He wrote, "There is not a single physical characteristic which all Negro stars have in common which would definitely identify them as Negroes. Jesse Owens, who has run faster and leaped farther than a human being has done before, does not have what is considered the Negroid type of calf, foot, and heel bones."[27] He would further comment on Owens, that "in all those characteristics presumptively associated with race or physical ability, Owens was Caucasoid rather than Negroid in type. Thus, his heel bone was relatively short, instead of long; his calf muscles had very long instead of short bellies; and his arches were high and strong instead of low and weak."[28] In a number of ways, Cobb was also challenging black views on black athletic abilities that, from a "positive" perspective held notions of innate physical skills and talents that essentialize African Americans albeit without the overtly negative racist stereotypes.

The Snub

No story regarding Blacks and the 1936 Olympics stands out as much as the infamous "snub." Much of the white and black press reported that Hitler snubbed Owens and other black athletes by refusing to shake their hands after they had won gold medals. This, of course, was interpreted along racial lines. Notwithstanding Hitler's deeply rooted racial prejudices, what actually happened was more complicated and ambiguous. On the first day of the Olympics, Hitler watched from his booth and after two German athletes and a Finnish athlete won gold medals, he invited them to his box for personal congratulations. Later, Cornelius Johnson won a gold medal in the high jump for the United States, but Hitler left before the U.S. national anthem was played, and it is unknown how deliberate his leaving was and whether he consciously did not want to publicly honor an African American athlete. The IOC's de Baillet-Latour warned Hitler to be impartial in his response to the winners, and, for whatever reason, Hitler no longer invited any athletes, German or otherwise, for personal congratulations after that. Although he would later falsely claim to be involved in this incident, Owens did not actually win a gold medal until the second day of the Olympics. It is unknown why the story in the media cited Owens rather than Johnson, but it was probably because Owens was the most famous of the black athletes in Berlin.[29]

The snub was seen from two perspectives. One perspective viewed the incident as validation of the racism that existed in Germany and why Hitler should be opposed. *The Crisis,* a leading African American publication, would write after the Olympics, "Cynics are trying to say they never expected Germany's Hitler to do anything except snub America's track ace, Jesse Owens . . . Most people—even those familiar with the Hitler creed on superior and inferior races—did not expect that the ruler of a great modern nation would so belittle himself as to refuse a sportsman-like handshake and word of commendation to winning athletes and guests of Germany, no matter what their color happened to be."[30] *The Crisis* would note that for African Americans, after the Hitler snub, "fascism now means something" if it did not before.[31] Another black newspaper, the *Washington Tribune,* stated, "A German paper said that the American team would have been poor without the Negroes. And they realized they could snub the Negroes and get away with it. Therefore, we should call upon the State Department to protest against the snub against the American team."[32]

A more radical reading of the incident not only saw Hitler's racism but also noted that it was not all that different from how African American athletes were treated in the United States. The *Philadelphia Tribune* wrote, "Newspapers are criticizing Hitler for not congratulating [Jesse] Owens, yet when he finishes running and comes back here to live among Nordics, will he not meet the same thing from them?"[33] The *Brown American* journal, in its August 1936 issue, pointed out the racial contradiction faced not by Germany but by the United States, noting that Hitler's emphasis on skin color as a criterion of character and status had a resonance across the Atlantic. As it astutely argued, "The great part of the 1936 Olympiad really happened in the United States. Here, where the solution of race is only a matter of mild degrees ahead of Germany, American newspapers were face-to-face with either condoning Hitler's lack of sportsmanship or actually conceding that the color of one's skin has nothing to do with the wearer's ability to stand up for his Nation."[34]

The black crusade against Nazism through the vehicle of Jesse Owens was muted to a significant degree by Owens's somewhat conservative political views. Only a few months after the Olympics, he participated in a Republican Party rally at which he stated, "I think Hitler's a noble man" in response to queries regarding his view of the infamous snub.[35] What made Owenss' statement particularly irksome to some African

Americans was that he had apparently also been critical of President Roosevelt and the Democratic Party. By the 1936 election, the voting black community had begun to shift its political alliance from the Republicans to the Democrats.

TABLE 5   **African American Medalists**

Name	Event	Medal
David Albritton	High jump	Silver
Cornelius Johnson	High jump	Gold
James LuValle	400–meter run	Bronze
Ralph Metcalfe	4x100–meter relay	Gold
	100–meter dash	Silver
Jesse Owens	100–meter dash	Gold
	200–meter dash	Gold
	Broad (long) jump	Gold
	4x100–meter relay	Gold
Frederick Pollard Jr	100–meter hurdles	Bronze
Matthew Robinson	200–meter dash	Silver
Archie Williams	400–meter run	Gold
Jack Wilson	Bantamweight boxing	Silver
John Woodruff	800–meter run	Gold

Source: Arthur A. Ashe Jr., *A Hard Road to Glory: A History of the African-American Athlete, 1919–1945.*

TABLE 6   **Gold Medals Won and Records Set by Jesse Owens at the 1936 Olympics**

Event	Record Set
100 meter	10.3 seconds
200 meter	20.7 seconds
long jump	26'5 1/4"

Source: Arthur A. Ashe Jr., *A Hard Road to Glory: A History of the African-American Athlete, 1919–1945.*

TABLE 7   **Achievements of African American Athletes at the 1936 Olympics**

Athlete	Event	Success
Jesse Owens	100 meter	Gold
Jesse Owens	200 meter	Gold
Jesse Owens	long jump	Gold
Jesse Owens	400-meter relay	Gold
Ralph Metcalfe	400-meter relay	Gold
Archie Williams	400 meter	Gold
John Woodruff	800 meter	Gold
Mack Robinson	200 meter	Silver
James Luvalle	400 meter	Bronze

Source: Arthur A. Ashe Jr., *A Hard Road to Glory: A History of the African-American Athlete, 1919–1945.*

The eighteen African Americans (sixteen men and two women) that went to Berlin to participate in the Games were, in many ways, agents of democracy. They represented not only the United States and its growing ideological conflict with international fascism but also a racial wedge who objectively and even consciously challenged racism in Germany and at home. Success—African American athletes won fourteen medals; nearly one-fourth of the fifty-six medals awarded the U.S. team in all events—brought attention and, it was hoped, a spotlight on the issue of black disenfranchisement and lack of civil rights.[36] Equally importantly, they won respect, even admiration from other athletes, some Germans, and many back home. However, it was the emerging mass movement of African Americans for civil and political rights outside of sports that realized the hopes and aspirations surging through the fists and feet of the black athletes.

Summary

In April 1947, a major breakthrough across racial lines occurred in the United States. Although a committee of baseball owners and officials had written a 1946 secret report recommending that Blacks not be admitted to the major leagues, which was voted 15–1 to support the conclusion, the time had come for a change. Despite a long history and discourse on the superiority of Whites in baseball, and a virtual ban on Blacks, Major League Baseball signed its first acknowledged player of African descent. The Brooklyn Dodgers owner, Branch Rickey, the only one to vote against the aforementioned report, signed the Montreal Royals' Jackie Robinson to play second. His debut, in which he scored the winning run, was on 15 April 1947, its racial significance captured in the *Boston Chronicle*'s 19 April 1947 banner headline, "TRIUMPH OF WHOLE RACE SEEN IN JACKIE'S DEBUT IN MAJOR-LEAGUE BALL."[37] Within a very short period, more Blacks were contracted to join the majors, closing an era of athletic segregation and leading to the demise of the Negro Leagues.

The end of segregation in baseball's major leagues could be linked to the new global attitude toward racism in the wake of the defeat of Nazism. After the fall of Hitler, the United States—and, later, South Africa—found itself under increasing criticism for its racial policies of segregation. As the cold war heated up, the Soviet Union and its allies would continuously point out the contradiction between U.S. statements and declarations about democracy and its obvious oppressive and discriminatory treatment of African Americans and other people of color. These criticisms were felt not only by the U.S. government but in more popular venues as well. In addition, the anti-racist resistance on the part of people of color and the postwar growth in the civil rights movement highlighted the hypocrisy.

10

Blacks in the Resistance Movement

[T]he greater the disparity in power between the dominant and subordinate and the more arbitrarily it is exercised, the more the public transcript of subordinates will take on a stereotyped, ritualistic cast. In other words, the more menacing the power, the thicker the mask.

—*James C. Scott*[1]

Unmasking the Opposition

In his provocative study *Domination and the Arts of Resistance,* James Scott examines what he terms public transcripts, that is, the public and visible interaction between the dominant and the subordinate. Affirming similar ground plowed by Frantz Fanon in *Black Skin, White Masks,* Scott argues and successfully demonstrates that while public transcripts provide the most immediate understanding of the power relationship between the powerful and the powerless, they veil a more critical engagement occurring beneath the surface in the hidden transcripts. From this framework, he goes on to do battle with the theory of hegemony, which, he contends, at best misunderstands the counteroppositional power that lies in both the performance of the public transcript and the empowering character of the hidden one. Neither an imprudent defiance of overwhelming power nor a complete ideological subjugation characterizes the subaltern's relationship to power, Scott argues. It is the space in between these two extremes that functions as more a continuum expressed in the dialectic between the hidden and the public, and there the counteropposition voice and actions of the oppressed can be found.

Scott's framework is highly useful in understanding the discursive nature and forms of black resistance to Nazism. Black opposition to the Nazis in Germany and the occupied lands was consistent though limited. It took on many forms from individual acts of sabotage to the dissemination of propaganda and illegal information to physical attacks and assassinations to official spying. Although all these activities are known to have happened, the size and effectiveness of the opposition are difficult to measure given the nature of the subject, and it is even thornier to try to disaggregate the role of people of African descent in these enterprises. On the one hand, Blacks participated in the resistance movement and resisted individually. On the other hand, they were also subjects of the organized resistance in some instances. And there is research indicating that at least some Blacks, particularly young ones, were rescued and either hidden or smuggled out of Germany by the movement.

Beyond anecdotal information, the principal sources for data on these activities have been either official testimonies given after the war and evidence from the organized resistance movement or individuals or official police and Nazi records.[2] All these sources are impeached to some degree, however, as they are prone to exaggeration and inflation as well as understatement on both sides. While the resistance movement may have had a tendency to overstate its achievements, the organizational imperative to be secretive and operate in small cells also meant that many activities were unknown and information about them lost forever with the death, both during and after the war, of resistance leaders.

In a similar way, police records, in one instance, reflected the effort to demonstrate law enforcement's efficacy and not dwell on the successes of the movement by down-playing just how successful the latter could be. However, the Nazis would also sweeten the numbers to try to make the same point about their own success at stopping or crushing the underground. Also, the fleeing Nazis destroyed many records as the war was ending to hide their crimes, including evidence of the murder of resistance forces. In any case, the data are highly problematic but remain the best available from official sources. Data collected by the researcher Gabriel Almond give some general indication of the nature of the resistance movement, in 1944, and how aggressive the state was in trying to destroy it. (See tables.)

Resistance against the Nazis across Europe varied considerably. From the massive and effective French underground to the relatively small German resistance movement, anti-Nazis fought back. Some risked life and limb to hide Jews and other enemies of the Nazi state, sometimes for years. Others joined the underground and waged a guerrilla war that included bombings, sabotage, assassinations, and virtually any act that would bring down Hitler. It is believed that the resistance movement in Germany played some role in rescuing and protecting certain Black youth, that is, many of the so-called Rhineland children, who were targets of sterilization and extermination by the Nazis.

Blacks in Europe, including Germany, were also engaged in resistance activities. African involvement in the French resistance movement is notable. After the war turned against the Germans and they began to retreat from Western Europe, Africans participated in the activities to destroy Nazi trains and railways, sabotage supply lines, and generally disrupt the German escape to the East. In August 1944, for example, 400 colonial prisoners and others who had been captured by the Nazis were freed from a train near Salbris, France. This group was then incorporated back into the attacks on the fleeing Germans. Stunning the Nazis, many of the black soldiers who survived the brutality

TABLE 8   **Consolidation of Statistics of Arrests
from the Regional Offices of the Gestapo
for January–March 1944**

	January	February	March	Total
Communism/Marxism	1,340	1,877	1,283	4,500
Reaction-Opposition	2,079	2,154	2,322	655

TABLE 9   **Consolidation of Statistics of Arrests
from the Regional Offices of the Gestapo for Germans
and for Foreigners April–June 1944**

	April		May		June		Total	
	Germ.	For.	Germ.	For.	Germ.	For.	Germ.	For.
Communism/	391	882	523	1,551	528	850	1442	3,283
Marxism	90	24	107	7	85	15	282	46
Reaction-Opposition	294	235	321	246	399	324	1,014	805
Treachery	937	628	1,204	709	2,285	913	4,426	2,250

and inhumanity of the northern French concentration camps and were liberated became guards over the Germans caught as the Allies advanced. And, as one researcher noted, "revenge was sought and delivered."[3]

While most of the black participants of the organized resistance inside and outside of Germany will forever remain unknown, there are a few who stand out and whose story survives. In many instances, black enemies of the state were killed instantly when caught by the Nazis. Some of those not murdered on the spot also managed to live through the ordeal of torture, beatings, and concentration camp existence. Johnny Voste, for instance, fought the Germans in the Netherlands and Belgium. He was captured and sent to Dachau in 1942. At liberation, he was the only Black there and may have been the only one to come through. He certainly was the only one to survive and live to tell about it.

Several other individuals stand out if only because enough information exists about their actions to locate them within the extended narrative of resistance against Nazism. While most Afro-Germans and Africans living in Germany donned the mask of survival and resisted through hidden transcripts, some were more public in their challenge to the state. This includes the activist Joseph Bile, who was forced to leave the country and continue to try to organize from abroad (see chapter 4), and the communist leader Hilarius Gilges. In France, where much but not all of the black resistance occurred, the singer and dancer Josephine Baker shines because she operated at such a high level of risk and her popularity as a global figure harnessed so many symbols of black achievement and success. She risked all of that, not to mention her very life, under extremely trying circumstances and managed not only to survive, but to do so with great style and panache. Finally, from about as far away as you could come, the Haitian Johnny

Nicholas, whose sense of adventure and courage was boundless, but whose story is unknown, provides a fitting close to this section. Nicholas embodied a never-say-die attitude that encapsulated the historical and contemporary ethos of black resistance, facing the worst that society could conjure and refusing to surrender either physically or spiritually.

Hilarius Gilges

Somewhere around a dozen SS men arrived as the evening was coming to an end. It was around 10 o'clock. They had been looking for and finally found their victim, a leader in the opposition to their authority. As his daughter recalls, this would be the last time his family would see him alive. Hilarius "Lari" Gilges was an early fatality of the Nazi regime in the Düsseldorf area—but certainly not the last. Only twenty-four when murdered, he became a hero and a martyr for many who would resist the fascists in the years to follow.

Not a lot is known about Gilges's early life. He was born on 4 March 1909 in Düsseldorf and was of mixed-race heritage. His mother, in a 1945 interview, noted that the family was working class. For Hilarius, his class upbringing and experiences and his racial uniqueness would inform his life activities as he grew up. Even in the pre-Hitler period, he was, as an Afro-German, often the target of racial taunts, insults, and slanders. These provocations would push him toward more radical politics during his teen years. According to his mother, he became active in the workers' movement at a young age. At only sixteen or seventeen, in 1926, Gilges joined the German Communist Youth Organization (KJVD). Reportedly, he was extremely commited to his political work in the party.

In addition to being a labor organizer, Gilges was a tap dancer and an actor. It is unknown how he became interested in tap dance, a form of dance with a distinct African American character—there is no evidence one way or the other that he was influenced by outside dancers. Even in this area, Gilges fought for justice and a progressive politics. When he was only twenty-one, around 1930, he became one of the cofounders of the leftist worker-entertainment group the Northwest Ran, in Düsseldorf. The Northwest Ran group, comprising actors, musicians, and other performers, organized anti-Nazi demonstrations and protests in an attempt to stem the growing tide of Nazism. By this time, the Nazi Party had become a serious force across the country including the Düsseldorf area. The agitation of the entertainment troup and his labor organizing in all the cities and villages of the low Rhine, had made Gilges well known beyond his hometown. These activities strengthened the hate of his enemies and their determination to rid themselves of this troublesome and even dangerous black man.

The situation heated up in 1931 as labor unrest grew and large demonstrations occurred at the Marz-Gedenfeier work site. At one of the protests, racists were able to provoke Gilges into a fight in which the police, who were politically reactionary, if not pro-Nazi, seized the opportunity to punish him. He was arrested and sentenced some weeks later by the country court in Düsseldorf. He was given one year in the area prison.

If the authorities believed that a year of incarceration would diminish Gilges's organizing activities, they were disabused of that notion fairly quickly after his release. Shortly after getting out of prison, he aggressively renewed his position as a leader of the labor movement in the area. In fact, according to his family, his activities grew as the danger of the Nazi takeover loomed larger and larger. Only months before the Nazis came to power, he was agitating and organizing through the party. In the 1932 elections, he traveled through nearly every city, town, and village attempting to mobilize against the coming fascist era.

When Hitler and the Nazis came to national power in January 1933, Gilges was at the top of the list of enemies of the state in the Düsseldorf area. He began to work both above ground and underground as the Nazis set out to destroy the left and any opposition that remained. In the face of death threats and other warnings, Gilges refused to back down or go into hiding. In addition to his commitment to his work, he also had a family by then. He was married and had two daughters.

One daughter, Franziska Helmuss, recalls with a deep sense of loss the night they came to get him and the aftermath. She remembers, on the night of June 20,

> My father was grabbed in front of my eyes. Twelve big SS officers dragged him out of the house. The next time I saw him was here [the Rhine river near Düsseldorf], floating under the bridge. He'd been stabbed 37 times and shot through the head . . . His funeral was well attended, but exclusively by women. The men were too afraid to be associated with him. The stonemason who made the gravestone for my father was incarcerated for five years in a Nazi concentration camp.[4]

According to his mother, Gilges's killers were known. She noted that one of his murderers was the notorious SS guard Carl Wüsthoff of Düsseldorf. The cruelty and torture involved in Gilges's murder expressed a vindictiveness that would characterize much of what was to follow for the next dozen years. Also, the fear that Helmuss described on the part of the men (and the bravery on the part of the women) would be repeated as the terrorist state consolidated itself and step-by-evil-step eliminated its perceived and real enemies.[5]

The city of Düsseldorf put up a monument to Gilges near the site where his body was found. To the very end, he refused to submit to the Nazi state. Although attacked by his foes for his politics and his black skin, he always viewed himself in the broadest terms and battled the Nazis on behalf of working-class people and the nation as a whole. The respect he earned was remembered by all who knew him. Maria Wacher, who was in Northwest Ran with him, sums up Gilges best when she says, simply, "he was a fighter."[6]

Josephine Baker

Born in St. Louis in 1906, Josephine Baker had a black and Indian heritage. Her mother, the former Carrie McDonald, was from South Carolina, and her father, Eddie Carson, was a drummer. They both worked in the theater and vaudeville, but Josephine would grow up only around her mother because Carson left a year after she was born. Josephine was lighter than anyone in the family, which made her distinct but contributed to what she felt was an unpleasant childhood.

When France declared war on Germany in September 1939 after the latter invaded Poland, the Deuxieme Bureau, the French military intelligence service, recruited Baker to become a spy.[7] She was a desirable choice because, as a well-known entertainer, she had legitimate reasons for moving around unsuspiciously. Her talents and willingness to participate would become even more urgent after France was occupied in May 1940 and by June 1940 was controlled by the Nazis. It is estimated that only about 2 percent of the population was actually involved in the resistance movement.[8] Baker joined the resistance from the very beginning.

She worked closely with and eventually became the lover of Jacques Abtey, the head of France's military counterintelligence operations in Paris.[9] Upon meeting Abtey, who operated under the nom de plume Jacques-François Hebert, for the first time to discuss her role, she told him, "France made me what I am. I will be grateful forever. The people of Paris have given me everything. They have given me their hearts, and I have given them mine. I am ready, Captain, to give them my life. You can use me as you wish."[10] Baker may also have been moved to act because she considered herself Jewish, a conversion that occurred during her marriage to Jean Lion, and this would also be an opportunity to strike a blow against the murderous anti-Semitism emanating from Germany.

The well-known and well-liked Baker would, as a spy, collect information from German officials and others at parties, embassy gatherings, and anywhere else useful data could be had. Charm was her business and with striking success she was able to pick up all types of information such as German troop locations, airfield operations, harbors, and army movements.[11] This intelligence she would pass on to Abtey, often written in invisible ink on her sheet music.[12]

By day, Baker worked at a Belgium refugee center and, in the evening, entertained at the Casino de Paris. At the latter, she performed for a while with Maurice Chevalier. In June, with the Nazis in command and beginning to round up Jews, many of whom were in the entertainment field, and some Blacks, Baker joined the flow of those who left Paris for what they felt, usually incorrectly, was safer turf in other parts of France. She left for her chateau in Dordogne (Les Milandes), storing gasoline in champagne bottles.[13] Over the next five years, she would carry out clandestine work not only in France but also in Portugal, Morocco, Algeria, Spain, Egypt, Syria, Palestine, Lebanon, and South America. She would end up spending a considerable amount of time in Lisbon, a major center of intelligence activities due to Portugal's neutral position. Technically, Baker and Abtey were part of the Free French military force rather than spies in the traditional sense of the term. They saw themselves as patriots doing their part to free France rather than as government employees simply carrying out their jobs. Information collected by Baker and Abtey went not only to French resistance and exile officials but also to U.S. authorities located in Casablanca. The Americans were more than pleased to have Baker attend embassy parties where she could pass on the extremely useful data that she had managed to gather in her endless travels. She would, however, have a falling out of sorts with the

Americans because of her anger over the segregation and racism that permeated U.S. military facilities, sites, gatherings, and general operations.

In 1941, Baker's espionage activities ground to a halt as she became ill. She developed peritonitis that in turn would grow into a nearly deadly blood infection called septicemia. She would have to have five major abdominal operations by 1946 before she was fully recovered. In fact, she became so ill that rumors circulated—spread, in part, by Maurice Chevalier, whom Baker had fallen out with because she accused him of collaborating with the enemy for continuing to perform in France—that she had actually died, leading to the African American poet Langston Hughes's being given his first assignment for the *Chicago Defender* to write her obituary. Although it was nearly two years before she was really up and mobile again, her improvement would be short-lived as she came down with paratyphoid, another debilitating illness. By early 1943, however, she was back to performing and espionage.

Even before the war ended, Baker won recognition for her work from General Charles de Gaulle. In the spring of 1943, for example, when de Gaulle arrived in Algiers, he presented her with the vaunted Cross of Lorraine (which she would later auction off for 350,000 Francs to raise money for the resistance cause). She was also commissioned a sub-lieutenant in the Women's Auxiliary of the French Air Force.[14] After the war, she received the treasured Medal of the Resistance.[15]

One notorious episode that reflected Baker's naivete and underscored her commitment as perhaps less ideological than personal was the stance she took toward Hitler's top ally in Europe, Italy's Bento Mussolini. She shocked not only many people in Europe but also many African Americans and Africans when she declared her support for the dictator, and, worse, endorsed his invasion of Ethiopia. She went as far as to declare that she would recruit Blacks to fight with the Italians.[16]

Her misplaced defense of Mussolini notwithstanding, Baker was an enormously daring individual who risked virtually all in the name of freedom and justice. Despised by her homeland, she found space for her talents and humanity in France, receiving in turn the country's adoration and generosity. After the war, she became a target of U.S. intelligence as well as the victim of accusations by the FBI and the red-baiting Senator Joseph McCarthy. While no radical and, in fact, keeping a very conscious distance from progressive groups, Baker was an unrelenting critic of U.S. racism and used many forums—though surprisingly not the performing stage—to expose racism against African Americans. Unlike Paul Robeson and W. E. B. Du Bois, Baker as an adopted and full citizen of France, could not be touched or have her travel restricted by the U.S. State Department. In the end, Baker lived her life to the fullest and, in the face of extraordinary times, rose to extraordinary heights.[17]

Johnny Nicholas

Hitler believed that Germany could win the war if it could develop the secret weapons he had Nazi scientists working on since 1938. He would refer to these weapons as *Vergeltungswaffen* (weapons of revenge). They would take the form of the V-1 (pilotless flying bomb) and the V-2 (the world's first guided missile). The V-2 stood forty-five feet high and when exploded created a hole thirty feet wide and twenty feet deep. When the RAF nearly destroyed the first $120 million production site at Peenemünde and killed 750 technicians and scientists, a hysterically enraged Hitler immediately called for a new location for production and testing of the weapons. That site would eventually be at Camp Dora (later called Camp Mittlebau). Dora, and the thirty-one subcamps that supported it, had more than 32,000 slave laborers—that would grow to more than 60,000—all within a twenty–mile area. At Dora, twenty-four hours a day, seven days a week, inmates were simply and literally worked to death. Any captive of the Nazis who arrived here grasped quickly and frightfully that this was the last stop in the system. Dora had started as a subcamp of the notorious Buchenwald in August 1943, becoming independent in October 1944. In the underground Kohnstein Mountain tunnels, a hell on earth was established that was run by Nazi scientists and engineers, and guarded by the dreaded SS.

It was here in this interminable purgatory that Prisoner No. 44451 pulled off one of the greatest deceptions of the war. Captured and (correctly) charged in November 1943 with being a high-level spy for the Allies, the detained prisoner was listed as *Nacht und Nebel* (Night and Fog). On 7 December 1941, Hitler himself issued the *Nacht und Nebel Erlass* (Night and Fog Decree), whose purpose was to take seized persons and have them disappear into the "night and fog," never to be heard from again.[18] No information was to be given about the person to family or anyone else, and all traces of these prisoners were to be erased. One Nazi offical responsible for carrying out this ruthless order, General Keitel Wilhelm, explained its purpose: "Efficient intimidation can only be achieved either by capital punishment or by measures by which the relatives of the criminal and the population do not know his fate."[19] For any other prisoner caught in this circumstance, life was effectively over. However, despite living under a perpetual sentence of Nacht und Nebel (NN), enduring constant threats to his life, and staring into the abyss time and time again, this inmate escaped death at least four times. This remarkable survivalist was the Haitian-born Jean Marcel Nicholas, better known to fellow prisoners and guards as the "American," Johnny Nicholas.

His story began on 20 October 1918 in Haiti. An "extremely bright" child, according to one of his teachers, "He would help anyone and completely forget about himself. All the time with such a good mood about him that you couldn't stop him."[20] Growing up in the jazz age and U.S imperialism (the country was occupied by the United States from 1915 to 1934), he was influenced by black American music and early Hollywood gangster movies, which undoubtedly fueled his love for excitement and adventure and pushed him toward his destiny of playing a risky role in the war. In 1938, at the age of twenty, he apparently joined the French Navy but was dismissed less than a year later after suffering an injury of some sort. This was only six months before the Germans declared war on France, invaded the country, and seized the capital in June 1940. Nicholas had spent time in Paris, part of it hanging out with medical students. He had no way of knowing that whatever details of medicine he picked up from these associations would save his life in a very few years.

In many ways, Nicholas's ascension to Ally spy was right out of central casting. He was not only tall, handsome, self-assured, and fearless, but his talents also included fluency in French, German, and English and a willingness to go to the edge. After being recruited and trained, he set up shop in Paris, posing, at least part of the time, as a gynecologist. He printed up a legal-appearing document that stated that he had a license to practice medicine with a degree from the University of Heidelberg.[21] As an "American gynecologist" with lots of women "patients," Nicholas was also a social hit and even hobnobbed with German officers at the various hot spots around Paris. His real job, however, was to assist pilots who had been shot down in France to escape back to England. This work was dangerous to say the least, and Nicholas relished it. He was stimulated by the perpetual thrill of tricking the Nazis as he stealthily moved his people through the dark nights from one hiding spot to another. Despite several brushes with the authorities, the intelligence tasks were going well until he was betrayed by an unexpected source.

In November 1943, the woman whom he had been seeing romantically had come to believe that he was cheating on her or, at least, preparing to cast her aside, probably a correct assumption. Nicholas was not involved in the kind of work out of which grows a traditional and healthy relationship, and he had a reputation as a ladies' man. Florence was an aspiring actress, a beautiful Parisian, and, most important, a critical player in the French resistance. She worked with Johnny in the Underground, sharing the risks and life-threatening activities that brought them together. After they had become emotionally involved, breaking a cardinal rule of the spy game, things began to deteriorate. In retaliation, and perhaps for other reasons, she turned him in to the Gestapo.

After being tortured, beaten, and held in several jails and prisons in France, Nicholas was put on a transport and sent to Germany. He would eventually serve time in the Buchenwald (January 1944–May 1944), Dora (May 1944–November 1944), and Rottlebrode (November 1944–April 1945) concentration camps, and even a day or two in Sachsenhausen and Ravensbreuck. Although, technically, he was not supposed to have any communication with the outside world, on 1 March 1944, Nicholas sent a postcard—the only note he would send during his captivity—to his brother Vildebart that read, "I am well. I can receive some parcels. Write to me in German. You can send me fresh or cooked vegetables as often as you wish. Send me some shaving soap and a toothbrush. I hope your wife is in good health. I would also be grateful for some tobacco."[22]

Although Nicholas was NN, his race does not seem to have been overwhelmingly central in how he was treated. While he was essentially sentenced to death under the NN order, he was not immediately killed. His blackness made him stand out among all the prisoners, yet he reportedly was not treated worse because he was black. One factor that appears to have been important was the belief that he was American (although not slated to be traded). It is difficult to know, but the Nazis may have believed that his Americanness would be useful at some point, and so let him live. His services as a "doctor," once he joined the infirmary, also made him valuable, the only commodity that the Nazis acknowledged. Finally, Nicholas's own wiles and ability to negotiate the best outcome for himself within the limits available was an important variable. This is not to say not that his race was ignored but that it was not the sole or principal determinant in defining his status. Of course, he was likely exoticized as the only black person in those camps, and his uniqueness at the camp would hardly go unnoticed. Nicholas exuberated in a profound sense of self-confidence and will to survive. These traits were a dividing line between life and death.

At Dora, the prisoners were malnourished, physically devastated, and forced to work sixteen-to-eighteen-hour days, which explains why the death rate was severe with easily half of the workers perishing within a short time, to be replaced by the next set of victims. Camp Dora, like the other concentration camps, established a camp infirmary (hospital is too generous a term) or *Revier*. Shortly after arriving, Nicholas reported to the infirmary and managed to convince Dr. Karl Kahr, who ran the woefully underresourced operation, that he too was a medical doctor and that he wanted a position as a prisoner-doctor. Distinct from many of the quacks and butchers who passed for physicians in the camps, Kahr valiantly and unsuccessfully attempted to provide a semblance of medical services to the desperate prisoners. The number of seriously ill and injured prisoners rose from fifty a day in August 1943 to over three hundred daily by the following winter.[23] The death toll was about 850 a month and rising rapidly.[24] As Kahr would lament years after the war, "The problem was there wasn't enough food for the prisoners and they worked too hard. Their resistance was so low that the medicines and vaccines didn't work. They had very little food for the prisoners. I hoped that in my position I would help improve it."[25] Whether Kahr, who would later call his period in the camp the "worst time of my life," believed Nicholas or not, he welcomed him into his little piece of horror.[26] In fact, as Kahr remembers, his staff was happy to have the only Negro in the camp, who was a sensation and celebrity of sorts, working in the Revier.[27] The fact that Nicholas spoke English, German, French, and a little Russian also was a plus. Kahr did not know a lot about Nicholas's personal life and wondered how as a downed pilot and a POW he ended up in a concentration camp.[28]

Although they fought a losing battle in the long run, assistant doctor Nicholas and Kahr were able to construct a hospital barracks. The first barracks, constructed in September 1944, was to hold 200 beds or rather 200 spots because the beds were not forthcoming. Nicholas's new position was key not only to his survival but to that of many other prisoners. As McCann et al. note, "Dr." Nicholas could "detour innocent prisoners out of the fatal-injection line and into some other line where they'd emerge to live another day. He could hand out—or deny—the slips that authorized a prisoner a day's 'convalescence' in his barracks instead of another twelve hours of agony in the tunnel. He often could lay his hands on extra rations, which he could use to keep one man alive or bribe another."[29]

The situation of Dora would dramatically deteriorate by late fall 1944. The advancing Russian army was forcing the Nazis to clear the eastern camps, including the massive death camp at Auschwitz, and to send surviving prisoners further into Germany itself to camps such as Dora. While thousands of exhausted, undernourished, and barely alive prisoners rolled nonstop into the camp, the Nazis provided even *fewer* resources needed for survival such as medicines, food, and clothes. Nicholas was in charge of the dispensary, a no-win situation in which he was forced to send 90 percent of the prisoners he saw back to work in subzero temperatures with only minimal treatment and medicine to give them. Although he was not trained in medicine formally, Nicholas's swift capacity to learn, his close friendships and discussions with medical students while in Paris, and his unrelenting effort to try to save as many as possible generated impressive skills in dealing with the injuries and illnesses that overwhelmed the prisoners at Dora.

After the war, former prisoners and guards would recall in interviews how this black doctor emerged to be so central in their lives. Edwin Katzeuellenbogen, a doctor at Buchenwald, recalls meeting Nicholas and that he "spoke American slang." He recalls that the doctors who were sent from Buchenwald to Dora "were prominent, mostly French physicians, and also an American Negro physician, 'Johnny.' "[30] Willi Burgdorf, a former Dora prisoner who also gave testimony after the war, erroneously believed that Nicholas had died working in the tunnels at Dora. He remembered him as a "mulatto" who had lived in France a long time and had told other inmates "he was working in the Secret Service."[31] Ferdinand Karpik, another inmate at Dachau and then Dora, had been told by Nicholas that he was an American officer and had been hiding out in France before being arrested. He did tell Karpik that he was an intelligence officer. The last time Karpik saw Nicholas was at Osthrode when he was being led away with others by the SS around 7 or 8 April 1945.[32]

Everyone, in postwar interviews, did not have favorable memories of Nicholas. Paul Maischen, who was a camp medic at Dora, was one. He testified, in reference to Nicholas, "The dispensary capa, a negro [sic], was so antagonistic to Ukrainians that in case a prisoner came to the dispensary and told there he was a Ukrainian, the negro [sic] chased him out with a club. It was well known that in the dispensary instead of thermometers thick clubs were used."[33] Walter Ulbright had been an inmate clerk at Rottlebrode. After getting into some trouble with camp officials at Dora around November 1944, Nicholas was transferred to Rottlebrode where he continued his duties as a doctor. Ulbright and Nicholas had a run-in over a patient. According to Ulbright, "When I learned from the prisoner, Alois Janz, who had been appointed as a night guard, that the physician Johnny Nicholas, had during the night put the Pole who was sick with the face erysipelas in the morgue, I at once awakened the physician and complained about it. He told me that this was a matter of his own, that the Pole had endangered the other sick and that he had to isolate him. I at once notified the S. D. G. Maischen [the camp medic], who took the Pole back to the dispensary."[34] The truth was that Nicholas's decision to take the ill and highly contagious prisoner, Janek, to the morgue was a correct one and it was Nicholas who brought him back the next morning. Both Maischein, who went on trial after the conflict for war crimes, and Ulbright were enemies of Nicholas.

These gripes notwithstanding, virtually all of those who worked with Nicholas lauded his efforts. After the war, not only did Kahr acknowledge Nicholas's effectiveness, but a number of survivors also testified to his lifesaving abilities. Jean Septfonds, for instance, was a French prisoner who had a bad and nearing fatal leg injury. Not only did Nicholas do minor but critical surgery on the leg and bandage it with paper, he clandestinely and dangerously provided Septfonds with a daily dose of soup. According to Septfonds, "If I had not gone to the Revier and to Johnny, I would not have returned to France."[35] Another prisoner-survivor, Jean Berger echoed Septfonds and stated, "[Nicholas] rendered numerous medical services to everybody."[36] Similar words came from Walter Pomaranski, who had suffered a terrible skull fracture while at Dora, but was patched up by Nicholas late one night. Somehow he sewed up Pomaranski's head wounds and even managed to give him a shot of morphine, a drug that was not that readily available for even the Nazis. Years later, Pomaranski would state, "If it wasn't for him, I might not have gotten out of Dora alive. He was either a very sincere man or a good actor."[37]

On 4 April 1945, Rottleberode was given the order to clear out and the Nazis began to march the prisoners, including Nicholas, deeper into Germany. In one of the worst massacres of the war, made more odious by the fact that the war was very much over, more than one thousand inmates were ruthlessly murdered. On Friday the 13th of April, after a grueling trek to the town of Gardelegen, the prisoners were told that they would spend the night there and be freed the next day. They were sent into a large barn where they were to sleep. Once they were trapped in the barn, the doors were locked and the Nazi guards and townspeople set the building on fire with everyone inside. This slaughter would continue for nearly twenty-four hours. The very few who somehow managed to crawl out of that inferno were shot on the spot. In total, 1,016 died. When this carnage was discovered shortly after by the Allied forces, the 102d U.S. Infantry Division, they were so incensed that they made the townspeople come out and participate in the burial of those who had died. A sign was erected that remains today. It states:

GARDELEGEN
MILITARY CEMETERY
HERE LIE 1016 ALLIED PRISONERS OF WAR WHO WERE MURDERED BY
THEIR CAPTORS.
THEY WERE BURIED BY CITIZENS OF GARDELEGEN WHO ARE
CHARGED WITH RESPONSIBILITY THAT GRAVES ARE FOREVER KEPT AS
GREEN AS THE MEMORY OF THESE UNFORTUNATES WILL BE KEPT IN
THE FREEDOM-LOVING HEARTS OF MEN EVERYWHERE.
ESTABLISHED UNDER SUPERVISION OF 102D INFANTRY DIVISION
UNITED STATES ARMY
VANDALISM WILL BE PUNISHED BY MAXIMUM PENALTIES UNDER
LAWS OF MILITARY GOVERNMENT
FRANK A. KEATING
MAJOR GENERAL U.S.A.
COMMANDING

As it turns out, Nicholas had at least one more death-defying miracle in him. Somehow Nicholas, who had been part of the prisoners' group, concluded that the move into the barn was a setup and managed to get away from the crowd despite being wounded and injured and barely standing himself. More crawling than walking at this point, Nicholas was also suffering from tuberculosis and blood poisoning. Although he eluded the Nazis for several days, he was recaptured and marched to Sachsenhausen concentration camp with about 150 other prisoners.

At Sachsenhausen, he and thousands of other inmates were scheduled to die, but the camp was low on poisonous gas and could not machine-gun people to death fast enough, so this camp was also evacuated as the Russian and American armies grew closer. Now, starting on 21 April, Nicholas and 40,000 inmates, in the midst of complete chaos and disarray, were off to Ravensbrueck. They arrived there the next day only to discover that it too was being cleared out. As he lay in his cell in indescribable agony, Nicholas was given a choice of either waiting for the Russians, who were very near, or leaving. Perhaps bitten too many times by Nazi treachery, Nicholas decided to join some of the others and hobbled out. On 3 May, about fifty miles from Ravensbrueck, Nicholas was found on the side of the road by an American tank unit near Lubz. Seven weeks later, the records show that he was admitted on 26 June to the Lariboisiere hospital in Paris run by the U.S. Army. His brother Vildebart soon had him switched to a French hospital, Hopital St. Antoine.

As he had all his adult life, Nicholas refused to give up the ghost despite having injuries and illnesses that would have killed most people. Unfortunately, this would be a battle, though bravely and tenaciously waged, he would lose. At around 2 A.M. on 4 September 1945, Nicholas died. He lies buried in the Cementary of Pantin in northeastern Paris.[38]

Summary

Much of the information on how people of African descent resisted the Nazis may be lost forever. Many have passed on perhaps never aware of the important contributions they made in not completely surrendering to the insanity of it all. The sophisticated arts of resistance were practiced out of necessity by the hundreds of thousands of people of African descent who had to deal with the Nazis and their war of death. Hitler, the Nazis, and the German people pushed the envelope of racism as far as it could go, but in the end they failed to destroy their chosen enemies either physically or, more important, spiritually.

With the defeat of Nazism, Germany, Europe, and, indeed, the international community entered a new phase. The birth of the United Nations, though difficult and shackled by the counterideology of national sovereignty, signaled a new discourse on race and racism. The UN Charter and subsequent leading documents would address this issue forthrightly. The loss and sacrifices by millions during the Nazi time were the foundations on which this emerging discourse was built. The millions of Jews, Gypsies, Russians, and Blacks, among others, who were targeted for state-controlled murder simply because of who they were had repulsed the global community and brought into being a human rights and anti–racist policy regime unprecedented in modern history.

Yet, even as policies and pronouncements against racism grew, so did the seeds of retrenchment and retreat. Within a very short time, the rhetoric of racism would recede as the cold war replaced the hot one. The antiblack racism that prevailed during the Hitler era, in Europe and beyond, would resurface in new but no less pernicious ways.

Part IV

Black Skins, German Masks

Blackness in Contemporary Germany

European (Dis)union

Racism and Antiracism in Contemporary Europe

Institutional racism is that which, covertly or overtly, resides in the policies, proce-dures, operations and culture of public or private institutions—reinforcing indi-vidual prejudices and being reinforced by them in turn.

—*A. Sivanandan*[1]

Race and Racism in Contemporary Europe

Unresolved issues of race and racism from the World War II era, inter alia, drive persist-ent racism, individual and institutional, in contemporary Europe. Sivanandan points to the structural dynamics of racism that are not reducible to simply individual prejudices even though they exist and are important. From police brutality to immigration poli-cies, contemporary European race relations are shaped by institutionalized discrimina-tion. Furthermore, many observers believe that circumstances are worsening. The scholar Kenan Malik theorizes that the "liberal hour" that emerged in the wake of Nazism generated a consensus in which biological views of race were thrown out and a liberal social democratic order was constructed in most modern European states. Racial and ethnic integration were on the agenda, and the welfare state was in full bloom. Laws were passed in the United Kingdom, France, and the United States that outlawed racial discrimination, and the United Nations, unlike its predecessor, the League of Nations, made antiracism a central tenet of its purpose.[2] The UNESCO studies on race in the 1950s and 1960s, for most students of the subject at the time, put the final nails in the coffin of the intellectual biological views of racism, the basis on which Nazism, Italian fascism, and other reactionary racist manifestations prior to War War II were built. UNESCO's "Third Statement on Race" argued that all humans "belong to a single species" and that there "is great genetic diversity within all human populations. Pure races—in the sense of genetically homogeneous populations—do not exist in the human species."[3] That racially halcyon time was short-lived, however, and as Malik observes, "Postwar liberalism was ... a temporary gap in history."[4] A paradigm shift occurred by the late 1960s, in the face of radical and even revolutionary subaltern challenges from below, and by the late 70s a new consensus had emerged of social retreat on the issues of equality and inclusion. In the recrudescentizing years of Reagan and Thatcher, social policy had come full circle, and by the 1990s, state-initiated policy and rhetoric of racial remediation through the vehicle of the welfare state was as dead as the Soviet Union and its crumbled domain.

The quiescent beasts began to rise. While the Nazis as a political force, and, for the most part, hard-core, state-centered Nazi ideology was overthrown in 1945, its physical elimination was never matched by an equal commitment to purging its philosophical and social roots. Indeed, denazification politics lasted only a very short time before the imperatives of the cold war surrendered the battle against racism to the struggle against communism. This meant that a popular campaign and strong policies to eradicate all vestiges of racism and ethnocentricism, including that of Negrophobia, was never seriously carried out. Europe (and the United States) was thus compromised by its own contradictory racial politics. By the 1990s, the white racial contract was once again operating at its most exclusive best.

The racial contract was functioning despite the fact that Europe, as noted, had never been all white. The historical and contemporary presence of people of color throughout the region challenges any notion that sees Europe as simply the evolution of white experiences, white contributions, and white legitimacy. White European dominance has always been contested space. This is not to minimize the impact of racism or the hegemonic authority of European Whites, but mainly to underscore that resistance to racism, white supremacy, and a white Eurocentrism has been constant. This resistance continues to manifest itself in the struggles against racist immigration policies, police violence and murders, assaults by right-wing extremists, and other social, cultural, and economic problems faced by people of color and ethnic minorities.

In many European nations, people of color are categorized under the generic label of "Blacks." This politically informed term includes people from or descendant from Africa, the Caribbean, Latin America, Asia, and the Middle East. While the term is being contested and is undergoing change (discussed later), it is still used to capture the broad array of peoples who have either historically resided in the region or recently immigrated, and who share the historical experience of colonialism and the contemporary reality of racism and ethnic discrimination. At the same time, the notion of specific black identities is different in each country. To be black in Germany, for instance, does not necessarily mean the same thing as being black in England, France, Hungary, or Italy. These differences stem from a fluid combination of official (state) definitions, cultural dictates, popular notions about who is in what group, and self-definitions.

In every nation in Europe, people of African descent can be found. Though, for the most part, their numbers are relatively small, they are important, and their prominence in a wide range of areas is growing. While many outside of Europe are perhaps generally aware that there are people of African descent in England and France, largely due to popular sports and music personalities, the experiences and social status of Afro-Caribbeans, Africans, and even African Americans in the Scandinavian countries, other parts of Western Europe, Southern Europe, and Central-Eastern Europe are unknown. Not only are there significant numbers of people of African descent in the region, they suffer from specific forms of racism aimed at dark-skinned African people.

Contemporary "Euroracism" is manifest not in the imposition of a brutalizing authoritarian state apparatus but in the even more insidious velvet glove of a discourse often expressed by social democratic and liberal state policies that target immigrants and migrants as the new scourge of Europe. At the same time, the criminalization of colored peoples and racist physical attacks affect citizens and the newly arrived alike. Euroracism links popular resentment and racial othering with new state policies that together curtail, if not eliminate altogether, progress on the racial front. Here the neoliberal state is a pivotal player in its willingness to concede to the political right the dominant articulation of an answer to the economic and social upheavals that have characterized many nations in Europe in the 1990s. On the one hand, economic and cultural globalization has destabilized fixed notions of work, play, and social life and sent people reeling in an attempt to find stability. On the other hand, the post–cold war era has taken away the long-indoctrinated enemy of either capitalism or socialism. Immigrants and others are caught in this squeeze.

Yet Europe finds itself at a crossroads. A 2000 UN report concluded that Europe is slated to lose population as it ages over the next five decades.[5] The report argues that Europe will need 700 million immigrants in order to maintain its present age structure. According to 1997 Eurostat forcasts, Italy will start to decline in 2008, Germany in 2013, Spain in 2014, and Finland in 2026 with the other EU members between 2030 and 2040 except for Luxemburg and Sweden. These estimates are based on the medium expectations rather than either the much lower or much higher forecast possibilities. Europe has already lost a significant proportion of its share of the world's population. While in 1950, 12 percent of the world lived in the EU states, only 4 percent will do so by 2050, and for all of Europe that number will be 7 or 8 percent. What all this means is that if Europe, particularly Western Europe, is to maintain a labor force that keeps it competitive in the global economy, it *must* recruit immigrants in unprecedented numbers. And it also means that a large percent, undoubtedly the majority, of those immigrants will be people from Africa, Asia, the Caribbean, and the Middle East. In other words, white Europe is staring down the barrel of a new racial configuration that brings not only economic and social changes but cultural and political ones as well.

While people from the different areas can expect to collectively face degrees of discrimination, the experiences will in some ways be very different depending on where people are from. Some authors have noted the phenomenon of "multiple racisms," that is, in a given society, different ethnoracial groups may experience racism in dissimilar and distinct ways, although all may suffer, at the same time, from a general form of racial prejudice and discrimination.[6] In Europe, it can be argued that those of African descent experience distinct expressions of racism that differ from those of Asians, the

Roma (Gypsies), or people from the Middle East. For example, the invective "nigger" is still hurled almost exclusively at people of African descent across the region.[7] The identification of specific forms of anti-dark-skinned racism and Negrophobia is by no means meant to diminish racism and other forms of intolerance visited upon other groups. The difference is not in terms of one form being more punitive or better or worse than another but in the specific historical-social contexts out of which particular groups emerged.

In addition to African-descended peoples, other groups suffering from racial and ethnic discrimination in the region include the Roma, Turks, Kurds, southern and eastern Asians, and Middle Easterners. The Roma, whom King Henry VIII called "Europe's most unwanted race," continued to endure unbridled discrimination and oppression throughout Europe.[8] In Central and Eastern Europe, in particular, the Roma experience physical attacks, nearly universal unemployment, and widespread attitudes that view them as less than human.[9]

The variety of peoples of color in Europe complicates our understanding of the different racial views that are embraced by Europeans. There is no one European view of race or racial differences. While Blacks in France from Africa and the Caribbean are seen (and see themselves) as French in every sense of the term, Africans who migrate rarely obtain German citizenship despite several generations of residency. In some instances, nationalism and ethnic differences among "white" Europeans, especially in Central and Eastern Europe, are more dominant conflicts than that of white versus black. Perhaps the most significant factor is the relatively small number of non-Whites in the region. In the United Kingdom, for example, Blacks constitute only about 5 percent of the population—with people of African descent less than half of that number—and are disproportionately concentrated in London, Bristol, Liverpool, and a few other major cities. Although people of color are playing increasingly visible roles, from entertainment and sports stars to elected officials and human rights leaders, their small numbers are no material threat to the lifestyles, employment, or general opportunities available to Whites. In other words, resistance mainly to colored immigrants is based more on ideological and politically derived notions and motives than on any concrete data that Whites are losing ground.

As noted, the term "black" is used politically to mean all people of color and not just those of African descent. The term is meant to capture the collective experience of imperialism, colonialism, and immigration. It emerged in a period when the number of people of color was small and the collective experience of adjusting to an often hostile environment rationalized the necessity of a broad tent under which all minorities could fit. Overcoming cultural, religious, language, and social differences was important to the leadership of the new communities even though such elision was often resisted at the community level. "Black" also emboldened a militant and sometimes radical position toward the state as it gave identity, dignity, and presence to the formerly colonialized and imperialized others. Strategically, the term mobilized a coalition-building model that valued collective response and resistance and a closing of ranks among those who were being commonly victimized in a general sense.

Times would change, however. "Black" as an all-inclusive category for all people of color is being contested. This reflects the increasingly different positions that various groups find themselves in regarding their socioeconomic and cultural status. In England, for instance, third-generation Afro-Caribbeans tend to be, on average, much more integrated and economically and socially secure than first-generation Pakistanis. "Black" is also being challenged on the ground that it disingenuously and dangerously collapses gender, class, and sexuality dynamics under the umbrella of race. This has led some to argue that the category "black" does not represent these different social locations and that it is more important to see each group in its own particular light. In discussing the relationship of the Asian community to the broader issue of black identity, Tariq Modood argues, "The choice, then, is not between a separatist Asian ethnicity and unity of the racially oppressed; the choice is between a political realism which accords dignity to ethnic groups on their own terms and a coercive ideological fantasy."[10] Although Modood does not interrogate the fabrication and fantasy of ethnic groups themselves, his point is salient, and exposes the real tension that exists. Also, a rising nationalist ideology among some people of African descent, in England, Switzerland, France, the Netherlands, and Germany, in particular, advocates a "people of African descent only" or a "people of African descent first" perspective. This can be seen by the growth in the region of nationalist groups such as the U.S.-based Nation of Islam, which has mosques and activists in England, France, Germany, Switzerland, and other states. Pan-Asian, Pan-Indian, and Pan-Arab perspectives also exist and further erode the umbrella identity of "black."

One difficulty in assessing the impact of racism on people of color is that few countries in Europe collect data that are racially useful; that is, census counts do not include racial categories. In some countries, such as France and Germany, it is illegal to collect such data. Researchers are left to calculate, in most instances, from immigration data and information given on nation of origin by respondents. Needless to say, calculating racial counts by nation of origin is highly problematic, particularly given that racial categories themselves are social constructions that are fluid and elastic in the first place. It is no more correct to conclude that an immigrant from South Africa or Jamaica is black than to believe that one from the United States or Canada is white.

Given these caveats, immigrant and census data and some independent studies give us some clue to the general numbers of racial minorities, particularly those of African descent, in Europe. According to research by the European Union, there are about 17 million immigrants in the fifteen member states of the European Community out of a total population of about 320 million. It is roughly estimated by the EU that about 6 million of those immigrants are from the developing world, the bulk of which are distributed in Germany, France, and the United Kingdom.[11] Some research shows that there are about 300,000 Afro-Germans with some estimates as high as 500,000.[12] In France, out of a population of 56.5 million, people of African descent constitute about 1 million.[13] And in the United Kingdom, the Afro-Caribbean population is about 1.6 percent (880,000 out of 52 million).[14]

While most Afro-Europeans are in the West, Central, Southern, and Eastern Europe contain tiny communities of African-descended peoples, many of whom are former students who never left or could not leave after the cold war. In Russia, Yugoslavia, Bulgaria, and other states, their presence has been noted in journalistic and even scholarly works.[15] In addition, there is a significant presence of African American expatriates, some ex-military, living in many states across Europe. During the cold war, the U.S. military presence in Europe was vast. The United States had more than 300,000 troops in the region during this period, mostly in West Germany. African Americans constituted a significant proportion of those forces. While most of the black American soldiers came home after their tour of duty, some stayed and settled in the region. In any case, many left children behind, though exact figures are difficult to determine.

Despite these recent developments, the European view on race and racism is in many ways still shaped by the experiences of World War II. As the scholars John Solomos and Les Black note, "the history of contemporary racism has been influenced in one way or another by the experience of fascism and the anti-Semitic political mobilizations which were a key feature of fascist movements.[16] To this insight, we can add the experiences of people of African descent.

Europe United and Divided

A Pan-European consciousness has emerged in recent years in a number of ways: the development of the euro; the NAFTA-like Maastricht Treaty; the increasing importance of regional institutions such as the European Union, the Council of Europe, and the European Parliament; the elimination of borders; and regional security institutions such as the Organization on Security and Cooperation in Europe (OSCE) and the U.S.-led North American Treaty Organization (NATO).[17] More than ever, a European identity is being promoted and nurtured among citizens of the region, with a concerted and calculated effort to minimize economic and political differences among states being coordinated by political leaders and policymakers. Those occurrences, however, coincide with a significant growth in racism, xenophobia, and racialized anti-immigrant passions. Both in rhetoric and in political and policy actions, a backlash against "Blacks" is evident in Western, Central, Southern, and Eastern Europe, with minorities of all colors under attack and on the defensive.

In the political arena, there has been a disturbing success on the part of racist and extremist political parties seeking elected office. While few in number, those previously on the margins have discovered the politics and populist language to draw many to an antigovernment, seemingly pro-working-class posture. These relatively new parties have gained mass audiences, media exposure, and quasi-legitimacy by winning elections and engaging conservative, liberal, and radical politicians on comparatively equal ground. Outside of mainstream political systems, racist and fascist organizations have experienced a growth spurt in recent years, becoming bolder (and often deadly) in physical attacks on racial minorities and immigrants that have made many areas of Europe unsafe for foreign travelers of color. These assaults have emerged in a context of virulent anti-immigration legislation that conservatives are seeking to put in place to discourage and reverse long-standing liberal immigration laws. In Western Europe, in particular, the seething anger toward immigrants (and those perceived to be immigrants) is finding a policy expression not only from right-wing politicians but ostensibly liberal ones as well.

Finally, it should be noted that racism and discrimination against Afro-Europeans are present in the social structures, particularly in the criminal justice systems, of the region. The prisons of Europe, while nowhere near approaching the explosion that characterizes the United States, reflect the racial disproportionalities that have filled U.S. jails and prisons to the brim with African Americans and Latinos. While disproportionate numbers of Afro-Europeans are being arrested and incarcerated or deported, police brutality against racial minorities—including murder—has skyrocketed.

From the Outside In: Rise of Racist and Neo-Fascist Parties

One of the most disturbing trends in recent years has been a growing support for racist and right-wing extremist political parties. Just as Hitler's National Socialist German Workers' Party recognized that it could seize power through the election process, its descendants have tried to implement a similar strategy. In some instances, the groups are split-offs from more violent fascist and even neo-Nazi organizations. In others, political leaders have advocated rigidly conservative and racist views to explain dislocations associated with such factors as economic globalization and political restructuring that have created massive instability in a number of states in Europe. Broad, postcommunist political transformations in the region have brought forth destabilized societies where it is easy to blame immigration and "others" for internal problems— popular views that have been exploited by opportunistic conservative political movements and parties.

According to Gly Ford, a minister of the European Parliament (MEP) who serves as the special rappateur for the European Parliament, since the 1983 by-elections in France when the French National Front (NF) won a surprising number of victories, more than ten million people have voted for extremist right and neo-Nazi parties.[18] The NF, headed by the rightist Jean-Marie Le Pen, was able to seize political control of four towns in France and had at least 275 regional councillors by the end of 1998.[19] In the late 1990s, the NF suffered a bitter split that took some of the wind out of its sails, but it remains a force in French politics. France is far from alone in confronting electoral challenges from the extreme right. In Austria, the Freedom Party (FP) won 28 percent of the vote in 1996 and grew to become the largest right-wing party in Europe. FP leaders have expressed admiration for Hitler and the SS, defended Nazi war criminals, and downplayed Nazi atrocities. In February 2000, the party garnered enough votes to become part of the ruling coalition government, a development that sparked condemnation and rebuke from political leaders across Europe and even in the United States. The outcry forced FP leader Jörg Haider to step down from playing a prominent role in the new government. In Belgium, the Vlaams Blok party, whose slogan is "Our own people first," won a number of electoral victories in the late 1990s. Similarly, in Denmark the Danish Peoples Party is increasing its share of the vote, partly on the basis of rhetoric against Muslims and immigrants of color. Other European parties that have succeeded in breaking through the electoral walls and made political gains include the Centrumdemokraten in the Netherlands and the Movimento Sociale Italiano in Italy. Although some of these parties have begun to lose support, they have become potent political forces. In addition, they not only are having an impact in their own states but are seeking power regionally. In 1999, there were thirty-two MEPs from six different extreme-right parties, organized into a number of blocs including the Group of the European Right.[20] Their role in the EP has been to resist antiracism efforts by liberals and progressives.

All indications are that the political right and concessions to the right from mainstream politicians will continue to grow in Europe. Economic and political upheavals sweeping most states in the Central and Eastern regions, and unstable economies in the West, do not bode well, although, interestingly, communists in some of the Eastern states have had a revitalization. Increasingly, there is popular support for blaming "others" for the woes facing all Europeans, rather than focusing on other causes of these dislocations. Politicians take advantage of the anxieties to build support for more conservative policies, and the parliamentary system of proportional representation facilitates inroads made by extremist forces. With as little as 5 percent of the vote, these parties gain political seats and a popular forum in which to spew their venom. In some small towns in France, for instance, extremist politicians have passed laws banning rap music and removed books on multiculturalism from the shelves of local public libraries.[21]

Racist Violence Grows

Spreading racist violence in Europe marked much of the 1990s. In recent years, there has been an increase in group and individual attacks on people of color and ethnic minorities—particularly Africans, Arabs, South Asians, and the Roma. The European Union reported that there were more than 12,000 racist incidents across Europe in 1996. According to the *European Race Audit*, which monitors issues of racism across the region, physical violence is rampant against immigrants and racial minorities. In Bulgaria, for example, five white teenagers were convicted in 1998 of the racist murder of a nineteen–year-old Roma. In Italy and Spain, homeless Africans were killed by racists in a series of attacks that escalated from the early 1990s.

One case that received international coverage in early 1999 was the racially motivated murder of a black teenager, Stephen Lawrence, in England. Coming home on the night of 22 April 1993, Lawrence and his friend Duwayne Brooks were attempting to catch a bus. When Lawrence stepped down the road to see if the bus was coming, he came across a group of five or six white youths who called him a "nigger" and then physically attacked him. Lawrence was stabbed twice in the chest and arm and, after running more than a hundred yards, died on the street. This horrible death shocked a nation and region where homicide still remains rare. Many believed that the sheer notoriety of the case would force authorities to expend every effort to catch the perpetrators of the crime.

From that point on, however, every phase of the investigation by the Metropolitan Police Service (MPS) was botched by either incompetent or uncaring neglect. At the base of this fiasco was a nagging and disturbing racism unconcerned that a black youth had been brutally murdered by a gang of racist brutes. Neither the police nor the Conservative Party in power at the time thought the case merited serious attention or further investigation. The police made no arrests although five suspects, who reportedly boasted to their friends about the killing, were quickly identified by witnesses and people in the neighborhood. Somehow, the police investigations turned up no witnesses other than Brooks even though press reports at the time identified a number of people who said they saw what happened. There was also no real physical evidence collected from the scene.

Lawrence's parents and others continue to press their case, however. At one point in 1996, three of the suspects were brought to trial in a private prosecution. But, due to lack of firm evidence and no assistance from the police, the suspects were acquitted and can never be tried again in regard to this case. Two other suspects were never even brought to trial. Despite these setbacks, the case continued to gain momentum and symbolized for many black Britons pervasive injustice, discrimination, and rising racism against people of color. The case was kept alive by the unwillingness of the black community to let it go. Activists throughout the country soon joined them, and the case became a cause célèbre for antiracists. Pressure was put on the Labor Party, and Tony Blair was forced, during his run for prime minister, to commit to establishing a commission of inquiry if a Labor government was elected. It was, and in 1997, he set up a high-level commission. After many months of testimony and investigation, the commission released its report in February 2000 and concluded, to a somewhat stunned nation, that "Stephen Lawrence was unlawfully killed in a completely unprovoked racist attack by five white youths."[22]

The inquiry produced a 459–page report with more than 12,000 pages of transcripts from eighty-eight witnesses. It is further estimated that there are more than 100,000 pages of supporting reports, statements, and other documentation. The release of the report received massive media coverage for days. The explosive exposé of institutional racism rocked all of England from top to bottom. In an unprecedented move, Blair went on the floor of the House of Commons and denounced "the racism that still exists in our society." Sir Paul Condon, head of Scotland Yard, also declared that "institutional racism" existed in his department and that a "sense of shame" had grown among police officers due to their failure to appropriately handle the Lawrence investigation.

While those who committed the Lawrence homicide were not formally punished, antiracist activists felt that they had won a tremendous victory anyway. The case brought together the greatest number of people ever mobilized around the issue of racist violence and institutional police racism. It was organized resistance by the Afro-Caribbean community and vast support from other communities of color and many white Britons that forced the issue into the popular domain. Just as the Rodney King beating in Los Angeles in 1994 was a catalyst for national mobilization around police brutality, the Lawrence case fired up hundreds of thousands across the United Kingdom to speak out against racist violence and state indifference to it.

Reformed Immigration Policy

On 21 June 1948, the SS *Empire Winrush* landed at Tilbury Docks in East London carrying 492 Jamaicans.[23] It was the beginning of a massive wave of Blacks from the Caribbean to England that would profoundly shape and racialize the nation's immigration policies and discourse on national identity. To address its labor shortage in the postwar period, England not only embraced a liberal immigration policy but aggressively sought colored immigrants. Less than a decade later, conservative media and politicians, such as the late ultraconservative MP Enoch Powell, would call for the reversal of the policies and for the deportation of England's Blacks and other people of color. In the last three decades, immigration of people of color from the developing world to the states of Europe has generated antagonism, inspiring political leaders of all ideological stripes, the major media, and right-wing social movements to target them as scapegoats for Europe's economic and social downturns.

Across Europe, immigration of racial minorities continued to be a feature of the late 1990s and into the new century. There are various reasons why immigrants are coming. While many came to find work, a large number simply came to be with their families. In the Netherlands, the number of Caribbean, African, and Middle Eastern immigrants has grown immensely. Official estimates count about 300,000 Surinamese, 260,000 Turks, and more than 200,000 Moroccans out of a total population of 15.5 million.[24] The non-European, foreign-born population continues to grow throughout the region, including Switzerland (18.9 percent), Austria (9 percent), Belgium (9 percent), Germany (8.8 percent), France (6 percent), and Denmark (4.2 percent).[25] Again, while not all of these immigrants are people of color, a disproportionately high number are, and they make up the new faces of present-day Europe. Their growth has unleashed a vicious legislative backlash against all immigrants with a racialized undertone as the foundation of opposition.

In nearly every European nation, immigration laws have been tightened. What has emerged is a center-right alliance and consensus seeking to close the doors on people from the global South, and, where possible, deport and reduce the colored populations already resident. In Austria, a new law was put in place in 1988 to stop refugees at the border. In Germany, there has been fierce conservative resistance to efforts to reform the nation's citizenship laws. In Switzerland, in a move reminiscent of California's 1994 Proposition 187, which outlawed medical and educational opportunities for children of "illegal" aliens, a new law was passed that requires physicians to deny medical service to those who are not legally in the country.[26]

Such policy battles will constitute perhaps the most serious confrontations that European states will face in the coming century. Calls for ethnic and racial purity, while impossible to implement, could if carried to their logical extension ignite atrocities of the worst kind, as witnessed in the ethnically driven breakup of Yugoslavia.

Antiracism Fights Back

The European-wide antiracist group, UNITED for Intercultural Action, had identified more than 1,700 organizations, more than 275 magazines, and 111 funding sources across the continent that are engaged in antiracist efforts.[27] This network has increasingly come together and successfully pressured policy changes at both the national and the regional levels. In addition to the quest for policy reform, the battle against racist organizations and movements, especially the neo-Nazi groups, has been very much on the agenda.

The network of nongovernmental organizations has worked closely with governmental agencies and institutions in recent years. In Strasbourg, in October 2000, 250 representatives of nongovernmental organizations gathered at the European preparatory conference (PrepCom) to debate and discuss issues of racism, racial discrimination, xenophobia, intolerance, anti-Semitism, and islamophobia. The conference was preparing for European NGO participation in the August–September 2001 UN World Conference Against Racism, Racial Discrimination, Xenophobia and Related Intolerance held in Durban. It was also building unity among Europeans engaged in antiracist work. The NGO meeting issued a strongly worded document, "Report from the Forum of Non- Governmental Organisations," that stated, in part:

> We reaffirmed our determination and commitment to combat all forms of racism, racial discrimination, xenophobia and intolerance, including anti-Semitism and islamophobia and all forms of religious intolerance, whether in their institutionalised form, resulting from doctrines and practices of so-called "racial superiority" or exclusivity or any other of the varied manifestations of such phenomena. We deplore the resurgence of racism, racial discrimination, xenophobia and intolerance, including anti-Semitism and islamophobia and all forms of religious intolerance, and a persistent climate of intolerance and acts of violence. Efforts undertaken by the international community to combat these phenomena are inadequate and must be reinforced. In particular, we are appalled by the recent electoral success in Europe of political parties disseminating and promoting racist and xenophobic ideology. When considering the various forms of racism, racial discrimination, xenophobia and intolerance, including anti-Semitism and islamophobia and all forms of religious intolerance, and ways to remedy them, the history of Europe, in particular slave trade, colonialism, and the Holocaust, has to be borne in mind.[28]

The report made 116 recommendations that were submitted to the meeting of states preparing for their participation in the parallel conference among states that also took place in South Africa. The recommendations were around the following themes: "Legal protection against racism and related discrimination at national, regional and international levels; Policies and practices to combat racism and related discrimination at subnational and national level; Education and awareness-raising to combat racism, related discrimination and extremism at local, national and international levels; Information, communication and the media; and Immigration and asylum."[29]

While the report and the recommendations covered a wide range of concerns and groups, such as the Roma, Kurds (Europe and the Middle East), Dalits (South Asia), and Burakumin (Japan), many of the Africans and other people of African descent living in Europe who attended the meeting felt that issues specific to antiblack, that is, Negrophobic, forms of racism were ignored or minimized. Although there was no opposition to the issues that were raised, this deeply felt exclusion inspired a follow-up meeting of Africans in Europe and from the Diaspora in Vienna in late April 2001.[30]

The issue of antiblackness resonates with many people of African descent in Europe who feel that this concern is often subsumed under the generic label of antiracism and not given its full due. The ability to respond to this concern, however, is circumscribed by several factors including the different status that Blacks have (citizen versus non-citizen), different definitions of blackness (racial communities versus immigrant/national communities), and different sizes of population (significant versus almost nonexistent). Language barriers, interracial family and relationships, and lack of resources also contribute. Most significant, there remains no ideological, political, or strategic paradigm regarding race and blackness on which unity exists, and one is not likely to emerge. All of these issues and more come together in the one country that has been the most in denial about its black past and present: Germany.

Breathing while Black

Linking the German Racial Past with the Present

Afro-Germans have no popularly acknowledged or recognized place in Germany history, few role models of African or Afro-European descent, and, until recently, no real sense of themselves as a community.

—*Tina Campt* [1]

The problem for us here in Germany is to bring these two identities together. Living here in Germany as Germans as well as having a feeling for your own history, your own kind, your own consciousness. The trick is to bring these two things together without going one way in overexaggeration.

—*Thomas Della* [2]

The date: 9 June 2000. The place: Dessau, Germany. The time: post–Cold War, reunited Germany. The body of Alberto Adriano is discovered. Barely alive, he had been maliciously attacked by three skinheads while walking through a park early that morning. According to one report, he had been kicked and beaten so viciously that he had only one eye left when he was found unconscious and naked. He died three days later in the hospital, leaving behind a wife and three children. Adriano was a German citizen. He was also of African descent, having been born in Mozambique.[3]

Adriano's murder begs numerous questions, How differently had the "black" presence changed since the Nazi period? How much had Germany changed since the Nazi era? Has an "Afro-German" or "black" identity formed and a community along with it? How do people of African descent in Germany view themselves in relation to the diaspora? What forms do black resistance take? These are flowing questions that are being answered in process. Even the issue of who is being discussed is up for grabs. No one knows for sure how many people of African descent reside in Germany today. Estimates of the number of Blacks in Germany (Africans, Afro-Germans, and others from the diaspora—vary from a European Parliament low of 50,000 to the Institute of Race Relations figure of 195,000 to a *Christian Science Monitor* report of 250,000 to as high as 500,000.[4] Given the tremendous influx of Africans during the 1990s, the number is probably somewhere between 200,000 and 400,000. In 1999, it was estimated that there were about 13,500 Africans in Berlin.[5] The number of people who fit the phenotype, however, is not the same as the number who identify themselves in a racially black manner. Whereas in the United Kingdom and the United States, there exists plenty of historical and ongoing data from surveys and polls regarding how people of African descent (to whatever degree) identify themselves and how those views have changed over time, this is not the case in Germany. As mentioned earlier, data are not collected along these lines and the notion of an Afro-German community is relatively new and undeveloped.

While the numbers are not clear, the political motion is. Both as an expression of internal reconstruction and the search for identity and in response to the level of racism manifest against Blacks, in particular, since the Berlin Wall came down, people of African descent in Germany have increasingly organized and mobilized to forge an Afro-German distinctiveness. This process is driven and complicated by a number of factors including the danger of racial violence, the hesitancy on the part of the state to address the issue, the difficulty of asserting a black identity in a nearly all-white environment, and internal differences among those who fall under the rubric of blackness. In negotiating this wide range of obstacles, a number of notable efforts have emerged that fundamentally challenge the mainstream German view of racial denial of the presence of the nation's black citizens. Within this context, the echoes of the antiblack Nazi past ring loud for some Afro-Germans and for the nation as a whole.

Building the Resistance

As noted earlier, a pivotal unifying and clarifying moment in the growing discursive movement for a black identity was the 1984 publication of *Farbe Bekennen* (*Showing Our Colors*). The book was written and edited by May Opitz, Katharina Oguntoye, and Dagmar Schultz and was the first extended work on black German history. It not only represented the insurgent voices of thirteen Afro-German women but expressed the incipient construction of an Afro-German identity and desire for community. It is difficult to overstate the importance of *Farbe Bekennen*. Grand transformations were occurring as the cold war was peaking under Reagan and Thatcher, Gorbachev's perestroika and glasnot were accelerating the downfall of the USSR, and the possibility of a united Germany loomed. In both East and West Germany, attacks on people of color and foreigners escalated and racist and neo-Nazi organizations began to network. The call for a greater unity among people of African descent was natural, and though not explicitly the purpose of the book, it was a clarion call for a new direction for black Germans. The book and two of its authors, May Opitz and Katharina Oguntoye, helped to found and develop two important organizations in the wake of *Farbe Bekennen*.

Opitz was a leading intellectual and organizer for the movement. Her poetry and tenacious spirit mobilized Afro-German energy and helped to instill the sense of black identity and black woman identity necessary to advance toward building a black community. In addition to her writing, she was politically active and helped to create Black History Month in Germany, beginning in 1990 and still going strong.[6] The community suffered a great loss, however, when she committed suicide on 9 August 1996 at the age of thirty-six. She had shortly before then been diagnosed with multiple sclerosis. Whether the cause was the illness or other pressures is not known for certain, but a number of Afro-Germans point out that suicide is actually a serious issue among Afro-Germans, especially the youth.

In 1986, the Black German Initiative (ISD) was formed. While it has sometimes been compared to a civil rights organization, its mission and agenda are not ideological, political, or focused on policy. Its founders were principally attempting to bring together people of African descent who were German citizens. (This would later change to include all those of African descent in Germany.) Its annual summer gathering, the *Bundesstreffen*, is mainly about bringing together Afro-Germans and Africans in Germany to meet and share experiences. Workshops are held on issues that participants are concerned about, but mostly it is a time to socialize and be among other Blacks, an opportunity that many do not have on a regular basis. Many of the participants bring their children or black children of their friends. White spouses and companions are left at home, for the most part, although it is apparently not unusual for people of color who are not of African ancestry to attend. The *Bundesstreffen* was critical for the generation who matured in the 1980s and were attempting to locate themselves in the changing environment, and it became a racial pilgrimage of sorts for many. It is easy to speculate that the gathering does not have the same meaning for the younger generation who have more outlets, personal and public, for carving a black identity—that is, if they feel the urgency to do so, which is not a given.

Around the same time that ISD formed, a number of black women had begun to meet, in 1985, to discuss ways to address the particular concerns that women of color faced in Germany. This wide range of concerns included sexual harassment, raising mixed-race children, and racism in the (white) feminist movement. ADEFRA was initially an acronym for Afro-Deutsch Fraülein, but later it was discovered that it is a word in Ethiopia meaning "woman who has courage," a more than fitting description of the women who created the organization.[7] The organization is mostly decentralized, although there have been some national meetings. ADEFRA has outreached to sisters throughout Europe as well as in the United States, such as the Black Womens Studies Institute in New York.

These organizations and stronger collaboration would be necessary as the growth of a neofascist network took off considerably after unification. For many Afro-Germans, as the journalist Paul Hockenos argues, the freedom from communism across Eastern Europe, including the former East Germany, was seen as a green light for the freedom to hate.

Under Attack and Fighting Back

Tragically, Adriano would join the list of about a hundred individuals who have died and many, many more who have been injured at the hands of neo-Nazis and other racists since the two Germanys became one again. The Adriano case galvanized a national outcry that had been building to address the issue of unbridled racist violence aimed at "foreigners" or those appearing to be so, although knowledge of one's German citizenship was unlikely to stop a racist attack. Adriano's killers—twenty-four–year-old Enrico Hilprecht, sixteen–year-old Christian Richter, and sixteen–year-old Frank Miethbauer— were eventually caught, tried, and convicted. According to the police, the three described their victim as a "foreigner pig."[8]

While the largest wave of attacks happened in the first few years of unification, incidents still occur too frequently. According to the Federal Office of Criminal Investigation, there were 750 incidents of far-right violence in 1999.[9] In Summer 2000 alone, according to the journalist Miranda Pyne,

> ten people were injured in a bombing in Düsseldorf—six of them Russian Jewish immigrants; two skinheads were arrested for injuring an African man in a racial attack; there was an arson attempt on a home for asylum seekers; two homeless men were kicked to death by young right-wing extremists; a memorial to a North African killed while fleeing racist attackers was vandalized in Berlin; and a 21–year-old German man was fined and given a five-month suspended sentence for punching a Hong Kong–born photojournalist attempting to cover racism in East Germany.[10]

For many, the murder of Adriano was Germany's new wake-up call. Antiracist organizations, including ISD and ADEFRA, supported mass public demonstrations against these attacks, and their calls were answered. In August 2000, 3,000 gathered in Munich; two months later, 30,000 gathered in Düsseldorf while more than 20,000 demonstrated in Dortmund.[11] These events involved not only activists but also government officials who felt the need to respond as well. While these gatherings did not focus solely on antiblack violence, the attacks were recognized as racial in nature. There was also a bigger protest that took place in Berlin. More than 200,000 people, the largest such protest in memory, came together to protest racism and call for tolerance. In an effort to demonstrate support for tolerance at the highest level, Chancellor Gerhard Schröder laid flowers and a wreath at the memorial established to commemorate Adriano. Schröder said, "We cannot and must not accept . . . that people are chased through the streets, beaten or even killed because of their language, religion or the color of their skin."[12]

Up until recently, Germany had banned only two political parties in its history: the successor to the Nazi Party, and the German Communist Party (in West Germany during the cold war). In 2000, however, a fierce national debate emerged over whether to outlaw the ultrareactionary National Democratic Party (NPD). The NPD, among others, was a leading voice shouting against "foreignization" and, at the same time, called for the restoration of German "territories" in France, Poland, the Czech Republic, parts of the former Soviet Union, and Austria.[13] Other extremist parties that have grown in influence and support in the country are the Republikaner and the German Peoples Party, and the National Front. One survey found that even among Germans in the so-called more tolerant West, 70 percent believe there are too many foreigners in the country. Another survey shows that at least 20 percent of Germans harbor feelings of hatred toward Blacks. The Government Commission for Foreigners has listed twenty-five towns as neo-Nazi centers and unsafe for foreigners, particularly foreigners of color.[14] The tension eventually led the government of Chancellor Schröder and President Johannes Rau of the Social Democratic Party (SPD) to ban the National Democratic Party (NPD), the aforementioned extreme-right-wing party with neo-Nazi connections.

A Black German Future

The Nazi past resonates in the black German present. One of the most egregious ironies of the postwar compensation issue is that those who served Nazism, whether willingly or not, such as German soldiers and unconvicted (or even convicted) war criminals, and their heirs receive pensions while most of the victims do not. It is notable that there is no time limit on applying for a war pension while the deadline for the original Bundesentschaedigungsgesetz (formally titled, the Federal Law for the Compensation of the Victims of National Socialist Persecution)—known as BEG—expired in 1969.[15] According to research, the German government pays ten times more annually to war criminals and former SS members, roughly 50,000, plus war veterans, than to Nazi victims. Half of the applicants for the BEG were denied.[16]

By some estimates more than $100 billion has been paid to victims of the Nazism. In the agreement signed by Germany, sixty-five German companies, and the United States in December 1999, the three parties committed to pay $5.2 billion for those forced to become slave laborers. Experts estimate that this includes perhaps as many as 1.7 million individuals.[17] The pact is consistent with the other deals made after the war to compensate those who had been victims of the Nazis.[18]

As for most Afro-Germans and other black sufferers, they have never received any reparations or compensation. BEG, signed on 10 September 1952, was an internal law to "compensate (1) residents of Germany, (2) emigrants from Germany, and (3) those who belong to the community of 'German language and culture.' Victims "must have had (1) territorial ties to Germany, (2) been persecuted on the grounds of political opposition, race, religion, or world view, and (3) either harmed physically or financially." To receive a monthly "injury to health" pension, victims must have been interned in a concentration camp for at least twelve months and have suffered a "not insignificant" injury to body and health. Importantly, BEG *did not cover* (1) forced or slave laborers, (2) all those who were harmed outside of Germany by Nazi killing squads, (3) victims of sterilization, (4) homosexuals, (5) "anti-socials," (6) communists, and (7) Gypsies. Afro-Germans and other people of African descent in Germany and the occupied lands fit categories 1, 2, 3, 4, 5, and 6, and possibly 7.

Theodor Michael, who has been a leader in fighting for compensation for Afro-Germans abused at the hands of the Nazis, states, "Most black victims have just given up because it is very hard for us to prove that we are entitled to compensation. The

Federal Compensation Law is very complicated."[19] He goes on to say that the "web of bureaucratic rules and complex legal procedures that black victims (most of them now well advanced in age) have to go through to claim compensation, is a put off."[20] The journalist Regina Jere-Malanda reports that black "victims of sterilizations have been asked to produce extensive documentation to prove their suffering (in this case, sterilization certificates and other medical documents to back the physical damage). Physical evidence alone is not enough. Why the authorities expect victims of such indelible harm to keep documents that remind them of their suffering, numbs the mind . . . [and] there have been very few success stories of black victims being compensated"[21]

Some Afro-Germans have gotten compensation. Michael fought successfully and helped his sister and brother both receive the compensation they deserved. They and Theodor, like many black Germans who were citizens, had their citizenship taken away during the Hitler years. Removal of citizenship was a category that required compensation under the postwar agreements. Yet many were turned away and did not have the resources or information to pursue their rightful claim. This issue remains a serious concern for the Afro-German community: as its resolution would indicate that the nation has come to grips, in part, with its past.

For black immigrants, despite changes that have occurred in the notoriously regressive German citizenship laws making it possible for long-term residents to obtain citizenship, many Africans are still under threat of being kicked out the country. Africans in Germany today are still facing forced deportations as the nation retreats on its commitments to refugees. On 30 November 1998, it deported twenty-six Togolese refugees and, one week later, on 7 December, it deported seventy-two Nigerians. In the case of the Nigerians, the government argued disingenuously that after the 1998 death of the dictator General Sani Abacha, it was safe for refugees to return home.[22]

These issues and others are shaping the development of the black community in Germany. In fact, it may be more proper to speak of several black communities in formation. The Afro-Germans who have citizenship, have a long history of presence in the country, and are fundamentally German in their cultural lives constitute a distinct group of Black people most of whom, but not all, are racially mixed. In a different situation are the African immigrants, from refugees to business people, who are in a state of transition: many will stay, marry, have children, and live out their lives in Germany but will, at best, assimilate the German culture with their own, as any other first-generation immigrants. Already there are dozens of organizations and projects that different African nationalities have established.[22] There is already an uneasy tension between these different collectivities as they attempt to negotiate similar racial space though from very different locations, histories, and perspectives. Finally, a third grouping of Blacks are those from other parts of the diaspora who reside in Germany but see themselves being there for only a limited time—though sometimes that time can be decades—and eventually leaving. More appropriatedly, they are expatriates who may have a strong but ultimately limited vested interest in the construction of community.

Despite these distinctions and tensions, the black community as a community continues to grow. The unity that was forged during the Nazi era as Blacks struggled to survive National Socialism echoes in contemporary Germany. Afro-Germans and other Blacks in Germany have reached out consistently in solidarity with other diasporian Blacks. Afro-British and African American influence, in the areas of music, politics, and scholarship, is strong. For the most part, however, the "exchange" has been one-way, and few in the diaspora have given attention to the process and development of black-ness in Germany. Yet, this imagining and forging of community proceeds, and, memo-ry, as a tool of resistance, is crucial to this process. Organizations like ADEFRA and the ISD, gatherings like the *Bundesstreffen*, programs like Black History Month, and publi-cations like *Afro Look* and *Afrekete* are all vehicles for building a conscious black pres-ence that challenges the nation to acknowledge, respect, and address its black past, present, and future.

Appendices

Appendix A

Nuremberg Laws

Law for the Protection of German Blood and German Honor (passed September 15, 1935)

Entirely convinced that the purity of German blood is essential to the further existence of the German people, and inspired by the uncompromising determination to safeguard the future of the German nation, the Reichstag has unanimously resolved upon the following law, which is promulgated herewith:

Section 1

1. Marriages between Jews and citizens of German or kindred blood are forbidden. Marriages concluded in defiance of this law are void, even if, for the purpose of evading this law, they were concluded abroad.
2. Proceedings for annulment may be initiated only by the Public Prosecutor.

Section 2

Sexual relations outside marriage between Jews and nationals of German or kindred blood are forbidden.

Section 3

Jews will not be permitted to employ female citizens of German or kindred blood as domestic servants.

Section 4

1. Jews are forbidden to display the Reich and national flag or the national colors.
2. On the other hand they are permitted to display the Jewish colors. The exercise of this right is protected by the State.

Section 5

1. A person who acts contrary to the prohibition of Section 1 will be punished with hard labour.

2. A person who acts contrary to the prohibition of Section 2 will be punished with imprisonment or with hard labour.

3. A person who acts contrary to the provisions of Sections 3 or 4 will be punished with imprisonment up to a year and with a fine, or with one of these penalties.

Section 6

The Reich Minister of the Interior in agreement with the Deputy Fuhrer and the Reich Minister of Justice will issue the legal and administrative regulations required for the enforcement and supplementing of this law.

Section 7

The law will become effective on the day after its promulgation; Section 3, however, not until 1 January 1936.

Appendix B

Nuremberg Laws

The Reich Citizenship Law (passed September 15, 1935)

Article 1

1. A subject of the State is a person who belongs to the protective union of the German Reich, and who therefore has particular obligations towards the Reich.

2. The status of subject is acquired in accordance with the provisions of the Reich and State Law of Citizenship.

Article 2

1. A citizen of the Reich is that subject only who is of German or kindred blood and who, through his conduct, shows that he is both desirous and fit to serve the German people and Reich faithfully.

2. The right to citizenship is acquired by the granting of Reich citizenship papers.

3. Only the citizen of the Reich enjoys full political rights in accordance with the provision of the laws.

Article 3

The Reich Minister of the Interior in conjunction with the Deputy of the Fuhrer will issue the necessary legal and administrative decrees for carrying out and supplementing this law.

The Reich Citizenship Law: First Regulation (passed November 14, 1935)

Article 1

1. Until further regulations regarding citizenship papers are issued, all subjects of German or kindred blood, who possessed the right to vote in the Reichstag elections at

the time the Citizenship Law came into effect, shall for the time being possess the rights of Reich citizens. The same shall be true of those to whom the Reich Minister of the Interior, in conjunction with the Deputy of the Fuhrer, has given preliminary citizenship.

2. The Reich Minister of the Interior, in conjunction with the Deputy of the Fuhrer, can withdraw the preliminary citizenship.

Article 2

1. The regulations in Article 1 are also valid for Reich subjects of mixed Jewish blood.

2. An individual of mixed Jewish blood is one who is descended from one or two grandparents who were racially full Jews, in so far as he or she does not count as a Jew according to Article 5, paragraph 2 One grandparent shall be considered as full-blooded if he or she belonged to the Jewish religious community.

Article 3

Only the Reich citizen, as bearer of full political rights, exercises the right to vote in political affairs or can hold public office. The Reich Minister of the Interior, or any agency empowered by him, can make exceptions during the transition period, with regard to occupation of public office. The affairs of religious organizations will not be affected.

Article 4

1. A Jew cannot be a citizen of the Reich. He has no right to vote in political affairs and he cannot occupy public office.

2. Jewish officials will retire as of December 31, 1935. If these officials served at the front in the world war, either for Germany or her allies, they will receive in full, until they reach the age limit, the pension to which they were entitled according to the salary they last received; they will, however, not advance in seniority. After reaching the age limit, their pensions will be calculated anew, according to the salary last received, on the basis of which their pension was computed.

3. The affairs of religious organizations will not be affected.

4. The conditions of service of teachers in Jewish public schools remain unchanged until new regulations for the Jewish school systems are issued.

Article 5

1. A Jew is anyone who is descended from at least three grandparents who are racially full Jews. Article 2, para. 2, second sentence will apply.

2. A Jew is also one who is descended from two full Jewish parents, if

(a) he belonged to the Jewish religious community at the time this law was issued, or joined the community later,

(b) he was married to a Jewish person, at the time the law was issued, or married one subsequently,

(c) he is the offspring of a marriage with a Jew, in the sense of Section 1, which was contracted after the Law for the Protection of German Blood and German Honor became effective,

(d) he is the offspring of an extramarital relationship with a Jew, according to Section I, and will be born out of wedlock after July 31, 1936.

Article 6

1. Requirements for the pureness of blood as laid down in Reich Law or in orders of the NSDAP and its echelons—not covered in Article 5—will not be affected.

2. Any other requirements for the pureness of blood, not covered in Article 5, can be made only by permission of the Reich Minister of the Interior and the Deputy Fuhrer. If any such demands have been made, they will be void as of January 1, 1936, if they have not been requested by the Reich Minister of the Interior in agreement with the Deputy Fuhrer. These requests must be made by the Reich Minister of the Interior.

Article 7

The Fuhrer and Reich Chancellor can grant exemptions from the regulations laid down in the law.

Notes

Introduction

1. Manuel Castells, *The Power of Identity: The Information Age—Economy, Society and Culture* (New York: Blackwell, 1997), 7.
2. Michael Burleigh and Wolfgang Wippermann, *The Racial State: Germany 1933–1945* (Cambridge: Cambridge University Press, 1991), 128–129.
3. There were other people of color and mixed-race individuals with heritage from Asia and the Middle East who were targeted by the Nazis. This study notes but can not examine their persecution which should be given the same serious investigation that is being attempted here.
4. Timothy Keegan, *Colonial South Africa and the Origin of the Racial Order: Reconsiderations in Southern African History* (Charlotte: University Press of Virginia), 1997.
5. Sander Gilman, *On Blackness without Blacks: Essays on the Image of the Black in Germany* (Boston: G. K. Hall, 1982).
6. William L. Shirer, *The Rise and Fall of the Third Reich: A History of Nazi Germany* (New York: Touchstone, 1990).
7. Daniel Jonah Goldhagen, *Hitler's Willing Executioners: Ordinary Germans and the Holocaust* (New York: Vintage, 1997).
8. For one analysis of how the U.S. Holocaust Memorial Museum reifies the commodification of the Holocaust, see Tim Cole, *Selling the Holocaust: From Auschwitz to Schindler How History Is Bought, Packaged and Sold* (New York: Routledge, 1999).
9. Ibid, 146–147.
10. Ibid, 147.
11. Ibid.
12. See beyondracism.com.
13. George M. Fredrickson, *The Comparative Imagination: On the History of Racism, Nationalism, and Social Movements* (Berkeley, CA: University of California Press, 1997).
14. See Tina Campt, "'Afro-German': The Convergence of Race, Sexuality, and Gender in the Formation of a German Ethnic Identity, 1919–1960," Cornell University, 1996; Charles Green, ed., *Globalization and Survival in the Black Diaspora: The New Urban Challenge* (Albany: State University of New York Press, 1997); Terri Sewell, *Black Tribunes: Black Political Participation in Britain* (London: Lawrence & Wishart, 1993), Lorenzo Morris, "African Immigrants in France: SOS Racisme vs. the National Front," in Georgia A. Persons, ed., *Race and Ethnicity in Comparative Perspective* (*National Political Science Review*, Volume 7), 20–36; and Ronald W. Walters, *Pan-Africanism in the African Diaspora: An Analysis of Modern Afrocentric Political Movements* (Detroit: Wayne State University Press, 1993).
15. Stuart Hall, *Culture, Media, Language: Working Papers in Cultural Studies, 1972–79* (London: Hutchinson, 1992); Stuart Hall and Paul du Gay, eds., *Questions of Cultural Identity* (London: Sage, 1996); Paul Gilroy, *Against Race: Imagining Political Culture Beyond the Color Line* (Cambridge: Belknap Press of Harvard University Press, 2000); and Paul Gilroy, *The Black Atlantic: Modernity and Double Consciousness* (Cambridge: Harvard University Press, 1993).
16. Martin A. Lee, *The Beast Reawakens* (New York: Routledge, 2000).
17. Uli Linke, *Blood and Nation: The European Aesthetics of Race* (Philadelphia: University of Pennsylvania Press, 1999), 207.

18. Rainer Pommerin, *Sterilisierung der Rheinlandbastrade: Das Schicksal einer farbigen Minderheit, 1918–1937* (Düsseldorf: Droste, 1979).
19. May Opitz, Katerina Oguntoye, and Dagmar Schultz, eds., *Showing Our Colors: Afro-German Women Speak Out* (Amherst: University of Massachusetts Press, 1992; Carol Aisha Blackshire-Belay, *The African-German Experience: Critical Essays* (Westport, CT: Praeger, 1996); Hans Massaquoi, *Destined to Witness: Growing Up Black in Nazi Germany* (New York: William Morrow, 1999); Katharina Oguntoye, *Eine Afro-Deutsche Geschichte: Zur Lebenssituation von Afrikanem und Afro-Deutschen in Deutschland, von 1888 bis 1950* [*An Afro-German History: The Situation of Africans and Afro-Germans in Germany, 1888–1950*] (Berlin: Hoho Verlag, 1997); John A. Williams, *Clifford's Blues* (Minneapolis: Coffee House Press, 1999); and *Black Survivors of the Holocaust*, Afro-Wisdom Films, 1997. It should be noted that there are some other works that are poorly written, badly researched, and nothing short of exploitative, such as Shermanita Camp, *Blacks in the Holocaust: An Untold and Striking Story of Survival of Seven Black Jazz Musicians in Hitler's Concentration Camp* (Hollywood, CA: Hallelujah Publications, 2000).
20. Camp *Blacks in the Holocaust.*
21. Paul Gilroy's *Against Race: Imaging Political Culture beyond the Color Line* (Cambridge: The Belknap Press of Harvard University Press, 2000).
22. See http://liberator.com/rh/.
23. See Sam Atsu Nove, *African-German Contacts: Directory of the African Communities in Germany* (Berlin: Redaktion & Gesamtherstellung, 1999).
24. See F. James Davis, *Who Is Black?: One Nation's Definition* (Philadelphia: Pennsylvania State University Press, 1991).
25. See Geoffrey Fox, *Hispanic Nation: Culture, Politics, and the Constructing of Identity* (New York: Birch Lane Press Book, 1996).
26. Amilcar Cabral, *Return to the Source: Selected Speeches of Amilcar Cabral* (New York: Africa Information Service, 1973), 68.
27. Opitz, *Showing Our Colors,* xxii.
28. Ruth W. Grant and Marion Orr, "Language, Race and Politics: From 'Black' to 'African American,'" *Politics and Society,* June 1996, 148. Also see Tom Smith, "Changing Racial Labels: From 'Colored' to 'Negro' to 'Black' to 'African American,'" *Public Opinion Quarterly,* winter 1992, 496–514; and Russell L. Adams, "Social Change and Cultural Politics," *Government & Politics,* March 1993, 23–27.
29. See Charles W. Mills, *The Racial Contract* (Ithaca, NY: Cornell University Press, 1997).
30. See Michael Omi and Howard Winant, *Racial Formation in the United States: From the 1960s to the 1980s* (New York: Routledge, 1986); and Howard Winant, *Racial Conditions: Politics, Theory, Comparisons* (Minneapolis: University of Minnesota Press, 1996).
31. William Drozdiak, "Payments Set for Ex-Slaves of Nazi Regime; Germany to Pay Aged Survivors," *Washington Post,* 24 March 2000, A13.

Chapter 1: "Look, a Negro!"

1. S. Craig Watkins, *Representing: Hip Hop Culture and the Production of Black Cinema* (Chicago: University of Chicago Press, 1998), 4.
2. Charles W. Mills, *The Racial Contract* (Ithaca, NY: Cornell University Press, 1997), 12.
3. Ibid., 13–14.
4. Ibid., 78.
5. Ibid., 64.
6. Harold Isaacs, "Color in World Affairs," *Foreign Affairs,* No. 47, 1969, 235.
7. Tina Campt, "African German/African American—Dialogue or Dialectic?: Reflections on the Dynamics of 'Intercultural Address,'" in Carol Aisha Blackshire-Belay, *The African-German Experience,* 77.
8. Goldhagen, *Hitler's Willing Executioners,* 48.
9. Wilhelm Reich, *The Mass Psychology of Fascism* (New York: Farrar, Straus, and Giroux, 1970).
10. François Bernier, "A New Division of the Earth," in Robert Bernasconi and Tommy L. Lott, eds., *The Idea of Race* (Indianapolis: Hackett, 2000), 1–2.
11. Stephen J. Gould, "The Geometer of Race," *Discover,* November 1994, 65.
12. Ibid.
13. Paul Gordon Lauren, *Power and Prejudice: The Politics and Diplomacy of Racial Discrimination* (Boulder, CO: Westview Press), 38.
14. De Gobineau, *Essay on the Inequality of Human Races* (*Essai sur l'inegalite des races humaines*), Vol. 1, 1–7.

15. Count Arthur de Gobineau, from his two-volume, *Essay on the Inequality of Human Races* (*Essai sur l'inegalite des races humaines*) Vol. 2, 502–523.
16. Immanual Kant, "'This fellow was quite black . . . a clear proof that what he said [was] stupid,'" in Emmanuel Chukwudi Eze, ed., *Race and the Enlightenment: A Reader* (New York: Blackwell, 2000), 55.
17. Mills, *The Racial Contract*, 71.
18. Robert Bernasconi and Tommy L. Lott, eds., *The Idea of Race: Readings in Philosophy* (Indianapolis: Hackett, Inc., 2000), 40.
19. Lauren, *Power and Prejudice*, 52.
20. Shirer, *The Rise and Fall of the Third Reich*, 109.
21. Ibid., 107.
22. Lauren, *Power and Prejudice*, 52.
23. See, for example, the British historian Thomas Carlyle's essay "Occasional Discourse on the Nigger Question," in *Fraser's Magazine*, No. 40, December 1849.
24. Robert Huttenback, *Racism and Empire* (Ithaca, NY: Cornell University Press, 1976, 277.
25. "From Colonial Racism to Nazi Population Policy," paper presented at the United States Holocaust Memorial Museum Conference on the Known, the Unknown, the Disputed, and the Reexamined, 5–8 December. From Session IV: "The Politics of Racial Health and Science," 2.
26. Alan James, "'Black': An Inquiry Into the Pejorative Associations of an English Word," *New Community*, spring–summer, 1981, 28.
27. Gilman, *On Blackness without Blacks*.
28. Christoph Meiners, "Ueber die grosse Verschiedenheit der Biegsamkeit und Unbiegsamkeit, der Harte und Weicheit der verschiedenen Stamme, und Racen der Mensche," *Gottingisches Magazin* 1, 1787, 230.
29. Gustav Jahoda, *Images of Savages: Ancient Roots of Modern Prejudice in Western Culture* (New York: Routledge, 1999), 65.
30. Ibid., 67.
31. Treaty of Versailles, 28 June 1919. Signatories of the treaty included the United States of America, Belgium, Bolivia, Brazil, British Empire, Canada, Australia, South Africa, New Zealand, India, China, Cuba, Ecuador, France, Greece, Guatemala, Haiti, Hedjaz, Honduras, Italy, Japan, Liberia, Nicaragua, Panama, Peru, Poland, Portugal, Roumania, Serb-Croat-Slovene State, Siam, Czecho-Slovakia, Uruguay. States invited to accede to the covenant were Argentine Republic, Chile, Colombia, Denmark, Netherlands, Norway, Paraguay, Persia, Salvador, Spain, Sweden, Switzerland, Venezuela.
32. Victor Perlo, *Super Profits and Crises: Modern U.S. Capitalism* (New York: International, 1988), 403–404.
33. C. L. R. James, "After Hitler, Our Turn," in C. L. R. James, *Spheres of Existence* (Westport, CT: Lawrence Hill, 1980), 37–38.
34. David Levering Lewis, ed., *W. E. B. Du Bois: A Reader* (New York: Henry Holt Books, 1995), 735.
35. Ibid., 736.
36. Ibid.
37. John Solomos and Les Black, *Racism and Society* (New York: St. Martin's Press, 1996), 168.
38. Susann Samples, "African Germans in the Third Reich," in Carol Aisha Blackshire-Belay, *The African-German Experience*, 57.
39. Omi and Winant, *Racial Formation*; and Winant, *Racial Conditions*.
40. Omi and Winant, *Racial Formation*, 68.
41. Margaret Somers and Gloria Gibson, "Reclaiming the Epistemological 'Other': Narrative and the Social Construction of Identity," in Craig Calhoun, ed., *Social Theory and the Politics of Identity* (Cambridge, MA: Blackwell, 1994), p. 59.
42. Lynne Duke, "S. African 'Coloreds' End Race Charade," *Washington Post*, 26 July 1998, A25–27.
43. George Mosse, *Toward the Final Solution: A History of European Racism* (New York: H. Fertig, 1985), xii.
44. "Black Survivors of the Holocaust."
45. Campt, "'Afro-German' The Convergence of Race, Sexuality, and Gender in the Formation of a German Ethnic Identity, 1919–1960," and Blackshire-Belay, *The African-German Experience*.
46. Tina M. Campt, "Afro-German Cultural Identity and the Politics of Positionality: Contests and Contexts in the Formation of a German Ethnic Identity," *New German Critique*, No. 58, 1993, 117.
47. She does note, however, how the interviewing process itself explores insights into diasporic relations and differences.

48. Massaquoi, *Destined to Witness*, 67.
49. "Growing Up Black in Nazi Germany," *The African Courier*, December 1999–January 2000, 27.
50. Walters, *Pan-Africanism*, 14–23.

Chapter 2: Negrophobia and Nationalism

1. Paul Rohrbach, *Deutsche Kolonialwirtschaft*, Vol. 1, Sudwest-Afrika, Berlin, 1907, 350; and Jon M. Bridgeman, *The Revolt of the Hereros* (Berkeley: University of California Press, 1981), 60–66.
2. John Newsinger, "Lord Greystroke and Darkest Africa: The Politics of Tarzan Stories," *Race and Class*, Vol. 28, No. 2, 1986, 70. For a broader discussion of the relationship between Tarzan and colonial conquest, see Graham J. Murphy, "Possession, Penetration, and Tarzan Comic Books," http://www.imagesjournal.com/issue07/features/tarzan.htm.
3. Joseph Conrad, *Heart of Darkness & Selections from the Congo Diary* (New York: Modern Library, 1999); Henry Stanley, *In Darkest Africa; or, The Quest, Rescue, and Retreat of Emin, Governor of Equatoria* (New York: Charles Scribner's Sons, 1890); and Rudyard Kipling, *Gunga Din and Other Favorite Poems* (New York: Dover, 1990).
4. Sarkis Atamian, *The Origin of Tarzan: The Mystery of Tarzan's Creation Solved* (Anchorage: Publications Consultants, 1997,35.
5. Edward Said, *Culture and Imperialism* (New York: Vintage, 1994), 22.
6. Catherine Jurca, "Tarzan, Lord of the Suburbs," *Modern Language Quarterly*, Vol. 57, No. 3, 1996, 492; and Sarkis Atamian, *The Origin of Tarzan: The Mystery of Tarzan's Creation Solved* (Anchorage, Alaska: Publications Consultants, 1997, 60.
7. Ibid., 492.
8. Murphy, "Possession."
9. Norman R. Bennett, *Africa and Europe: From Roman Times to National Independence* (New York: Africana, 1984), 67.
10. Olayinka Oludipe, "A History of More than a Century: The Origins of the African Diaspora in Berlin," *The African Courier*, February–March 1999, p. 5.
11. "From Colonial Racism to Nazi Population Policy," U.S. Holocaust Memorial Museum conference, 5–8 December 1993, 11.
12. Helmut Walser Smith, "The Talk of Genocide, the Rhetoric of Miscegenation: Notes on Debates in the German Reichstag Concerning Southwest Africa, 1904–14," in Sara Friedrichsmeyer, Sara Lennox, and Susanne Zantop, *The Imperialist Imagination: German Colonialism and Its Legacy* (Ann Arbor: University of Michigan Press, 1998), 116–121.
13. Ibid., 122.
14. Ibid., 111, 122.
15. Ibid., 112, 114–115.
16. Sven Lindqvist, *"Exterminate All the Brutes": One Man's Odyssey into the Heart of Darkness and the Origins of European Genocide* (New York: New Press, 1992), 157.
17. See Raphael Lemkin, *Axis Rule in Occupied Europe: Laws of Occupation, Analysis of Government, Proposals for Redress* (Washington, DC: Carnegie Endowment for International Peace, 1944).
18. Ibid., 49.
19. For a rich and insightful discussion of the politics of the discourse on genocide, see Ward Churchill, *A Little Matter of Genocide: Holocaust and Denial in the Americas, 1492 to the Present* (San Francisco: City Light Books, 1997).
20. Opitz, *Showing Our Colors*, 19–37.
21. Smith, "Talk of Genocide," 100.
22. Lindovist, "Exterminate," 150.
23. Len Cooper, "Aryan Nation: Germany's Cruel African Heritage," *Washington Post*, 20 February 1994, C3.
24. Ibid.
25. Regina Jere-Malanda, "Forgotten: Black Victims of Hitler's Germany," *New African*, October 1999, 20.
26. Smith, "Talk of Genocide," 110.
27. Eugen Fischer, *Die Rehobother Bastards und das Bastardierungsproblem beim Menschen* (*The Rehoboth Bastards and the Bastardization Problem in Man*): (Jena, G. Fischer, 1913).
28. Cooper, "Aryan Nation," C3.
29. "From Colonial Racism to Nazi Population Policy," 6; and Burleigh and Wippermann, 38.
30. Fischer, *Rehoboth Bastards*, 302.
31. Fischer, *Rehoboth Bastards*.

32. "From Colonial Racism to Nazi Population Policy," 7–8.
33. Lee, *Beast Reawakens,* 112.
34. Cooper, "Aryan Nation."
35. "From Colonial Racism to Nazi Population Policy," 17.
36. Sterling Johnson, *Black Globalism: The International Politics of a Non-State Nation* (Brookfield, VT: Ashgate, 1998), 79.
37. Ibid., 80.
38. Louis R. Harlan, *Booker T. Washington: The Wizard of Tuskegee, 1901–1915* (New York: Oxford University Press, 1983), 267.
39. Ibid,., 268, and Johnson, *Black Globalism,* 81.
40. Harlan, *Booker T. Washington,* 268.
41. Ibid., 268–269.
42. W. E. B. Du Bois, *International Tribute to William E. B. Du Bois* (New York: United Nations, Center Against Apartheid, 1982), 48.
43. Roi Ottley, *No Green Pastures* (New York: Charles Scribner's Sons, 1951), 151.
44. Jahoda, *Images of Savages,* 27.
45. Opitz, *Showing Our Colors,* 3–4; and Edward Scobie, "The Black in Western Europe," in Ivan Van Sertima, ed., *African Presence in Early Europe* (New Brunswick: Transaction, 1996), 199.
46. Oludipe, "History of More than Century," 5.
47. Paulette Reed-Anderson, *Eine Geschichte von mehr als 100 Jahren: Die Anfange der Afrikanischen Diaspora in Berlin* [*A History of More than 100 Years: That Beginning of the African Diaspora in Berlin*], Berlin, fall 1994, 8.
48. Ibid.
49. Interview with Theodor Michael, 7 May 2000.
50. Massaquoi, *Destined to Witness,* 8–9.
51. Ibid., 10.
52. Ibid, Interview with Michael.
53. Ibid.
54. Oludipe, "History of More than Century," 5.
55. Rachel L. Swarns, "Gaborone Journal; Africa Rejoices as a Wandering Soul Finds Rest," *New York Times,* 6 October 2000.
56. Oludipe, "History of More than Century," 5.
57. Richard D. Altick, *The Shows of London* (Cambridge: Belknap, 1978), 269.
58. Abiola Sinclair, "The Story of Saartijie Baartman, the Hottentot Venus," *Black History Magazine,* No. 6, 1999, 49.
59. Stephen Jay Gould, *The Flamingo's Smile: Reflections in Natural History* (New York: Norton, 1985), 291–301.
60. Sinclair, "Story of Saartjie Baartman," 43.
61. Altick, *Shows of London,* 269.
62. Ibid., 270.
63. Stephen Jay Gould, *Mismeasure of Man* (New York: Norton, 1996), 69.
64. Altick, *Shows of London,* 272.
65. "Bring Back the Hottentot Venus," *Weekly Mail & Guardian,* 15 June 1995.
66. Ronald Takaki, *A Different Mirror: A History of Multicultural America* (Boston: Little, Brown, 1993), 30.
67. Phillips Verner Bradford and Harvey Blume, *Ota Benga: The Pygmy in the Zoo* (New York: St. Martin's Press, 1992), 106.
68. Letter from McGee to Verner, 21 October 1903, in *Ota Benga: Pygmy in the Zoo,* 240.
69. Bradford and Blume, *Ota Benga,* 113–114.
70. See letter from A. E. R., *New York Globe,* 12 September 1906.
71. "No Aid from M'Clellen," *New York Evening Post,* 11 September 1906, and "African Pygmy's Fate Is Still Undecided," *New York Times,* 18 September 1906.
72. Bernth Lindfors, "Charles Dickens and the Zulus," in Bernth Lindfors, ed., *Africans on Stage: Studies in Ethnological Show Business* (Bloomington: Indiana University Press, 1999), 62–80; and Charles Dickens, "The Noble Savage," *Household Words,* 11 June 1853, 337–339.
73. Jeffrey P. Green, "A Revelation in Strange Humanity: Six Congo Pygmies in Britain, 1905–1907," in Bernth Lindfors, *Africans on Stage: Studies in Ethnological Show Business* (Bloomington: Indiana University Press, 1999), 177.
74. Massaquoi, *Destined to Witness,* 25.

75. Ibid., 61.
76. Marilyn Kern-Foxworth, *Aunt Jemima, Uncle Ben, and Rastus: Blacks in Advertising, Yesterday, Today, and Tomorrow* (Westport, CT: Praeger, 1994); Diane Roberts, *The Myth of Aunt Jemima: Representations of Race and Religion* (New York: Routledge, 1994); and Jan Nederveen Pieterse, *White on Black: Images of Africa and Blacks in Western Popular Culture* (New Haven, CT: Yale University Press, 1992).
77. Kern-Foxworth, *Aunt Jemima*, 30.
78. Allison Blakely, *Russia and the Negro: Blacks in Russian History and Thought* (Washington, DC: Howard University Press).
79. *Der Artist, Central-Organ de Circus, Variete-Buhnen, reisenden Kapellen und Ensembles*, quoted in Rainer E. Lotz, *Black People: Entertainers of African Descent in Europe, and Germany* (Bonn: Birgit Lotz Verlag, 1997), 12.
80. Oludipe, "History of More than Century," 5.
81. John Lovell Jr., *Black Song: The Forge and the Flame, The Story of How the Afro-American Spritual Was Hammered Out* (New York: Macmillian, 1972), 402–410.
82. See Robert Hill, *The Marcus Garvey and Universal Negro Improvement Association Papers, November 1927 to August 1940, Vol. 7* (Los Angeles: University of California Press, 1990), 212.
83. W. E. B. Du Bois, "The Winds of Time," *Chicago Defender*, 17 January 1948, 15.
84. W. E. B. Du Bois, *The Autobiography of W. E. B. Du Bois: A Soliloquy on Viewing My Life from the Last Decade of Its First Century* (New York: International, 1968), 62.
85. Julius Lester, ed., *The Seventh Son: The Thought and Writings of W. E. B. Du Bois*, Vol. I (New York: Random House, 1971, 3.
86. Interview with Michael, 7 May 2000.
87. Manning Marable, *W. E. B Du Bois: Black Radical Democrat* (Boston: Twayne, 1986), 16.
88. Du Bois, *Autobiography*, 160–162.
89. Ibid.
90. Marable, *Du Bois*, 17.
91. Ibid.
92. Du Bois, *Autobiography*, 285; and Lester, *Seventh Son*, 67.
93. David L. Lewis, *W. E. B. Du Bois: Biography of a Race, 1868–1919* (New York: Henry Holt, 1993), 141.
94. Lester, *Seventh Son*, 453.
95. W. E. B. Du Bois, "World War and the Color Line," *The Crisis*, November 1914, 28–30.
96. Ibid.

Chapter 3: Soldiers of Misfortune, Children of Misfortune

1. Alfred Werner, "Germany's New Pariahs," *The Crisis*, May 1952, 293.
2. George Mosse, *Toward the Final Solution: A History of European Racism* (New York: H. Fertig, 1978), 176.
3. Adam Hochschild, *King Leopold's Ghost: A Story of Greed, Terror, and Heroism in Colonial Africa* (New York: Houghton Mifflin, 1999).
4. Neal Acherson, *Los Angeles Times*, 10 January 1999; Giles Foden, *The Guardian* (London), 24 April 1999; Jeremy Harding, *New York Times*, 20 September 1998; Gail Gerhart, *Foreign Affairs*, March–April, 1999; *The Economist*, 11 September 1999; and *Financial Times*, 3 April 1999.
5. Richard Taylor, "The Monster Who Plundered the Congo," *Boston Globe*, 16 September 1998.
6. *The Economist*, 11 September 1999.
7. http://www.bookwire.com/nbcc/awards1998.html.
8. Hochschild, *King Leopold's Ghost*, 102–114; 152–158.
9. Ibid., 1.
10. Ibid., 2. It should be noted that other writers have referred to Morel as a great "humanitarian." See Lewis H. Gann and Peter Duignan, *The Rulers of German Africa, 1884–1914* (Stanford, CA: Stanford University Press, 1977), 34.
11. Hochschild, *king Leopold's Ghost*, 2.
12. Ibid., 187.
13. Tamara Straus, "King Leopold's Ghost Makes a Comeback," 24 September 1999 (downloaded), Alternet web site.
14. Taylor, "The Monster."
15. Treaty of Versailles, Articles 428 and 429.
16. Interview with Michael, 7 May 2000.

17. In many cases, "black" was used by scholars and researchers to refer to all troops of color. In this work, it will be noted when that usage is applied as opposed to "black" referring to only people of African descent.

18. Gann and Duignan, *Rulers of German Africa,* 115–120.

19. Adolph Hitler, *Mein Kampf* (New York: Houghton Mifflin, 1943), 644–645.

20. Lauren, *Power and Prejudice,* 112.

21. Opitz, *Showing Our Colors,* 41. Pommerin claims that there were 19,000 occupation troops in the Rhineland in 1924. At various times, an effort was made to distinguish racially (skin color) northern Africans from sub-Saharan Africans, with the former being perhaps more acceptable than the latter. Ottley says in the years 1919 and 1921, France had about 85,000 men stationed in Germany, of which between 40,000 and 45,000 were from Africa—Algeria, Morocco, Tunisia, Madagasca, and Senegal (about 10,000).

22. Edmund D. Morel, *King Leopold's Rule in Africa* (New York: Funk and Wagnalls, 1905); E. D. Morel, *Great Britain and the Congo: The Pillage of the Congo Basin* (New York: H. Fertig, 1969); E. D. Morel, *Red Rubber: The Story of the Rubber Slave Trade Flourishing on the Congo in the Year of Grace 1906* (New York: Negro Universities Press, 1969); and E. D. Morel, *E. D. Morel's History of the Congo Reform Movement* (Oxford: Clarendon Press, 1968).

23. Hochschild, *King Leopold's Ghost,* 345.

24. W. S. Adams, *Edwardian Portraits* (London: Secker & Warburg, 1957); Catherine Ann Cline, *E. D. Morel 1873–1924: The Strategies of Protest* (Belfast: Blackstaff Press, 1980); F. Seymour Cocks, *E. D. Morel: the Man and His Work* (London: George Allen & Unwin, 1920); and A. J. P. Taylor, *The Trouble Makers: Dissent over Foreign Policy 1792 - 1939* (London: Hamish Hamilton, 1957).

25. Edmund Morel, *The Black Man's Burden* (Manchester: National Labour Press, 1920).

26. Hochschild, *King Leopold's Ghost,* 210.

27. Robert C. Reinders, "Racialism on the Left: E. D. Morel and the 'Black Horror on the Rhine,'" *International Review of Social History,* No. 13, 1968, 4.

28. Ibid., 5.

29. Edward Morel, "Black Scourge in Europe, Sexual Horror Let Loose by France on Rhine, Disappearance of Young German Girls," *Daily Herald,* 9 April 1920.

30. J. Ellis Barker, "The Colored French Troops in Germany," *Current History,* July 1921, 599.

31. Ibid.; E. D. Morel, "The Employment of Black Troops in Europe," *Nation,* 17 March 1920; Edmund Morel, "The Prostitution of the Rhineland," *Foreign Affairs,* June 1921; Edmund Morel, "Horror on the Rhine," *Foreign Affairs,* August 1920.

32. Morel, "The Employment of Black Troops in Europe," 893.

33. Reinders, "Racialism on the Left," 20.

34. Barker, "Colored French Troops," 597.

35. Ibid., 597–598.

36. Ibid., 596.

37. Ibid., 595.

38. Ibid., 599.

39. Ibid.

40. Peter Fryer, *Staying Power: The History of Black People in Britain* (London: Pluto Press, 1984), 317.

41. Ibid., 317–318.

42. Hochschild, *King Leopold's Ghost,* 287.

43. Keith Nelson, "The 'Black Horror on the Rhine': Race as a Factor in Post–World War I Diplomacy," *Journal of Modern History,* No. 42, 1970, 616.

44. Sean Dennis Cashman, *African Americans and the Quest for Civil Rights, 1900–1990* (New York: New York University Press, 1991), 29–31.

45. Nelson, "Black Horror on the Rhine," 620–621.

46. Hochschild, *King Leopold's Ghost,* 241.

47. Lester, *Seventh Son,* 457.

48. Fryer, *Staying Power,* 318.

49. Reinders, "Racialism on the Left," 17. Wayne F. Cooper, *The Passion of Claude McKay: Selected Poetry and Prose, 1912–1948* (New York: Schocken Books, 1973), 55–57.

50. "The Rhine's Black Horror Faded," *Literary Digest,* 25 June 1921, 14.

51. Ibid, Reinders, "Racialism on the Left," 27.

52. Hochschild, *King Leopold's Ghost,* 210.

53. Barker, "Colored French Troops," 595–596.

54. Ibid., 594.
55. Ibid.
56. Solomos and Black, *Racism and Society*, 173.
57. Mosse, *Toward the Final Solution*, 176; Shirer, *Rise and Fall*, 123.
58. Mosse, *Toward the Final Solution*, 176–177.
59. Pommerin, "Sterisierung," 10; and Samples, "African Germans in the Third Reich," 53.
60. *Black Survivors of the Holocaust*, Shooting Script, 6 June 1997, 3.
61. Len Cooper, "Aryan Nation," C3.
62. Pommerin, "Sterisierung," 23, 25, 28.
63. Opitz, *Showing Our Colors*, 49.
64. Len Cooper, "Aryan Nation," C3.
65. Hitler, *Mein Kampf*, 188.
66. Shirer, *Rise and Fall*, 81.
67. Ibid., 80–81.
68. Werner, "Germany's New Pariahs," 291.
69. Hitler, *Mein Kampf*, 629.
70. Ibid., 325.
71. See U.S. Holocaust Memorial Museum, Photo Archives, Designation # 634.7077, W/S # 17609.
72. Hitler, *Mein Kampf*, 624.
73. Ibid.
74. Ibid., 388.
75. Ibid., 438.
76. Ibid., 439.
77. Ibid., 439–440.
78. Ibid., 430.
79. Ibid., 644.
80. Ibid, Solomos and Black, *Racism and Society*, 146, and Hitler, *Mein Kampf*, 260.
81. Cooper, "Aryan Nation," C3.
82. Reed-Anderson, *Eine Geschichte von meht als 100 Jahran*, 8.
83. Ibid.
84. Interview with Michael, 7 May 2000.
85. A copy of the original list is in the possession of the author.
86. Charles Henry, *Ralph Bunche: Model Negro or American Other?* (New York: New York University Press, 1999), 77; and James R. Hooker, *Black Revolutionary: George Padmore's Path from Communism to Pan-Africanism* (New York: Praeger, 1967), 6–9.
87. Hooker, *Black Revolutionary*, 17.
88. It has been falsely asserted by the journalist Ottley that 1,000 attended this conference. He also got the date wrong, citing 1931 instead of 1930. Ottley, *No Green Pastures*, 64.
89. Hooker, *Black Revolutionary*, 17.
90. Interview with Michael, in Cologne, 7 May 2000.
91. Hooker, *Black Revolutionary*, 19.
92. Interview with Michael, 7 May 2000.
93. Fryer, *Staying Power*, 335.
94. C. L. R. James, *Spheres of Existence: Selected Writings* (London: Allison & Busby, 1980), 227.
95. Lauren, *Power and Prejudice*, 125–126.
96. Hooker, *Black Revolutionary*, 24–25.
97. David Levering Lewis, ed., *W. E. B. Du Bois: A Reader* (New York: Henry Holt, 1995), 697.
98. See Theodore Kornweibel Jr., *"Seeing Red": Federal Campaigns against Black Militancy, 1919–1925* (Bloomington: Indiana University Press, 1999).
99. Lou Potter, *Liberators: Fighting on Two Fronts in World War II* (New York: Harcourt Brace Jovanovich, 1992), 24.
100. Morris J. MacGregor Jr. and Bernard C. Nalty, eds., *Blacks in the United States Armed Forces – Basic Documents*, vol. 4 (Wilmington, DE: Scholarly Resources, 1977), 282.
101. Potter, *Liberators*, 26.
102. Lester, *Seventh Son*, 80–81.
103. W. E. B. Du Bois, *Dusk of Dawn: An Essay toward an Autobiography of a Race Concept* (New Brunswick, NJ: Transaction, 1992), 286–287.
104. Shirer, *Rise and Fall*, 185.

Chapter 4: Hitler's Black Dilemmas

1. Opitz, *Showing Our Colors*, 62.
2. Ottley, *No Green Pastures*, 161.
3. Ibid.
4. Ibid., 152.
5. Ibid., 162.
6. Ibid., 152.
7. Samples, *African Germans*, 56.
8. Ibid., 57.
9. Ottley, *No Green Pastures*, 51.
10. Samples, *African Germans*, 53.
11. Kelly Miller, "Hitler—The German Klu Klux," *Norfolk Journal and Guide*, 1 April 1933, 3.
12. *Black Survivors of the Holocaust.*
13. Tina Campt, Pascal Grosse, and Yara-Colette Lemke-Muniz de Faria, "Blacks, Germans, and the Politics of Imperial Imagination, 1920–60," in Sara Friedrichsmeyer, Sara Lennox, and Susanne Zantop, *The Imperialist Imagination: German Colonialism and Its Legacy* (Ann Arbor: University of Michigan Press, 1998), 217.
14. Ibid., 218.
15. Ibid.
16. Samples, *African Germans*, 58.
17. Campt, Grosse, and Lemke-Muniz de Faria, "Blacks, Germans, and Politics," 215.
18. Ibid., 217.
19. Pommerin, *Sterilizierung*, 55.
20. Samples, *African Germans*, 55.
21. Massaquoi, *Destined to Witness*, xvi.
22. Samples, *African Germans*, 59.
23. John Hope Franklin, *From Slavery to Freedom: A History of Negro American*, 3rd ed. (New York: Vintage, 1969), 480; and Arthur F. Raper, *The Tragedy of Lynching* (New York: Dover, 1970), 481.
24. See Azza Salama Layton, *International Politics and Civil Rights Policies in the United States, 1941–1960* (New York: Cambridge University Press, 2000).
25. Henrich Krieger, "How to Wipe Out the American Negro," *Washington Tribune*, 11 August 1936.
26. "From Colonial Racism to Nazi Population Policy," 3.
27. Ibid., 4.
28. Ibid., 5.
29. Massaquoi, *Destined to Witness*. There are other autobiographical and biographical works being produced that address the post-war era and, in particular,. the experiences of black women including Ika Hugel-Marshall and Baerbel Kampmann. See Ika Hugel-Marshall, *Invisible Woman: Growing Up Black in Germany* (New York: Continuum, 2001) and Harald Gerunde: *Eine von uns: Als Schwarze in Deutschland geboren* [*One of Us: Being born Black in Germany*] (Wuppertal, Germany: Peter Hammer Verlag, 2000).
30. Campt, Grosse, and Lemke-Muniz de Faria, "Blacks, Germans, and Politics," 218.
31. "Nazi Colorphobia Flares Anew; Newspaper Takes Rap at American Negroes," *Norfolk Journal and Guide*, 13 March 1937, 4.
32. Ben Austin, http://www.mtsu.edu/~baustin/nurmberg.html. For more on Plessy v. Ferguson, see Charles Lofgen, *The Plessy Case: A Legal-Historical Interpretation* (New York: Oxford University Press, 1987).
33. Norman H. Baynes, ed., *The Speeches of Adolf Hitler* (New York: Oxford University Press, 1942), 731–732.
34. See additional orders passed including the Second Order (21 December 1935), Third Order (14 June 1938), Fourth Order (25 July 1938), Fifth Order (27 September 1938), and Sixth Order (30 October 1938). Helmut Krausnick and Martin Broszat, *Anatomy of the SS State* (London: Granada, 1973), 53–54.
35. Wilhelm Stuckart and Hans Globke, *Kommentare zur deutschen Rassengesetzgebung* [*Commentaries to the German Race-Legislation*], Vol. 1, Munich, 1936, cited in Campt, "'Afro-German' The Convergence of Race, Sexuality, and Gender in the Formation of a German Ethnic Identity, 1919–1960," 165.
36. Stuckart and Globke, *Kommentare*, 55; and Burleigh and Wippermann, *Racial State*, 50.
37. Ben Magubane, "Racism in the Age of Europe," research paper presented to the South African National Conference on Racism, October 2000, 5–6. http://www.sahrc.org.za/main_frameset.htm.

38. Davis, *Who Is Black?* and Scott L. Malcolmson, *One Drop of Blood: The American Misadventure of Race* (New York: Farrar, Straus, and Giroux, 2000).
39. Kennedy, 59–60.
40. Ibid., 60.
41. Ibid., 48–50.
42. Ibid.,, 50.
43. Ibid.
44. Ian F. Haney Lopez, *White By Law: The Legal Construction of Race* (New York: New York University Press, 1996), 4.
45. Samples, *African Germans*, 60–61.
46. *Black Survivors of the Holocaust*, 12.
47. Robert N. Proctor, *Racial Hygiene: Medicine under the Nazis* (London: Harvard University Press, 1988), 114.
48. Burleigh and Wippermann, *Racial State*, 202.
49. Ibid., 230.
50. Campt, "African German/African American—Dialogue or Dialectic?," 79.
51. Ibid.
52. *Black Survivors of the Holocaust*.
53. Ibid, 9.
54. Massaquoi interview, April 7, 2000.
55. Krausnick and Broszat, *Anatomy of SS State*, 46.
56. Ibid., Campt, "African German/African American—Dialogue or Dialectic?," 80.
57. Although this is an extremely provocative story, no further information on Baarn is available. See "Negro Nazi Spy Trapped in S. America," *Amsterdam News*, 24 August 1944, 1A, 10B.
58. Leila J. Rupp, "Mother of the Volk: The Image of Women in Nazi Ideology," *Signs*, winter 1977, 362–363.
59. Adolf Hitler, in Anne Marie Koeppen, ed., *Das deutsche Landfrauenbuch* (Berlin: Reichsnahrstand Verlag, 1937). Cited in Rupp, 364.
60. See Lisa Pine, "Girls in Uniform: Nazi Girl's Movement," *History Today*, March 1999.
61. *Opportunity*, letter to editor, March 1935, 71.
62. Ottley. *No Green Pastures*, 54.
63. "Africans in Germany Living in Terror, French Report," *Norfolk Journal and Guide*, 20 October 1934, 5.
64. Ibid.
65. Tyler Stovall, *Paris Noir: African Americans in the City of Light* (New York: Houghton Mifflin, 1996), 119.
66. Ibid., 121.
67. Michael Fabre, *From Harlem to Paris: Black American Writers in France, 1840–1980* (Chicago: University of Illinois Press, 1993), 65–66.
68. Stovall, *Paris Noir*, 119.
69. Ibid., 122.
70. Ibid., 124.
71. Ibid., 125.
72. Ibid., 126.
73. Ibid.
74. Ibid.
75. Ibid.
76. Ibid.
77. Langston Hughes, "Beaumont to Detroit, 1943." *Common Ground*, fall 1943, 104.
78. John Welch, "Twelve Years under Hitler," *Pittsburgh Courier*, 1944, 6.
79. Samples, *African Germans*, 57.
80. Matthew E. Gardner, "Germany Plots for Africa," *The Voice of Ethiopia*, 28 January 1939, 7.
81. Kelly Miller, "Hitler—The German Ku Klux," *Norfolk Journal and Guide*, 7 April 1933, 3.
82. Kelly Miller, "Race Prejudice in Germany and America," *Opportunity*, April 1993, 102–105.
83. "Jewish Massacre Feared Soon in Germany," *Washington Tribune*, 10 March 1933, 10.
84. "Vichy Asks Africans for Labor in Germany," *Afro-American*, 8 August 1942, 3.
85. "Nazi Prepare to Rid Reich of Colored People," *Afro-American*, 6 February 1943, 3.
86. Frank P. Model, "Elmer Spyglass, Salesman for Democracy," *Pittsburgh Courier*, 26 March 1955.
87. Winston McDowell, "Race and Ethnicity during the Harlem Jobs Campaign, 1932–1935," *Journal of Negro History*, summer–autumn 1984, 134–146.

88. L. D. Reddick, "What Hitler Says about the Negro," *Opportunity,* April 1933, 108.

89. Justin Raimondo, "Behind the Headlines," 28 April 2000, antiwar.com.

90. Lawrence Dennis and Maximilian St. George, *A Trial on Trial: The Great Sedition Trial of 1944* (Torrance, CA: Institute for Historical Review, 1984), 33–34.

91. Raimondo, "Behind the Headlines."

92. Ibid.

93. Dennis and St. George, *A Trial on Trial,* 35.

94. Adolph L. Reed Jr., *W. E. B. Du Bois and American Political Thought: Fabianism and the Color Line* (New York: Oxford University Press, 1997), 78.

95. David Levering Lewis, *W. E. B. Du Bois: The Fight for Equality and the American Century, 1919–1963* (New York: Henry Holt), 199.

96. Werner Sollors, "W. E. B. Du Bois in Nazi Germany: A Surprising, Prescient Visitor," *Chronicle of Higher Education,* 12 November 1999, B4.

97. Lewis, *W. E. B. Du Bois: The Fight for Equality and the American Century, 1919–1963,* 396.

98. Ibid., 395–396.

99. Sollors, "W. E. B. Du Bois in Nazi Germany," B4.

100. Ibid., B5.

101. Ibid.

102. W. E. B. Du Bois, *Pittsburgh Courier,* December 5, 1936.

103. Sollors, "W. E. B. Du Bois in Nazi Germany," B5.

104. Lewis, *W. E. B. Du Bois: A Reader,* 735.

105. Ibid.

106. Ibid., 401.

107. W. E. B. Du Bois, *Pittsburgh Courier,* 12 December 1936.

108. Ibid.

109. Sollors, "W. E. B. Du Bois in Nazi Germany," B5.

110. Lewis, *W. E. B. Du Bois: A Reader,* 734.

111. Ibid., 734.

112. Sollors, "W. E. B. Du Bois in Nazi Germany," B5.

113. Lewis, *W. E. B. Du Bois: The Fight for Equality and the American Century, 1919–1963,* 398.

114. Ibid., 399.

115. W. E. B. Du Bois, "The German Case against the Jews," *Pittsburgh Courier,* 2 January 1937.

116. W. E. B. Du Bois, "As the Crow Flies," *Amsterdam News,* 12 April 1941, 1, 16.

117. Ibid., 16.

Chapter 5: Made in America, Perfected in Germany

1. Burleigh and Wippermann, *Racial State,* 128–129.

2. Ibid., "From Colonial Racism to Nazi Population Policy," 9.

3. William H. Tucker, *The Science and Politics of Racial Research* (Chicago: University of Chicago, 1994), 49.

4. Ibid.

5. Daniel J. Kevles, *In the Name of Eugenics: Genetics and the Uses of Human Heredity* (Cambridge: Harvard University Press, 1995), 116.

6. Tucker, *Science and Politics of Racial Research,* 111.

7. Charles Davenport, *State Laws Limiting Marriage Selection in Light of Eugenics,* (Cold Spring Harbor, NY: Eugenics Records Office, 1913), 43.

8. Dorothy Roberts, *Killing the Black Body: Race, Reproduction, and Meaning of Liberty* (New York: Vintage Books, 1997), 66.

9. Philip Reilly, *Surgical Solution: A History of Involuntary Sterilization in the United States* (Baltimore: Johns Hopkins University, 1991), 28.

10. Dorothy Roberts, *Killing the Black Body,* 65.

11. Ibid., 66.

12. Ibid.

13. Ibid., 70.

14. Ibid., 65; Richard J. Herrnstein and Charles Murray, *The Bell Curve: Intelligence and Class Structure in American Life* (New York: Free Press, 1994), 127–266; and Edward East, *Heredity and Human Affairs* (New York: Scribner, 1929), 306.

15. Dorothy Roberts, *Killing the Black Body,* 71.

16. "German Eugenics, 1934," *Eugenical News,* No. 19, 1934, 140.

17. Tucker, *Science and Politics of Racial Research*, 112.

18. Ibid., 123.

19. Ibid., 124.

20. Ibid., 113.

21. Kevles, *In Name of Eugenics*, 117.

22. "From Colonial Racism to Nazi Population Policy," 5.

23. Reilly, *Surgical Solutions*, 105.

24. Tucker, *Science and Politics of Racial Research*, 111.

25. Ibid.

26. Kevles, *In Name of Eugenics*, 117.

27. Opitz, *Showing Our Colors*, 48.

28. Dorothy Roberts, *Killing the Black Body*, 68.

29. Tucker, *Science and Politics of Racial Research*, 120.

30. Ibid., 116.

31. Ibid., 117.

32. Burleigh and Wippermann, *Racial State*, 129.

33. Kevles, *In Name of Eugenics*, 117.

34. Campt, "African German/African American—Dialogue or Dialectic?," 73.

35. Ibid., 73.

36. Benno Muller-Hill, *Murderous Science: Elimination by Scientific Selection of Jews, Gypsies, and Others, Germany 1933–1945* (New York: Oxford University Press, 1988), 32.

37. Burleigh and Wippermann, *Racial State*, 49.

38. Ibid., 129.

39. Ibid., 130.

40. Massaquoi, *Destined to Witness*, 112–113.

41. Henry Friedlander, *Origins of Nazi Genocide: From Euthanasia to the Final Solution* (Durham: University of North Carolina Press, 1995), 247.

42. Kevles, *In Name of Eugenics*, 117.

43. Ibid., Burleigh and Wippermann, *Racial State*, 130; and Pommerin, "Sterilisierung," 78.

44. Ibid., Burleigh and Wippermann, *Racial State*.

45. Friedlander, *Origins of Nazi Genocide*, 246.

46. "From Colonial Racism to Nazi Population Policy," 5.

47. Ibid., Friedlander, 246.

48. Len Cooper, "Aryan Nation," C3.

49. Opitz, 57, *Showing Our Colors*, 65–66.

50. Reichministerium des Innern report, document from U.S. Holocaust Memorial Museum, 2 June 1937.

51. Reichsministerium des Innern, document from U.S. Holocaust Memorial Museum, 17 June 1937.

52. Reichsministerium des Innern, document from U.S. Holocaust Memorial Museum, 19 June 1937.

53. *Black Survivors of the Holocaust*, 3.

54. Kevles, *In Name of Eugenics*, 118.

55. "Fears Nazis Will Teach Prejudices," *Washington Afro-American*, 17 February 1934, 1.

56. See William L. Clay, *Just Permanent Interests: Black Americans in Congress, 1870–1991* (New York: Amistad, 1992).

Chapter 6: Behind the Wire

1. Williams's novel revolves around the experiences of a gay, African American jazz musician who is arrested in 1933 soon after Hitler comes to power and sent to Dachau. He remains in the concentration camp for the entire twelve years that the Nazis are in power. John Williams, *Clifford's Blues* (Minneapolis: Coffee House Press, 1999), 12.

2. Michel Foucault, *Discipline & Punishment: The Birth of the Prison* (New York: Vintage Books, 1995), 11.

3. Ibid., 16.

4. Bob Moore and Kent Fedorowich, *Prisoners of War and Their Captors in World War II* (Washington, DC: Berg, 1996).

5. Homer Smith, *Black Man in Red Russia: A Memoir* (Chicago: Johnson, 1964).

6. Bob Moore and Kent Fedorowich, "Prisoners of War in the Second World War: An Overview," in Bob Moore and Kent Fedorowich, *Prisoners of War and Their Captors in World War II* (Washington, DC: Berg, 1996), 1.

7. Charles A. Stenger, "American Prisoners of War in World War I, World War II, Korea, and Vietnam: Statistical Data concerning Numbers Captured, Repatriated, and Still Alive as of January 1, 1992," in Tom Bird, *American POWs of World War I: Forgotten Men Tell Their Stories* (Westport, CT: Praeger, 1992), 140; and Mitchell G. Bard, "American Victims of the Holocaust," in Bird, 131.

8. Interview with Paulette Reed-Anderson.

9. "World War II Prisoners of War Punchcards," electronic database, Office of the Provost Marshall General, Records Group 389, National Archives and Records Administration, College Park, MD. See also *American Prisoners of War and Civilian Internees: Records Relating to Personal Participation in World War II*, Reference Information Paper 80, National Archives and Records Administration, Washington, DC, 1982.

10. Ibid.

11. Myron Echenberg, *Colonial Conscripts: The Tirailleurs Senegalais in French West Africa, 1857–1960* (London: J. Currey, 1991), 94.

12. Ibid.

13. Regina Jere-Malanda, "Forgotten: Black Victims of Hitler's Germany," *New African*, October 1999, 20.

14. Moore and Fedorowich, "Prisoners of War in the Second World War: An Overview," 11.

15. Ottley, *No Green Pastures*, 163.

16. David Killingray, "Africans and African Americans in Enemy Hands," in Moore and Fedorowich, *Prisoners of War and Their Captors in World War II*, 181.

17. Ibid., 181; and Echenberg, *Colonial Conscripts*, 88, 191 n. 8.

18. "The Black Star: On the Fate of African-Germans under National Socialism," lecture, Koln University, African Studies Program, Marianne Bechhause-Gerst, 29 November 1995.

19. Robert W. Kesting, "Forgotten Victims: Blacks in the Holocaust," *Journal of Negro History*, winter 1992, 32.

20. Killingray, "Africans and African Americans," 188–189.

21. Nancy Lawler, *Soldiers of Misfortune: Ivorien Tirailleurs of World War II* (Athens: Ohio University Press, 1992), 102.

22. Killingray, "Africans and African Americans," 182.

23. Bill Reed, *"Hot From Harlem:" Profiles in Classic African-American Entertainment* (Kearney, NE: Morris, 1998), 56.

24. Lou Potter with William Miles and Nina Rosenblum, *Liberators: Fighting on Two Fronts in World War II* (New York: Harcourt Brace Jovanovich, 1992).

25. Sean Dennis Cashman, *African Americans and the Quest for Civil Rights, 1900–1990* (New York: New York University Press, 1991), 73.

26. "Memorandum of Telephone Statement from Dr. Lowrie," 16 January 1942. In author's possession.

27. Memorandum, U.S. Holocaust Memorial Museum, undated. In author's possession.

28. Ottley, *No Green Pastures*, 163.

29. Charles H. Houston, "The Negro Soldier," *The Nation*, 21 October 1944, 496.

30. L. J. Perry, "Hitler Gang Helps South Abuse Negro," *Amsterdam News*, 10 February 1945, A1, B11.

31. Private First Class Harold Lawrence, letter to the *Pittsburgh Courier*, 21 August 1944.

32. See Sam King, *Climbing Up the Rough Side of the Mountain* (London: Miinerva Press, 1998); Robert N. Murray, *Lest We Forget: The Experiences of World War II Westindian Ex-Service Personnel* (Nottinghamshire, England: Nottingham Westindian Combined Ex-Services Association, 1996); and Ben Bousquet and Colin Douglas, *West Indian Women at War: British Racism in World War II* (London: Lawrence & Wishart, 1991).

33. See Graham Smith, *When Jim Crow Met John Bull: Black Americans in World War II* (New York: St. Martin's Press, 1988).

34. Killingray, "Africans and African Americans," 183; Bousquet and Douglas, *West Indian Women at War*; King, *Climbing Up*; and Murray, *Lest We Forget*.

35. See Mike Philips and Trevor Philips, *Winrush: The Irresistible Rise of Multi-Racial Britain* (New York: HarperCollins, 1998), 31–32.

36. Gilroy, *Against Race*, 303–304.

37. Solomos and Black, *Racism and Society*, 171.

38. Kesting, "Forgotten Victims," 31–32; and "Summary Worksheet," War Crimes Branch, U.S. Army, 16 July 1945.

39. Kesting, "Forgotten Victims," 31.

40. Killingray, "Africans and African Americans," 187.

41. U.S. Holocaust Memorial Museum document. In author's possession.

42. Konnilyn G. Feig, *Hitler's Death Camps: The Sanity of Madness* (New York: Holmes and Meire, 1981).

43. Paulette Reed-Anderson, interview on Friday, 28 April 2000, Berlin, Germany. Also, see letter to Dr. Julia Okpara, dated 24 February 1998, in author's possession.

44. Ibid.

45. Records in author's possession.

46. See record from Gedenkstatte und Museum Sachsenhausen, in author's possession. Dated 2 March 2000.

47. Mitchell G. Bard, *Forgotten Victims: The Abandonment of Americans in Hitler's Camps* (Boulder, CO: Westview Press, 1994), 165.

48. Marc Hillel and Clarissa Henry, *Of Pure Blood* (New York: McGraw Hill, 1976), 173.

49. Rita Rodriquez, "Musicians Queried on Acts Abroad," *New York Amsterdam News*, 25 March 1944, 1A; and Julius J. Adams, "Nazi Internment Camp Victim Tells Story of His Adventures in Foreign Countries," *New York Amsterdam News*, 15 April 1944, 7A.

50. Ibid.

51. Rodriquez, "Musicians Queried."

52. "The Black Star: On the Fate of African-Germans under National Socialism," lecture, Koln University, African Studies Program, Marianne Bechhause-Gerst, 29 November 1995.

53. Interview with Michael, 7 May 2000.

54. See Theodor Michael, "*Einige Biographische Bemerkungen zu Mohamad Husen,*" [*Some Biographical Remarks Regarding Mohamad Husen*] 24 November 1999. In author's possession.

55. Paulette Reed-Anderson, "Memorial Service in Memory of Mohamed Husen, an African Victim of National Socialist Tyranny," *African Courier*, No. 12, December 1999–January 2000, 24.

56. Bechhause-Gerst, lecture, Koln University, 29 November 1995.

57. Commemoration to the Memory of the African Mohamed Husen, Victim of the National Socialist Tyranny, program, 24 November 1999.

58. Gilroy, *Against Race*, 302.

59. See Nazi propaganda photo, USHMM Photo Archives, Desig # 634.7077, W/S #17509.

60. Monica C. Rothschild-Boros, *In the Shadow of the Tower: The Works of Josef Nassy 1942–1945*, Art Exhibit Guidebook, undated, 8.

61. Ibid.

62. Ibid., 9.

63. Ibid.

64. Ibid.

65. Ferdinand Protzman, "Nassy's 'Images of Internment,'" *Washington Post*, 1 June 1997, G7.

66. Jere-Malanda, "Forgotten," 20.

67. *Black Survivors of the Holocaust.*

68. Jessie Chaney Smith, ed., *Notable Black American Women* (Detroit: Gale Research, 1992), 1056–1057.

69. Linda Dahl, *Stormy Weather: The Music and Lives of a Century of Jazzwomen* (New York: Pantheon, 1984), 81. Also, see D. Antoinette Handy, *Black Women in American Bands and Orchestras* (Lanham, MD: Scarecrow Press, 1998); D. Antoinette Handy, *The International Sweethearts of Rhythm* (Lanham, MD: Scarecrow Press, 1998); Sally Placksin: *American Women in Jazz, 1900 to the Present: Their Words, Lives, and Music* (New York, Seaview Books, 1982); and Sherrie Tucker: *Swing Shift: "All-Girl" Bands of the 1940s* (Durham: Duke University Press, 2000).

70. Reed, "Hot from Harlem," 61.

71. Ibid., 61–62.

72. Valaida Snow, "I've Met No Color Bar," *Chicago Defender*, 7 October 1934.

73. Reed, "Hot from Harlem," 61.

74. Ibid.

75. Mario Charles, "The Age of a Jazzwoman: Valada Snow, 1900–1956," *Journal of Negro History*, Vol. 80, Issue 4, autumn, 1995, 185.

76. Rosetta Reitz, "Hot Snow: Valaida Snow (Queen of the Trumpet Sings & Swings)," *Black American Literature Review*, winter, 1982, 158.

77. Dahl, *Stormy Weather*, 81

78. Will Friedwald, *Jazz Singing: America's Great Voices from Bessie Smith to Bebop and Beyond* (New York: Charles Scribner's Sons, 1990), 352.

79. Krin Gabbard, "Signifying the Phallus: Mo' Better Blues and Representations of the Jazz Trumpet," in Krin Gabbard, ed., *Representing Jazz* (Durham: Duke University Press, 1995), 109.

80. Friedwald, *Jazz Singing*, 352.

81. Ibid.
82. Valaida, Volume 1, 1935–1937, Harlequin Records, United Kingdom, 1992; and Valaida, Volume II, 1935–1940, Harlequin Records, United Kingdom, 1992.
83. Reed, "Hot from Harlem," 240, n. 42.
84. Ibid., 67.
85. Ibid., Dahl, *Stormy Weather*, 81–82.
86. Ibid., 81.
87. Reed, "Hot from Harlem," 68.
88. Shirer, *Rise and Fall*, 697.
89. Reed, "Hot from Harlem," 68.
90. National Archives database.
91. Dahl, *Stormy Weather*, 82.
92. Marten Clausen, Liner Notes, "Valaida, Vol. II, 1935–1940," Harlequin Records, Czech Republic, 1992.
93. Reitz, "Hot Snow," 159.
94. Ibid.
95. Ibid.
96. Valaida Snow, "I Came Back from the Dead," liner notes, *Hot Snow*, Rosetta Records.
97. Reitz, "Hot Snow," 159.
98. Ibid.
99. *Pittsburgh Courier*, 7 September 1946.
100. Dahl, *Stormy Weather*, 213
101. Ibid., 257.
102. Reed, "Hot from Harlem," 58.
103. Carman Moore, *Village Voice*, 19 February 1982, 79–80.
104. Walters, *Pan-Africanism*, 75.
105. For more on Negritude, see Abiola Irele, "Negritude or Black Cultural Nationalism," *Journal of Modern African Studies*, 3, December 1965; Norman R. Shapiro, ed., *Negritude: Black Poetry from Africa and the Caribbean* (Stonington, CT: October House, 1970); and Leopold Senghor, *Negritude et Humanisme* (Paris: Le Seuil, 1964).
106. Killingray, "Africans and African Americans," 189.
107. Janice Spleth, *Leopold Sedar Senghor* (Boston: Twayne, 1985), 11.
108. Ibid.; and Janet G. Vaillant, *Black, French, and African: A Life of Leopold Sedar Senghor* (Cambridge: Harvard University Press, 1990), 167.
109. See Leopold Sedar Senghor, "Hosties Noires," in S. Okechukwu Mezu, *The Poetry of Leopold Sedar Senghor* (London: Heinemann Press, 1973), 29–45.
110. Vaillant, *Black, French, and African*, 173.
111. Ibid., 176.
112. Senghor, "Hosties Noires," 43.
113. Vaillant, *Black, French, and African*, 176.
114. Ibid., 177.
115. Info on the report. Note that the title is wrong. It should be *Liberators* and not *The Liberators*.
116. Daniel Allentuck, "Black Soldiers and the Death Camps," *Lies of Our Times*, May 1993.
117. Jeff Bradley, "Black Troops First to Reach Death Camp," *Denver Post*, 7 March 1993.
118. Potter, *Liberators*, 217.
119. Ibid., 218.
120. "Black Liberators of the Holocaust," *New York Newsday*, 22 October 1992.
121. "Black Soldiers Gave the Gift of Life," *Jewish Week*, 6–12 November 1992.
122. "Black Liberators of the Holocaust."
123. Richard Bernstein, "Doubts Mar PBS Film of Black Army Unit," *New York Times*, 2 March 1993.
124. Killingray, "Africans and African Americans," 191.
125. See L. W. F. Grundlingh, "The Participation of South African Blacks in the Second World War," unpublished thesis, Rand Afrikaans University, 1986.
126. Killingray, "Africans and African Americans," 194.
127. Gleeson, 203–206.

Chapter 7: Imagining Blackness

1. Shirer, *Rise and Fall*, 241.
2. Ibid.

3. Murray Edelman, *From Art to Politics: How Artistic Creations Shape Political Conceptions* (Chicago: University of Chicago Press, 1995), 48.
4. See Rainer E. Lotz, *Black People: Entertainers of African Descent in Europe, and Germany* (Bonn: Birgit Lotz Verlag, 1997).
5. Ibid., 302.
6. Josephine Baker, *Les Memoirs de Josephine Baker, Recueillis et Adaptes par Marcel Sauvage* [*The Mémoirs of Josephine Baker, Introverted and Adapted by Marcel Sauvage*] (Paris: KRA, 1927), 59–60.
7. Lotz, *Black People*, 372.
8. Gabrielle Edgcomb, *From Swastika to Jim Crow: Refugee Scholars at Black Colleges* (Malabar, FL: Krieger, 1993), 53.
9. Stefan Kuhl, *The Nazi Connection: Eugenics, American Racism, and German National Socialism* (New York: Oxford University Press, 1994), 98–99.
10. Ibid., 99.
11. Tom Bogle, *Toms, Coons, Mulattoes, Mammies & Bucks: An Interpretative History of Blacks in American Films* (New York: Continuum, 1989); Nelson George, *Blackface: Reflections on African Americans and the Movies* (New York: HarperCollins, 1994); Manthia Diawara, ed., *Black American Cinema* (New York: Routledge, 1993); Ed Guerrero, *Framing Blackness: The African Americans Image in Film* (Philadelphia: Temple University Press, 1993); and Jesse Rhines, *Black Film, White Money* (New Brunswick, NJ: Rutgers University Press, 1996).
12. Bogle, *Toms, Coons*, 102.
13. Alain Patrice Nganang, *"Der koloniale Sehnsuchtsfilm: Vom lieben Afrikaner deutscher Filme der NS-Zeit,"* ("The Colonial Longing Film of the Dear African of German Films of the NS Time"), unpublished paper, August 2000.
14. Edward Said, *Culture and Imperialism* (New York: Vintage, 1994), 68.
15. Sabine Hake, "Mapping the Native Body: On Africa and the Colonial Film in the Third Reich," in Friedrichsmeyer, Lennox, and Zantop, *The Imperialist Imagination*, 174.
16. Woodruff D. Smith, *The German Colonial Empire* (Chapel Hill: University of North Carolina Press, 1978), 233.
17. David Welch, *Progaganda and the German Cinema, 1933–1945* (New York: Oxford University Press, 1983), 273.
18. Hake, "Mapping the Native Body," 177.
19. Ibid., 164.
20. Ibid., 166.
21. Ibid., 181.
22. Samples, "African Germans," 63.
23. Ibid.
24. Ibid.
25. John Welch, "Twelve Years under Hitler," 6.
26. Samples, "African Germans," 61.
27. Hake, "Mapping the Native Body," 170.
28. "'Germanin' entsteht im Suden," *Film-Kurier*, 26 May 1942.
29. "The Black Star: On the Fate of African-Germans under National Socialism," lecture, Koln University, African Studies Program, Marianne Bechhause-Gerst, 29 November 1995.
30. David Irving, *The Trail of the Fox* (New York: E. P. Dutton, 1997), 59.
31. Ibid., 60.
32. Opitz, *Showing Our Colors*, 70.
33. Gilroy, *Against Race*, 298.
34. Hake, "Mapping the Native Body," 170.
35. *Black Survivors of the Holocaust.*
36. Opitz, *Showing Our Colors*, 69.
37. Ibid.
38. Neil A. Wynn, *The Afro-American and the Second World War* (New York: Holmes & Meier, 1993), 83.
39. "The Big Negro Drum of Promoting Colonialism: The German Africa-Show, 1935–1943," undated. Document from the U.S. Holocaust Memorial Museum in author's possession.
40. Campt, Grosse, and Lemke-Muniz de Faria, "Blacks, Germans, and Politics," 218–220.
41. Ibid., 219, 221.
42. "The Big Negro Drum of Promoting Colonialism: The German Africa-Show, 1935–1943."
43. Solomos and Black, *Racism and Society*, 175.

Chapter 8: "Nigger Music Must Disappear"

1. Langston Hughes, *Weary Blues* (New York: Knopf, 1926), 25.
2. Mike Zwerin, *La Tristesse de Saint Louis: Jazz under the Nazis* (New York: Beech Tree Books, 1987), p. 14.
3. Kathy J. Ogren, *The Jazz Revolution: Twenties America and the Meaning of Jazz* (New York: Oxford University Press, 1989), 121.
4. Theodor W. Adorno, "Perennial Fashion—Jazz," in *Prisms* (Cambridge: MIT Press, 1982), 121.
5. Ibid., 123.
6. Lee B. Brown, "Adorno's Critique of Popular Music: The Case of Jazz Music," *Journal of Aesthetic Education*, spring 1992, 20.
7. Ibid., 24.
8. Ibid., 28.
9. Leroi Jones, *Blues People: The Negro Experience in White America and the Music That Developed From It* (New York: Morrow Quill Paperbacks, 1963), 143.
10. Michael Bernard-Donais, "Jazz, Rock 'n' Roll, Rap and Politics," *Journal of Popular Culture*, [date], 127–128.
11. Solomos and Black, *Racism and Society*, 170.
12. Michael H. Kater, *Different Drummers: Jazz in the Culture of Nazi Germany* (New York: Oxford University Press, 1992), 9.
13. Ibid., 12.
14. Paulette Reed-Anderson, *Eine Geschichte von mehr als 100 Jahren: Die Anfänge der Afrikanischen Diaspora in Berlin* [*A History of More Than 100 Years: The Beginning of the African Diaspora in Berlin*] (Berlin: Die Auslaenderbeauftragte des Berliner Senats (Commissioner for Foreigners' Affairs), Fall 1994, 8.
15. Lotz, *Black People*, 283.
16. Ibid., 284.
17. Ibid., xvi.
18. Ibid., xvii.
19. Kater, *Different Drummers*, 19.
20. Ibid., 24.
21. Ibid., 21.
22. Ibid., 22.
23. Ibid., 30. See n. 11.
24. Ibid., 30.
25. Zwerin, *La Tristesse de Saint Louis*, 120.
26. Kater, *Different Drummers*, 23.
27. "Reich Bars Radio Jazz to Safeguard 'Culture,'" *New York Times*, 13 October 1935; and "Nazis Reject Jazz," *New York Times*, 18 March 1933. S. Frederick Starr, *Red and Hot: The Fate of Jazz in the Soviet Union* (New York: Limelight Editions, 1985), 174.
28. Kater, *Different Drummers*, 39.
29. Ibid., 138.
30. Zwerin, *La Tristesse de Saint Louis*, 120.
31. Kater, *Different Drummers*, 53–54.
32. Zwerin, *La Tristesse de Saint Louis*, 31–32.
33. Kater, *Different Drummers*, 50.
34. Interview with Hans Massaquoi.
35. Starr, *Red and Hot*, 175.
36. Ibid., 174–175.
37. Solomos and Black, *Racism and Society*, 171.
38. Kater, *Different Drummers*, 136.
39. Massaquoi interview, 7 April 2000.
40. Ibid.
41. Ibid.
42. olomos and Black, *Racism and Society*, 171.
43. Kater, *Different Drummers*, 149.
44. Zwerin, *La Tristesse de Saint Louis*, 22–23, 55.
45. Kater, *Different Drummers*, 20.
46. Ibid., 22.

47. Starr, *Red and Hot,* 174.
48. Kater, *Different Drummers,* 23.
49. Steve Holtje and Nancy Ann Lee, ed., *Music Hound Jazz: The Essential Album Guide* (Detroit: Visible Ink, 1998), 948.
50. Zwerin, *La Tristesse de Saint Louis,*169.
51. Stovall, *Paris Noir,* 49.
52. Zwerin, *La Tristesse de Saint Louis,*101.
53. Kater, *Different Drummers,* 147.
54. Ibid., 147.
55. Ibid., 148.
56. Stovall, *Paris Noir,* 123–124.
57. Ibid., 158–159.
58. Ibid., 124.
59. Zwerin, *La Tristesse de Saint Louis,*102.
60. John Welch, "Twelve Years under Hitler," 6.
61. Stovall, *Paris Noir,* 124.
62. Ottley, *No Green Pasture,* 163–164.
63. Starr, *Red and Hot,* 185.
64. Cole, *Selling the Holocaust,* 105.
65. Zwerin, *La Tristesse de Saint Louis,*29.
66. Ibid., 73.
67. Ibid.
68. Ibid., 73–74.
69. Ibid.
70. Eric Vogel, "Jazz in a Nazi Concentration Camp," *Downbeat,* 7 December 1961, 22.
71. "Nazi 'Clear' Us of Jazz; Blame Jews," Norfolk *Journal and Guide, 21* December 1935.
72. Kater, *Different Drummers,* 30.

Chapter 9: Punched Out and Overrun

1. *Black Survivors of the Holocaust.*
2. Paulette Reed-Anderson, *Metropole, Menschen, Nahaufnahme: Afrikaner in Berlin* [*Metropolis, People, Close-up: Africans in Berlin*] (Berlin, 1996), 22.
3. Massaquoi, *Destined to Witness,* 135–140.
4. Hitler, *Mein Kampf,* 409–410.
5. Bogle, *Toms, Coons,* 17.
6. Joe Louis, *Joe Louis: My Life* (Hopewell, NJ: Ecco Press, 1978), 137.
7. Massaquoi, *Destined to Witness,* 114–120.
8. *The Crisis,* October 1936 issue (a reprint of an article in *Der Weltkampf*)
9. ESPN, Sunday, 14 November 1999.
10. Louis, *Joe Louis,* 144.
11. U.S. Holocaust Memorial Museum website, http://www.ushmm.org.
12. "Boycott the Olympics," *Baltimore Afro-American,* 15 December 1934, 1.
13. "Stay Out of Nazi Olympics," *The Crisis,* September 1935, 273.
14. *Chicago Defender,* 14 December 1935.
15. *Philadelphia Tribune,* 19 December 1935.
16. Ernest Lee Jahncke, letter to Count Henri Baillet-Latour, president of IOC, 25 November 1935.
17. Committee on Fair Play in Sports, New York, 15 November 1935.
18. See Heinrich Krieger, "How to Wipe Out the American Negro," *Washington Tribune,* 11 August 1936, 4, and, "Nazi Colorphobia Flares Anew; Newspaper Takes Rap at American Negroes," *Norfolk Journal and Guide,"* 13 March 1937, 1.
19. Memorial website.
20. Arthur A. Ashe, Jr., *A Hard Road to Glory: A History of the African American Athlete, 1919–1945* (New York: Warner Books, 1988), 82.
21. Ibid., 83.
22. *Norfolk Journal and Guide,* 8 June 1935.
23. Ashe, *A Hard Road to Glory ,* 87.
24. William N. Wallace, "Marty Glickman, Blocked at '36 Olympics, Dies at 83," *New York Times,* 4 January 2001.
25. Ashe, *A Hard Road to Glory,* 85.

26. Dean B. Cromwell, *Championship Technique in Track and Field* (New York: Whittlesey House/ McGraw-Hill, 1941), 6.
27. William Montague Cobb, "Race and Runners," *Journal of Health and Physical Education,* January 1936, 54, 56.
28. Cobb, "Physical Anthropology of the American Negro," *American Journal of Physical Anthropology,* June 1942, 169.
29. Ashe, *A Hard Road to Glory* , 85.
30. "Small Acts from a Small Man, *The Crisis,* September 1936, 273.
31. "Fascism Now Means Something," *The Crisis,* September 1936, 273.
32. "The Hitler Snub Deliberate," *Washington Tribune,* 7 August 1936, 4; "Hitler's Aryan Superman Myth Is Exploded as Colored Americans Stampede Olympics, *Philadelphia Tribune,* 8 August 1936, 1; and "Hitler Won't Shake Hands," *Baltimore Afro-American,* 8 August 1936, 1.
33. "Hitler and Owens," *Philadelphia Tribune,* August 13, 1936, 13.
34. "Hitler's Contribution," *Brown American,* August 1936, 8.
35. "Hitler Praised above Roosevelt by Jesse Owens at G.O.P. Rally," *Philadelphia Tribune,* 29 October 1936, 2.
36. *New York Amsterdam News,* August 8, 1936.
37. Quoted in Ashe, *A Hard Road to Glory* , 10.

Chapter 10: Blacks in the Resistance Movement

1. James C. Scott, *Domination and the Arts of Resistance: Hidden Transcripts* (New Haven, CT: Yale University Press, 1990), 3.
2. See Gabriel A. Almond, "The Size and Composition of the Anti-Nazi Opposition in Germany," *PS: Political Science & Politics,* September 1999.
3. Killingray, "Africans and African Americans," 190.
4. *Black Survivors of the Holocaust,* 11.
5. "Hilarious Gilges, An Explanation by His Mother Given in 1945," Archive of the VVN Düsseldorf (No.) 4007, in author's possession.
6. *Black Survivors of the Holocaust.*
7. Phyllis Rose, *Jazz Cleopatra: Josephine Baker in Her Time* (New York: Doubleday, 1989), 183.
8. Ibid., 181.
9. Ibid., 183.
10. Ibid., 183–184.
11. Ibid., 184.
12. Ibid., 187.
13. Ibid., 185.
14. Ibid., 202–204.
15. Ibid., 205.
16. Lynn Haney, *Naked at the Feast: A Biography of Josephine Baker* (New York: Dodd, Mead, 1981), 258.
17. Mary L. Dudziak, "Josephine Baker, Racial Protest, and the Cold War," *Journal of American History,* September 1994, 543–570.
18. Shirer, *Rise and Fall,* 957.
19. Ibid.
20. Hugh Wray McCann and David C. Smith, *The Search for Johnny Nicholas* (London: Sphere Books, 1982), 123.
21. Ibid., 34.
22. Ibid., 144
23. Ibid., 183.
24. Ibid., 185.
25. Ibid., 188.
26. Ibid., 187.
27. Ibid., 188.
28. Testimony of Karl Kahr, Dachau Detachment, 7708th War Crimes Group, U.S. Army, 29 April 1947.
29. McCann, *The Search for Johnny Nicholas,* 204.
30. Testimony of Edwin Katzeuellenbogen, Dachau Detachment, 7708th War Crimes Group, U.S. Army, 14 August 1947.
31. Testimony of Willi Burgdorf, Dachau Detachment, 7708th War Crimes Group, U.S. Army, 8–9 July 1947.

32. Testimony of Ferdinand Karpik, Dachau Detachment, 7708th War Crimes Group, U.S. Army, 21 May 1947.
33. Testimony of Paul Maischen, 16 September 1947.
34. Sworn statement of Walter Ulbright, undated.
35. McCann, *The Search for Johnny Nicholas,* 217.
36. Ibid., 218.
37. Ibid., 220.
38. Ibid., 325–359.

Chapter 11: European (Dis)union

1. A. Sivanandan, "Seize the Time," *Campaign against Racism & Fascism,* February–March 1999, 2.
2. For a history of the United Nations activities and policies against racism, see Michael Banton, *International Action against Racial Discrimination* (Oxford: Clarendon Press, 1996).
3. UNESCO International Scholars, "Proposals on the Biological Aspects of Race," Moscow, August 1964, in Daniela Gioseffi, *On Prejudice: A Global Perspective* (New York: Anchor Books, 1993), 621.
4. Kenan Malik, *The Meaning of Race: Race, History and Culture in Western Society* (New York: New York University Press, 1996), 10.
5. "Replacement Migration: Is It a Solution to Declining Populations," United Nations Population Division, Department of Economic and Social Affairs, United Nations Secretariat, 21 March 2000.
6. David Goldberg, ed., *Anatomy of Racism* (Minneapolis: University of Minnesota Press, 1990).
7. Paul Hockenos, *Free to Hate: The Rise of the Right in Post-Communist Eastern Europe* (New York: Routledge, 1993), 149.
8. Amanda Sebestyen, "'Europe's Most Unwanted Race,'" *CARF,* February–March 1999, 14.
9. See Isabel Fonseca, *Bury Me Standing: The Gypsies and Their Journey* (New York: Vintage, 1995).
10. Tariq Modood, "'Black,' Racial Equality, and Asian Identity," *New Community,* Vol. 14, No. 3, 1988, 403.
11. Glyn Ford, *Report on the Findings of the Inquiry,* (Luxembourg: European Parliament, Committee of Inquiry on Racism and Xenophobia, Office for Offical Publications of the European Communities, 1991), 119.
12. Blackshire-Belay, *African-German Experience,* ix; and Liz Fekete and Frances Webber, *Inside Racist Europe* (London: Institute of Race Relations, 1994), 47.
13. Fekete and Webber, 45.
14. David Owen, *Black People in Great Britain* (Coventry: Centre for Research in Ethnic Relations of the Economic and Social Research Council, 1994), 1.
15. See Paul Hockenos, *Free to Hate: The Rise of the Right in Post-Communist Eastern Europe* (New York: Routledge, 1993).
16. Solomos and Black, *Racism and Society,* 50.
17. This unity was on display in the Kosovo conflict where Europe united against one of its own. See Julie Mertus, *Kosovo: How Myths and Truths Started a War* (Berkeley: University of California Press, 1999).
18. Ford, *Report on the Findings.*
19. Ibid.
10. Ibid.
21. Ibid.
22. See Stephen Lawrence Inquiry, http://www.official-documents.co.uk/document/cm42/4262/4262.htm.
23. Kathleen Paul, *Whitewashing Britain: Race and Citizenship in the Postwar Era* (Ithaca, NY: Cornell University, 1997), 111.
24. Eugene Robinson, "Blending In, or Wiping Out?: Immigration Tests a European Society," *Washington Post,* 5 July 1998.
25. "Dutch Diversity," *Washington Post,* July 5, 1998.
26. *European Race Audit,* February 1998.
27. See *European Address Book against Racism,* Edition 2000, United for Intercultural Action, Amsterdam, 2000.
28. "Report from the Forum of Non-Governmental Organisations," Conference of Europe, EURO-CONF, (2000)8, Conference 2000–2001\NGOFORUM\documents\eng-euroconf00–8, 11 October 2000, 2.
29. Ibid., 5.
30. See Vienna Declaration http://www.icare.to wcar caucus pages African/African Descent caucus.

Chapter 12: Breathing while Black

1. Tina M. Campt, "Afro-German Cultural Identity and the Politics of Positionality: Contests and Contexts in the Formation of a German Ethnic Identity," in Friedrichsmeyer, Lennox, and Zantop, *Imperialist Imagination*, 112.
2. Miranda Pyne, "Dreadlocks and Lederhosen: Black Germans under Siege," 5 December 2000. At Africana.com website. Downloaded 1 March 2001.
3. Ibid.
4. See Tina Campt, "Afro-German Cultural Identity," in Friedrichsmeyer, Lennox, and Zantop, *Imperialist Imagination*, 110; and Karin Obermeier, "Afro-German Women: Recording Their Own History," *New German Critique* No. 46, winter 1989, 172–180.
5. Lucian Kim, "Grappling with Being Black . . . and German," *Christian Science Monitor*, 4 February 1999.
6. Kwame Appiah, "Berlin Celebrates 10th Anniversary of the Black History Month," *African Courier*, February–March 1999, 1.
7. Interview with Ekpenyong Ani and Judy Gummich, 5 August 2000.
8. "Echoes from Germany's Past: Neo-Nazis Sentenced in Vicious Racial Murder," *Toronto Star*, 31 August 2000.
9. Peter Finn, "Wrestling with a Legacy of Hate," *Toronto Star*, 6 August 2000.
10. Pyne, "Dreadlocks and Lederhosen."
11. Pyne.
12. Pyne.
13. Hockenos, *Free to Hate*, 52.
14. See Rand C. Lewis, *The Neo-Nazis and German Unification* (Westport, CT: Praeger, 1996).
ı. See German Compensation for National Socialist Crimes http://www.ushrom.org/assets/frg.htm.
15. See, Benjamin Ferencz, *Less than Slaves: Jewish Forced Labor and the Quest for Compensation* (Cambridge: Harvard University Press, 1979); Henrik G. Van Damm, "Reparations in the Federal Republic," in Walter Stahl, *The Politics of Postwar Germany* (New York: Praeger Press, 1963); and Ronald Zweig, *German Reparations and the Jewish World: A History of the Claims Conference* (Boulder, CO: Westview Press, 1987).
16. William Drozdiak, "Germans Reach Settlement with Slave Laborers," *Washington Post*, 18 December 1999.
17. Daniel J. Wakin, "Germany Agrees to Pay $5 Billion to Nazi-Era Slave Laborers," *New York Times*, 17 July 2000.
18. Regina Jere-Malanda, "Forgotten: Black Victims of Hitler's Germany," *New African*, October 1999, 19.
19. Ibid.
20. Ibid.
21. Ken Kamara, "Massive Deportations of African Asylum Seekers Attracts Sharp Criticism," *African Courier*, February–March 1999, 1.
22. Sam Atsu Nove, *African-German Contacts, 1999/2000* (Berlin: Redaktion & Gesamtherstellung, 1999).

Bibliography

Books and Chapters in Books

Adams, W. S., *Edwardian Portraits* (London: Secker & Warburg, 1957).

Adorno, Theodor W., "Perennial Fashion—Jazz," in *Prisms* (Cambridge: MIT Press, 1982).

Altick, Richard D., *The Shows of London* (Cambridge: Belknap, 1978).

Ashe, Arthur A., Jr., *A Hard Road to Glory: A History of the African American Athlete, 1919-1945* (New York: Warner Books, 1988).

Atamian, Sarkis, *The Origin of Tarzan: The Mystery of Tarzan's Creation Solved* (Anchorage: Publications Consultants, 1997).

Baker, Josephine, *Les Memoirs de Josephine Baker, Recueillis et Adaptes par Marcel Sauvage* [The Memoirs of Josephine Baker, Collected and Adapted by Marcel Sauvage] (Paris: KRA, 1927).

Banton, Michael, *International Action against Racial Discrimination* (Oxford: Clarendon Press, 1996).

Bard, Mitchell G., *Forgotten Victims: The Abandonment of Americans in Hitler's Camps* (Boulder, CO: Westview Press, 1994).

Baynes, Norman H., ed., *The Speeches of Adolf Hitler* (New York: Oxford University Press, 1942).

Bennett, Norman R., *Africa and Europe: From Roman Times to National Independence* (New York: Africana, 1984).

Bernasconi, Robert, and Tommy L. Lott, eds., *The Idea of Race: Readings in Philosophy* (Indianapolis: Hackett, Inc., 2000).

Bernier, Francois, "A New Division of the Earth," in Robert Bernasconi and Tommy L. Lott, eds., *The Idea of Race* (Indianapolis: Hackett, 2000).

Blackshire-Belay, Carol Aisha, *The African-German Experience: Critical Essays* (Westport, CT: Praeger, 1996).

Blakely, Allison, *Russia and the Negro: Blacks in Russian History and Thought* (Washington: Howard University Press).

Bogle, Tom, *Toms, Coons, Mulattoes, Mammies & Bucks: An Interpretative History of Blacks in American Films* (New York: Continuum, 1989).

Bousquet, Ben, and Colin Douglas, *West Indian Women at War: British Racism in World War II* (London: Lawrence & Wishart, 1991).

Bradford, Phillips Verner, and Harvey Blume, *Ota Benga: The Pygmy in the Zoo* (New York: St. Martin's Press, 1992).

Bridgeman, Jon M., *The Revolt of the Hereros* (Berkeley: University of California Press, 1981).

Burleigh, Michael, and Wolfgang Wippermann, *The Racial State: Germany 1933-1945* (Cambridge: Cambridge University Press, 1991).

Cabral, Amilcar, *Return to the Source: Selected Speeches of Amilcar Cabral* (New York: Africa Information Service, 1973).

Camp, Shermanita, *Blacks in the Holocaust: An Untold and Striking Story of Survival of Seven Black Jazz Musicians in Hitler's Concentration Camp* (Hollywood, CA: Hallelujah Publications, 2000).

Campt, Tina, "African German/African American—Dialogue or Dialectic?: Reflections on the Dynamics of 'Intercultural Address,'" in Carol Aisha Blackshire-Belay, *The African-German Experience: Critical Essays* (Westport, CT: Praeger, 1996).

Campt, Tina, Pascal Grosse, and Yara-Colette Lemke-Muniz de Faria, "Blacks, German, and the Politics of Imperial Imagination, 1920-60," in Sara Friedrichsmeyer, Sara Lennox, and Susanne Zantop, *The*

Imperialist Imagination: German Colonialism and Its Legacy (Ann Arbor: University of Michigan Press, 1998).

Cashman, Sean Dennis, *African Americans and the Quest for Civil Rights, 1900-1990* (New York: New York University Press, 1991).

Castells, Manuel, *The Power of Identity: The Information Age—Economy, Society and Culture* (New York: Blackwell, 1997).

Churchill, Ward, *A Little Matter of Genocide: Holocaust and Denial in the Americas, 1492 to the Present* (San Francisco: City Light Books, 1997).

Clay, William L., *Just Permanent Interests: Black Americans in Congress, 1870-1991* (New York: Amistad, 1992).

Cline, Catherine Ann, *E. D. Morel 1873-1924: The Strategies of Protest* (Belfast: Blackstaff Press, 1980).

Cole, Tim, *Selling the Holocaust: From Auschwitz to Schindler How History Is Bought, Packaged and Sold* (New York: Routledge, 1999).

Conrad, Joseph, *Heart of Darkness & Selections from the Congo Diary* (New York: Modern Library, 1999).

Cooper, Wayne F., *The Passion of Claude McKay: Selected Poetry and Prose, 1912-1948* (New York: Schocken Books, 1973).

Cromwell, Dean B., *Championship Technique in Track and Field* (New York: Whittlesey House/McGraw-Hill, 1941).

Dahl, Linda, *Stormy Weather: The Music and Lives of a Century of Jazzwomen* (New York: Pantheon, 1984).

Davenport, Charles, *State Laws Limiting Marriage Selection in Light of Eugenics* (Cold Spring Harbor, NY: Eugenics Records Office, 19130.

Davis, F. James, *Who Is Black?: One Nation's Definition* (Philadelphia: Pennsylvania State University Press, 1991).

Dennis, Lawrence, and Maximilian St. George, *A Trial On Trial: The Great Sedition Trial of 1944* (Torrance, CA: Institute for Historical Review, 1984).

Diawara, Manthia, ed., *Black American Cinema* (New York: Routledge, 1993).

Du Bois, W. E. B., *Dusk of Dawn: An Essay toward an Autobiography of a Race Concept* (New Brunswick, NJ: Transaction, 1992).

———, *The Autobiography of W. E. B. Du Bois: A Soliloquy on Viewing My Life from the Last Decade of Its First Century* (New York: International, 1968).

———, *International Tribute to William E. B. Du Bois* (New York: United Nations, Center Against Apartheid, 1982).

East, Edward, *Heredity and Human Affairs* (New York: Scribner, 1929).

Echenberg, Myron, *Colonial Conscripts: The Tirailleurs Senegalais in French West Africa, 1857-1960* (London: J. Currey, 1991).

Edelman, Murray, *From Art to Politics: How Artistic Creations Shape Political Conceptions* (Chicago: University of Chicago Press, 1995).

Edgcomb, Gabrielle, *From Swastika to Jim Crow: Refugee Scholars at Black Colleges* (Malabar, FL: Krieger, 1993).

Fabre, Michael, *From Harlem to Paris: Black American Writers in France, 1840-1980* (Chicago: University of Illinois Press, 1993).

Feig, Konnilyn G., *Hitler's Death Camps: The Sanity of Madness* (New York: Holmes and Meire, 1981).

Ferencz, Benjamin, *Less Than Slaves: Jewish Forced Labor and the Quest for Compensation* (Cambridge, MA: Harvard University Press, 1979).

Fischer, Eugen, *Die Rehobother Bastards und das Bastardierungsproblem beim Menschen* [The Rehoboth Bastards and the Bastardization Problem in Man] (Jena, 1913).

Fonseca, Isabel, *Bury Me Standing: The Gypsies and Their Journey* (New York: Vintage, 1995).

Ford, Glyn, *Report on the Findings of the Inquiry* (Luxembourg: European Parliament, Committee of Inquiry on Racism and Xenophobia, Office for Official Publications of the European Communities, 1991).

Foucault, Michel, *Discipline & Punishment: The Birth of the Prison* (New York: Vintage Books, 1995).

Fox, Geoffrey, *Hispanic Nation: Culture, Politics, and the Constructing of Identity* (New York: Birch Lane Press Book, 1996).

Franklin, John Hope, *From Slavery to Freedom: A History of Negro Americans*, 3d ed. (New York: Vintage, 1969), 480; and Arthur F. Raper, *The Tragedy of Lynching* (New York: Dover, 1970).

Fredrickson, George M., *The Comparative Imagination: On the History of Racism, Nationalism, and Social Movements* (Berkeley, CA: University of California Press, 1997).

Friedlander, Henry, *Origins of Nazi Genocide: From Euthanasia to the Final Solution* (Durham: University of North Carolina Press, 1995).

Friedrichsmeyer, Sara, Sara Lennox, and Susanne Zantop, *The Imperialist Imagination: German Colonialism and Its Legacy* (Ann Arbor: University of Michigan Press, 1998).

Friedwald, Will, *Jazz Singing: America's Great Voices from Bessie Smith to Bebop and Beyond* (New York: Charles Scribner's Sons, 1990).

Fryer, Peter, *Staying Power: The History of Black People in Britain* (London: Pluto Press, 1984).

Gabbard, Krin, "Signifying the Phallus: Mo' Better Blues and Representations of the Jazz Trumpet," in Krin Gabbard, ed., *Representing Jazz* (Durham: Duke University Press, 1995).

Gann, Lewis H., and Peter Duignan, *The Rulers of German Africa, 1884-1914* (Stanford, CA: Stanford University Press, 1977).

George, Nelson, *Blackface: Reflections on African Americans and the Movies* (New York: HarperCollins, 1994).

Gerunde, Harald, *Eine von uns: Als Schwarze in Deutschland geboren* [*One of Us: Being Born Black in Germany*] (Wuppertal, Germany: Peter Hammer Verlag, 2000).

Gilman, Sander, *On Blackness without Blacks: Essays on the Image of the Black in Germany* (Boston: G. K. Hall, 1982).

Gilroy, Paul, *The Black Atlantic: Modernity and Double Consciousness* (Cambridge: Harvard University Press, 1993).

——— *Against Race: Imaging Political Culture Beyond the Color Line* (Cambridge: Belknap Press of Harvard University Press, 2000).

Gioseffi, Daniela, *On Prejudice: A Global Perspective* (New York: Anchor Books, 1993).

de Gobineau, Count Arthur, *Essay on the Inequality of Human Races* (*Essai sur l'inegalite des races humaines*), Vol. 1.

———,*Essay on the Inequality of Human Races* (*Essai sur l'inegalite des races humaines*), Vol. 2.

Goldberg, David, ed., *Anatomy of Racism* (Minneapolis: University of Minnesota Press, 1990).

Goldhagen, Daniel Jonah, *Hitler's Willing Executioners: Ordinary Germans and the Holocaust* (New York: Vintage, 1997).

Gould, Stephen Jay, *Mismeasure of Man* (New York: Norton, 1996).

———, *The Flamingo's Smile: Reflections in Natural History* (New York: Norton, 1985).

Green, Charles, ed., *Globalization and Survival in the Black Diaspora: The New Urban Challenge* (Albany, NY: State University of New York Press, 1997).

Green, Jeffrey P., "A Revelation in Strange Humanity: Six Congo Pygmies in Britain, 1905-1907," in Bernth Lindfors, *Africans on Stage: Studies in Ethnological Show Business* (Bloomington: Indiana University Press, 1999).

Guerrero, Ed, *Framing Blackness: The African Americans Image in Film* (Philadelphia: Temple University Press, 1993).

Hall, Stuart, *Culture, Media, Language: Working Papers in Cultural Studies, 1972-79* (London: Hutchinson, 1992).

Hall, Stuart, and Paul du Gay, eds., *Questions of Cultural Identity* (London: Sage, 1996).

Handy, D. Antoinette, *Black Women in American Bands and Orchestras* (Lanham, MD: Scarecrow Press, 1998);

———, *The International Sweethearts of Rhythm* (Lanham, MD: Scarecrow Press, 1998).

Haney, Lynn, *Naked at the Feast: A Biography of Josephine Baker* (New York: Dodd, Mead, 1981).

Harlan, Louis R., *Booker T. Washington: The Wizard of Tuskegee, 1901-1915* (New York: Oxford University Press, 1983).

Henry, Charles, *Ralph Bunche: Model Negro or American Other?* (New York: New York University Press, 1999).

Herrnstein, Richard J., and Charles Murray, *The Bell Curve: Intelligence and Class Structure in American Life* (New York: Free Press, 1994).

Hill, Robert, *The Marcus Garvey and Universal Negro Improvement Association Papers, November 1927 to August 1940, Vol. 7* (Los Angeles: University of California Press, 1990).

Hillel, Marc, and Clarissa Henry, *Of Pure Blood* (New York: McGraw Hill, 1976).

Hitler, Adolf, *Mein Kampf* (New York: Houghton, Mifflin, 1943).

Hochschild, Adam, *King Leopold's Ghost: A Story of Greed, Terror, and Heroism in Colonial Africa* (New York: Houghton Mifflin, 1999).

Hockenos, Paul, *Free to Hate: The Rise of the Right in Post-Communist Europe* (New York: Routledge, 1993).

Holtje, Steve, and Nancy Ann Lee, ed., *Music Hound Jazz: The Essential Album Guide* (Detroit: Visible Ink, 1998).

Hooker, James R., *Black Revolutionary: George Padmore's Path From Communism to Pan-Africanism* (New York: Praeger, 1967).

Hugel-Marshall, Ika, *Invisible Woman: Growing Up Black in Germany* (New York: Continuum, 2001).

Hughes, Langston, *Weary Blues* (New York: Knopf, 1926).

Huttenback, Robert, *Racism and Empire* (Ithaca: Cornell University Press, 1976).

Irving, David, *The Trail of the Fox* (New York: E. P. Dutton, 1997).

Jahoda, Gustav, *Images of Savages: Ancient Roots of Modern Prejudice in Western Culture* (New York: Routledge, 1999).

James, C. L. R., *Spheres of Existence: Selected Writings* (London: Allison & Busby, 1980).

Johnson, Sterling, *Black Globalism: The International Politics of a Non-State Nation* (Brookfield, VT: Ashgate, 1998).

Jones, Leroi, *Blues People: The Negro Experience in White America and the Music That Developed From It* (New York: Morrow Quill Paperbacks, 1963).

Kant, Immanual, "'This fellow was quite black ... a clear proof that what he said [was] stupid,'" in Emmanuel Chukwudi Eze, ed., *Race and the Enlightenment: A Reader* (New York: Blackwell, 2000).

Kater, Michael H., *Different Drummers: Jazz in the Culture of Nazi Germany* (New York: Oxford University Press, 1992).

Keegan, Timothy, *Colonial South Africa and the Origin of the Racial Order: Reconsiderations in Southern African History* (Charlotte: University Press of Virginia), 1997.

Kennedy, Stetson, *Jim Crow Guide: The Way It Was* (Boca Raton FL: Florida Atlantic University Press, 1990).

Kern-Foxworth, Marilyn, *Aunt Jemima, Uncle Ben, and Rastus: Blacks in Advertising, Yesterday, Today, and Tomorrow* (Westport, CT: Praeger, 1994).

Kevles, Daniel J., *In the Name of Eugenics: Genetics and the Uses of Human Heredity* (Cambridge: Harvard University Press, 1995).

Killingray, David, "Africans and African Americans in Enemy Hands," in Bob Moore and Kent Fedorowich, *Prisoners of War and Their Captors in World War II* (Washington, DC: Berg Press, 1996).

King, Sam, *Climbing Up the Rough Side of the Mountain* (London: Minerva Press, 1998).

Kipling, Runyard, *Gunga Din and Other Favorite Poems* (New York: Dover, 1990).

Koeppen, Anne Marie, ed., *Das deutsche Landfrauenbuch* (Berlin: Reichsnahrstand Verlag, 1937). Cited in Rupp.

Kornweibel, Jr., Theodore, *"Seeing Red": Federal Campaigns against Black Militancy, 1919-1925* (Bloomington: Indiana University Press, 1999).

Krausnick, Helmut, and Martin Broszat, *Anatomy of the SS State* (London: Granada, 1973).

Kuhl, Stefan, *The Nazi Connection: Eugenics, American Racism, and German National Socialism* (New York: Oxford University Press, 1994).

Lauren, Paul Gordon, *Power and Prejudice: The Politics and Diplomacy of Racial Discrimination* (Boulder, CO: Westview Press).

Lawler, Nancy, *Soldiers of Misfortune: Ivorien Tirailleurs of World War II* (Athens: Ohio University Press, 1992).

Layton, Azza Salama, *International Politics and Civil Rights Policies in the United States, 1941-1960* (New York: Cambridge University Press, 2000).

Lee, Martin A., *The Beast Reawakens* (New York: Routledge, 2000).

Lemkin, Raphael, *Axis Rule in Occupied Europe: Laws of Occupation, Analysis of Government, Proposals for Redress* (Washington, DC: Carnegie Endowment for International Peace, 1944).

Lester, Julius, ed., *The Seventh Son: The Thought and Writings of W. E. B. Du Bois*, vol. I (New York: Random House, 1971.

Lewis, David Levering, ed., *W. E. B. Du Bois: A Reader* (New York: Henry Holt, 1995).

Lewis, David Levering, *W. E. B. Du Bois: Biography of a Race, 1868-1919* (New York: Henry Holt, 1993).

_____, *W. E. B. Du Bois: The Fight for Equality and the American Century, 1919-1963* (New York: Henry Holt and Company, 2000).

Lewis, Rand C., *The Neo-Nazis and German Unification* (Westport, CT: Praeger, 1996).

Lindfors, Bernth, "Charles Dickens and the Zulus," in Bernth Lindfors, ed., *Africans on Stage: Studies in Ethnological Show Business* (Bloomington: Indiana University Press, 1999).

Lindovist, Sven, *"Exterminate All the Brutes": One Man's Odyssey into the Heart of Darkness and the Origins of European Genocide* (New York: New Press, 1992).

Linke, Uli, *Blood and Nation: The European Aesthetics of Race* (Philadelphia: University of Pennsylvania Press, 1999).

Lofgen, Charles, *The Plessy Case: A Legal-Historical Interpretation* (New York: Oxford University Press, 1987).

Lopez, Ian F. Haney, *White by Law: The Legal Construction of Race* (New York: New York University Press, 1996).

Lotz, Rainer E., *Black People: Entertainers of African Descent in Europe, and Germany* (Bonn: Birgit Lotz Verlag, 1997).

Lovell, John, Jr., *Black Song: The Forge and the Flame, The Story of How the Afro-American Spiritual Was Hammered Out* (New York: Macmillian, 1972).

Louis, Joe, *Joe Louis: My Life* (Hopewell, NJ: Ecco Press, 1978).

MacGregor, Jr., Morris J., and Bernard C. Nalty, eds., *Blacks in the United States Armed Forces—Basic Documents*, vol. 4 (Wilmington, DE: Scholarly Resources, 1977).

Malcolmson, Scott L., *One Drop of Blood: The American Misadventure of Race* (New York: Farrar, Straus, and Giroux, 2000).

Malik, Kenan, *The Meaning of Race: Race, History and Culture in Western Society* (New York: New York University Press, 1996).

Marable, Manning, *W. E. B. Du Bois Black Radical Democrat* (Boston: Twayne, 1986).

Massaquoi, Hans, *Destined to Witness: Growing Up Black in Nazi Germany* (New York: William Morrow, 1999).

McCann, Hugh Wray, and David C. Smith, *The Search for Johnny Nicholas* (London: Sphere Books, 1982).

Mertus, Julie, *Kosovo: How Myths and Truths Started a War* (Berkeley, CA: University of California Press, 1999).

Mezu, S. Okechukwu, *The Poetry of Leopold Sedar Senghor* (London: Heinemann Press, 1973).

Mills, Charles W., *The Racial Contract* (Ithaca, NY: Cornell University Press, 1997).

Moore, Bob, and Kent Fedorowich, *Prisoners of War and Their Captors in World War II* (Washington, DC: Berg, 1996).

_____, "Prisoners of War in the Second World War: An Overview," in Bob Moore and Kent Fedorowich, *Prisoners of War and Their Captors in World War II* (Washington, DC: Berg, 1996).

Morel, E. D., *E. D. Morel's History of the Congo Reform Movement* (Oxford: Clarendon Press, 1968).

———, *Great Britain and the Congo: The Pillage of the Congo Basin* (New York: H. Fertig, 1969).

———, *Red Rubber; the Story of the Rubber Slave Trade Flourishing on the Congo in the Year of Grace 1906* (New York: Negro Universities Press, 1969).

Morel, Edmund D., *King Leopold's Rule in Africa* (New York: Funk and Wagnalls, 1905).

Mosse, George, *Toward the Final Solution: A History of European Racism* (New York: H. Fertig, 1978).

Murray, Robert N., *Lest We Forget: The Experiences of World War II Westindian Ex-Service Personnel* (Nottinghamshire, England: Nottingham Westindian Combined Ex-Services Association, 1996).

Muller-Hill, Benno, *Murderous Science: Elimination by Scientific Selection of Jews, Gypsies, and Others, Germany 1933-1945* (New York: Oxford University Press, 1988).

Nove, Sam Atsu, *African-German Contacts: Directory of the African Communities in Germany, 1999/2000* (Berlin: Redaktion & Gesamtherstellung, 1999).

Ogren, Kathy J., *The Jazz Revolution: Twenties America and the Meaning of Jazz* (New York: Oxford University Press, 1989).

Oguntoye, Katharina, *Eine Afro-Deutsche Geschichte: Zur Lebenssituation von Afrikanem und Afro-Deutschen in Deutschland, von 1888 bis 1950* [*An Afro-German History: The Situation of Africans and Afro-Germans in Germany, 1888-1950*] (Berlin: Hoho Verlag, 1997);

Omi, Michael, and Howard Winant, *Racial Formation in the United States: From the 1960s to the 1980s* (New York: Routledge, 1986).

Opitz, May, Katerina Oguntoye, and Dagmar Schultz, eds., *Showing Our Colors: Afro-German Women Speak Out* (Amherst: University of Massachusetts Press, 1992).

Ottley, Roi, *No Green Pastures* (New York: Charles Scribner's Sons, 1951).

Owen, David, *Black People in Great Britain* (Coventry: Centre for Research in Ethnic Relations of the Economic and Social Research Council, 1994).

Paul, Kathleen, *Whitewashing Britain: Race and Citizenship in the Postwar Era* (Ithaca, NY: Cornell University, 1997).

Perlo, Victor, *Super Profits and Crises: Modern U.S. Capitalism* (New York: International, 1988).

Philips, Mike, and Trevor Philips, *Winrush: The Irresistible Rise of Multi-Racial Britain* (New York: HarperCollins, 1998).

Pieterse, Jan Nederveen, *White on Black: Images of Africa and Blacks in Western Popular Culture* (New Haven, CT: Yale University Press, 1992).

Placksin, Sally: *American Women in Jazz, 1900 to the Present: Their Words, Lives, and Music* (New York: Seaview Books, 1982).

Pommerin, Rainer, *Sterilisierung der Rheinlandbastrade: Das Schicksal einer farbigen Minderheit, 1918-1937* (Dusseldorf: Droste, 1979).

Potter, Lou, *Liberators: Fighting on Two Fronts in World War II* (New York: Harcourt Brace Jovanovich, 1992).

Proctor, Robert N., *Racial Hygiene: Medicine under the Nazis* (London: Harvard University Press, 1988).

Reed, Jr., Adolph L., *W. E. B. Du Bois and American Political Thought: Fabianism and the Color Line* (New York: Oxford University Press, 1997).

Reed, Bill, *"Hot from Harlem:" Profiles in Classic African-American Entertainment* (Kearney, NE: Morris Publishing, 1998).

Die Auslaenderbeauftragte des Berliner Senats (Commissioer for Foreigners' Affairs), *Eine Geschichte von mehr als 100 Jahren: Die Anfange der Afrikanischen Diaspora in Berlin* [A History of More Than 100 years: That Beginning of the African Diaspora in Berlin] Berlin, Fall 1994.

Reich, Wilhelm, *The Mass Psychology of Fascism* (New York: Farrar, Straus, and Giroux, 1970).

Reilly, Philip, *Surgical Solution: A History of Involuntary Sterilization in the United States* (Baltimore: Johns Hopkins University Press, 1991).

Rhines, Jesse, *Black Film, White Money* (New Brunswick, NJ: Rutgers University Press, 1996).

Roberts, Diane, *The Myth of Aunt Jemima: Representations of Race and Religion* (New York: Routledge, 1994).

Roberts, Dorothy, *Killing the Black Body: Race, Reproduction, and Meaning of Liberty* (New York: Vintage Books, 1997).

Rose, Phyllis, *Jazz Cleopatra: Josephine Baker in Her Time* (New York: Doubleday, 1989).

Said, Edward, *Culture and Imperialism* (New York: Vintage, 1994).

Samples, Susann, "African Germans in the Third Reich," in Carol Aisha Blackshire-Belay, *The African-German Experience: Critical Essays* (Westport, CT: Praeger, 1996).

Scobie, Edward, "The Black in Western Europe," in Ivan Van Sertima, ed., *African Presence in Early Europe* (New Brunswick: Transaction, 1996).

Scott, James C., *Domination and the Arts of Resistance: Hidden Transcripts* (New Haven, CT: Yale University Press, 1990).

Senghor, Leopold Sedar, *Negritude et Humanisme* (Paris: Le Seuil, 1964).

Sewell, Terri, *Black Tribunes: Black Political Participation in Britain* (London: Lawrence & Wishart, 1993).

Shapiro, Norman R., ed., *Negritude: Black Poetry from Africa and the Caribbean* (Stonington, CT: October House, 1970).

Shirer, William, *The Rise and Fall of the Third Reich: A History of Nazi Germany* (New York: Touchstone, 1990).

Smith, Graham, *When Jim Crow Met John Bull: Black Americans in World War II* (New York: St. Martin's Press, 1988).

Smith, Helmut Walser, "The Talk of Genocide, the Rhetoric of Miscegenation: Notes on Debates in the German Reichstag Concerning Southwest Africa, 1904-14," in Sara Friedrichsmeyer, Sara Lennox, and Susanne Zantop, *The Imperialist Imagination: German Colonialism and Its Legacy* (Ann Arbor: University of Michigan Press, 1998).

Smith, Homer, *Black Man in Red Russia: A Memoir* (Chicago: Johnson, 1964).

Smith, Jessie Chaney, ed., *Notable Black American Women* (Detroit: Gale Research, 1992).

Smith, Woodruff D., *The German Colonial Empire* (Chapel Hill: University of North Carolina Press, 1978).

Solomos, John, and Les Black, *Racism and Society* (New York: St. Martin's Press, 1996).

Somers, Margaret, and Gloria Gibson, "Reclaiming the Epistemological 'Other': Narrative and the Social Construction of Identity," in Craig Calhoun, ed., *Social Theory and the Politics of Identity* (Cambridge, MA: Blackwell, 1994).

Spleth, Janice, *Leopold Sedar Senghor* (Boston: Twayne, 1985).

Starr, S. Frederick, *Red and Hot: The Fate of Jazz in the Soviet Union* (New York: Limelight Editions, 1985).

Stanley, Henry, *In Darkest Africa; or, The Quest, Rescue, and Retreat of Emin, Governor of Equatoria* (New York: C. Scribner's Sons, 1890).

Stovall, Tyler, *Paris Noir: African Americans in the City of Light* (New York: Houghton Mifflin, 1996).

Stuckart, Wilhelm, and Hans Globke, *Kommentare zur deutschen Rassengesetzgebung* [*Commentaries to the German Race-Legislation*], Vol. 1, Munich, 1936.

Takaki, Ronald, *A Different Mirror: A History of Multicultural America* (Boston: Little, Brown, 1993).

Taylor, A. J. P., *The Trouble Makers: Dissent over Foreign Policy 1792–1939* (London: Hamish Hamilton, 1957).

Tucker, Sherrie, *Swing Shift: "All-Girl" Bands of the 1940s* (Durham: Duke University Press, 2000).

Tucker, William H., *The Science and Politics of Racial Research* (Chicago: University of Chicago, 1994).

Vaillant, Janet G., *Black, French, and African: A Life of Leopold Sedar Senghor* (Cambridge: Harvard University Press, 1990).

G. Van Damm, Janet G., "Reparations in the Federal Republic," in Walter Stahl, *The Politics of Postwar Germany* (New York: Praeger Press, 1963).

Walters, Ronald W., *Pan-Africanism in the African Diaspora: An Analysis of Modern Afrocentric Political Movements* (Detroit: Wayne State University Press, 1993).

Watkins, S. Craig, *Representing: Hip Hop Culture and the Production of Black Cinema* (Chicago: University of Chicago Press, 1998).

Welch, David, *Progaganda and the German Cinema, 1933-1945* (New York: Oxford University Press, 1983).

Williams, John A., *Clifford's Blues* (Minneapolis: Coffee House Press, 1999).

Winant, Howard, *Racial Conditions: Politics, Theory, Comparisons* (Minneapolis: University of Minnesota Press, 1996).

Zweig, Ronald, *German Reparations and the Jewish World: A History of the Claims Conference* (Boulder, CO: Westview Press, 1987).

Zwerin, Mike, *La Tristesse de Saint Louis: Jazz under the Nazis* (New York: Beech Tree Books, 1987).

Articles

Acherson, Neal, *Los Angeles Times*, 10 January 1999.

Adams, Julius J., "Nazi Internment Camp Victim Tells Story of His Adventures in Foreign Countries," *New York Amsterdam News*, 15 April 1944.

Adams, Russell L., "Social Change and Cultural Politics," *Government & Politics*, March 1993.

"Africans in Germany Living in Terror, French Report," *Norfolk Journal and Guide*, 20 October 1934.

"African Pygmy's Fate Is Still Undecided," *New York Times*, 18 September 1906.

Allentuck, Daniel, "Black Soldiers and the Death Camps," *Lies of Our Times*, May 1993.

Almond, Gabriel A., "The Size and Composition of the Anti-Nazi Opposition in Germany," *PS: Political Science & Politics*, September 1999.

Appiah, Kwame, "Berlin Celebrates 10th Anniversary of the Black History Month," *The African Courier*, February–March 1999.

Austin, Ben, http://www.mtsu.edu/~baustin/nurmberg.html.

Barker, J. Ellis, "The Colored French Troops in Germany," *Current History*, July 1921.

Bernard-Donais, Michael, "Jazz, Rock 'n' Roll, Rap and Politics," *Journal of Popular Culture*, [date].

Bernstein, Richard, "Doubts Mar PBS Film of Black Army Unit," *New York Times*, 1 March 1993.

"Black Liberators of the Holocaust," *New York Newsday*, 22 October 1992.

"Black Soldiers Gave the Gift of Life," *The Jewish Week*, 6-12 November 1992.

Black Survivors of the Holocaust, Shooting Script, 6 June 1997.

"Boycott the Olympics," *Baltimore Afro-American*, 15 December 1934.

Bradley, Jeff, "Black Troops First to Reach Death Camp," *Denver Post*, 7 March 1993.

"Bring Back the Hottentot Venus," *Weekly Mall & Guardian*, 15 June 1995.

Brown, Lee B., "Adorno's Critique of Popular Music: The Case of Jazz Music," *Journal of Aesthetic Education*, Spring 1992.

Campt, Tina, "Afro-German Cultural Identity and the Politics of Positionality: Contests and Contexts in the Formation of a German Ethnic Identity," in Friedrichsmeyer, Lennox, and Zantop, 110; and Karin Obermeier, "Afro-German Women: Recording Their Own History," *New German Critique* No. 46, Winter 1989.

Carlyle, Thomas, "Occasional Discourse on the Nigger Question," *Fraser's Magazine*, No. 40, December 1849.

Charles, Mario, "The Age of a Jazzwoman: Valaida Snow, 1900-1956," *Journal of Negro History*, Vol. 80, Issue 4, Autumn 1995.

Cobb, William Montague, "Physical Anthropology of the American Negro," *American Journal of Physical Anthropology*, June 1942.

———, "Race and Runners," *Journal of Health and Physical Education*, January 1936.

Cooper, Len, "Aryan Nation: Germany's Cruel African Heritage," *Washington Post*, 20 February 1994.

Dickens, Charles, "The Noble Savage," *Household Words*, 11 June 1853.

Drozdiak, William, "Germans Reach Settlement with Slave Laborers," *Washington Post*, 18 December 1999.

———, "Payments Set For Ex-Slaves of Nazi Regime; Germany to Pay Aged Survivors," *Washington Post*, 24 March 2000.

Du Bois, W. E. B., "As the Crow Flies," *Amsterdam News*, 12 April 1941.

———, "The German Case against the Jews," *Pittsburgh Courier*, 2 January 1937.

———, "The Winds of Time," *Chicago Defender*, 17 January 1948.

————, *Pittsburgh Courier,* 12 December 1936.

————, *Pittsburgh Courier,* 5 December 1936.

————, "World War and the Color Line," *The Crisis,* November 1914.

Duke, Lynne, "S. African 'Coloreds' End Race Charade," *Washington Post,* 26 July 1998.

"Dutch Diversity," *Washington Post,* 5 July 1998.

"Echoes From Germany's Past: Neo-Nazis Sentenced in Vicious Racial Murder," *Toronto Star,* 31 August 2000.

"Fascism Now Means Something," *The Crisis,* September 1936.

"Fears Nazis Will Teach Prejudices," *Washington Afro-American,* 17 February 1934.

Financial Times, 3 April 1999.

Finn, Peter, "Wrestling with a Legacy of Hate," *Toronto Star,* August 6, 2000.

Foden, Giles, *The Guardian* (London), 24 April 1999.

Gardner, Matthew E., "Germany Plots for Africa," *The Voice of Ethiopia,* 28 January 1939.

"German Eugenics, 1934," *Eugenical News,* No. 19, 1934.

"'Germanin' entsteht im Suden," *Film-Kurier,* 26 May 1942.

"Hilarious Gilges, An Explanation by His Mother Given in 1945," Archive of the VVN Düsseldorf (No.) 4007, in author's possession.

Gould, Stephen Jay, "The Geometer of Race," *Discover,* November 1994.

Grant, Ruth W., and Marion Orr, "Language, Race and Politics: From 'Black' to 'African American,'" *Politics and Society,* June 1996.

"Growing up Black in Nazi Germany," *The African Courier,* December 1999–January 2000.

Harding, Jeremy, *New York Times,* 20 September 1998.

"Hitler and Owens," *Philadelphia Tribune,* 13 August 1936.

"Hitler Praised above Roosevelt by Jesse Owens at G.O.P. Rally," *Philadelphia Tribune,* 29 October 1936.

"The Hitler Snub Deliberate," *Washington Tribune,* 7 August 1936.

"Hitler Won't Shake Hands," *Baltimore Afro-American,* 8 August 1936.

"Hitler's Aryan Superman Myth is Exploded as Colored Americans Stampede Olympics, *Philadelphia Tribune,* 8 August 1936.

"Hitler's Contribution," *Brown American,* August 1936.

Houston, Charles H., "The Negro Soldier," *The Nation,* 21 October 1944.

Hughes, Langston, "Beaumont to Detroit, 1943," *Common Ground,* fall 1943.

Irele, Abiola, "Negritude or Black Cultural Nationalism," *Journal of Modern African Studies,* No. 3, December 1965.

Isaacs, Harold, "Color in World Affairs," *Foreign Affairs,* No. 47, 1969.

James, Alan, "'Black': An Inquiry into the Pejorative Associations of an English Word," *New Community,* spring-summer, 1981.

Jere-Malanda, Regina, "Forgotten: Black Victims of Hitler's Germany," *New African,* October 1999.

"Jewish Massacre Feared Soon in Germany," *Washington Tribune,* 10 March 1933.

Jurca, Catherine, "Tarzan, Lord of the Suburbs," *Modern Language Quarterly,* Vol. 57, No. 3, 1996.

Kamara, Ken, "Massive Deportations of African Asylum Seekers Attracts Sharp Criticism," *The African Courier,* February-March 1999.

Kesting, Robert W., "Forgotten Victims: Blacks in the Holocaust," *The Journal of Negro History,* winter 1992.

Kim, Lucian, "Grappling with Being Black . . . and German," Christian Science Monitor, 4 February 1999.

Krieger, Heinrich, "How to Wipe Out the American Negro," *Washington Tribune,* 11 August 1936.

McDowell, Winston, "Race and Ethnicity during the Harlem Jobs Campaign, 1932-1935," *Journal of Negro History,* summer–autumn 1984.

Michael, Theodor, "*Einige Biographische Bemerkungen zu Mohamad Husen,*" ["Some Biographical Remarks regarding Mohamad Husen"] November 24, 1999. In author's possession.

Miller, Kelly, "Hitler—The German Ku Klux," *Norfolk Journal and Guide,* 7 April 1933.

————, "Race Prejudice in Germany and America," *Opportunity,* April 1993.

Model, Frank P., "Elmer Spyglass, Salesman for Democracy," *Pittsburgh Courier,* 26 March 1955.

Modood, Tariq, "'Black,' Racial Equality, and Asian Identity," *New Community,* XIV, No. 3, 1988.

Morel, E. D., "The Employment of Black Troops in Europe," *Nation,* 17 March 1920.

Morel, Edmund, "Horror on the Rhine," *Foreign Affairs,* August 1920.

————, "The Prostitution of the Rhineland," *Foreign Affairs,* June 1921;

————, "Black Scourge in Europe, Sexual Horror Let Loose by France on Rhine, Disappearance of Young German Girls," *Daily Herald,* 9 April 1920.

Morris, Lorenzo, "African Immigrants in France: SOS Racisme vs. the National Front," in Georgia A. Persons, ed., *Race and Ethnicity in Comparative Perspective* (*National Political Science Review*, Vol. 7).

Murphy, Graham J., "Possession, Penetration, and Tarzan Comic Books," http://www.imagesjournal.com/issue07/features/tarzan.htm.

"Nazi 'Clear' Us of Jazz; Blame Jews," Norfolk *Journal and Guide*, 21 December 1935.

"Nazi Colorphobia Flares Anew; Newspaper Takes Rap at American Negroes," *Norfolk Journal and Guide*, 13 March 1937.

"Nazi Prepare to Rid Reich of Colored People," *Afro-American*, 6 February 1943.

"Nazis Reject Jazz," *New York Times*, 18 March 1933.

"Negro Nazi Spy Trapped in S. America," *Amsterdam News*, 24 August 1944, 1A.

Nelson, Keith, "The 'Black Horror on the Rhine': Race as a Factor in Post–World War I Diplomacy," *Journal of Modern History*, No. 42, 1970.

Newsinger, John, "Lord Greystroke and Darkest Africa: The Politics of Tarzan Stories," *Race and Class*, Vol. 28, No. 2, 1986.

Nganang, Alain Patrice, *"Der koloniale Sehnsuchtsfilm: Vom lieben Afrikaner deutscher Filme der NS-Zeit,"* ("The Colonial Longing Film of the Dear African of German Films of the NS Time"), unpublished paper, August 2000.

"No Aid From M'Clellen," *New York Evening Post*, 11 September 1906.

Oludipe, Olayinka, "A History of More Than a Century: The Origins of the African Diaspora in Berlin," *The African Courier*, February–March 1999.

Perry, L. J., "Hitler Gang Helps South Abuse Negro," *Amsterdam News*, 10 February 1945.

Pine, Lisa, "Girls in Uniform: Nazi Girl's Movement," *History Today*, March 1999.

Protzman, Ferdinand, "Nassy's 'Images of Internment,'" *Washington Post*, 1 June 1997.

Pyne, Miranda, "Dreadlocks and Lederhosen: Black Germans Under Siege," 5 December 2000. At Africana.com web site. Downloaded 1 March 2001.

Raimondo, Justin, "Behind the Headlines," 28 April 2000, antiwar.com.

Reddick, L. D., "What Hitler Says about the Negro," *Opportunity*, April 1933.

Reed-Anderson, Paulette, "Memorial Service in Memory of Mohamed Husen, an African Victim of National Socialist Tyranny," *The African Courier*, No. 12, December 1999–January 2000.

"Reich Bars Radio Jazz to Safeguard 'Culture,'" *New York Times*, 13 October 1935.

Robert C. Reinders, "Racialism on the Left: E. E. Morel and the 'Black Horror on the Rhine,'" *International Review of Social History*, No. 13, 1968.

Reitz, Rosetta, "Hot Snow: Valaida Snow (Queen of the Trumpet Sings & Swings)," *Black American Literature Review*, winter 1982.

"The Rhine's Black Horror Faded," *Literary Digest*, 25 June 1921.

Robinson, Eugene, "Blending In, Or Wiping Out?: Immigration Tests a European Society," *Washington Post*, 5 July 1998.

Rodriquez, Rita, "Musicians Queried On Acts Abroad," *New York Amsterdam News*, 25 March 1944.

Rohrbach, Paul, *Deutsche Kolonialwirtschaft*, Vol. 1, Sudwest-Afrika, Berlin, 1907.

Rupp, Leila J., "Mother of the Volk: The Image of Women in Nazi Ideology," *Signs*, winter 1977.

Sebestyen, Amanda, "'Europe's Most Unwanted Race,'" *Campaign Against Racism & Fascism*, February/March 1999.

Sinclair, Abiola, "The Story of Saartijie Baartman, the Hottentot Venus," *Black History Magazine*, No. 6, 1999.

Sivanandan, A., "Seize the Time," *Campaign against Racism & Fascism*, February–March 1999.

"Small Acts from a Small Man, *The Crisis*, September 1936.

Smith, Tom, "Changing Racial Labels: From 'Colored' to 'Negro' to 'Black' to 'African American,'" *Public Opinion Quarterly*, winter 1992.

Snow, Valaida, "I Came Back from The Dead," Liner Notes, *Hot Snow*, Rosetta Records.

———, "I've Met No Color Bar," *Chicago Defender*, 7 October 1934.

Sollors, Werner, "W. E. B. Du Bois in Nazi Germany: A Surprising, Prescient Visitor," *The Chronicle of Higher Education*, 12 November 1999.

"Stay Out of Nazi Olympics," *Crisis*, September 1935.

Straus, Tamara, "King Leopold's Ghost Makes a Comeback," 24 September 1999 (downloaded), Alternet Web site.

Swarns, Rachel L., "Gaborone Journal; Africa Rejoices as a Wandering Soul Finds Rest, *New York Times*, 6 October 2000.

Taylor, Richard, "The Monster Who Plundered the Congo," *The Boston Globe*, 16 September 1998.

"Vichy Asks Africans for Labor in Germany," *Afro-American*, 8 August 1942.

Vogel, Eric, "Jazz in a Nazi Concentration Camp," *Downbeat,* 7 December 1961.

Wakin, Daniel J., "Germany Agrees to Pay $5 Billion to Nazi-Era Slave Laborers," *New York Times,* 17 July 2000.

William N. Wallace, "Marty Glickman, Blocked at '36 Olympics, Dies at 83," *New York Times,* 4 January 2001.

Welch, John, "Twelve Years under Hitler," *Pittsburgh Courier,* 1944.

Werner, Alfred, "Germany's New Pariahs," *The Crisis,* May 1952.

Newspapers Consulted

The African Courier
Afro-American
Chicago Defender
Chicago Tribune
The Crisis
The Economist
Foreign Affairs
Los Angeles Times
New York Amsterdam News
New York Globe
New York Times
Norfolk Journal and Guide
Opportunity
Philadelphia Tribune
Pittsburgh Courier
Village Voice
Washington Post
Washington Tribune

Government Reports, Unpublished Papers, and Letters

American Prisoners of War and Civilian Internees: Records Relating to Personal Participation in World War II, Reference Information Paper 80, National Archives and Records Administration, Washington, DC, 1982.

Bechhause-Gerst, Marianne, lecture, Koln University, African Studies Program, 29 November 1995.

"The Big Negro Drum of Promoting Colonialism: The German Africa-Show, 1935-1943," undated. Document from the U.S. Holocaust Memorial Museum in author's possession.

"The Black Star: On the Fate of African-Germans Under National Socialism," lecture, Koln University, African Studies Program, Marianne Bechhause-Gerst, 29 November 1995. Document from the U.S. Holocaust Memorial Museum in author's possession.

Campt, Tina, "'Afro-German' The Convergence of Race, Sexuality, and Gender in the Formation of a German Ethnic Identity, 1919–1960," dissertation, Cornell University, 1996.

Commemoration to the Memory of the African Mohamed Husen, Victim of the National Socialist Tyranny, program, 24 November 1999.

Committee on Fair Play in Sports, letter, New York, 15 November 1935.

"From Colonial Racism to Nazi Population Policy," paper presented at the United States Holocaust Memorial Museum Conference on the Known, the Unknown, the Disputed, and the Reexamined, December 5–8, 1993. Document from the U.S. Holocaust Memorial Museum in author's possession.

Grundlingh, L. W. F., "The Participation of South African Blacks in the Second World War," unpublished thesis, Rand Afrikaans University, 1986.

Jahncke, Ernest Lee, letter to Count Henri Baillet-Latour, President IOC, 25 November 1935.

Lawrence, Harold, letter to the *Pittsburgh Courier,* 21 August 1944.

Magubane, Ben, "Racism in the Age of Europe," research paper presented to the South African National Conference on Racism, October, 2000, 5–6. http://www.sahrc.org.za/main_frameset.htm.

"Memorandum of Telephone Statement from Dr. Lowrie," 16 January 1942. Document from the U.S. Holocaust Memorial Museum in author's possession.

Reichministerium des Innern report, document from U.S. Holocaust Memorial Museum, 2 June 1937.

———, document from U.S. Holocaust Memorial Museum, 17 June 1937.

———, document from U.S. Holocaust Memorial Museum, 19 June 1937.

"Report from the Forum of Non- Governmental Organisations," Conference of Europe, EUROCONF, (2000)8, Conference 2000-2001\NGOFORUM\documents\eng-euroconf00-8, 11 October 2000.

Rothschild-Boros, Monica C., *In the Shadow of the Tower: The Works of Josef Nassy 1942-1945,* Art Exhibit Guidebook, undated.

Sworn statement of Walter Ulbright, undated. Document from the U.S. Holocaust Memorial Museum in author's possession.

"Summary Worksheet," War Crimes Branch, U.S. Army, 16 July 1945.

Testimony of Edwin Katzeuellenbogen, Dachau Detachment, 7708th War Crimes Group, U.S. Army, 14 August 1947. Document from the U.S. Holocaust Memorial Museum in author's possession.

Testimony of Ferdinand Karpik, Dachau Detachment, 7708th War Crimes Group, U.S. Army, 21 May 1947. Document from the U.S. Holocaust Memorial Museum in author's possession.

Testimony of Karl Kahr, Dachau Detachment, 7708th War Crimes Group, U.S. Army, 29 April 1947. Document from the U.S. Holocaust Memorial Museum in author's possession.

Testimony of Paul Maischen, 16 September 1947.

Testimony of Willi Burgdorf, Dachau Detachment, 7708th War Crimes Group, U.S. Army, 8-9 July 1947.

"World War II Prisoners of War Punchcards," electronic database, Office of the Provost Marshall General, Records Group 389, National Archives and Records Administration, College Park, MD.

Index